English Grammar and Composition

Second Course

John E. Warriner

FRANKLIN EDITION

Harcourt Brace Jovanovich, Publishers

Orlando   New York   Chicago   San Diego   Atlanta   Dallas

THE SERIES:

English Grammar and Composition: First Course
English Grammar and Composition: Second Course
English Grammar and Composition: Third Course
English Grammar and Composition: Fourth Course
English Grammar and Composition: Fifth Course
English Grammar and Composition: Complete Course
Test booklet and teacher's manual for each above title.

CORRELATED SERIES:

English Workshop: First Course
English Workshop: Second Course
English Workshop: Third Course
English Workshop: Fourth Course
English Workshop: Fifth Course
English Workshop: Review Course

Composition: Models and Exercises, First Course
Composition: Models and Exercises, Second Course
Composition: Models and Exercises, Third Course
Composition: Models and Exercises, Fourth Course
Composition: Models and Exercises, Fifth Course
**Advanced Composition: A Book of Models for Writing, Complete
   Course**

Vocabulary Workshop: First Course
Vocabulary Workshop: Second Course
Vocabulary Workshop: Third Course
Vocabulary Workshop: Fourth Course
Vocabulary Workshop: Fifth Course
Vocabulary Workshop: Complete Course

John E. Warriner taught English for thirty-two years in junior and senior high schools and in college. He is chief author of the *English Grammar and Composition* series, coauthor of the *English Workshop* series, general editor of the *Composition: Models and Exercises* series, and editor of *Short Stories: Characters in Conflict.* His co-authors have all been active in English education.

Printed in the United States of America

ISBN   0-15-311881-4

To the Student

A long time ago when education did not have to be so complicated as it must be today, the main subjects in school were referred to as the three R's: reading, 'riting, and 'rithmetic. As a familiar song says, they were "taught to the tune of a hickory stick." The hickory stick, fortunately, is not much used any more, but the three R's remain. Two of them, reading and writing, make up a large part of the school subject called English.

If someone were to ask you the unlikely question, "What do you do in English?" your reply might be something like this: "In English we read stories and poems and stuff like that. We learn about nouns and verbs and, well, subjects and predicates, I guess. We write our own stories and poems and themes. And we give talks in front of the class." This answer is a fairly good account of what you do in English.

A teacher, however, would use different terms in answering the same question. Instead of mentioning just stories and poems, a teacher might say you study *literature*. Noun, verb, subject, and predicate are terms used in the study of *grammar*. Writing stories, poems, and themes is practicing written *composition*. Talks in front of the class are a means of improving your *speech*. The four main areas of English, then, are literature, grammar, composition, and speech.

This book deals mainly with the last three of the four areas, grammar, composition, and speech. To use a language well, you need to know how it works. By studying grammar, you learn how the language works. This knowledge will help you to improve both your writing and your speech.

Although you write much less often than you speak, written composition demands a large amount of English time because writing is hard to learn. Each year in school, you will be expected to do more written work in most of your classes, but it is only in English class that you learn how to write.

By writing well, you communicate with others. By speaking (and listening) well, you also communicate with others. Speech skills are a vital part of your education because you spend so much of every day talking with others.

Mastering the three areas in this textbook—grammar, composition, and speech—is not an easy task. However, you can do it if you have sound guidance. Your teacher is your most helpful guide, but your textbook is also an important guide. Study it, follow the rules, do the practice exercises, and whenever you write or speak put to use what you have learned. You will find your work will improve steadily.

J. W.

Contents

9. Correct Use of Verbs 158

Principal Parts of Regular and
Irregular Verbs

10. Correct Use of Pronouns 179

Nominative and Objective Cases

11. Correct Use of Modifiers 189

Choice, Comparison, Placement

PART THREE: Mechanics

PART FOUR: Sentence Structure

15. Learning "Sentence Sense"   275
Fragments and Run-on Sentences

16. Sentence Combining and Revising   293
Correcting Choppy and Monotonous Styles of Writing

PART FIVE: Composition

24. The Library 481

The Dewey Decimal System,
The Card Catalogue,
Reference Books

25. Vocabulary 496

Context, Word Analysis,
Word Choice

26. Spelling   526
Improving Your Spelling

PART SEVEN: Speaking and Listening

27. Speaking   555
Announcements and Reports,
Delivering a Speech, Evaluating
a Speech

Grammar

PART ONE

Chapter 1

The Sentence

Subject and Predicate

Suppose that you began to read a story that opened as follows:

Awakened in study hall John leaped from his seat into the balcony above him came the marching band led by the drum major playing the "Star-Spangled Banner" on his tall hat a great plume nodded to John it was a rude awakening.

Your difficulty in understanding the story comes not from a failure to understand the words but from a failure to understand the writer's units of thought. If the writer told the story to you, the meaning could be conveyed by vocal expression and by pauses at the right places. But writing differs from speaking in that writers have only their words and punctuation as a method of communication. Thus it is the duty of writers to use patterns which their readers are familiar with—to write complete sentences that are set off clearly by punctuation.

There is a second important difference between speaking and writing. In conversation you often leave a sentence unfinished and begin it over again. You think as you speak. In writing, you have to think *before* you begin. Writing requires more care than informal speaking.

1a. A *sentence* is a group of words expressing a complete thought.

A sentence begins with a capital letter and concludes with an end mark: a period or a question mark or an exclamation point. Sometimes a group of words looks like a sentence when it is not. You must examine the group of words closely to be sure that it expresses a complete thought. Reading it aloud will help you.

NOT A SENTENCE   The music of Scott Joplin.
                  [This is not a complete thought. What about the music of Scott Joplin?]

SENTENCE   The music of Scott Joplin has become popular again.

NOT A SENTENCE   Upon hearing José Feliciano.
                  [The thought is not complete. Who heard Feliciano? What was the response?]

SENTENCE   Upon hearing José Feliciano, the audience applauded.

NOT A SENTENCE   After she worked a long time.
                  [The thought is not complete. What happened after she worked a long time?]

SENTENCE   After she worked a long time, Louise Nevelson completed the sculpture.

EXERCISE 1. Number your paper 1–20. Read the following groups of words and decide which are sentences and which are not. (Capital letters and end punctuation marks have been purposely omitted.) If a group of words is a sentence, copy it after the proper number, adding a capital letter and end punctuation. If the group of words is not a sentence, write *NS* after the proper number; then add whatever is necessary to complete the thought and make it a sentence.

EXAMPLES   1. living alone in the mountains
          1. *NS   Living alone in the mountains, the couple make their own furniture and clothes.*
          2. classes in mountain climbing are beginning this week
          2. *Classes in mountain climbing are beginning this week.*

1. catching the baseball with both hands
2. in the back of the room stood a tall pile of boxes
3. a long narrow passage with a trapdoor at each end
4. after waiting for six hours
5. the gymnasium is open
6. last night there were six television commercials every half-hour
7. instead of calling the doctor about her sore throat
8. beneath the tall ceiling of the church
9. are you careless about shutting off unnecessary lights
10. doing the multiplication tables
11. practice your writing
12. her sister studies engineering at the college
13. discussing the dance in February
14. probably forty guests
15. the governor was elected
16. when the chorus began singing
17. she is tired
18. after the frightening movie when the lights were still dim
19. beneath the truck on the highway
20. everyone shared the remaining cookies

EXERCISE 2. Number your paper 1–20. Opposite each number on your paper, write *S* if the group of words is a sentence and *NS* if it is not a sentence.

1. One of the best-known women in our history is Sacajawea. 2. A member of the Lemhi band of the Shoshoni Indians. 3. She is famous for her role as interpreter for the Lewis and Clark expedition. 4. Which was seeking the Northwest Passage. 5. In 1800 the Lemhis had encountered a war party of the Hidatsa. 6. Who captured some of the Lemhis, including Sacajawea. 7. Later, with Charbonneau, her French-Canadian husband, and their two-month-old son. 8. Sacajawea joined the Lewis and Clark expedition in what is now North Dakota. 9. Her knowledge of Indian languages enabled the explorers to communicate with various tribes. 10. Sacajawea also hunted up wild foods. 11. And once saved valuable instruments during a storm. 12. As they traveled further. 13. The explorers came across the Lemhis. 14. From whom Sacajawea had been separated years before. 15. The Lemhis helped the explorers. 16. By giving them guidance.

17. After they returned from the expedition. 18. Clark tried to establish Sacajawea and Charbonneau in St. Louis. 19. However, the couple moved back to Sacajawea's native land. 20. Where this famous woman died in 1812.

EXERCISE 3. The following groups of words are not sentences. On your paper, add to each group whatever is necessary to make an interesting sentence.

1. on the last day of summer
2. found only in the country
3. a tall woman
4. burning out of control
5. in our tree house
6. the lonely house on the hill
7. which performed many tricks
8. during the last recess

9. when the teacher boarded the bus
10. with her hat pulled down over her eyes

THE SUBJECT

You have learned that a sentence is a group of words expressing a complete thought. In order to express a complete thought, a sentence must have a subject and a predicate.

1b. The *subject* of a sentence is the part about which something is being said.

subject
A long line of people | waited to see Poitier's movie.
subject
Standing in the line were | several groups of students.

Since the subject is that part of the sentence about which something is being said, you can usually locate it by asking yourself *Who?* or *What?* Who waited to see the movie? Who was standing in the line? Notice that the subject comes at the beginning of the first example above and at the end of the second.

In the subject part of each sentence above, one word stands out as essential: in the first sentence, *line;* in the second sentence, *groups.* These two words, which cannot be removed from the subject parts of the sentences, are called *simple subjects.* The simple subject and the other words that belong with it are called the *complete subject.*

1c. The *simple subject* is the main word in the complete subject.

The simple subjects below are printed in heavy type.

complete subject
My **date** for the dance | arrived late.

complete subject
The long, hard **trip** across the desert | was finally over.

complete subject
Pacing back and forth in the cage was | a hungry **tiger.**

When the subject is only one word or one name, the complete subject and the simple subject are the same.

complete subject
Patsy Mink | was elected to office in Hawaii.
She || was chosen congresswoman.

EXERCISE 4. Number your paper 1–10. After each number, copy the complete subject from the corresponding sentence. Then underline the simple subject.

EXAMPLE 1. The time for the takeoff approached.
1. *The* <u>*time*</u> *for the takeoff*

1. A thick fog covered the airport.
2. Many planes had been grounded.
3. The one with the hospital supplies had to get through.
4. The pilot of the plane had a great deal of experience.
5. The plane taxied slowly down the runway.
6. Everyone in the control tower waited breathlessly.
7. The plane picked up speed.
8. Down the runway sped the aircraft.
9. It gradually rose from the ground.
10. The plane with its precious cargo was in the air at last.

As has been pointed out, the most important word in the complete subject is the simple subject. Without the simple subject there could be no sentence. From now on in this book, the word *subject* will refer to the simple subject.

EXERCISE 5. Number your paper 1–20. After the

proper number, copy the subject (simple subject) of each sentence. Ask yourself what or whom the sentence says something about.

1. Mark Twain wrote many entertaining stories. 2. Among them is "The Celebrated Jumping Frog of Calaveras County." 3. One of the characters in this story will apparently believe anything. 4. In a broken-down mining camp, this character meets Mr. Simon Wheeler. 5. To the kindly old man, he asks a simple question. 6. Instead of a simple answer, Mr. Wheeler gives a long, fantastic, and funny reply. 7. This reply is in the form of a humorous tall tale. 8. The tale features Jim Smiley, the owner of a very athletic frog. 9. Mr. Smiley trained this frog for jumping contests. 10. Confidently, the owner gambled his money on the frog's leaping ability. 11. Soon someone challenged Smiley's frog. 12. The challenger, however, did not have a jumping frog for the contest. 13. To Smiley, this was no problem. 14. In a nearby swamp, he found a frog for the challenger. 15. Each creature was held on the starting line. 16. Then, with a shout, each man released his frog. 17. But Smiley's famous frog never jumped. 18. The ordinary toad from the swamp easily won the contest. 19. Smiley had been fooled by a trick. 20. You will enjoy reading this farfetched account.

THE PREDICATE

The subject is one of the two essential parts of a sentence; the other essential part is the predicate.

1d. The *predicate* of a sentence is the part which says something about the subject.

predicate
N. Scott Momaday | wrote several books.

predicate
My whole family | heard Marian Anderson sing.

predicate
On either side of me were | my two best friends.

To find the predicate in a sentence, ask, *What is being said about the subject?* or *What happened?* In the normal order of an English sentence, the predicate follows the subject, but in some sentences the predicate comes before the subject. (See the sentence above.)

The Simple Predicate, or Verb

Just as the simple subject is the most important part of the complete subject, so the simple predicate is the most important part of the complete predicate. The simple predicate is usually called the *verb* of the sentence.

1e. The *simple predicate,* or *verb,* is the main word or group of words in the predicate.

In each of the following sentences the simple predicate, or verb, is in heavy type.

complete subject   *complete predicate*
The movie star | **signed** autographs for hours.

complete subject   *complete predicate*
A whirlwind | **swept** through the town.

complete subject   *complete predicate*
The trees | **sagged** with the weight of the ice.

The simple predicate may be a one-word verb, or it may be a verb of more than one word, such as *has signed, did sweep, will be sagging.* When the simple predicate has more than one word, it is called a *verb phrase.* Note the verb phrases in heavy type in the following sentences.

The famous novel *Frankenstein* **was written** by Mary Woolstonecraft Shelley.

After the concert, the guitarist **will be signing** autographs.

Your vocabulary **can be increased** by study of the origins of words.

The complete predicate, which consists of the verb or verb phrase and the other words that belong with it, usually comes after the subject, but it sometimes can appear at the beginning of a sentence as in the following sentences.

       complete predicate   *complete subject*

There on its back **was** | a large **tortoise.**

       complete predicate   *complete subject*

At the top of the tree **is** | a bird's **nest.**

The subject may come in the middle of the predicate so that part of the predicate is on one side of the subject and the rest is on the other side. In the following examples, the complete predicate is in heavy type:

During the winter many birds **fly south.**

Do sparrows **fly south?**

The words *not* and *never,* which are frequently used with verbs, are not verbs. They are never part of a verb or verb phrase.

She **did** not **believe** me.

We **had** never **met.**

From now on in this book, the simple predicate will be called the verb.

EXERCISE 6. Number your paper 1–10. Copy the complete predicates from the following sentences. Then underline the verbs or verb phrases twice.

EXAMPLE   1. A ton and a half of groceries may seem like a big order for a family of five.

1. _may seem_ like a big order for a family of five.

1. Such a big order is possible, however, in the village of Pang.
2. This small village is located near the Arctic Circle.
3. The people of Pang receive their groceries once a year.
4. A supply ship makes a visit once a year to Pang.
5. In spring, families order their year's supply of groceries by mail.
6. The huge order is delivered to Pang a few months later.
7. The people store the groceries in their homes.
8. Frozen food is kept outdoors.
9. Too costly for most residents is the air-freight charge of two dollars a kilogram.
10. Villagers also can hunt for wild game or can fish in the icy water.

EXERCISE 7. Number your paper 1–20. After the proper number, copy the verb or verb phrase in each of the following sentences.

1. At one time the _exemplum_ was a popular tale. 2. The _exemplum_ is a tale with a moral. 3. One popular _exemplum_ is told by the Pardoner in Chaucer's _Canterbury Tales_. 4. According to the story, three young men were looking for Death. 5. During their search they met an old man. 6. He directed them to an oak tree. 7. There they would find Death. 8. The young men hurried to the tree. 9. But the only thing under the tree was a heap of gold. 10. Now the young men no longer looked for Death. 11. Instead they thought of the money. 12. Each wanted all the money for himself. 13. The youngest of the men was sent into town on an errand. 14. On his return he was killed by the other two. 15. Then these two drank a

toast to their good fortune. **16.** Soon they too died. **17.** The youngest man had poisoned their wine. **18.** Thus all three men found Death. **19.** Greed is the source of much evil. **20.** This, of course, is the moral of the *exemplum*.

EXERCISE 8. Copy the subject and the verb from each of the following sentences. Underline the subject once and the verb twice.

EXAMPLE   1. In 1665 a great plague killed 68,000 people in London alone.
           1. *plague killed*

1. The next year a great fire destroyed 13,200 homes.
2. These two catastrophes are recorded in the diaries of the time.
3. Samuel Pepys is one of the most famous diarists of England.
4. A firsthand account of the plague and the fire was given in his diary.
5. Most families in London suffered some loss from the fire.
6. At first the fire seemed very small.
7. In fact, during the first night of the fire, Pepys slept quite peacefully.
8. Why were the people fleeing their homes and shops?
9. Pepys suggested a plan to the king for stopping the progress of the fire.
10. Houses around the fire were pulled down.

EXERCISE 9. Find the subject and the verb in each sentence and write them on your paper after the proper number.

1. Carla's mother drove us to the theater.
2. The bumblebee carries pollen from one plant to another.

3. A strong, gusting wind is blowing out to sea this morning.
4. My sister accidentally left her car keys inside the locked car.
5. From Maine to California the bicyclists made a cross-country journey.
6. The Medusa of Greek mythology was one of three Gorgons, terrible in appearance.
7. For many centuries she has been pictured with her head of snakes.
8. The picture of Medusa with her snaky hair appears in many books on mythology.
9. According to myth, a glance at the Medusa would turn a mortal to stone.
10. She was slain with the aid of the goddess Athena.

EXERCISE 10. Some of the word groups below are complete subjects and some are complete predicates. On your paper, add whatever part is needed to make each a sentence. Then underline the simple subject once and the verb twice.

EXAMPLE   1. worked throughout the night
1. *The people of the circus worked throughout the night.*

1. the jukebox at the corner drugstore
2. should never be eaten by anyone
3. are mysterious creatures
4. the old house on our block
5. some residents of Sacramento
6. raced down the track
7. suddenly turned toward us
8. my favorite singer
9. the woman with the deft hands and the hearty laugh
10. discovered a cave in the hills behind the old, abandoned sawmill

THE SENTENCE BASE

You have been studying the two most important parts of the sentence: the subject and the verb. Because these two parts are essential to the sentence, they are called the *sentence base*. All other parts of the sentence are attached to the sentence base.

SENTENCE BASE **Dogs play.**

SENTENCE BASE WITH OTHER PARTS ATTACHED Every day two frisky **dogs** named Bison and Stark **play** for hours on our front lawn.

The parts that were added give additional information, but they would be meaningless without the sentence base.

EXERCISE 11. Here are ten sentence bases. Add other parts to them. Notice how the sentence base holds the other parts together.

EXAMPLE 1. Snow covered.
         1. *Last night a ten-inch snow covered Nashville.*

1. Wind howled.
2. Plane soared.
3. Dog growls.
4. Group played.
5. Cannon was roaring.
6. Sun set.
7. Woman stared.
8. Cat leaped.
9. Guests were waiting.
10. Time has passed.

COMPOUND SUBJECTS AND COMPOUND VERBS

Many times more than one subject is being talked about.

ONE SUBJECT **Alicia** carried her book.

TWO SUBJECTS	**Alicia** and **Joy** carried their books.
THREE SUBJECTS	**Alicia, Joy,** and **Carmen** carried their books.
ONE SUBJECT	**New York City** is our destination.
TWO SUBJECTS	Either **New York City** or **Niagara Falls** is our destination.

Notice that when two or more subjects have the same verb, a connecting word—*and* or *or*—is used between them. The connected subjects are referred to as a *compound subject*.

1f. A *compound subject* consists of two or more connected subjects that have the same verb. The usual connecting words are *and* and *or*.

The **Senate** and the **House** are in session. [There are two subjects—*Senate* and *House*—which are joined by a connecting word—*and*—and have the same verb—*are*.]

EXERCISE 12. On your paper, copy the compound subjects from the following sentences, together with the connecting word. Then list the verb or verb phrase which goes with both subjects.

EXAMPLE 1. Cicely Tyson and Paul Winfield starred in a film together.
    1. *Cicely Tyson and Paul Winfield*—*starred*

1. Hawaii and Alaska were the last states admitted to the Union.
2. Books and money were donated to our library.
3. The *Pinta,* the *Niña,* and the *Santa Maria* left Spain for the New World.
4. Pencils or pens may be used on this test.

5. Scarlett O'Hara and Melanie Wilkes were created by Margaret Mitchell.
6. At that time the twist and the bossa nova were popular dances.
7. Almost immediately the lightning and the thunder ceased.
8. Either Cal or Sue must pay the bill for the broken slide projector.
9. In the streets were old people, young people, and children.
10. *Re-, com-,* and *pro-* are common prefixes.

Just as a sentence may have a compound subject, so it may have a compound verb.

1g. A *compound verb* consists of two or more connected verbs that have the same subject.

ONE VERB	Surfing **has become** a very popular sport.
COMPOUND VERB	The dog **barked** and **growled** at the thief. [There are two verbs— *barked, growled*—joined by *and.* Both verbs have the same subject— *dog.*]
COMPOUND VERB	The man **was convicted** but later **was found** innocent of the crime. [There are two verb phrases— *was convicted, was found*—joined by *but.* Both verb phrases have the same subject— *man.*]

EXERCISE 13. Copy the compound verb from each of the following sentences, together with the connecting word. Then write the subject of the verb.

EXAMPLE 1. The stranded party lighted a bonfire

and waved their shirts to the circling plane.
  1. *lighted and waved—party*

1. Karen practiced her serve and won the tournament.
2. St. Augustine, Florida, was founded in 1565 and is the oldest city in the United States.
3. According to mythology, Arachne angered Minerva and was changed into a spider.
4. Martina Arroyo has sung in major American opera halls and has made appearances abroad.
5. The fire was set by a careless person or was started by lightning.
6. During public hangings, thieves circulated among the spectators and robbed them.
7. Ynes Mexia explored the wilds of South America and brought back rare tropical plants.
8. Jim Rice autographed baseballs and made a short speech.
9. General Lee won the fight but lost the war.
10. Many people have gone to Blackbeard Island near Georgia and have searched for treasure.

Sometimes you will see a sentence which has a compound subject and a compound verb. In such a sentence both of the subjects go with both of the verbs.

$$\overset{\text{s}}{\text{The captain}} \text{ and the } \overset{\text{s}}{\text{crew}} \overset{\text{v}}{\text{battled}} \text{ the storm}$$
and $\overset{\text{v}}{\text{prayed}}$ for better weather. [Notice that both *captain* and *crew* perform both actions— *battled* and *prayed*.]

EXERCISE 14. Copy the following sentences on your paper, underlining the subjects once and the verbs or verb phrases twice.

EXAMPLE   1. Several fine poems and novels were written by the Brontë sisters.
          1. Several fine <u>poems</u> and <u>novels</u> <u>were</u> <u>written</u> by the Brontë sisters.

1. Charlotte and Emily are the most famous Brontë sisters.
2. Originally they wrote and published their works under pen names.
3. *Jane Eyre* and *Wuthering Heights* are their well-known books.
4. In Charlotte Brontë's novel, Jane Eyre endured and overcame many hardships.
5. Emily Brontë's *Wuthering Heights* saddens me and makes me tearful.
6. Catherine Earnshaw and Heathcliff stand as unforgettable characters.
7. As children they wandered and explored the moor.
8. Catherine loved Heathcliff but married Edgar.
9. *Jane Eyre* and *Wuthering Heights* became movies.
10. I watch the movies and then read the books again.

EXERCISE 15. Using titles, words, and characters of songs, books, and poems, write ten sentences, five with compound subjects and five with compound predicates. Underline subjects once and verbs twice.

EXAMPLE   1. <u>Frankie</u> and <u>Johnny</u> <u>were</u> sweethearts.

EXERCISE 16. Number your paper 1–10 and make complete sentences by adding predicates to the subjects provided below. Seek sentence variety by using some compound predicates. You may also add to the subjects, making them compound if you wish. Underline the subject once and the verb twice. Capitalize the first word of each sentence.

EXAMPLE 1. the troops
1. *Toward sunset the troops reached camp.*

1. the lively chimpanzee
2. the theater on the corner
3. a crowd of autograph seekers
4. our star basketball player
5. a lazy turtle
6. the star of the show
7. the results of the contest
8. Anita
9. five astronauts
10. the reporter

CLASSIFYING SENTENCES BY PURPOSE

1h. Sentences may be classified according to their purpose. There are four kinds of sentences.[1]

(1) A *declarative sentence* **makes a statement. It is followed by a period.**

EXAMPLES Miriam Colon founded the Puerto Rican Traveling Theatre.
Amelia Earhart was born in 1897.
Curiosity is the beginning of knowledge.

(2) An *interrogative sentence* **asks a question. It is followed by a question mark.**

EXAMPLES What do you know about glaciers?
Why do we see only one side of the moon?
Who was the mother of Perseus?

---

[1] The classification of sentences according to structure (simple, compound, complex) is taught in Chapter 7.

(3) An *imperative sentence* **gives a command or makes a request. It is followed by a period. Strong commands are followed by exclamation points.**

EXAMPLES   Do your homework each night.
Watch out!
Finish your work, John.

At first glance none of these sentences seems to have any subject. But, of course, the person addressed in each case is the subject. The subject *you,* then, is said to be understood in all these sentences.

(You) do your homework each night.
(You) watch out!
John, (you) finish your work, please.

(4) An *exclamatory sentence* **shows excitement or expresses strong feeling. It is followed by an exclamation point.**

EXAMPLES   What a sight the sunset is!
They're off!
Sarah won the portable radio!

Junior high students have a tendency to overuse the exclamatory sentence. Be sure to save your exclamation points for sentences which really do show emotion. If overused, the exclamatory sentence loses its significance.

EXERCISE 17. Below are ten famous quotations. Number your paper 1–10. After each number, write the kind of sentence it is and give the punctuation mark that should follow the sentence.

EXAMPLE 1. Speak softly and carry a big stick
                      —THEODORE ROOSEVELT
    1. *imperative.*

1. I have nothing to offer but blood, toil, tears, and sweat — SIR WINSTON CHURCHILL
2. Tact is after all a kind of mindreading
   — SARAH ORNE JEWETT
3. O, that this too too solid flesh would melt,
   Thaw, and resolve itself into a dew
   — WILLIAM SHAKESPEARE
4. The history of every country begins in the heart of a man or a woman — WILLA CATHER
5. What happiness is there which is not purchased with more or less of pain — MARGARET OLIPHANT
6. Bring me my bow of burning gold — WILLIAM BLAKE
7. No one can make you feel inferior without your consent — ELEANOR ROOSEVELT
8. Since when was genius found respectable
   — ELIZABETH BARRETT BROWNING
9. If you do not think about the future, you cannot have one — JOHN GALSWORTHY
10. An expert is one who knows more and more about less and less — NICHOLAS MURRAY BUTLER

DIAGRAMING THE SUBJECT AND VERB

A diagram shows the structure of a sentence as a kind of picture. Making a diagram of the subject and verb is a way of showing that you understand these two parts of the sentence.

PATTERN

subject	verb

EXAMPLES   Lions roar.

Lions	roar

People speak.

Notice that the parts of the sentence base — the subject and verb — are placed on a horizontal line with a vertical line separating the subject from the verb. The capital marking the beginning of the sentence is used, but not the punctuation.

To diagram a sentence, you first pick out the subject and the verb and then write them on the horizontal line, separated by a crossing vertical line.

EXAMPLES   1. The energetic reporter dashed to the fire.

reporter	dashed

2. Have you been studying for the final test?

you	Have been studying

3. Listen to the beautiful music.

(you)	Listen

EXERCISE 18.   Diagram the simple subjects and verbs in the following sentences. Omit all other words from your diagram. Use a ruler and leave plenty of space between the diagrams.

1. Midas is a character in Greek mythology.

2. He was the king of Phrygia.
3. Dionysus gave Midas a strange power.
4. With this power, Midas could turn anything into gold.
5. The secret dwelt in his touch.
6. For a while, this gift pleased Midas.
7. Soon it became a curse.
8. Do you know why?
9. Read the story of King Midas in a mythology book.
10. Today, people with "the Midas touch" can make money in any project at all.

The following example shows how to diagram a sentence with a compound subject. Notice the position of the joining word *and*.

EXAMPLE   Vines and weeds grew over the old well.

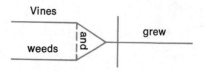

To diagram a sentence with a compound verb, you follow a similar pattern.

EXAMPLE   The model walked across the platform and turned around.

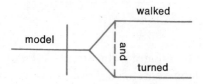

If the sentence has both a compound subject and a compound verb, it is diagramed this way.

EXAMPLE Ken and Dick dived into the water and swam across the pool.

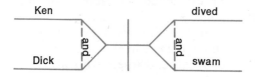

EXERCISE 19. Diagram the simple subjects and verbs or verb phrases in the following sentences.

/ 1. We ran to the railroad station and barely caught the train.
/ 2. The students and the faculty combined their efforts and defeated the proposal.
3. The plane circled above the landing field but did not descend.
√ 4. Pencil and paper are needed for tomorrow's assignment.
5. The actress and her costar prepared for the scene.
6. The students either wrote in ink or typed their compositions.
7. The President and the Congress approved the bill and provided the necessary money.
8. In the evening the crickets and frogs make loud noises.
√ 9. She will write or will call this week.
√ 10. The workers and the management argued for hours and reached an agreement.

REVIEW EXERCISE A. *Oral Drill.* One student should identify the complete subject; another, the complete predicate. A third student should point out the simple subject; and a fourth student, the verb or verb phrase. Some sentences have compound subjects and verbs.

1. Collies and German shepherds guard and herd sheep.

2. One German shepherd responded to one hundred commands.
3. Another dog could do about one hundred and fifty things.
4. People at the Gaines Research Center called Tubby the most useful animal in the United States.
5. It herded cattle, gathered firewood, and carried messages.
6. The trainer would scatter fifteen objects on the floor.
7. The dog would bring each object on command and drop it at the trainer's feet.
8. It hardly ever missed a command.
9. Other dogs have become famous for their intelligence.
10. Lassie and Rin Tin Tin are known to many movie fans.

REVIEW EXERCISE B. Copy the following sentences on your paper. Separate the complete subject from the complete predicate with a vertical line. Then underline the simple subject once and the verb twice.

EXAMPLE 1. Legends and folk tales have been repeated and enjoyed throughout the Americas.
1. _Legends_ and _folk tales_ | _have been repeated_ and _enjoyed_ throughout the Americas.

1. The Chorotega people lived in Nicoya, in Costa Rica, hundreds of years ago.
2. A lovely folk tale tells the story of Nicoya's treasure and praises Princess Nosara for keeping it from the enemy.
3. The warriors of the Chireños landed on the Nicoyan peninsula and attacked the Chorotegas.
4. The Indians of Nicoya were surprised and could not react quickly.

5. Nosara grabbed the treasure in her father's house.
6. Nosara and her suitor took a bow and arrow and fled into the woods.
7. The two ran from the enemy all night and at last reached a river.
8. The brave girl dashed into the mountains, hid the treasure, and returned to the river.
9. The enemy killed the princess and her friend.
10. The murderous tribe never found the gold.

REVIEW EXERCISE C. Copy the following sentences, putting in the correct end punctuation. Then underline the simple subject once and the verb twice. (Be able to tell what kind of sentence each one is.)

EXAMPLE   1. Look at the skywriting.
                    1. (*you*) <u>*Look*</u> at the skywriting.

1. The most important problem for the world is air pollution
2. How many times does the moon go around the earth in a month
3. Think about the problem of hunger
4. Despite its huge body, the rhinoceros has a very small brain
5. Can you give a definition for *amity*
6. How wondrous the sky appears at night
7. Consider the effect of humans on nature
8. Many large museums in America have pottery by Maria Martinez from New Mexico
9. What animals hibernate in the winter
10. What a fantastic world lies beneath the waves

Chapter 2

The Parts of Speech

Noun, Pronoun, Adjective

There are many thousands of different words in the English language. But there are only eight different *kinds* of words. These eight kinds, which are called "parts of speech," are the *noun, pronoun, adjective, verb, adverb, preposition, conjunction,* and *interjection.* In this chapter you will study three of these eight parts of speech: the *noun,* the *pronoun,* and the *adjective.*

THE NOUN

One of the first things that happened to you after you were born was that you were given a name. And the first words that you learned to speak were names of things. If you were to travel to a foreign country, where a language other than English is spoken, you would again find yourself inquiring, "What's that called?" Knowing the names of things is basic to communication. A word which names is called a *noun.*

2a. A *noun* is a word used to name a person, place, thing, or idea.

Persons Helen Hayes, Dr. Lacy, child, architect

Places Wyoming, Mexico, Europe, home, city
Things money, shell, wind, worm, desk
Ideas courage, love, freedom, sorrow, luck

Notice that some kinds of nouns name things which you can see, while others do not. The nouns which name unseen things, like ideas, are more difficult to identify.

EXERCISE 1. Number your paper 1–13. Pick out fifty nouns from the following sentences. (*Who* and *all* are not nouns.)

1. Planets and moons only reflect light.
2. Early settlers of Utah were the Mormons.
3. Many people in the world are still trying to gain independence.
4. Women in the United States were given the right to vote over sixty years ago.
5. Rome was destroyed by barbarians in the fifth century.
6. Both children and adults enjoy the story of the proud emperor who walked down the streets of a village in invisible clothes.
7. The crowd gathered in the arena to see gymnasts from all over the world compete for top honors.
8. In one museum the paintings and drawings of a monkey were exhibited.
9. The rights of the people are protected by the Constitution.
10. The history of the English language is a fascinating subject for students.
11. The koala, an animal found chiefly in Australia, climbs trees to eat leaves.
12. Many presidents of our country have been lawyers as well as politicians.
13. Our government is a republic rather than a true democracy.

EXERCISE 2. Number your paper 1–10. Pick out the forty nouns from the following famous lines of poetry. List each noun in order after the proper number. (The words *I, me, you, your, him, it,* and *whom* are not nouns.)

EXAMPLE   1. Sir Patrick Spens is the best sailor
That sails upon the sea. – UNKNOWN
1. *Sir Patrick Spens, sailor, sea*

1. Friends, Romans, countrymen, lend me your ears;
I come to bury Caesar, not to praise him.
– WILLIAM SHAKESPEARE
2. The birthday of my life
Is come, my love is come to me.
– CHRISTINA ROSSETTI
3. Beauty is in the eye of the beholder.
– MARGARET WOLFE HUNGERFORD
4. A thing of beauty is a joy forever. . . .
– JOHN KEATS
5. It was many and many a year ago,
In a kingdom by the sea,
That a maiden there lived whom you may know
By the name of Annabel Lee. . . .
– EDGAR ALLAN POE
6. I lift my lamp beside the golden door.
– EMMA LAZARUS
7. Here a star, and there a star,
Some lose their way!
Here a mist, and there a mist,
Afterwards – Day!
– EMILY DICKINSON
8. The paths of glory lead but to the grave.
– THOMAS GRAY
9. The weapon that you fought with was a word,
And with that word you stabbed me to the heart.
– MARY ELIZABETH COLERIDGE
10. The quality of mercy is not strain'd,
It droppeth as the gentle rain from heaven
Upon the place beneath. – WILLIAM SHAKESPEARE

Compound Nouns

Sometimes a single noun is made up of two or more words. These words may be written as a single word (safeguard), as two words (safe deposit), or with a hyphen (safe-conduct). Nouns that are names of particular people or things also often consist of more than one word: Rose Fitzgerald Kennedy (a three-word noun), Buckingham Palace (a two-word noun), *The Adventures of Huckleberry Finn* (the name of a book; a five-word noun). The only way to be sure how a word is written is to look it up in your dictionary.

Proper Nouns and Common Nouns

There are two main classes of nouns: common nouns and proper nouns. While the common noun names a class of person, place, or thing, the proper noun names a particular person, place, or thing. The proper noun begins with a capital letter; if it consists of more than one word, each important word is capitalized (*Declaration of Independence*).

COMMON NOUNS	PROPER NOUNS
poem	"To a Skylark"
country	Kenya
man	Roberto Clemente
ship	*Adventurer*
newspaper	*New York Times*
ocean	Pacific Ocean
street	Market Street
date	November 6, 1982
city	Los Angeles

EXERCISE 3. Number your paper 1–10. After each number, list the nouns you find in the corresponding sentence. (Note: *one* and *their* are not nouns.)

EXAMPLE 1. Forests come in many different shapes, kinds, and sizes.
1. *forests, shapes, kinds, sizes*

1. Trees in a tropical jungle have an ample supply of water.
2. Rain forests usually are located in tropical regions.
3. However, one rain forest is on a peninsula in the northwestern state of Washington.
4. Along the coast of California grow the famous redwoods, the tallest trees in the world.
5. The woods in Canada contain mostly evergreens, which adapt well to a cold climate.
6. Woods in the temperate zones have evergreens and also trees that shed leaves, like oaks, beeches, and maples.
7. The giant Douglas fir, an evergreen tree, is a valuable source of lumber.
8. Many other types of plants are dependent on trees for their life.
9. Forests swarm with insects, mammals, birds, and reptiles.
10. A national park such as Sequoia National Park protects large areas of forest.

REVIEW EXERCISE A. Make two columns on your paper. Label one column *Proper Nouns* and the other column *Common Nouns*. Under the appropriate heading, list the nouns from the following paragraph. Be sure to capitalize all proper nouns.

Each day several thousand people visit the lincoln memorial in washington. The monument was designed by henry bacon and was dedicated on memorial day. Located in west potomac park, the lincoln memorial consists of a large marble hall which encloses a life-like statue of abraham lincoln. The figure, which was made from twenty-eight blocks of white marble by daniel chester french, a distinguished sculptor, is sitting in a large armchair as if in deep meditation. On the north wall is found a famous passage from an inaugural address by lincoln, and on the south wall is inscribed the gettysburg address.

THE PRONOUN

Once you can recognize nouns, you can learn to identify pronouns. A *pronoun* is a word that stands for a noun. Without pronouns we would be forced to repeat the same nouns again and again.

> When Kelly saw the signal, Kelly pointed the signal out to Teresa.
> When Kelly saw the signal, **she** pointed **it** out to Teresa.

2b. A *pronoun* is a word used in place of one or of more than one noun.

Name the nouns which the pronouns in the following sentences stand for.

1. Gail read the book and returned **it** to the library.
2. The models bought **themselves** new dresses.
3. "Students," the teacher said, "**you** should keep vocabulary notebooks."
4. Sharon and Pat went fishing. **Both** caught six bass.

The noun that a pronoun stands for is called the *antecedent*. This noun is not always stated.

> *antecedent*　　*pron.*　　　*pron.*
> **Catherine** told **her** father **she** would be late.

> *antecedent*　　*pron.*
> **Juanita,** did **you** do the lesson?

> **You** can't sleep now. [no antecedent stated]

There are several kinds of pronouns. These are the *personal pronouns:*

> I, me, mine, my, myself
> you, your, yours, yourself, yourselves
> he, him, his, himself
> she, her, hers, herself
> it, its, itself
> we, us, our, ours, ourselves
> they, them, their, theirs, themselves

In this book pronouns that come directly before nouns and show possession (*my, his, her, its, your, their*) are called *possessive pronouns.* Your teacher may prefer that you call them *possessive adjectives.*

Make sure that you learn to spell *its* and *their.* Neither *hisself* nor *theirselves* is standard; avoid them.[1]

Other common pronouns are

> who, whom, whoever, whomever
> everybody, everyone, someone, somebody
> no one, nobody, none, others

The following words are pronouns when they are used in the place of nouns:

> what, which, whatever, whichever, whose
> this, that, these, those
> one, each, some, any, other, another
> .many, more, much, most
> both, several, few, all, either, neither

EXERCISE 4. Number your paper 1–10. After each number, list the pronouns in the corresponding sen-

---

[1] *Standard* and *nonstandard* are the terms used in this book to describe kinds of usage. This book teaches standard English. The word *standard* suggests a model with which things can be compared. In this case, the model — standard English — is the set of usage conventions most widely accepted by English-speaking people. All other kinds of usage are called *nonstandard* English. These are variations in usage that are not acceptable in formal writing and formal speaking.

tence. After each pronoun, write the noun or nouns that the pronoun refers to.

EXAMPLE 1. Linda saw the shoes in the window, and she decided to try them on.
1. *she — Linda*
them — shoes

1. Four thousand years ago, a potter scratched a triangle on a vessel to identify it.
2. By marking the vessel, the potter was saying, "This is mine and makes me proud."
3. Furthermore, the artisan was declaring, "If you, the buyer, want another work like it, come to me."
4. The triangle was a symbol of quality, and it is the earliest example of a trademark yet discovered.
5. Early carpenters created distinctive marks and used them to identify products as theirs.
6. In England, silversmiths' guilds tested the quality of precious metals in their great halls.
7. When the members of a guild found a sample to be pure, they would brand it with a stamp.
8. The term *hallmark* comes from this process, and it means "the highest quality."
9. Today, over a million products have their own registered trademarks to help us, the consumers, identify them.
10. Wouldn't shopping be difficult if no products had trademarks to distinguish themselves from other ones?

EXERCISE 5. Copy the following paragraphs, filling in the blanks with appropriate pronouns. If necessary, refer to the lists of pronouns on page 34.

Let —— tell —— about the travel experience of —— of my friends, Mary Tam. —— was taking a group tour through the dense Austabian forests.

After traveling for hours at night through wilderness, —— in the group wanted to make camp, but the guide insisted that —— continue on. Finally, —— agreed to travel for just one more hour.

Soon —— were rewarded for the trip. At the edge of the forest, the guide pointed to the top of a large tree where several koalas were feeding. —— of the animals swung from one tree to ——.

The tour group watched —— from the ground. —— dared to speak a word. The koalas munched happily on the leaves of the trees. —— held onto branches with their sharp claws. —— of the animals carried a cub on her back. —— was feeding the cub while she also fed ——. Although —— of the koalas have been hunted ruthlessly, a —— of the animals thrive within remote Australian forests. —— of the tour members marveled at the unique appearance of the koalas. —— look different from any animal in the world.

EXERCISE 6. Number your paper 1–10. List the pronouns after the proper number. Circle the possessive pronouns.

EXAMPLE 1. What do you know about her life?

1. *What, you,* (*her*)

1. On our way home from school, we heard the sirens of twelve fire engines.
2. Rats are the ugliest creatures one could imagine; they are also very dangerous.
3. Both of them were delighted to see their names in the newspaper.
4. They give us a swimming lesson during each of the gym periods.
5. Do you think she noticed the ink stain on my new plaid shirt?
6. Most of your efforts in school will help you later on in college and in a career.

7. He immediately complimented them on their beautiful dancing.
8. Please tell me if someone is going to make breakfast for all of us.
9. Because everyone is rooting for the underdog team, I am cheering for the team favored to win.
10. She and Dan like summer best, but I can't wait for it to be over.

REVIEW EXERCISE B. Number your paper 1–10. Copy the pronouns from each sentence after the corresponding number. Circle all possessive pronouns.

1. All of us saw Rosemary Casals play tennis.
2. Many of the spectators watching in the stands play tennis themselves.
3. Who would not like to be on the court playing during one of the sets?
4. Casals began to play, and the crowd was awed by the strength of her serve.
5. People were amazed that anyone could play with that much stamina.
6. Casals played such a strong game that she seemed to be rewarding us for our support.
7. Did you know that Rosemary Casals played in many of the tennis tournaments?
8. I remembered that Casals had won my admiration by fighting for equal rights for women in professional tennis.
9. Several people in the audience showed by their enthusiasm that they had enjoyed watching the games.
10. We met them for dinner after the tournament.

THE ADJECTIVE

Jennie goes fishing, and after an exciting struggle she reels in a trout over twenty inches long and weighing almost five pounds. She will not be content with describing her catch merely as a trout. Rather, she will call it a *large* trout or even a *huge* trout.

Allen and Sonia have just finished the final exam for the history course they are taking. Neither of them will be satisfied with saying merely that it was a test. Rather, they will describe the test as being *long* or *difficult* or even *unfair!*

Usually we are not satisfied with just naming things — *trout, test*. We like to make a noun more definite by describing it in some way. The words which we use to make a noun more definite are called *adjectives*. When a noun is described by an adjective, it is said to be *modified*. Since a pronoun may be used in place of a noun, it too may be described, or modified, by an adjective.

2c. An *adjective* is a word used to modify a noun or a pronoun.

An adjective often answers one of these questions: *What kind? Which one? How much or how many?*

WHAT KIND?	WHICH ONE?	HOW MUCH? OR HOW MANY?
a *tall* woman	the *other* one	*five* times
a *steep* mountain	*this* year	*many* mistakes
a *long* hike	the *last* answer	*several* others
an *eager* clerk	*those* people	*no* supplies
a *tired* dog	*that* dress	*few* marbles

The most frequently used adjectives are *a, an, the*. These little words are called *articles*.

EXERCISE 7. Copy the following sentences, filling in the blanks with adjectives which answer the questions given.

EXAMPLE   1. We bought food for *how many?* guests, but *how many?* people attended our *which one?* party.

1. *We bought food for fifty guests, but ninety people attended our last party.*

1. Although they corrected *how many?* mistakes, they made *how many?* others.
2. *Which one?* night *how many?* friends investigated a *what kind?* house.
3. A *what kind?* donkey carried a *what kind?* load for *how many?* days.
4. We had only a *how much?* amount of gasoline by the time we reached the *which one?* town.
5. During the *what kind?* winter we entertained ourselves by reading *how many?* books.

In Exercise 7 all adjectives preceded the nouns which they modified. Sometimes, however, the adjective follows the word it modifies. Note the position of the adjectives in the following sentences. An arrow is drawn from the adjective to the word it modifies.

Each one of the students brought **used books** for the auction.

The **books,** although **old** and **worn,** were quickly bought.

EXERCISE 8. Copy the following sentences, underlining the adjectives. Then draw an arrow from each adjective to the noun which it modifies. Do not underline *a, an,* and *the,* but remember that they are adjectives.

EXAMPLE   1. It was a rainy day when the tired troops returned from the battle.

1. *It was a rainy day when the tired troops returned from the battle.*

1. Melville described whaling in his famous novel *Moby Dick.*
2. Whaling used to be considered an exciting and romantic adventure.
3. Whalers took long voyages on sailing ships with tall masts.
4. Modern whaling is a different kind of adventure.
5. Today, ships that hunt for whales are huge floating factories.
6. Sharp harpoons are shot from guns and carry an explosive tip.
7. In the previous century, the products of whaling had great value, but today the products are not in much demand.
8. Some types of whales are becoming a rare sight in the oceans of the world.
9. Of the nine species of whales, six are now on the list of endangered species.
10. Citizens, both young and old, have been working for a long time to protect whales.

EXERCISE 9. There are twenty-five adjectives in the following paragraph. Make a list of them as they appear. Do not list articles.

1. The ancient Greeks and Romans worshiped twelve major gods. 2. The one with the most power was Zeus, or Jupiter, who lived on a high mountain, Mount Olympus. 3. From the cloudy peak he surveyed the various affairs of the world. 4. He rode in a great chariot which was drawn by four white horses. 5. Whenever he liked, he called for a great assembly of the gods. 6. At the huge assembly one would find Poseidon, or Neptune, the god of the sea; Hades, or Pluto, the god of the shadowy land of the dead; Hera, or Juno, the beautiful but quarrelsome wife of Zeus; Apollo, the handsome god of the sun; Diana, the swift goddess of the hunt, who in time became known as the goddess of the moon; Hermes, or Mercury, the

swift messenger of the gods; Hestia, or Vesta, the goddess of the hearth, who became a special protector of the home; Ares, or Mars, the dreadful god of war; Athena, or Minerva, the favorite daughter of Zeus, who was noted for great wisdom; Hephaestus, or Vulcan, the ugly god, who was the useful god of fire and of the forge; and Aphrodite, or Venus, the lovely goddess of beauty.

EXERCISE 10. Except for *a, an,* and *the,* the following sentences contain no adjectives. Rewrite them and, wherever possible, add interesting adjectives to modify the nouns and pronouns.

EXAMPLE 1. The dog performed tricks.

1. *The small, short-haired dog performed many unusual tricks.*

1. Lisa bought a balloon for her sister.
2. The door opened, and a woman was standing there.
3. We rode for miles before we spotted the park.
4. Juan collects pencils and coins.
5. We watched the fireworks from our window.
6. The cold forced people indoors.
7. The lineman picked off the pass and ran yards for a touchdown.
8. The skater glided around the rink.
9. After running for hours, Sandra led all of the runners.
10. The sisters have become stars.

Proper Adjectives

When you speak of the poetry of Homer, you use a proper noun, but when you say *Homeric* poetry, you use a proper adjective. A proper adjective is formed from a proper noun, and like a proper noun, it begins with a capital letter.

PROPER NOUN	PROPER ADJECTIVE
Mexico	Mexican capital
Africa	African nations
China	Chinese calendar

EXERCISE 11. Number your paper 1–10. If a sentence contains a proper noun, copy the noun after the corresponding number. If the sentence contains a proper adjective, copy both the adjective and the noun it modifies. Some sentences contain both proper nouns and proper adjectives.

EXAMPLE 1. Many French words were added to the English language after the invasion of the Normans in 1066.
1. *French words, English language, Normans*

1. A friend in Japan sent some beautiful Japanese dinnerware to my parents.
2. The professor of African literature gave a lecture on the novels of Camara Laye, a writer who was born in Guinea.
3. Marian McPartland, a jazz pianist from New York City, played several of the songs that Scott Joplin wrote.
4. The remains of several Roman roads can be seen in England today.
5. American tourists in Holland enjoy going to a shoe factory where they can see the traditional wooden shoes being made.
6. The Shakespearean actors were dressed in Elizabethan costumes.
7. During the press conference, the President commented on the Congressional vote.
8. In swimming class this week we are learning to do the Australian crawl.
9. Two Italian dishes which Americans enjoy are lasagna and spaghetti.

10. Many writers have based stories and poems on the Arthurian legend.

Changing Parts of Speech

Sometimes nouns are used as adjectives: *Marian's* book, *airplane* ride, *school* mascot. *Marian, airplane,* and *school* are nouns, but they act like adjectives when they are put in front of nouns. Because the part of speech is determined by the way in which the word is used in a sentence, in parts-of-speech exercises, label as adjectives all nouns used in this way.

Words like *each, some,* and *whose* are sometimes pronouns and sometimes adjectives, depending on their use in a sentence. When they are used in place of nouns, they are pronouns; when they modify nouns, they are adjectives. If they are adjectives, they always precede a noun.

PRONOUN **Each** did the assignment.
ADJECTIVE **Each** person did the assignment.
PRONOUN **Some** have gone to their dressing rooms.
ADJECTIVE **Some** actors have gone to their dressing rooms.
PRONOUN **Whose** are these?
ADJECTIVE **Whose** gloves are these?

EXERCISE 12. In each of the following sentences, decide whether the word in italics is used as an adjective or a pronoun. Number your paper 1–10. Beside the number, write *adj.* when the word is an adjective and *pron.* when the word is a pronoun.

EXAMPLE   1. Do *whatever* is best.
            1. *pron.*

1. *Both* missed the target.
2. We stuffed a Christmas stocking with fruit and toys for *each* one of the children.

3. *Many* high schools offer driver training.
4. *One* should study about a state or country before visiting it.
5. *Some* kinds of seaweed are used in making ice cream.
6. After several days in Paris, *each* of the tourists flew to London.
7. The detective questioned *both* suspects for hours.
8. Sandra found *another* way to work the problem.
9. Last summer *many* of us learned to play tennis.
10. The unicorn is a mythical animal which has only *one* horn.

REVIEW EXERCISE C. There are twenty adjectives in the following sentences. Write the adjectives in each sentence after the corresponding number on your paper. Do not list articles. Be careful not to confuse adjectives with pronouns.

1. There is an interesting tribal legend which tells how people gained possession of fire. 2. According to this story, fire originally belonged to the bears. 3. Then one day the bears went into a deep forest and left the fire on the ground. 4. Soon there were few flames. 5. And the pitiful voice of the fire cried out, "Feed me, or I will die!" 6. As it happened, there were several people who heard the anxious cry of the fire. 7. They picked up one stick from the north and another stick from the south. 8. They took two others from the east and the west. 9. Then they placed these four sticks on the dying fire. 10. Immediately large flames shot up.

11. When the bears returned, they did not recognize their old friend, the fire. 12. They went away and left it to die. 13. But when some of the people who had cared for the fire saw its great loneliness, they picked it up and took it with them. 14. Since that day fire has belonged to people, who use it in many ways.

DIAGRAMING NOUNS AND ADJECTIVES

Diagraming, as you recall from Chapter 1, is a way of showing that you understand the relationship between words and groups of words. When you first studied the adjective, you drew an arrow from the adjective to the noun that it modified. This relationship can also be expressed in a diagram.

PATTERN

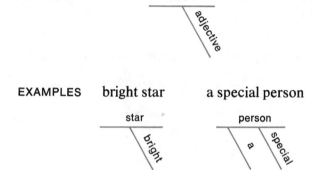

EXAMPLES bright star   a special person

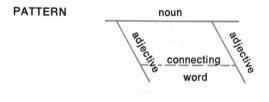

Two or more adjectives joined by a connecting word are diagramed this way.

PATTERN

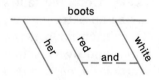

EXAMPLE her red and white boots

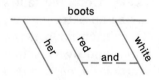

Notice that possessive pronouns are diagramed like adjectives.

EXERCISE 13. Diagram the following items. Use a ruler and allow plenty of space between diagrams.

1. mighty warrior
2. big blue ox
3. a narrow path
4. long, exciting movie
5. his one purpose
6. the last one
7. blue and silver streamers
8. many others
9. my final offer
10. the slow but persistent turtle

EXERCISE 14. Diagram the following sentences.

EXAMPLE   1. A funny clown performed.

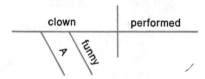

1. Our Swedish visitor arrived.
2. Several answers were given.
3. The angry dog growled.
4. Each one agreed.
5. Our problem has been solved.
6. The small, shy boy won.
7. The poor but generous woman helped.
8. A house and a large barn have burned.
9. The noisy crowd jeered and shouted.
10. My favorite candidate will speak.

REVIEW EXERCISE D. Copy the following paragraph on your paper, leaving an extra line of space between lines of writing. Over each noun, write *n.;* over each pronoun, write *pron.;* and over each adjective, write *adj.* Disregard the articles *a, an,* and *the.*

Charles Drew developed techniques that made it possible to separate and preserve blood. His research saved numerous lives during World War II. After he received his medical degrees, he taught at Howard University in the capital. He set up centers in which blood could be stored. The British government asked him to develop a storage system in England. During the war, Dr. Drew was director of an important effort for the American Red Cross which involved donation of blood. Dr. Drew was also chief surgeon at Freedman's Hospital. We are indebted to this scientist for great contributions. Many people we know have needed blood and owe their lives to his methods.

REVIEW EXERCISE E. Diagram the following sentences.

1. Every minute counts.
2. Many famous performers attended.
3. Five days and five nights passed.
4. The powerful motor shook and roared.
5. The golden clock struck.
6. A few people have left.
7. Several dark clouds can be seen.
8. The ventriloquist and the dummy talked and sang.
9. My favorite comedian is performing.
10. The black and white horses have been sold.

Chapter 3

The Parts of Speech

Verb, Adverb, Preposition, Conjunction, Interjection

In Chapter 2 you studied two of the workhorses of the sentence—the *noun* and the *pronoun*—and the part of speech which makes the noun or pronoun more definite—the *adjective*. In this chapter you will learn about the other workhorse of the sentence—the *verb*—and the remaining four parts of speech—*adverb, preposition, conjunction,* and *interjection.*

THE VERB

You know that a verb is one of the parts of a sentence base. It helps to make a statement about its subject. Some verbs do this by expressing the action of the subject: girl *ran;* monkey *chatters;* sun *sets.* Other verbs help to make a statement without expressing action: I *am* an eighth-grader; this *is* good; she *seems* happy.

3a. A *verb* is a word that expresses action or otherwise helps to make a statement.

Action Verbs

The action expressed by a verb may be physical action or mental action.

PHYSICAL ACTION   jump, shout, search, carry, run
MENTAL ACTION   worry, think, believe, imagine

The action verbs in the following sentences are in heavy type.

Langston Hughes **wrote** volumes of poetry.
Julia Child **makes** gourmet cooking fun.
A distinguished cinematographer, James Wong Howe, **filmed** the movie.
We **listened** to the *Jupiter Symphony* by Mozart.
They **watch** all of Julie Andrews' movies.
She **remembered** the song.

EXERCISE 1.   Number your paper 1–11. Copy after the proper number the verb or verbs in each sentence. There are a total of twenty verbs in the passage. They are all action verbs.

1. In the winter, our house makes strange noises. **2.** Doors on old brass hinges creak as they open and close. **3.** Pipes in the basement shudder when the hot water heater starts up. **4.** Loose floorboards crack from the weight of footsteps. **5.** The rustle of window curtains whispers softly when the winds blow outside. **6.** The old china cabinet rattles noisily each time a truck passes by. **7.** Beams and rafters in the attic strain and groan during the cold, windy nights. **8.** Often, members of my family sit silently and listen for these noises of the house. **9.** We disconnect the television and the appliances. **10.** Each of us makes a list of the various sounds. **11.** Sometimes we pretend that ghosts lurk upstairs and cause the eerie noises.

Linking Verbs

Many important verbs do not express action. They do help to make a statement, but they do this by acting as a link between the subject, which normally comes before the verb, and a word in the predicate, which usually follows the verb. They link their subjects with nouns or adjectives in the predicate.

The star's name **is** Ruby Dee. [name = Ruby Dee]
Marie Curie **became** a famous scientist. [Marie Curie = scientist]
Wild animals **remain** free on the great animal reserves in Africa. [free animals]
The student from Germany **seemed** lonely and unhappy. [lonely and unhappy student]
The watermelon **looks** ripe. [ripe watermelon]

The verb most commonly used as a linking verb is the verb *be*. You should memorize its various forms.

Forms of the Verb Be

am, is, are, was, were, be, being, been

Any verb ending in *be* or *been* is a form of *be: shall be, will be, can be, might be, has been, have been, had been, would have been, might have been,* etc.

In addition to *be,* there are several other verbs which are often used as linking verbs:

seem, appear, look
become, grow
taste, feel, smell, sound
remain, stay

EXERCISE 2. Copy the following sentences, inserting a linking verb in each blank. Use a different verb for each blank. Be prepared to tell what words the verb links.

EXAMPLE 1. Judith Jamison —— calm during the première of the dance.
1. *Judith Jamison* <u>remained</u> *calm during the première of the dance.* [*Remained* links *Jamison* and *calm.*]

1. An unabridged dictionary —— heavy.
2. *Dracula* —— a weird novel.
3. The pine cones —— festive after they were painted silver and gold.
4. The orange —— a little too sweet.
5. In many fairy tales a horrible beast —— a handsome prince.
6. After a rain the streets —— fresh and clean once again.
7. Did she —— in Florida long?
8. The skier —— more daring with each jump she made.
9. We —— quiet during the concert.
10. These roses —— sweet.

Most of the verbs that you studied as linking verbs may also be used as action verbs. Whether a verb is used to express action or to link words depends on its meaning in a given sentence.

LINKING The tiger **looked** tame.
ACTION The tiger **looked** for something to eat.
LINKING The soup **tasted** good.
ACTION I **tasted** the soup.
LINKING She **grew** tired of playing.
ACTION She **grew** into a fine woman.

EXERCISE 3. In the sentences below the same verb is used as a linking verb and as an action verb. When the verb is used as an action verb, copy it. When it is used as a linking verb, copy it and the words it links.

EXAMPLES 1. Ms. Hughes appeared quite angry.
1. *appeared, Ms. Hughes – angry*

2. Ms. Hughes appeared suddenly in the door.
2. *appeared*

1. At the queen's order, her servant tasted the food.
2. The food tasted safe.
3. The taster looked happy after the experiment.
4. Therefore the queen looked upon her with favor.
5. On another occasion the food looked good.
6. The queen again looked at her official taster.
7. The poor woman felt numb with fear.
8. She felt a sudden chill throughout her body.
9. A dinner bell sounded in the banquet hall.
10. Because the taster knew this food had been poisoned, the bell sounded ominous to her.

EXERCISE 4. Write two sentences for each of the following verbs. In the first sentence use the verb as a linking verb; in the second, use it as an action verb.

1. smells   3. taste   5. looks
2. appeared   4. feel

EXERCISE 5. Number your paper 1–16. After the proper number, make a list of the verbs that appear on that line. If the verb is a linking verb, list also the words which the verb links.

1 "Big Bad John" is a ballad which every-
2 one likes. According to the song, John wanders
3 into a mining town. No one there knows anything
4 about his past, although many rumors spread
5 among the people. They think that John was once
6 a bad man; they give him the name "Big Bad
7 John." Still, he seems a hard worker.
8   Then one day he becomes a hero to the towns-
9 people. The mine caves in, and all hope for the
10 safety of the miners appears futile. But John seems
11 confident. He smells the smoke and the fumes,
12 then braces the broken supports of the mine. The

13 other miners scramble to freedom while John dies
14 below. The miners never forget his sacrifice. They
15 place a marker over the mine shaft: "At the bot-
16 tom of this mine lies a big, big man."

Helping Verbs

So far in this chapter you have been studying one-
word verbs, sometimes called *main verbs*. Without
these verbs there could be no sentences. Frequently,
though, the main verb is accompanied by other verbs
called *helping verbs*. The main verb and the helping
verbs make up a *verb phrase*. Each of the main verbs
below is made into a verb phrase through the use of
helping verbs. Notice that the main verb may change
its form when a helping verb is added.

MAIN VERB **crawl**
VERB PHRASE **will crawl**
MAIN VERB **listen**
VERB PHRASE **have been listening**
MAIN VERB **find**
VERB PHRASE **would have been found**

You see that a verb phrase consists of a main verb
preceded by one or more helping verbs. Here is a list
of the most commonly used helping verbs.

be (am, is, are, etc.)	shall	should	must
has	will	would	do
have	can	could	did
had	may	might	does

The verb *be* in its various forms is the most frequently used helping verb. *Be* used as a helping verb
is very easy to distinguish from *be* used as a linking
verb. When *be* is used as a helping verb, there is always a main verb used with it; but when *be* is used as a
linking verb, it is itself the main verb.

HELPING VERB	**are found**
LINKING VERB	**are**
HELPING VERB	**have been tasted**
LINKING VERB	**have been**

The following sentences contain verb phrases. The helping verbs and the main verbs are in heavy type; the main verbs are also underlined.

Seiji Ozawa **has been <u>praised</u>** for his fine conducting.

His recordings **should be <u>heard</u>** by anyone interested in classical music.

He **will <u>conduct</u>** many outstanding orchestras.

He **is <u>making</u>** music important to young people.

EXERCISE 6. Copy the verb phrases as they appear in the exercise.

People have been dancing the polka for more than a hundred years. The dance as it is known today has been attributed to a young serving girl from Czechoslovakia whose identity was lost long ago. Because of its grace and beauty, the polka's popularity was established quickly. Soon after it was danced in Prague, people everywhere were doing the polka. The music of the polka can be enjoyed by both the dancers and the listeners. When polka music is being played, no one can remain still.

Sometimes the verb phrase is interrupted by other parts of speech, as in the examples below.

Because of the fog, we **could** not **see** the road.
Parachuting **has** quickly **become** an important sport.
People **may** someday **communicate** with dolphins.
How much **do** you **know** about Lucy Stone, the suffragist?
Have you ever **read** a biography of Elizabeth I?

EXERCISE 7. There are twenty verb phrases in the following paragraph. Number your paper 1–20. After the proper number, list the verb phrases that appear on that line. Some of the verb phrases are interrupted by other parts of speech. If a verb phrase begins on one line and ends on another, list it for the line on which it begins.

1   The boomerang has long interested people. It
2   was developed by the aborigines of Australia and
3   may be used for amusement, hunting, or war. A
4   different kind of boomerang is used for each pur-
5   pose. We in America have usually misunderstood
6   the boomerang. The kind of boomerang which
7   will return to its owner after it has been thrown
8   is used almost entirely for amusement. This kind
9   of boomerang can hurt an inexperienced thrower.
10 But the aborigines of Australia do not use this
11 type of boomerang for hunting. They have de-
12 veloped one which will move near the ground
13 for many feet and then suddenly will fly upward
14 at a great speed. With this kind of weapon the
15 natives can surprise the game that they are hunt-
16 ing. The boomerang which is used in war can
17 be thrown only by a strong person. This weapon
18 will easily break the arm of a person who is
19 standing five hundred feet from the thrower. It
20 may even inflict a fatal wound.

REVIEW EXERCISE A. Number your paper 1–18. After the proper number, list the verbs and the verb phrases that appear on that line. If a verb phrase begins on one line and ends on another, list it for the line on which it begins. After each action verb or verb phrase, write *a.v.;* after each linking verb or verb phrase, write *l.v.*

1   The term *Viking* was used for all sailors of the
2   North, whether they were Norwegians, Swedes,

3   or Danes. The Vikings were a fierce people who
4   roamed the seas for about three hundred years.
5   For several centuries people considered them the
6   scourge of Europe because they invaded and
7   pillaged the countries to the south. They wor-
8   shiped such fierce gods as Thor and Odin, and
9   they believed that they should die in battle. When
10 Vikings died, they went to Valhalla, where they
11 could eternally enjoy battles and banquets. The
12 Vikings thought Valhalla was a very happy place.
13 Each day the warriors would go out to the battle-
14 field and would receive wounds time and time
15 again. But at the end of each day they would all
16 meet back at the banquet hall, where their wounds
17 would promptly heal and they could boast about
18 their great bravery in battle.

REVIEW EXERCISE B. Number your paper 1–10 and copy the sentences below, writing on every other line of your paper. Some of the words are italicized; underline them. Over each word that you underline, write an abbreviation to show which part of speech it is: *n.* for noun, *pron.* for pronoun, *adj.* for adjective, *a.v.* for action verb, and *l.v.* for linking verb. Treat proper names and verb phrases as one word.

EXAMPLE   1. *Mary McLeod Bethune is* a *major figure* in American history.

              n.   *l.v.*   *adj.*

      1. <u>*Mary McLeod Bethune*</u> <u>*is*</u> a <u>*major*</u>

        n.

      <u>*figure*</u> in American history.

1. Mary Bethune *dedicated* her *life* to helping *young* people.
2. In her *early years* she *began* a teaching *career.*
3. In 1904 *she moved* to Florida and *opened* a *school* of *her* own.
4. The school eventually *became* the Bethune-Cookman College, and *Bethune* served as its *president.*

5. In 1930 Bethune *was invited* to a *presidential conference* on child health and protection.
6. Then, during Roosevelt's *administration, she helped* in the establishment of the *National Youth Administration.*
7. Her *outstanding efforts* impressed Roosevelt, and *he established* an *important* office on minority affairs.
8. This office *granted funds* to *serious students* so they could continue *their* education.
9. In 1945 she *was* an observer at the *conference* that *organized* the *United Nations.*
10. Bethune *remained* interested in education, and her *notable* efforts earned her *national recognition.*

THE ADVERB

3b. An *adverb* is a word used to modify a verb, an adjective, or another adverb.

An adverb usually answers one of these questions: *Where? When? How? To what extent (how much or how long)?* These are some of the questions a newspaper reporter tries to answer when covering a story.

WHERE?
The fire started **here.**

The couple was married **nearby.**
The thief fell **down.**

WHEN?
The police inspector arrived **promptly.**

Then the suspects were questioned.
The detective takes notes **daily.**

HOW?
The accident occurred **suddenly.**
The Prime Minister spoke **carefully.**
The train stopped **abruptly.**

TO WHAT EXTENT (HOW MUCH OR HOW LONG)?
We should **never** become upset.
The escaped convicts ran **far.**
She has **scarcely** begun the lesson.

(1) An adverb modifies a verb more often than it modifies an adjective or an adverb.

Notice in the following examples how the adverb makes the meaning of the verb more definite.

The man crawled **down.** [The adverb tells *where* the man crawled.]
He crawled **slowly.** [The adverb tells *how* he crawled.]
Now we are busy. [The adverb tells *when* we are busy.]
The speaker droned on **endlessly.** [The adverb tells *to what extent* the speaker droned.]

Adverbs are sometimes used to ask questions.

Where are you going?
How did you do on the test?

EXERCISE 8. Number your paper 1–10. Write an adverb for each blank. After each adverb, write what the adverb tells: *Where? When? How?* or *To what extent (how much)?* the action was done.

Use a different adverb for each blank and include all four kinds.

1. We waved —— and ran ——.
2. The scissors cut ——.
3. A clue was found ——.
4. —— the so-called ghost appeared.
5. Our friends could —— wait.
6. —— will the doctor get ——?
7. —— the climbers —— climbed Lookout Mountain.
8. Lena's kite flew —— than the others and rode the wind more ——.
9. The dog moaned —— as the girl —— washed it.
10. The author typed —— as the story unfolded in her mind.

EXERCISE 9. The following sentences contain twenty adverbs, all modifying verbs. Number your paper 1–9. After the proper number, copy the adverbs in that sentence.

1. The snowstorm has completely blocked traffic and has temporarily grounded airplanes.
2. How can you develop into a strong runner now?
3. Yesterday three police officers secretly followed the suspect.
4. The doctor came immediately, but the patient had already recovered.
5. Gymnastics has recently attracted many students, and the equipment is always in use.
6. The coach argued violently, but the umpire calmly threw him out of the game.
7. February is never a warm month in Maine.
8. Her luncheon was received well, and her speech was applauded loudly afterward.
9. Today astronomers can accurately chart the course of planets, yet the motions of some celestial bodies are still a mystery.

(2) An adverb sometimes modifies an adjective.

An adverb is sometimes needed to make the meaning of an adjective more definite. An *extremely* good dancer is quite different from a *fairly* good dancer.

The skaters put on a **very** exciting show. [The adjective *exciting* modifies the noun *show;* then the adverb tells *how exciting* the show was.]

An **unusually** fast starter, Karen easily won the hurdles event. [The adjective *fast* modifies the noun *starter;* then the adverb tells *how fast* the starter was.]

Our committee is **especially** busy at this time of year. [The adjective *busy* modifies the noun *committee;* then the adverb tells *how busy* the committee is.]

EXERCISE 10. Number your paper 1–10. Copy the adverbs that modify adjectives in each sentence. After each adverb, list on your paper the adjective it modifies.

EXAMPLE   1. Because there are so many kangaroos in Australia, the kangaroo has become the national animal.
    1. *so, many*

1. Kangaroos are extremely fast animals.
2. Kangaroos seem very graceful when they are leaping about.
3. But they look quite awkward when they are still.
4. Their back legs are extremely long.
5. Their front legs are too short to be of much use in moving about.
6. The baby kangaroo, called a "joey," is hardly longer than an inch at birth.
7. It looks thoroughly contented in its mother's pouch.
8. Some kangaroos are unusually small even after they have reached their full growth.
9. One kind is no larger than a rabbit.
10. The great red kangaroo, the largest variety, is surprisingly tall.

EXERCISE 11. The adverb *very* is used far too often to modify adjectives. Write an adverb to modify each adjective below. Do not use *very*.

EXAMPLE   1. beautiful
    1. *unbelievably beautiful*

1. light
2. narrow
3. happy
4. tidy
5. daring

6. awkward
7. true
8. dishonest
9. tired
10. sweet

(3) An adverb occasionally modifies another adverb.

Elena finished the problem **more** quickly than I did. [The adverb *quickly* modifies the verb *finished* and is, in turn, modified by the adverb *more,* which tells *how quickly* Elena finished the problem.]

Our guest left **quite** abruptly. [The adverb *abruptly* modifies the verb *left* and is modified by *quite,* which tells *how abruptly* our guest left.]

EXERCISE 12. Number your paper 1–10. From the following sentences list opposite the proper number only the adverbs which modify other adverbs. Then, after each adverb, write the adverb that it modifies.

EXAMPLE 1. The fingerprint is most certainly an aid in verifying the identity of a criminal.
1. *most, certainly*

1. Before 1900, fingerprinting was very rarely used by the police.
2. As a matter of fact, the use of fingerprinting was almost entirely confined to verifying personal identification.
3. People used their fingerprints quite often to protect themselves from forgers.
4. As a means of identification the fingerprint has been fairly consistently used for at least two thousand years.
5. The walls of caves show quite undeniably that primitive people were also interested in the use of fingerprints.
6. So fingerprinting has been used much longer than we ordinarily think.
7. Finally, around 1900, it was established that a fingerprint very clearly distinguishes one individual from all others.
8. The many studies of classifications of fingerprints

were most enthusiastically welcomed by Scotland Yard, and, later, fingerprinting was adopted by the FBI.

9. Today the classification of fingerprints is so well developed that an expert can locate a particular set of prints in minutes by finding the class to which the prints belong.

10. We realize that the expert works quite rapidly when we remember that the files contain millions of fingerprints.

REVIEW EXERCISE C. Number your paper 1–10. Make a list of the adverbs in the order that they appear in the exercise. After each adverb, write the word or expression that the adverb modifies. Some sentences have more than one adverb.

EXAMPLE   1. The suspect fidgeted quite noticeably.
1. *quite, noticeably*
noticeably, fidgeted

1. After we had finished packing our gear, a terribly violent thunderstorm began in the Amazon Valley.
2. While the storm raged outside, we sat down in our tent to review our research findings on animal life.
3. We found that one very strange frog in the Amazon Valley has a most unusual method of escaping capture.
4. If a snake suddenly attacks it, the frog cleverly expands like a balloon and the snake is not able to swallow it.
5. Another kind of frog has an equally strange escape mechanism.
6. If attacked, it secretes a highly potent poison which completely paralyzes its enemies, allowing the frog to escape.
7. In the Amazon Valley we often found grasshoppers that were surprisingly large.
8. Some were even bigger than our hands.

9. In contrast, some frogs were much smaller than the ends of our fingers.
10. We had been unusually well rewarded during our stay in the Amazon Valley.

DIAGRAMING VERBS AND ADVERBS

The verb, like the noun and pronoun, always appears on a horizontal line. The adverb is diagramed on a slanting line under the word it modifies.

1. An adverb modifying a verb:

EXAMPLES   studies hard   does not exercise daily

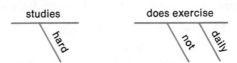

2. An adverb modifying an adjective:

EXAMPLES
    extremely strong wind   much better swimmer

3. An adverb modifying another adverb:

EXAMPLES   tried rather hard   flew almost too high

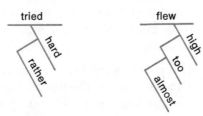

EXERCISE 13. Diagram the following groups of words. Use a ruler and leave plenty of space between diagrams.

1. answered quickly
2. badly worn sail
3. listened quite intently
4. worked very late
5. dangerously sharp curve
6. never plans very carefully
7. walked proudly away
8. somewhat rickety bridge
9. may possibly happen
10. drove rather slowly

EXERCISE 14. Diagram the following sentences. Use a ruler and leave plenty of space between diagrams.

1. The plane landed smoothly.
2. The guide limped noticeably.
3. The extremely nervous passenger collapsed.
4. Our turn finally came.
5. They tried very hard.
6. The shutters rattled quite noisily.
7. The almost new automobile had been slightly damaged.
8. We are definitely leaving tomorrow.
9. The tired motorist drove much too far.
10. The unbelievably slow turtle got there first.

THE PREPOSITION

3c. A *preposition* is a word used to show the relationship of a noun or a pronoun to some other word in the sentence.

Notice how a change in the preposition changes the relationship between *package* and *tree* in each of the following sentences.

The package **under** the tree is mine.
The package **in** the tree is mine.
The package **near** the tree is mine.

Learn to recognize the following words, which are commonly used as prepositions.

Commonly Used Prepositions

aboard	behind	from	throughout
about	below	in	to
above	beneath	into	toward
across	beside	like	under
after	between	near	underneath
against	beyond	of	until
along	but (except)	off	unto
amid	by	on	up
among	down	over	upon
around	during	past	with
at	except	since	within
before	for	through	without

Occasionally you will find compound prepositions —prepositions of more than one word. A compound preposition may be considered as one word.

Compound Prepositions

because of	according to
on account of	instead of
in spite of	out of

EXERCISE 15. Number your paper 1–10. Make a list of the prepositions as they appear in the following sentences. Several of these prepositions will be compound prepositions.

1. In Roman mythology, Vulcan was the god of fire.
2. According to legend he once had a bad fall.
3. His father, Jupiter, kicked him out of heaven.
4. From Mount Olympus, the home of Jupiter, Vulcan fell to the earth.
5. He fell through space like a meteor, and his descent lasted for an entire day.

6. He fell to earth with such force that he broke one of his legs.
7. After his injury Vulcan was called the lame god.
8. He remained on earth and made a new life for himself.
9. Eventually he climbed to the top of Mount Etna in Sicily and established a great forge there.
10. With his forge he created many beautiful golden objects.

A preposition is always followed by a noun or pronoun, which it relates to another word in the sentence. The noun or pronoun following the preposition is called the *object* of the preposition. Words that modify the object may come between the preposition and the object. Taken together, the preposition, its object, and the modifiers of the object are called a *prepositional phrase.*

EXAMPLE across the dusty prairie [The entire prepositional phrase includes the preposition (*across*), its object (*prairie*), and two adjectives modifying the object (*the, dusty*).]

EXERCISE 16. Each of the following sentences contains a prepositional phrase. Number your paper 1–10, and after the proper number, copy the phrase. Underline the prepositions.

EXAMPLE 1. Walt Whitman wrote a very moving poem, "O Captain! My Captain!" about Abraham Lincoln.
    1. *about Abraham Lincoln*

1. In this poem the ship's captain represents Abraham Lincoln.
2. The ship has just completed a voyage through rough weather.

3. On the shore, people celebrate the ship's safe arrival.
4. One member of the ship's crew addresses his captain.
5. "For you they call, the swaying mass, their eager faces turning. . . ."
6. Everyone except the captain can hear the rejoicing.
7. He has died during the voyage.
8. The ship represents the ship of state.
9. And the ship's voyage across rough seas symbolizes the war.
10. Lincoln, the captain, directed his ship toward a safe harbor.

Sometimes the same word may be used as a preposition or an adverb. It is easy to tell the adverb from the preposition if you remember that a preposition must always be followed by a noun or pronoun object.

ADVERB The plane circled above.
PREPOSITION The plane circled above our heads. [Note the object of the preposition — *heads*.]
ADVERB We remained within.
PREPOSITION We remained within the shelter. [Note the object of the preposition — *shelter*.]

EXERCISE 17. Use each of the following words in a sentence, first as an adverb, then as a preposition. Underline the designated word.

EXAMPLE 1. across
1. *"Why can't I swim across?" the child questioned.*
   At one time people were afraid to venture across the ocean.

1. below   3. down   5. within
2. aboard   4. underneath

You must also be careful not to confuse a prepositional phrase beginning with *to* (*to town, to her club*,
etc.) with a verb form beginning with *to* (*to run, to
be seen, to have completed*, etc.). Remember again
that a prepositional phrase always ends with a noun
or pronoun.

THE CONJUNCTION

3d. A *conjunction* **is a word which joins words or groups
of words.**

Conjunctions joining single words:

> brush **and** paint
> hot **or** cold
> small **but** comfortable

Conjunctions joining groups of words:

> through a forest **and** across a river
> wanted to notify **but** not to alarm
> camping out **or** staying in motels

Conjunctions joining groups of words that are sentences:

> The stars seem motionless, **but** actually they
> are moving rapidly through space.
> One leader was very powerful, **and** the other
> was very weak.
> Sharon typed her paper herself, **or** she had her
> sister type it for her.

Conjunctions are of three kinds: *coordinating, correlative*, and *subordinating*.

The *coordinating conjunctions* are *and, but, or,
nor, for*, and *yet*.

> The cave explorers carried ropes **and** torches.

> You may take the test now, **or** you may wait until later.
>
> Our auction was very successful, **for** every student brought something to be sold.

Notice that when *for* is used as a conjunction, it connects groups of words that are sentences. On all other occasions it is used as a preposition.

CONJUNCTION We wrote to the tourist bureau, **for** we wanted information on places to visit.

PREPOSITION We waited patiently **for** a reply.

Correlative conjunctions are always found in pairs and have other words dividing them: *either . . . or, neither . . . nor, both . . . and, not only . . . but also.*

> Our class will furnish **either** the punch **or** the cookies for the party.
>
> **Both** cats **and** dogs make good pets.
>
> Claire Boothe Luce was **not only** a playwright **but also** an ambassador.

Subordinating conjunctions occur in complex sentences. They are explained on pages 103–04.

EXERCISE 18. Number your paper 1–10. Write after each number a coordinating or correlative conjunction to fill the blanks in the corresponding sentence.

1. We will play —— badminton —— volleyball.
2. Paul Bunyan —— Babe, his Blue Ox, are part of American folklore.
3. We read —— —— our texts —— —— the books in the library.
4. I'm not sure whether it was Charlotte Brontë —— George Eliot who wrote *Silas Marner*.
5. Phyllis McGinley wrote poetry —— published essays.

6. —— Los Angeles —— San Diego is the capital of California.
7. My parents are going shopping, —— I am staying at home.
8. —— the seal —— the porpoise enjoy showing off for people.
9. The happy winner of the skating contest waved her hands —— threw her cap into the air.
10. The freshman did not win the race, —— had he expected to win it.

EXERCISE 19. Make a list of the twenty coordinating and correlative conjunctions as they appear in the exercise below. Be able to tell what words or groups of words each conjunction joins. Treat a pair of correlative conjunctions as one conjunction.

The intelligence of dogs and cats has often been compared. Some people say that the dog is smarter, but others argue that the cat is brighter. Certainly the dog performs tricks more readily than the cat, for it is especially interested in pleasing its owner. The cat, on the other hand, neither tries nor wishes to please its owner. The cat is an independent animal, but the dog is dependent on its owner for affection and attention. The only work a cat will do for its owner is to catch mice or rats, and that kind of work is fun.

There are many common misunderstandings about both dogs and cats. Most people believe that the mother dog or cat teaches its offspring by showing them how something is done. Actually, the offspring do not learn by watching their mother but by doing what their mother does. The mother takes the offspring along and allows them to take part in an activity. Of course, the mother not only puts its offspring into a learning situation but also urges them on.

Another false belief is that a cat will always chase and kill mice. We know that this idea is wrong, for an experiment has shown it so. When a young kitten and a mouse were put into a cage together, the kitten neither chased the mouse nor tried to harm it in any way. In fact, the kitten and the mouse became great friends. They played together happily, and neither was harmed. So *Peter Churchmouse,* the old story about the mouse and the kitten who were friends, is possible after all.

THE INTERJECTION

3e. An *interjection* is a word which expresses emotion and which is not related grammatically to other words in the sentence.

> **Oh!** You surprised me.
> **Wow!** Am I tired!
> **Well,** I did my best.

DETERMINING PARTS OF SPEECH

You have now finished a study of the eight parts of speech. On the next page is a chart which briefly summarizes what you have learned.

3f. A word's use determines its part of speech.

Although words are given as examples of particular parts of speech in the chart below, you cannot really tell what part of speech a word is until you know how the word is used in a sentence. You've seen in your study of Chapters 2 and 3 that the same word can be used as a pronoun and an adjective or as an adverb and a preposition. Only when you see how a word is used in a sentence can you label it as a particular part of speech.

> **Each** did his part. [pronoun]
> **Each** student baked a cake. [adjective]

The tired shoppers sat **down** for a while. [adverb]
The ball rolled **down** the hill. [preposition]
A member of the crew has spotted **land.** [noun]
The pilot can **land** here safely. [verb]

SUMMARY

Rule	Part of Speech	Use	Examples
2a	noun	names	Wilma, cave, Asia
2b	pronoun	takes the place of a noun	she, ourselves, who, anyone
2c	adjective	modifies a noun or pronoun	sick, tiny, purple, smooth
3a	verb	shows action or helps to make a statement	play, study, were, become
3b	adverb	modifies a verb, an adjective, or another adverb	very, too, usually, quickly
3c	preposition	relates a noun or pronoun to another word; begins a prepositional phrase	beside [her] to [town] for [John] with [them]
3d	conjunction	joins words	and, but, or
3e	interjection	shows strong feeling	Well! Wow! Oh!

REVIEW EXERCISE D. Number your paper 1–20. After each number, copy the italicized word from the corresponding sentence. Then write the part of speech of the word. Be prepared to explain your answer to the class.

EXAMPLES
1. That is a good *date* for the festival.
   1. *date — noun*
2. Does Diane still *date* Ted?
   2. *date — verb*

1. The package is too heavy *for* him.
2. He had to set the package down, *for* it was too heavy to carry.
3. One night we tried to count the *stars,* but finally we lost count.
4. My favorite actress *stars* in this movie.
5. *Some* have agreed to work in the booths.
6. *Some* booths will feature unusual contests and prizes.
7. The girl walked *along* gaily next to her parents.
8. Julio and José walked down a path that runs *along* the lake.
9. Do you know where *my* coat is?
10. *My!* What an unusual painting!
11. The *still* water reflected her image clearly.
12. Are you *still* looking for your sister?
13. There are *many* who will help the committee with the project.
14. Mae and I found *many* different shells on the beach.
15. People who do not exercise *tire* easily.
16. My parents bought a new *tire* before we left on our vacation.
17. An airport is located *nearby.*
18. We are staying in a *nearby* hotel.
19. At the first port twenty-seven passengers climbed *aboard.*
20. While we were *aboard* the ship, we rested and enjoyed ourselves.

REVIEW EXERCISE E. Write a short sentence for each of the following, using the word as the part of speech that is indicated. Underline the word in your sentence.

EXAMPLE   1. *attempts* as a noun
           1. *The Wright brothers' first* <u>attempts</u> *at flying ended in failure.*

 1. *shade* as a verb
 2. *today* as an adverb
 3. *all* as an adjective
 4. *plans* as a noun
 5. *over* as an adverb
 6. *tour* as a verb
 7. *several* as a pronoun
 8. *within* as a preposition
 9. *look* as an interjection
10. *for* as a conjunction

REVIEW EXERCISE F. Number your paper 1–50. From the following paragraphs, copy after the proper number each of the italicized words. After each word, write its part of speech. Be able to explain your answer by giving the *use* of the word in the sentence. Use the following abbreviations:

n.	noun	*adv.*	adverb
pron.	pronoun	*prep.*	preposition
v.	verb	*conj.*	conjunction
adj.	adjective	*interj.*	interjection

(1) *People* have (2) *always* enjoyed playing tricks on (3) *me.* (4) *Yesterday* during (5) *lunch* one of my friends (6) *said* that (7) *she* (8) *had* a (9) *difficult* problem (10) *for* me. The problem went something (11) *like* this: "There are (12) *two* (13) *rabbits*—a big rabbit (14) *and* a little rabbit. The (15) *little* rabbit (16) *is* the big rabbit's son, (17) *but* the big rabbit is (18) *not* the little rabbit's (19) *father.* What relation are (20) *they?"*

I (21) *thought* (22) *about* the (23) *problem* (24) *throughout* lunch. (25) *Later* I thought about it (26) *during* science class. As a matter of fact, I didn't notice when my (27) *teacher* (28) *called* on me to answer. I considered every (29) *possible* answer, but none (30) *seemed* right. (31) *Finally* the (32) *bell* (33) *rang* and I (34) *rushed* over (35) *to* my friend's (36) *desk.* "What's the answer?" I (37) *begged.*

(38) *"Well,* the big rabbit is (39) *obviously* the little rabbit's mother," my friend knowingly (40) *replied.*

(41) *"What!* (42) *You* mean the answer was that simple!" I (43) *groaned.* "You've (44) *tricked* me for the (45) *last* time." And (46) *no one* did trick (47) *me* (48) *again* (49) *until* the (50) *next* day.

The Phrase

Prepositional and Participial Phrases

In Chapters 2 and 3 you studied single-word modifiers: the adjective and the adverb. A whole group of words may also act as a modifier. Just as a verb phrase acts as a single verb, so an adjective phrase acts as a single adjective, and an adverb phrase acts as a single adverb. As modifiers, phrases play an important part in our sentences. This chapter will focus on how to identify and use phrases in writing.

4a. A phrase is a group of related words that is used as a single part of speech and does not contain a verb and its subject.

You have already studied the *verb phrase,* which is introduced by a helping verb (*have* bought). You have also been introduced to the *prepositional phrase.* In this chapter you will learn more about the prepositional phrase, and you will meet a new kind of phrase —the *participial phrase.*

THE PREPOSITIONAL PHRASE

4b. A *prepositional phrase* is a group of words that begins with a preposition and usually ends with a noun or pronoun.

In the following examples, the prepositional phrases are in heavy type.

We prepared treats **for them.**
During the night the horse ran off.
Marian wore white pajamas **with red stripes.**

Of course, a single prepositional phrase may contain two or more objects.

The dish is filled **with nuts and rice cookies.**
The group traveled **through Spain and Italy.**

EXERCISE 1. Number your paper 1–13, using every other line. Write after each number the prepositional phrases in the corresponding sentence. There are twenty-five phrases.

1. The daily schedule prepared by the camp directors was followed from dawn until late evening.
2. We were awakened at six by a bugle, played with cold fingers by a sleepy camper.
3. Linda Sanchez sometimes woke the camp in the morning with her saxophone.
4. Standing attentively outside our cabins, we shivered in the early morning breeze coming across the lake.
5. After exercises, everyone swam in the icy water.
6. Fearing death from freezing, we raced back and dressed for breakfast.
7. Inspection followed the cleaning of cabins.
8. Activity period included classes in painting, crafts, music, drama, and folklore.
9. The rest of the morning was devoted to sports.
10. After lunch, we spent an hour in our cabins.
11. Then we had two hours of water sports.
12. The time between water sports and dinner was free.
13. At night, talented campers and counselors entertained us, and we sang songs.

The Adjective Phrase

Some prepositional phrases are called *adjective phrases* because they act like adjectives; that is, they modify nouns and pronouns.

4c. An *adjective phrase* is a prepositional phrase that modifies a noun or pronoun.

Notice that the adjectives and adjective phrases in heavy type in the following sentences do the same work: they modify a noun.

ADJECTIVE   The **lighthouse** beacon stayed on all night.

ADJECTIVE PHRASE   The beacon **from the lighthouse** stayed on all night.

ADJECTIVE   Their **varsity** players are bigger than our players.

ADJECTIVE PHRASE   The players **on their varsity** are bigger than our players.

ADJECTIVE   I met some **Asian** students.

ADJECTIVE PHRASE   I met some students **from Asia.**

Like the adjective, an adjective phrase is usually located next to the word it modifies. But while the adjective generally precedes the word it modifies, the adjective phrase usually follows the word it modifies.

EXERCISE 2. Each of the following sentences contains an adjective phrase. Number your paper 1–10. After the proper number, copy the phrase and the noun or pronoun it modifies.

EXAMPLE   1. The snow on the highway was five feet deep.
    1. *on the highway, snow*

1. The strait between the Pacific Ocean and San Francisco Bay is called the Golden Gate.
2. The Golden Gate Bridge spans this narrow body of water.
3. San Francisco was once a small village on the bay but is now a busy metropolitan center.
4. The California Gold Rush of 1849 swelled San Francisco's population.
5. The 1906 earthquake destroyed the homes of many people.
6. Today sightseers from many different nations crowd San Francisco's streets.
7. Some of the streets are very steep.
8. San Francisco's Chinatown and Fisherman's Wharf are two attractions for visitors.
9. This city beside the bay has many charms.
10. Do you know any songs about San Francisco?

EXERCISE 3. Construct sentences using each of the following word groups as an adjective phrase. Underline the noun or pronoun that the adjective phrase modifies.

EXAMPLE 1. on the hill
1. *The single <u>tree</u> on the hill looks lonely.*

1. around the corner
2. near the school
3. like them
4. through the woods
5. under the big tent
6. for our dog
7. with colorful lights
8. in the band
9. under the rock
10. at the dock

Sometimes one adjective phrase follows another. The second phrase usually modifies the object in the first phrase.

Sicily is an island **off the coast of Italy.**

EXERCISE 4. Each sentence below contains two adjective phrases. Number your paper 1–10, and copy the phrases after the proper numbers. After each phrase, copy the word it modifies.

EXAMPLE   1. Lynn wrote a research paper on monsters in Scotland.
1. *on monsters, paper*
in Scotland, monsters

1. Many of us in the class wished that we could speak a foreign language.
2. Jeanette suggested that we already knew several words from languages of other countries.
3. "We all know the sounds of animals around the world," she said.
4. "Surely dogs in countries outside the United States must go *bow-wow* or *arf-arf.*"
5. We were shocked when the European exchange student in the back of the room said that this was wrong.
6. "The bark of a dog in Italy," she said, "is pronounced *bu-bu.*"
7. "When a dog in the country of Spain barks, it goes *how-how.*"
8. "The French, the people on the other side of the border, pronounce a dog's bark *wah-wah.*"
9. We learned that the sounds of other animals throughout the world were not our familiar ones either.
10. Why is it that the people from every land except our own completely mispronounce animal sounds?

The Adverb Phrase

When a prepositional phrase is used as an adverb to modify a verb, adjective, or adverb, it is called an *adverb phrase.* Like a single-word adverb, the adverb phrase answers the questions *How? When? Where? To what extent?*

4d. An *adverb phrase* is a prepositional phrase that modifies a verb, an adjective, or an adverb.

> The snow fell **like feathers.** [The adverb phrase modifies the verb *fell,* telling *how* the snow fell.]
>
> Her dress is too long **in the back.** [The adverb phrase modifies the adjective *long,* telling *where* the dress is too long.]
>
> We arrived early **in the morning.** [The adverb phrase modifies the adverb *early,* telling *when* we were early.]

Adverb phrases modify verbs more often than they modify adjectives and adverbs.

EXERCISE 5. Each sentence below contains an adverb phrase. Number your paper 1–10. After the proper number, write the adverb phrase from each sentence. Then write the verb, adjective, or adverb that the phrase modifies.

EXAMPLE   1. The first coffeehouses were built in Egypt.
                1. *in Egypt, were built*

1. The first English coffeehouse opened in 1650.
2. Soon coffeehouses were popular beyond belief.
3. Almost everyone went to the coffeehouse.
4. At such a place one learned the latest gossip.
5. People sat late into the night drinking coffee and talking.
6. They never shied away from a discussion.
7. Instead they argued on every occasion.
8. They were witty in their arguments.
9. For thirty years Will's Coffee House was often crowded.
10. The famous writers John Dryden and Joseph Addison could often be found at Will's.

EXERCISE 6. Construct sentences in which you use the following phrases as adverbs modifying verbs. Underline the word modified.

EXAMPLE 1. during the night
1. *During the night a bear <u>ate</u> our food.*

1. about a year ago
2. through the storm
3. in the shower
4. down the street
5. beside the detective
6. outside the shelter
7. by my friends
8. above the clouds
9. after many hours
10. without any books

Like adjective phrases, adverb phrases often appear one after the other, usually modifying the same word.

Animals move **to a warm place during the winter months.**

The adjective phrase almost always follows immediately after the word it modifies, but the adverb phrase may be separated from the word it modifies by other words. Adverb phrases may be moved about in the sentence.

For many centuries people searched **for a way** to make gold.

People searched **for many centuries for a way** to make gold.

For a way to make gold, people searched **for many centuries.**

EXERCISE 7. Number your paper 1–7. Write after the proper number the adverb phrase (phrases) in each sentence. After each phrase, write the word it modifies.

1. Mount Vernon is interesting for its history.
2. It is near Washington, D.C.
3. The house was named Mount Vernon by Lawrence

Washington, who lived there for many years.
4. Somewhat later, George and Martha Washington moved to Mount Vernon.
5. After Washington's death the house passed through several hands.
6. In 1858, it was bought by the Mount Vernon Ladies Association, who restored it.
7. The buildings and grounds are open to the general public.

DIAGRAMING ADJECTIVE AND ADVERB PHRASES

An adjective or adverb phrase is diagramed below the word it modifies. Write the preposition on a line slanting down from the modified word. Then write the object of the preposition (the noun or pronoun following the preposition) in the phrase on a horizontal line leading from the slanting line. Modifiers within a phrase are diagramed in the usual way.

PATTERNS

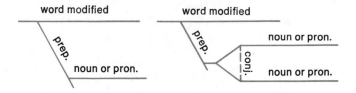

EXAMPLES   1. walked along the road

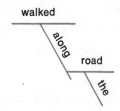

2. paintings by famous artists

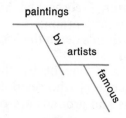

3. went with Hollis and Dave

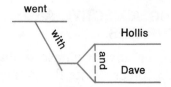

When a prepositional phrase modifies the object of another prepositional phrase, the diagram looks like this:

EXAMPLE   camped on top of a mountain

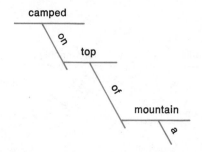

EXERCISE 8. Diagram the following word groups which contain prepositional phrases. Use a ruler and leave plenty of space between diagrams.

1. invited to the celebrations
2. everyone but her
3. date of the wedding
4. a glimpse of the famous ruler

5. was by my favorite actor and actress
6. hiked for twenty miles
7. one of the people in the room
8. the day before the trial
9. read about King Midas and his golden touch
10. drove to a village near Paris

EXERCISE 9. Diagram the following sentences, each of which contains an adjective phrase or an adverb phrase or both.

EXAMPLE   The company of actors performed in front of a large audience.

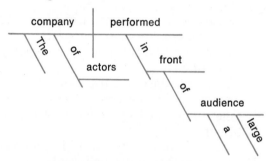

1. The film was made in Spain.
2. The number of whales is decreasing.
3. One of the candidates withdrew from the race.
4. Ocean tides are controlled by the moon.
5. Pompeii was destroyed by a volcano.
6. Citrus fruits are grown in California and Florida.
7. Many historic events have been decided by sudden changes in the weather.
8. The defeat of the Spanish Armada resulted from a violent ocean storm.
9. Some familiar animals can be found only in zoos.
10. Hundreds of species have vanished from the earth.

REVIEW EXERCISE A. List in order the adjective and adverb phrases in the following sentences. Before each phrase, write the number of the sentence in which it occurs. After each phrase, write the word or expression it modifies. Be ready to tell whether it is an adjective or an adverb phrase.

EXAMPLE   1. Through the years our understanding of the word *travel* has changed.
1. *Through the years, has changed*
1. *of the word, understanding*

1. Few of us know that our word *travel* comes from the French term *travailler,* which means "to work hard."
2. Until recent times, *travel* was associated with pain or agony.
3. During your spare time, read a few accounts of the traveling conditions of the past.
4. Before the days of modern transportation, travel was not easy.
5. One might start on a trip to a neighboring state or country and never arrive there.
6. One often faced the dangers of bandits and wild beasts.
7. One certainly met with discouragement from nasty weather and rough roads.
8. For many centuries a traveler often relied on hospitality in the homes of strangers.
9. The laws of hospitality required that the hosts be generous with their food and possessions.
10. If a traveler was not allowed into the house, the hosts believed they would suffer misfortune.

THE PARTICIPLE

Besides the eight parts of speech that you have learned, our language contains another kind of word — the *verbal.* A verbal is a word that is formed from a verb but is used in sentences as another part of speech. One kind of verbal is the *participle.*

4e. A *participle* is a verb form used as an adjective.

There are two kinds of participles—present participles and past participles. Present participles end in *–ing*. Past participles often end in *–ed, –d,* or *–t*.

> The horses **trotting** past were not frightened by the crowd. [*Trotting,* a form of the verb *trot,* modifies, like an adjective, the noun *horses— trotting horses.*]
>
> **Buried** by pirates, the treasure was undiscovered for centuries. [*Buried,* a form of the verb *bury,* modifies, like an adjective, the noun *treasure— buried treasure.*]

Do not confuse participles used as in the examples above with participles used in a verb phrase.

PARTICIPLE	**Broken,** the toy still ran.
VERB PHRASE	The toy **was broken** but still ran.
PARTICIPLE	**Planning** their trip, the class learned some geography.
VERB PHRASE	While they **were planning** their trip, the class learned some geography.

Think of the participle in a verb phrase as part of a verb, not as an adjective.

EXERCISE 10. Number your paper 1–10. After the proper number, copy the participle (participles) from each of the following sentences. After each participle, write the noun it modifies. Be prepared to tell whether the participle is a present participle or a past participle.

EXAMPLE 1. We heard the wind howling around the house.
  1. *howling, wind*

1. Toys, broken and mutilated, were all around the room.
2. Grinning broadly, Julia obviously brought good news.

3. The roof, blazing furiously, soon collapsed.
4. The shoes, tattered and stained, had been left on the cobbler's doorstep.
5. For years the shack stood there, quite deserted.
6. Sighing happily, she folded and put away the letter.
7. I watched the dog charging toward me.
8. Singing and dancing, the people of New Orleans paraded through the streets.
9. The crowd, cheering wildly, applauded the performance.
10. Recently published, this book is not yet available in paperback.

THE PARTICIPIAL PHRASE

When a participle introduces a group of related words that act together as an adjective, this word group is called a *participial phrase*.

4f. A *participial phrase* is a group of related words that contains a participle and that acts as an adjective.

A prepositional phrase often follows the participle. When it does, it is considered a part of the participial phrase. In the examples below all the words in heavy type are part of the participial phrase. An arrow is drawn from each participial phrase to the word that it modifies.

Seeing itself in the mirror, the duck seemed bewildered.

It stood in front of the mirror, **watching its image closely.**

Then, **disgusted with the other duck,** it began to peck the mirror.

Finally, **giving up in dismay,** it backed cautiously away from its strange opponent.

EXERCISE 11. Number your paper 1–10. After the proper number, copy the participial phrase and the noun or pronoun that it modifies.

1. Defeated badly, the team walked slowly from the field.
2. Looking over the audience, Carolyn saw several familiar faces.
3. A bear, standing in the road, stopped traffic.
4. The heavy rains predicted by the weather bureau did not come.
5. Washed overboard by an enormous wave, the skipper was rescued by the crew.
6. The family left early, forgetting to lock the back door of the house.
7. Grabbing the snake by its tail, Melissa flung it into the bushes.
8. Mailed on March 4, your letter did not arrive until April 1.
9. We offered a ride into town to two students waiting for the bus.
10. Named for her mother, Catherine has always been called Katie.

EXERCISE 12. From each of the following sentences, copy the participial phrase. After the phrase, write the word or words that it modifies.

1. Noted for her beauty, Venus was sought by all the gods as a wife.
2. Jupiter, knowing her charms, nevertheless married her to Vulcan, the ugliest of the gods.
3. Bathed in radiant light, Venus brought love and joy wherever she went.
4. Mars, known to the Greeks as Ares, was the god of war.

5. Terrified by Ares' power, the Greeks did not like to worship him.
6. They saw both land and people destroyed by him.
7. Observing his path, they said that Ares left blood, devastation, and grief behind him.
8. The Romans, having great respect for Mars, made him one of their three chief deities.
9. They imagined him dressed in shining armor.
10. Mars, supposed to be the father of the founders of Rome, has a month named after him.

EXERCISE 13. Use the following participial phrases in sentences of your own. Place each phrase as close as possible to the noun or pronoun that it modifies. If you use a participial phrase to begin a sentence, put a comma after the phrase, and follow it closely with the word that is modified.

EXAMPLE   1. waiting for the train
            1. *Waiting for the train, we walked up and down the platform.*

1. published every week
2. standing in the long line for tickets
3. wearing a green silk scarf
4. left by herself for a few minutes
5. planning the escape
6. hidden in a safe place
7. swinging from tree to tree
8. confused by all the questions
9. written in a strange language
10. hearing the clock strike twelve and seeing all the lights go out

REVIEW EXERCISE B. The following sentences contain prepositional and participial phrases. Number your paper 1–20. After the proper number, copy a phrase, and write the word or words that it modifies.

Then write what kind of phrase it is: *prep.* or *part.* List one phrase for each sentence; do not list separately prepositional phrases that are part of participial phrases.

EXAMPLE   1. Seeing her from a distance, I did not recognize my friend.
            1. *Seeing her from a distance — I — part.*

1. I bought the novel with the beautiful cover, but I did not enjoy the story.
2. Expecting an exciting tale, I was disappointed.
3. Destroyed by floods in 1980, the village has not been rebuilt.
4. Hilda and Ann, realizing the danger, shouted a warning.
5. After the field trip, everyone wrote a report.
6. Pressing the small button on the side panel, I accidentally erased the computer's memory bank.
7. These mysterious animals, hidden in the deep forest, have defied capture.
8. Lions are growing scarce, but they still roam freely in African game preserves.
9. Forming a circle, elephants will protect a sick comrade.
10. The horse has contributed a great deal to our civilization.
11. In 1910, Blanch S. Scott became the first woman professional airplane pilot.
12. Stopped by a traffic officer, the driver started an argument.
13. Without elevators, skyscrapers would not have been possible.
14. The touchdown play was a long pass thrown with superb accuracy.
15. A line of 180 million atoms would be two centimeters long.
16. Harvard, established in 1636, is America's oldest college.
17. Harriet King won the national fencing championship for two consecutive years.

18. Our girls' basketball team, coached by Mrs. Walcott, did not lose a game.
19. Other drivers, honking their horns behind us, angered my father.
20. We found the missing keys under the doormat.

REVIEW EXERCISE C. Rewrite each of the following incomplete sentences by adding the kind of phrase indicated in parentheses. You must invent the new phrase yourself.

EXAMPLE 1. —— we waited at the corner. (*adverb phrase*)
1. *For hours we waited at the corner.*
2. Police questioned the man ——. (*participial phrase*)
2. *Police questioned the man standing by the telephone booth.*

1. The ferryboat —— crossed the channel. (*participial phrase*)
2. —— we will decorate the gym. (*adverb phrase*)
3. The refrigerator —— breaks down often. (*adjective phrase*)
4. —— we pulled the fire alarm. (*participial phrase*)
5. The letter was covered with stamps ——. (*adjective phrase*)
6. —— the driver was ready for the race. (*participial phrase*)
7. The look on her face made me suspicious ——. (*adverb phrase*)
8. The item comes with a guarantee ——. (*adjective phrase*)
9. The vacuum cleaner sent up a cloud of dust ——. (*participial phrase*)
10. The majority rules ——. (*adverb phrase*)

Chapter **5**

The Clause

Independent and Subordinate Clauses

In Chapter 4 you studied the phrase, a group of related words without a verb and its subject. In a sentence there may also be groups of related words called *clauses,* that do contain a verb and its subject.

PHRASES **on the tugboat** [no subject or verb]
have been laughing [no subject]

CLAUSES **as the tugboat crossed the river** [a verb — *crossed* — and its subject — *tugboat*]
who have been laughing [a verb — *have been laughing* — and its subject — *who*]

5a. A *clause* is a group of words that contains a verb and its subject and is used as a part of a sentence.

THE INDEPENDENT CLAUSE

5b. An *independent* (or *main*) *clause* expresses a complete thought and can stand by itself as a sentence.

If you can recognize a sentence, you will have no trouble recognizing independent clauses. Independent clauses are sentences when they stand alone. They are usually called independent clauses only when they are part of a sentence.

SENTENCE **I baked her a cake.**

INDEPENDENT CLAUSE Since it was my mother's birthday, **I baked her a cake.**

Study the following sentences, in which the independent clauses are in heavy type. Notice that a sentence may have more than one independent clause. (See the third sentence.)

If you have worked with the soil, **you are familiar with humus.**

Humus **comes from a Latin word** that means "earth."

Humilis **means "on the ground," and from this Latin word we derive the word "humility."**

When you are humble, **you are "on the ground."**

THE SUBORDINATE CLAUSE

While an independent clause can stand alone as a complete thought, a subordinate clause cannot stand alone.

SENTENCE Writers gathered at the home of Gertrude Stein when she lived in Paris.

INDEPENDENT CLAUSE Writers gathered at the home of Gertrude Stein. [can stand alone]

SUBORDINATE CLAUSE when she lived in Paris [cannot stand alone]

5c. A *subordinate* (or *dependent*) *clause* **does not express a complete thought and cannot stand alone.**

The word *subordinate* means "lesser in rank or importance." Since a subordinate clause cannot stand by itself, it is considered "below the rank" of an independent clause.

Study the following sentences, which contain subordinate clauses set in heavy type. Notice that the subordinate clauses all contain verbs and their subjects.

Some subordinate clauses begin with words like *since, when, if,* or *as.* (You will learn more about these words later on in this chapter.)

           S   V

As the monster appeared from beneath a huge rock, all of us in the movie theater held our breath.

         S   V

Since most plants die without light, we moved our houseplants closer to the window.

Some subordinate clauses begin with words like *who, which,* or *that.* (You will learn more about these words later on in this chapter.)

          S   V

The animals **that I saw in the game preserve** were protected from hunters.

       S   V

Michelle, **who was on the debating team last year,** won her argument with the teacher.

      S   V

People **who live in glass houses** should not throw stones.

Notice, in the last two examples, that the word *who* is both the introductory word in the clause and the subject of the clause.

EXERCISE 1. Some of the following expressions are sentences, although they are written without capital letters and periods; some are subordinate clauses; and some are phrases. Number your paper 1–20. If the expression is a sentence, write *S* after the proper number; if a subordinate clause, write *C;* if a phrase, write *P*.

1. we built a swimming pool
2. on the front page
3. if everyone has voted
4. which was sold at the auction
5. after many years
6. during the bad snowstorm
7. the celebrity wore dark glasses
8. as our supplies were giving out
9. who escaped without harm
10. in the dolphin's tank
11. when the ship docked at Rotterdam
12. would have been found
13. since the last time we met
14. down the middle
15. in the meantime everyone can rehearse
16. if the train is not late
17. as I stood on the platform
18. near the zoo
19. everyone cheered
20. when the rain has stopped

EXERCISE 2. Copy the subordinate clause from each of the following sentences. Underline the subject of the clause once and the verb twice.

EXAMPLE   1. In history class we learned about the plague that spread across Europe in the fourteenth century.

   1. *that spread* across Europe in the fourteenth century.

1. In October, 1347, trading ships arrived on the Mediterranean island of Sicily from Caffa, which was a port city on the Black Sea.
2. As they emerged from the boats, many of the sailors carried a strange illness.
3. No medicine could save the sailors, who died quickly and painfully.

4. In the same year many other people became sick and died as plague spread across Sicily and Europe.
5. Even doctors caught the illness when they hurried to the bedsides of sick patients.
6. If a person traveled to another city in Europe, the disease probably traveled too.
7. The fast-spreading, deadly plague terrified the survivors, who thought the world was coming to an end.
8. Since it originated in the Black Sea area, the plague was called the Black Death.
9. No one is sure of the total number of people who died from the dreaded plague.
10. Since medicine offers new ways for controlling plague, the spread of this disease is unlikely today.

EXERCISE 3. Add an independent clause to each of the following subordinate clauses, and write the whole sentence on your paper. Draw one line under the subject of each clause and two lines under the verb.

EXAMPLES 1. who arrived early
            1. *She is the woman who arrived early.*
            2. when the music stopped
            2. *When the music stopped, the party ended.*

1. when I awoke this morning
2. if my teacher approves
3. since the record was made
4. if it is cold tomorrow
5. who waited in line
6. as she began to shoot
7. when we performed on stage
8. who gave the report
9. since the weather was good
10. that I bought yesterday

THE ADJECTIVE CLAUSE

Like an adjective or an adjective phrase, a clause may modify a noun or a pronoun. In the word groups below you see first an adjective phrase, then an adjective clause.

ADJECTIVE PHRASE the woman **in the car**
ADJECTIVE CLAUSE the woman **who is in the car**
ADJECTIVE PHRASE a tree **with red blossoms**
ADJECTIVE CLAUSE a tree **which has red blossoms**
ADJECTIVE PHRASE a day **for fishing**
ADJECTIVE CLAUSE a day **that was made for fishing**

5d. An *adjective clause* is a subordinate clause used as an adjective to modify a noun or pronoun.

Observe how the adjective clauses in the following sentences modify nouns or pronouns. Notice that adjective clauses usually follow immediately after the words that they modify.

Helen Keller was the remarkable woman **who overcame blindness and deafness.**

Ms. Jackson showed slides **that she had taken in Turkey.**

The ones **whose flight was delayed** spent the night in Detroit.

The Relative Pronoun

Adjective clauses are easy to identify because they are almost always introduced by a special kind of pronoun: the *relative pronoun. Who, whom, whose, which,* and *that* are called *relative* pronouns because they *relate* to another word or idea in the sentence.

Leonardo da Vinci was the artist **who painted the *Mona Lisa.*** [The relative pronoun *who*

begins the clause and relates to the noun *artist*.]
Everything **that could be done** was done.
[The relative pronoun *that* begins the clause
and relates to the pronoun *everything*.]

EXERCISE 4. Copy the adjective clauses from the
following sentences. Circle the relative pronouns.
After each clause, write the word that the pronoun
relates, or refers, to.

EXAMPLE 1. Our neighbors have a dog that is called
Juno.
1. (that) *is called Juno, dog*

1. Antonyms are words which have opposite meanings.
2. Skin diving is a sport that is now becoming very popular.
3. Pluto, which is the farthest planet from Earth, takes 248 years to revolve once around the sun.
4. A scholarship was awarded to the one whose short story was judged best.
5. The Secretary of Labor who served during World War II was Frances Perkins.
6. The source of energy which holds the greatest promise is solar energy.
7. Gwendolyn Brooks, who for many years has been Poet Laureate of Illinois, was born in Kansas.
8. In *Walden,* Thoreau relates the lessons that he learned from living alone.
9. Athena was the Greek goddess who sprang from the head of her father.
10. Doctors are people whom the world will always need.

Sometimes the relative pronoun is preceded by a
preposition. The preposition has actually been moved
from the end of the clause to the beginning. Many
writers think that the clause sounds better with the
preposition at the beginning.

the day <u>which</u> we looked forward to
the day to <u>which</u> we looked forward

my friend, <u>whom</u> I would do anything for
my friend, for <u>whom</u> I would do anything

the politician <u>whose</u> speech the public is interested in
the politician in <u>whose</u> speech the public is interested

When you are looking for an adjective clause, remember that the relative pronoun may be preceded by a preposition.

EXERCISE 5. Write the adjective clause from each of the following sentences. Circle the relative pronouns.

1. Coco Chanel is the woman for whom the perfume is named.
2. Grendel, the monster that Beowulf slew, had devoured many people.
3. The Festival Casals, about which we have heard so much, was established by Pablo Casals in Puerto Rico in 1957.
4. Ella Fitzgerald, who started singing in New York City, is famous throughout the world.
5. Christopher Marlowe wrote of Helen of Troy, "Was this the face that launched a thousand ships...?"
6. Margery was one of the students who scored well on the test.
7. In the play *My Fair Lady,* Eliza Doolittle, a poor flower merchant, becomes a woman whom everyone admires.
8. The Kinderhook was the creek in which we found the small striped bass.
9. Janet Flanner, whose pen name was Genêt, wrote dispatches from Paris.

10. The early settlers were brave people to whom we owe a great deal.

EXERCISE 6. Complete each sentence by supplying an adjective clause for the blank. Write the complete sentence on your paper. Remember that a clause must have a subject and a verb. Underline each relative pronoun.

EXAMPLE 1. Gray clouds —— are called stratus clouds.
1. *Gray clouds that form a broad layer are called stratus clouds.*

1. Our class put on a play ——.
2. The ship —— is the largest one I have ever seen.
3. Dogs —— do many things for people.
4. The police officer quickly filled out a ticket for the car ——.
5. The woman —— was once a trapeze artist.
6. The paintings —— are very costly.
7. We listened to music ——.
8. Dolores' aunt introduced her to a professional soccer player ——.
9. Our school newspaper —— is read by all the students.
10. We handed our tickets to the usher ——.

EXERCISE 7. The following paragraphs contain ten adjective clauses. Copy each adjective clause as it appears. After each clause, write the word that it modifies.

EXAMPLE 1. Dogs that are trained carefully at the Seeing Eye Foundation help the blind to lead happy, active lives.
1. *that are trained carefully at the Seeing Eye Foundation—Dogs*

Dogs that are chosen as guide dogs for the blind do not begin their Seeing Eye training until they are mature. From the age of ten weeks to fourteen months, they are cared for by children who are members of a 4-H organization. Then they are taken to the Seeing Eye Foundation, which carefully trains them for three months.

Each week that they are there, they are graded on fifteen items. They are judged on their responses to commands and on their behavior in various situations which might tend to distract them. They must learn not only to be obedient but also to reason well enough to delay obedience in situations which might bring injury to their masters. They must learn to avoid the obstacles that their blind masters cannot see. Dogs are color-blind, and they obviously cannot tell the color of a traffic light; therefore they patiently wait and then move across a street with the crowd that is standing around them.

By the time that the dog and the owner have finished their training together, the owner is able to have absolute faith in the dog. And the dog is happy because of the affection which it receives from its owner.

THE ADVERB CLAUSE

Like an adverb or an adverb phrase, a subordinate clause may modify a verb, adjective, or adverb. Such a clause is called an *adverb clause*.

ADVERB PHRASE   **During the cold winter months** many animals hibernate.

ADVERB CLAUSE   **When the weather turns cold,** many animals hibernate.

5e. An *adverb clause* is a subordinate clause used as an adverb.

An adverb clause may tell *how, when, where, why, to what extent* (*how much* or *how long*), or *under what conditions* the action of the verb is done.

> The truck moves **as if it has a heavy load.** [The adverb clause tells *how* the truck *moves.*]
> There was a great sea wave **when the volcano erupted.** [The adverb clause tells *when* there *was* a great sea wave.]
> We stood **where we could see all of the track.** [The adverb clause tells *where* we *stood.*]
> **Because the day was very hot,** the cool water felt good. [The adverb clause tells *why* the water felt *good.*]
> We worked **until we were completely worn out.** [The adverb clause tells *how long* we *worked.*]
> **If it does not rain tomorrow,** we will go to see Crater Lake. [The adverb clause tells *under what condition* we *will go* to see Crater Lake.]

As these examples show, the adverb clause may come at various places in the sentence. When it comes at the beginning, it is usually followed by a comma.

The Subordinating Conjunction

In Chapter 3 you learned to recognize two kinds of conjunctions: coordinating conjunctions, like *and* and *but,* and correlative conjunctions, like *either . . . or* and *neither . . . nor.* There is a third kind of conjunction, called a *subordinating conjunction,* which introduces an adverb clause. Just as a relative pronoun, like *who* or *which,* introduces an adjective clause, so a subordinating conjunction, like *since* or *if,* introduces an adverb clause.

The following words are commonly used to begin

adverb clauses. Remember that *after, before, since, until,* and *as* may also be used as prepositions.

Subordinating Conjunctions

after	before	until
although	if	when
as	in order that	whenever
as if	since	where
as though	so that	wherever
as long as	than	while
as soon as	though	
because	unless	

EXERCISE 8. Copy the adverb clause from each of the following sentences. Circle the subordinating conjunction and draw one line under the subject and two lines under the verb of each clause. Be prepared to tell what word the clause modifies.

EXAMPLE 1. We read stories before we go to bed.
   1. (before) we go to bed

1. When divers explore the beds of rivers and lakes, they often find fossils.
2. At the end of seven grueling rounds, the old fighter felt as if hundred-pound weights were chained to his gloves.
3. After Mona had searched for several days, she found just the right gift.
4. The women changed into flat-heeled shoes so that they could walk more easily.
5. The twins had never seen a waterfall until their aunt took them to Niagara Falls.
6. Because Sandra was interested in folk music, she did a research paper on the old ballad "Barbara Allan."
7. We sang songs as we rode back from the game.

8. Some animals would become extinct if they were not protected by law.
9. The students collected various kinds of rocks while they were on their field trip.
10. Whenever any kind of danger threatens, the baby kangaroo jumps into its mother's pouch.

EXERCISE 9. There are ten adverb clauses in the following paragraph. Write the number of the line on which the clause begins. Then write the clause. In each clause underline the subject once and the verb twice.

1   What animals would you name if you were
2 told to make a list of the ten smartest animals
3 in the world? After you had considered the matter
4 for a few minutes, you would probably name the
5 monkey, the dog, and several other animals.
6 Perhaps the horse would also be one of your
7 choices, since you have often heard the expression
8 "horse sense." As you listed the animals, you
9 would probably not think of the donkey. Al-
10 though everyone considers the donkey a rather
11 dumb animal, its intelligence is superior to that
12 of the brightest horse. When we think of the
13 noble-looking horse, we think of its intelligence.
14 But there are many animals that surpass the horse
15 in intelligence. The horse is a nervous creature
16 that tends to go berserk whenever it is exposed to
17 any strange situation. Because the horse is so
18 emotional, it has to wear blinders on either side
19 of its eyes so that it will not be distracted. When
20 you make out a list of the brightest animals, don't
21 just list your favorites.

EXERCISE 10. Add an adverb clause to each of the following sentences (independent clauses). Copy the entire sentence on your paper. Then circle the subordinating conjunctions, and underline the subject of each adverb clause once and the verb twice. Remember that your adverb clauses will tell *how, when, where, why, how much,* or *under what conditions.*

EXAMPLE   1. The rain finally stopped.
           1. (*After*) our <u>yard</u> <u>was flooded</u>, the rain finally stopped.

1. The dog barked.
2. Our team won.
3. The crew on the ship worked hard.
4. Amy speaks German well.
5. We built a sauna, a Finnish bathhouse, in our backyard.
6. The Steins have gone to Mexico for a week.
7. Ruby finished her homework early.
8. I was almost asleep.
9. Lois wants to be a veterinarian.
10. Everyone enjoyed the meal.

REVIEW EXERCISE A. Each of the following quotations contains either an adjective or an adverb clause. Copy the clause after the proper number. Write *adj. clause* or *adv. clause* where appropriate.

1. Your own property is concerned when your neighbor's house is on fire. — HORACE
2. If wishes were horses, beggars would ride.
                           — ENGLISH PROVERB
3. All that glitters is not gold. — ENGLISH PROVERB
4. Never answer a letter while you are angry.
                           — CHINESE PROVERB
5. You gain strength, courage and confidence by every experience in which you really stop to look fear in the face. — ELEANOR ROOSEVELT
6. Everything in nature is a cause from which there flows some effect. — SPINOZA
7. It is foolish to tear one's hair in grief, as if sorrow would be made less by baldness. — CICERO

8. God helps those who help themselves.
— ALGERNON SIDNEY
9. Every fact that is learned becomes a key to other facts. — E. L. YOUMANS
10. When one has been threatened with a great injustice, one accepts a smaller [injustice] as a favor. — JANE WELSH CARLYLE

REVIEW EXERCISE B. There are twenty subordinate clauses — ten adjective clauses and ten adverb clauses — in the following paragraphs. Write the number of the line in which the first word of the clause appears. Then write the clause. Write *adj. clause* after each adjective clause and *adv. clause* after each adverb clause.

1   Robert Browning, who was a poet of the Vic-
2 torian period, wrote a poem about Childe Roland,
3 a daring knight who set out on a dangerous quest
4 for the Dark Tower. Many brave knights had
5 been killed because they had searched for the
6 Tower, but Roland was determined not to rest
7 until he found it.
8   After Roland had searched for years, he came
9 upon an old man who pointed the way to the
10 Tower. Following the old man's directions,
11 Roland found himself in a land which was hor-
12 rible beyond belief. As he passed across the eerie
13 wasteland, he saw all around him the signs of
14 savage struggles that had taken place there in the
15 past. Although Roland now felt doomed, he rode
16 on. He saw sights that would have convinced the
17 bravest of knights to turn back. But Roland would
18 not give up while he had strength to continue.
19   Finally, when he had become discouraged, a
20 large black bird swooped down over his head. As
21 he watched it fly away, he saw in the distance the

22 place for which he was searching. Lying in a val-
23 ley, the Dark Tower loomed up before him as a
24 rocky shelf might appear to a sailor at the very
25 moment that his ship crashes into it. While
26 Roland paused to look, he heard ringing in his
27 ears the names of all those who had died in the
28 quest for the Tower. Then, on the hillsides, he saw
29 in a sheet of flame the figures of the knights who
30 had perished. But, in spite of the horror, Roland
31 raised his horn to his lips and blew: *"Childe*
32 *Roland to the Dark Tower came."*

REVIEW EXERCISE C. Number your paper from 1 to
10, and copy the subordinate clause in each of the
following sentences. Then label each subordinate
clause as *adj. clause* or *adv. clause.*

1. People who enjoy animals are interested in facts and stories about them.
2. Flying fish can glide through the air because they are supported by air currents.
3. If you could unravel a spider web into a straight thread, it could measure up to 480 kilometers.
4. Crocodiles and alligators are the only reptiles that have loud voices.
5. The tortoises that live in the Galapagos Islands can live 190 years.
6. Although all snakes can shake their tails, only the rattlesnake has a noisemaker.
7. Swifts, which are the world's fastest birds, can fly 320 kilometers an hour.
8. The male seahorse carries the eggs of the female in a pouch that is like the pouch of a kangaroo.
9. When hatching time comes, the baby seahorses leave the male's pouch.
10. Human beings, who are fifteen times larger than cats, have 206 bones, but cats have 230.

Chapter **6**

The Sentence Base

**Direct and Indirect Objects,
Subject Complements**

As you learned in Chapter 1, every sentence
has a sentence base. The sentence base always consists of at least a verb and its subject. In many sentences this subject-verb base is enough.

      s   v
John shouted.
      s   v
The squirrels scampered across the campus.

The sentence base usually has another part, in
addition to the subject and verb, called a *complement*.
The word *complement* means "completer." A complement completes the meaning begun by the subject
and verb. Notice that the following word groups are
not complete, even though they have subjects and
verbs.

      s   v
Marlene brought [what?]
s v
I met [whom?]
      s   v
Her friend is [what?]

Here a complement completes the meaning of each.

S   V   C
Marlene brought a cake.
S V C
I met Carlos.
   S V   C
Her friend is a painter.

6a. A *complement* is a word or group of words that completes the meaning begun by the subject and verb.

Jody redecorated her **room.** [*Room* completes the meaning by telling *what* Jody redecorated.]

My aunt sent **me** a **postcard** from Amsterdam. [*Me* and *postcard* complete the meaning by telling *what* was sent and *to whom.*]

I asked **what he wanted.** [The group of words *what he wanted* completes the meaning by telling *what* I asked.]

The Ephron sisters are humorous **writers.** [*Writers* completes the meaning by telling something about the subject *sisters.*]

The *Mona Lisa* is very **famous.** [*Famous* completes the meaning by describing the subject *Mona Lisa.*]

In the sentences above you see two kinds of complements. In sentences 1, 2, and 3 you see complements which are affected by the action of the verb. In sentences 4 and 5 you see complements which refer to the subject. A noun, a pronoun, or an adjective can serve as a complement. But an adverb can never be a complement.

The bus is **here.** [*Here* is an adverb, not a complement.]

A complement, like a subject, is never in a prepositional phrase.

Sarah is reading the **dictionary.** [*Dictionary* is a complement; it completes the meaning begun by the subject and verb.]

Sarah is thumbing through the dictionary. [*Dictionary* is in the phrase "through the dictionary"; it is not a complement.]

Helen is an expert **skier** and **skater.** [*Skier* and *skater* are complements; they complete the meaning begun by the subject and verb.]

Helen is in Colorado. [*Colorado* is in the phrase "in Colorado"; it is not a complement.]

EXERCISE 1. Make three columns on your paper. Label the first *Subject,* the second *Verb,* and the third *Complement.* Write in the appropriate columns these three parts of the base of each sentence. Remember that a complement is never in a prepositional phrase.

1. We usually take the bus to school.
2. The driver of a school bus must be pleasant.
3. The distance between school and home is not long.
4. The walk from school is uncomfortable in bad weather.
5. Usually I meet one of my friends at the corner.
6. On Mondays everyone in school seems sleepy.
7. A seat in the last row is sometimes desirable.
8. Jan and Flo have always been good friends.
9. Can you remember the name of the principal?
10. Alice bought a loaf of bread on her way home.
11. Sometimes we read a story in the afternoon.
12. This new book is full of animal adventures.
13. Did anyone guess the ending of the story?
14. My brother borrows a lot of library books.
15. His overdue book is a very long novel.

EXERCISE 2. Make three columns on your paper. Label the first *Subject,* the second *Verb,* and the third *Complement.* Find the base of each sentence, and enter the parts in the appropriate columns. Remember that a complement is never in a prepositional phrase.

1. In Shakespeare's time, plays were very popular in England.
2. Many people watched plays at the Globe Theater in London.
3. William Shakespeare was one of the owners of the Globe.
4. The playhouse looked quite different from most of our modern theaters.
5. It was a building with eight sides.
6. The building contained an inner courtyard.
7. The stage was a large platform at one end of the courtyard.
8. Many people in the audience did not have seats during a performance.
9. The people without seats filled the courtyard in front of the stage.
10. Many of them watched the action of the play from a position next to the stage.

EXERCISE 3. Write five sentences using the following sentence bases. Add enough words to make *interesting* sentences.

SUBJECT	VERB	COMPLEMENT
girl	delivered	telegram
days	are	long
Pam	won	contest
runner	appeared	tired
Venus	is	planet

DIRECT AND INDIRECT OBJECTS

There are two kinds of complements which are affected by the action of the verb: the *direct object* and the *indirect object*.

6b. The *direct object* receives the action expressed by the verb or names the result of the action.

> Dorothea Lange photographed **farmers** in the Midwest during the Depression. [*Farmers* is the direct object; it receives the action of the verb *photographed.*]
>
> Lange built an impressive **collection.** [*Collection* is the direct object; it names the result of the action *built.*]

Direct objects follow action verbs only. They answer the question *What?* or *Whom?* after an action verb. Lange, in the first sentence, photographed whom? She photographed *farmers;* therefore, *farmers* is the direct object. In the second sentence, Lange built what? She built a *collection;* therefore, *collection* is the direct object.

EXERCISE 4. Number your paper 1–10. Copy the action verb and its object in each sentence. Say the verb to yourself and ask *What?* or *Whom?* Remember that objects are complements and will never be in a prepositional phrase.

1. The Cheyennes gave great respect to the older members of their tribe.
2. We watched a performance of Lorraine Hansberry's *A Raisin in the Sun.*
3. The United States celebrates several holidays on Mondays.
4. Cyrano wore a hat with a large plume.
5. Are you helping or hurting the environment?
6. At the end of the press conference, the mayor thanked the reporters for their patience.
7. Did you believe her version of the story?
8. The scientists discovered prehistoric animals buried in the snow.
9. Mayor Fiorello La Guardia governed New York City during the Depression.

10. Has the government changed the size of the dollar bill?

6c. The *indirect object* of the verb precedes the direct object and tells to whom or what or for whom or what the action of the verb is done.

> The speaker gave **us** her opinion. [*Us* is the indirect object because it tells *to whom* the speaker gave her opinion.]
>
> My parents bought our **boat** a new sail. [*Boat* is the indirect object because it tells *for what* my parents bought a new sail.]

Notice that the sentences above have a direct object as well as an indirect object. This is usually the case. The indirect object normally precedes the direct object.

> The guide gave **me** clear **directions**. [*Me* is the indirect object; *directions* is the direct object.]

The indirect object, like the direct object, is never in a prepositional phrase.

> She sent her **mother** some of her earnings. [*Mother* is an indirect object, telling *to whom* she sent some of her earnings.]
>
> She sent some of her earnings to her mother. [*Mother* is not an indirect object; it is in the prepositional phrase "to her mother" and is the object of the preposition *to*.]

EXERCISE 5. Number your paper 1–10. Copy the direct and indirect objects from the following sentences. Write *d.o.* after each direct object and *i.o.* after each indirect object. Not every sentence has an indirect object.

1. Her parents wired her the money she needed.
2. They directed me to the nearest drugstore.

3. Celia sent the landlord a check for rent.
4. The guide showed the tourists the best places to eat.
5. Someone deliberately gave us poor advice.
6. Unfortunately, we had lost two of our tickets.
7. We sent our relatives some handmade Christmas cards.
8. We admired the exchange student's accent.
9. Becky and Amy taught themselves a lesson about bicycling at night.
10. In European countries, you must carry your passport for identification.

REVIEW EXERCISE A. The following sentences contain ten direct objects and five indirect objects. Number your paper 1–10. After the proper number, write the objects in the corresponding sentence. Label direct objects *d.o.* and indirect objects *i.o.*

1. Mr. Luis told us many interesting stories about his childhood in Puerto Rico.
2. Yesterday's mathematics assignment on decimals was very difficult, and no one in the class finished it.
3. Allow yourselves more time for your homework assignments.
4. Television viewers in our country can watch events as they happen in any other part of the world.
5. Who told you that ridiculous story about the gorilla in the gymnasium?
6. A permanent member of the United Nations Security Council can veto any resolution.
7. The Panama Canal greatly shortened the trip by boat between Europe and Australia.
8. Rudolph Diesel's first motor exploded during his experiments and nearly killed him.
9. The jeweler, Mrs. Adams, offered me a hundred dollars for my pearl necklace.

10. I brought her my antique silver bracelet, but she was not interested in it.

DIAGRAMING DIRECT AND INDIRECT OBJECTS

All complements except the indirect object are diagramed on the main horizontal line with the subject and the verb as part of the sentence base. The direct object is diagramed on the horizontal line with a vertical line preceding it. The vertical line stops at the horizontal line to distinguish it from the line separating the subject and the verb.

PATTERNS

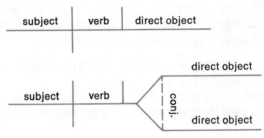

EXAMPLES   1. The rain cleaned the street.

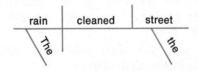

2. We sold lemonade and cookies.

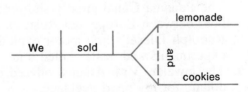

EXERCISE 6. Diagram the following sentences, which contain direct objects. Use a ruler and leave plenty of space between diagrams.

1. We completed our assignment.
2. The quarterback made the touchdown.
3. The distinguished conductor directed his own composition.
4. Our class collects leaves and rocks.
5. The audience saw a serious one-act play and two amusing skits.
6. The school of fish paid no attention to the diver.
7. I have heard programs from Germany on my shortwave set.
8. Billie read several articles on surfboarding and water skiing.
9. A few people still plant corn by the light of the moon.
10. We grow orchids and tulips in our greenhouse.

To diagram an indirect object, write it on a short horizontal line below the verb. Connect it to the verb by a slanted line.

PATTERNS

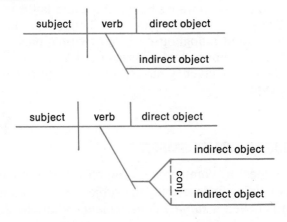

EXAMPLES   1. The artist showed me his painting.

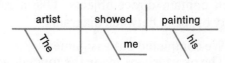

2. The company gave Jan and John summer jobs.

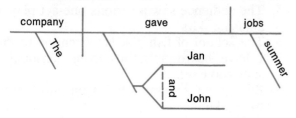

EXERCISE 7. Diagram the following sentences. Not every sentence has an indirect object.

1. The lifeguard gave us lessons.
2. Cara's sister taught her the rules.
3. The cashier handed the children balloons.
4. The judges awarded Jean and Rae the prizes.
5. Snow gives motorists and pedestrians trouble.
6. At the dime store we bought Japanese lanterns.
7. The police sold my parents tickets to the dance.
8. Josie built a doghouse for her two puppies.
9. Ms. Thompson lent Charles her binoculars.
10. Have you given your report on the pyramids of Egypt?

SUBJECT COMPLEMENTS

Sometimes a complement completes the meaning by explaining or describing the subject. Such a complement is called a *subject complement*. While the direct and the indirect object can follow action verbs only, the subject complement can follow linking verbs only. (If you need to review the list of linking verbs, turn to page 50.)

6d. A *subject complement* is a word which follows a linking verb and refers to (explains or describes) the subject.

> Alice Tseng is a **teacher.** [*Teacher* follows the linking verb *is;* it explains something about *Alice Tseng.*]
>
> We are the **ones.** [*Ones* follows the linking verb *are;* it refers to the subject *we.*]
>
> A lemon tastes **sour.** [*Sour* follows the linking verb *tastes;* it describes *lemon* — sour lemon.]
>
> The weather looked **good.** [*Good* follows the linking verb *looked;* it describes *weather.*]

Nouns, pronouns, and adjectives can serve as subject complements.

Predicate Nominatives and Predicate Adjectives

There are two kinds of subject complements — *predicate nominatives* and *predicate adjectives.*

(1) If the subject complement is a noun or a pronoun, it is called a *predicate nominative.*

EXAMPLES   Tuesday is my **birthday.** [*Birthday* is a predicate nominative. It is a noun referring to the subject *Tuesday.*]

He is **one** of the best players. [*One* is a predicate nominative. It is a pronoun referring to the subject *he.*]

Like subjects and objects, predicate nominatives never appear in a prepositional phrase.

The result was a **declaration** of war. [The predicate nominative is *declaration,* not *war.* Not only is *war* part of a prepositional phrase, but the *result* was just a *declaration,* not the war itself.]

(2) If the subject complement is an adjective, it is called a *predicate adjective*. A predicate adjective modifies the subject.

EXAMPLES   An atomic reactor is very **powerful.** [*Powerful* is a predicate adjective modifying the subject *reactor.*]

This ground looks **swampy.** [*Swampy* is a predicate adjective modifying the subject *ground.*]

EXERCISE 8. Copy the linking verb and the subject complement from each of the following sentences. If the complement is a predicate nominative (noun or pronoun), write *p.n.* after it. If it is a predicate adjective, write *p.a.* after it.

1. My glasses are dirty.
2. "I am the one who called you yesterday," Consuelo said.
3. Many public buildings in the East are proof of I. M. Pei's architectural skill.
4. The downtown mall appeared especially busy today.
5. Kay Tomlinson seems happy with the results of the election.
6. The patient felt heavy to the stretcher-bearers.
7. Antarctica is larger in size than Europe or Australia.
8. The clown's makeup became a mask behind which he hid all of his sorrow.
9. Some words, like *cavern* and *meander,* sound especially melodious.

10. While the mountain lion looked around for food, the young fawn remained perfectly still.

Some verbs, like *look, grow,* and *feel,* may be used as either linking verbs or action verbs. They are followed by a predicate nominative or a predicate adjective only when they are used as linking verbs. They are followed by objects only when they are used as action verbs.

LINKING VERB   The swimmer **felt happy.** [*Happy* is a predicate adjective after the linking verb *felt.*]

ACTION VERB   The swimmer **felt the water.** [*Water* is a direct object after the action verb *felt.*]

EXERCISE 9. Six of the sentences in this exercise contain a subject complement — predicate nominative or predicate adjective. If a sentence has a subject complement, copy the complement after the proper number; if not, leave the space blank after the number.

1. After the guests had left, the house seemed very lonely.
2. Seals grow very playful before feeding time.
3. The injured woman felt her right leg.
4. The fossil bones discovered by the divers were those of a gigantic bird which once lived in Florida.
5. At first the drums sounded loud.
6. The employer looked carefully at all the applications.
7. Roots of plants grow toward water.
8. The chemistry students looked quite afraid when they discovered that they had accidentally concocted an explosive.
9. Virginia Dare was the first child born to English parents in the New World.

10. A picture of a ski jumper was on the cover of our literature book.

Number your paper 1–12. List after the proper number the fifteen subject complements in this exercise. Be sure your words follow a linking verb and refer to the verb's subject.

1. Many members of the gourd family are popular with amateur gardeners.
2. Some fruits of gourd plants taste sweet, but others seem bitter.
3. The gourd plant, a type of vine, can be easy to grow.
4. The watermelon is a very popular gourd fruit.
5. After selecting a watermelon, we want to see whether it looks ripe inside.
6. If the seeds are black and the flesh is a rich pink, the melon will be good.
7. Nothing could be better.
8. The squash is a less popular fruit of the gourd family.
9. The pumpkin, a close relative of the squash, long ago became an American favorite.
10. To some people, squash looks strange.
11. Some people will eat acorn squash but will not touch crookneck squash, which is very nutritious.
12. Perhaps someday squash will be a treat like pumpkin pie.

DIAGRAMING SUBJECT COMPLEMENTS

A subject complement is diagramed somewhat like a direct object. But the short vertical line separating it from the verb is slanted toward the subject to show that the complement refers to the subject.

PATTERNS

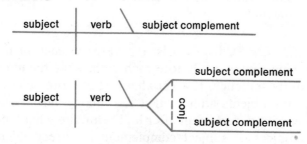

EXAMPLES   1. The dancers are graceful.

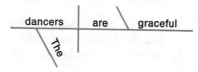

2. The contestants are Joan and Dean.

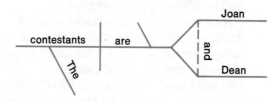

EXERCISE 10.   Diagram the following sentences.

1. The lights were dim.
2. Who are they?
3. The girls became lifeguards.
4. The cave was cold and damp.
5. Our speaker was a teacher and a writer.
6. We felt qualified for the job.
7. One of the most daring explorers of the sixteenth century was Sir Francis Drake.
8. The chimpanzees seem happy in their new environment.
9. My shoes looked worn and dusty after the long walk.

10. John Donne was a famous poet and a great preacher.

REVIEW EXERCISE C. List the verbs in each of the following sentences. Before each verb, write the number of its sentence. If a verb has one or more objects, write the objects after it. If it is a linking verb, write the subject complement after it. Then write what kind each object or subject complement is: direct object (*d.o.*); indirect object (*i.o.*); predicate adjective (*p.a.*); predicate nominative (*p.n.*).

EXAMPLE   1. I have never seen a bald eagle, but its picture is very common.
        1. *have seen, bald eagle   d.o.*
        1. *is, common   p.a.*

1. On one side of a quarter, you will find a bald eagle with outspread wings.
2. The bald eagle is our national symbol.
3. Because bald eagles steal fish from other birds, many citizens would prefer another symbol.
4. The wild turkey was a candidate.
5. The bald eagle has many good qualities.
6. This native of North America looks far nobler than many birds.
7. Its strength seems enormous, and its eyesight is extraordinary.
8. From a distance of nearly five kilometers, a bald eagle can spot a fish.
9. It is one of the few animals that take only one mate during a lifetime.
10. These are only a few of the interesting facts about the bald eagle.
11. Bald eagles give bird watchers great enjoyment.
12. The bald eagle was once common in many sections of our country.
13. Although it is unlawful, some people hunt the bald eagle.

14. Today we find bald eagles principally in Florida and Alaska.
15. Our country offers them protection.

REVIEW EXERCISE D. Diagram these sentences.

1. The lifeguard gave the rescued boy artificial respiration.
2. We deposited our money at the bank.
3. You seem very cheerful today.
4. Her mother was a leading ballerina with a famous ballet troupe.
5. Don and Maria acted the parts of Romeo and Juliet.
6. The origin of the gypsies remains a great mystery.
7. The girls made themselves bracelets and necklaces for the dress rehearsal.
8. Two of the most famous canals in the world are the Suez Canal and the Panama Canal.
9. We proudly displayed our best paintings along the sidewalk.
10. The clown's shoes were long and wide.

REVIEW EXERCISE E. Fill the blanks in the following paragraph with words which will make a funny or ridiculous story. Copy on your paper the words that you want in the blanks. After each word, write what kind of complement it is: *p.n., p.a., d.o.,* or *i.o.*

Yesterday I looked out my window and thought I saw a ——. But when I got outside I realized that it was a ——. It looked —— and ——. It gave —— a ——. Then I became —— and ran back inside. When I opened the —— fifteen minutes later, it was still there. Finally I decided that it was not ——. I went back outside and offered it a ——. Now it follows me wherever I go.

Chapter 7

The Kinds of Sentence Structure

Simple, Compound, Complex, and Compound-Complex Sentences

In Chapter 1 you learned that sentences may be classified according to their purpose: *declarative, interrogative, imperative,* and *exclamatory.* Another way to classify sentences is according to their construction, the kind and number of their clauses. In this chapter you will study the four kinds of sentences that result from this classification: *simple, compound, complex,* and *compound-complex.*

THE SIMPLE SENTENCE

From your study of clauses in Chapter 5, you will remember that a clause is a sentence part which contains a verb and its subject. An independent clause expresses a complete thought and may stand alone. A subordinate clause does not express a complete thought and cannot stand alone. When an independent clause stands alone with no other clauses attached to it, it is called a simple sentence.

7a. A *simple sentence* has one independent clause and no subordinate clauses.

In the examples below, the subjects and verbs are printed in heavy type. Notice that a simple sentence may have a compound subject (sentence 2) or a compound verb (sentence 3) or both (sentence 4).

EXAMPLES   The **hair stylist gave** John a new look.

Beth Heiden and **Sheila Young won** Olympic medals. [compound subject: *Beth Heiden* and *Sheila Young*]

Lawrence caught the ball but then **dropped** it. [compound verb: *caught* but *dropped*]

The **astronomer** and her **assistant studied** the heavens and **wrote** reports on their findings. [compound subject: *astronomer* and *assistant;* compound verb: *studied* and *wrote*]

EXERCISE 1. After the proper number, copy the subjects and the verbs from the following simple sentences. Some of the sentences have compound subjects and verbs.

EXAMPLE   1. The first baseball games were quite different from those of today.
1. *games, were*

1. No system or set of rules governed baseball in the early days.
2. Youngsters in knickers gathered in lots near the town hall.
3. They used barrel staves for bats.
4. Sometimes stumps or posts served as bases.
5. The number of bases depended on the amount of space available.
6. The first college game was played in 1859 and was won by Amherst College.
7. According to the rules for this first college game, the game ended, not after nine innings, but after the scoring of seventy-five runs by one team.

8. The War Between the States made baseball popular and spread a knowledge of the rules and practices of the game throughout the United States.
9. Soldiers waiting for battle and prisoners waiting for the war to end staged baseball games to break the monotony.
10. After the war, the soldiers, remembering the excitement of the game, continued to play it.

THE COMPOUND SENTENCE

Sometimes two or more independent clauses appear in the same sentence without any subordinate clauses. Such a sentence is called a *compound sentence*.

7b. A *compound sentence* has two or more independent clauses but no subordinate clauses.

The independent clauses are usually joined by coordinating conjunctions: *and, but, or, nor, for*.

EXAMPLES **Thad prepared the slides, and Inés examined them.** [two independent clauses joined by the conjunction *and*]

According to legend, Betsy Ross made our first flag, but there is little evidence. [two independent clauses joined by the conjunction *but*]

The whistle blew, the drums rolled, and the crowd cheered. [three independent clauses, the last two joined by the conjunction *and*]

EXERCISE 2. Number your paper 1–10. After each number, write the subject and verb of the first independent clause, the coordinating conjunction, and the subject and verb of the next clause. Insert a comma before the conjunction. Underline subjects once and verbs twice.

EXAMPLE   1. A director of a theater-in-the-round visited our class, and we listened to his humorous stories for almost an hour.
1. <u>director</u> <u>visited,</u> and <u>we</u> <u>listened</u>

1. Many strange things happen backstage during a performance, but the audience usually does not know about them.
2. Audiences at theaters-in-the-round add to the director's problems, for they are seated very close to the stage.
3. Members of the audience sometimes use stage ashtrays, or they hang their coats on the actors' coat racks.
4. Sometimes these actions are overlooked by the stagehands, and the results can be very challenging for the actors.
5. The main clue in a certain mystery play depended on a scarf left lying on the stage floor, but the audience had gathered on the stage during intermission.
6. During the scene after the intermission, the detective in the play counted three scarves instead of one, but the actor showed no surprise.
7. Directors are not always able to predict the reactions of the audience, nor can they always control the audience.
8. During the performance of another mystery drama, a spectator in the front row became too excited about the action of the play, for at one point, leaping up on the stage, the spectator tackled the killer.
9. The workers in charge of properties are usually alert and efficient, but they do sometimes make mistakes.
10. In the most dramatic scene of one production of *Romeo and Juliet,* the character Juliet prepared to kill herself with a dagger, but unfortunately there was no dagger on the stage.

Distinguishing Between Compound Sentences and Simple Sentences with Compound Subjects or Verbs

Although it consists of two or more subjects joined by a conjunction, a compound subject is still one subject. A compound verb is still one verb. A simple sentence, which has only one subject and one verb, is still a simple sentence even when its subject or verb is compound. Do not confuse a simple sentence containing a compound subject or a compound verb with a compound sentence, which has a subject and verb in each of its independent clauses.

> SIMPLE SENTENCE   Bill and Joe increased their speed and passed the other runners. [compound subject and verb]
>
> COMPOUND SENTENCE   Bill led half the way, and then Joe took the lead.

EXERCISE 3. Number your paper 1–10. Copy the subjects and verbs in the following sentences. Underline subjects once and verbs twice. Then write *S.* if the sentence is a simple sentence or *Cd.* if it is a compound sentence.

> EXAMPLES   1. Many adventurers have followed the tracks of the abominable snowmen and have published reports on their findings.
>
>   1. *adventurers* *have followed*, *have published* S.
>
>   2. Some believe in the existence of the snowmen, and others call the snowmen fakes.
>
>   2. *some believe, others call* Cd.

1. The snowmen supposedly inhabit the Himalaya

Mountains, and they are usually called yetis by the natives of the Himalayan area.

2. Snowmen have been known for centuries in legend and literature, but their existence has never been proved.
3. According to accounts, the Sherpas living on the lower Himalayas often hear the strange whistle of the yetis at night, and, on going outside in the morning, they find yeti tracks in the snow.
4. One explorer found a so-called yeti hand and offered it as evidence of the snowmen's existence.
5. Other kinds of evidence, such as yeti scalps, have been offered, but many of these things have been proved fakes.
6. Some people have reported encounters with the yetis and have described their appearance.
7. The yeti supposedly resembles a large monkey or ape, and he has a large pointed head with sunken eyes.
8. He is covered with grayish hair, but the hair is definitely not like animal fur.
9. Many of the reports about the snowmen are probably hoaxes, but others come from people of unquestionable honesty.
10. Perhaps someday explorers or Sherpas will capture one of the yetis, and then scientists will unravel the mystery of the abominable snowmen.

DIAGRAMING COMPOUND SENTENCES

If you can diagram a simple sentence, then you can easily learn to diagram a compound sentence, for the independent clauses in a compound sentence are diagramed like simple sentences. The second clause is diagramed below the first and is joined to it by a coordinating conjunction diagramed as shown. The coordinating conjunction is placed on the horizontal line.

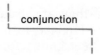

EXAMPLE The quarterback threw a good pass, but the end did not catch it.

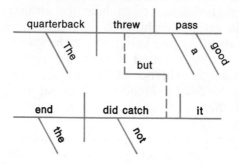

EXERCISE 4. Diagram the following compound sentences.

1. I want a motorboat, but Jan prefers a sailboat.
2. The bus stopped at the restaurant, and everyone got off.
3. Our club is very small, but it is growing.
4. Shall we meet you at the station, or will you take a taxi?
5. In Arizona the temperature is often high, but the humidity always remains low.

THE COMPLEX SENTENCE

Like a compound sentence, a complex sentence contains more than one clause. But unlike the compound sentence, the complex sentence has at least one subordinate clause.

7c. A *complex sentence* **has one independent clause and at least one subordinate clause.**

A subordinate clause may be an adjective clause (see page 98) or an adverb clause (see pages 102–03).

Adjective clauses begin with a relative pronoun: *who, whom, whose, which, that.* Adverb clauses begin with subordinating conjunctions: *after, although, because, if, until, when,* etc.

In the examples below, the subordinate clauses are printed in heavy type.

EXAMPLE   **When I watch Martha Graham's dances,** I feel like studying dance.

One independent clause   I feel like studying dance
Subordinate clause   When I watch Martha Graham's dances

EXAMPLE   Some of the sailors **who took part in the mutiny on the British ship *Bounty*** settled Pitcairn Island.

One independent clause   Some of the sailors settled Pitcairn Island
Subordinate clause   who took part in the mutiny on the British ship *Bounty*

EXAMPLE   **Since the ballads that have come down to us are usually sad,** ballad singers often dress in black or other somber colors.

One independent clause   ballad singers often dress in black or other somber colors
Two subordinate clauses   Since the ballads are usually sad   that have come down to us

EXERCISE 5.   Copy the following complex sentences. Draw one line under each independent clause and two lines under each subordinate clause. Circle subordinating conjunctions and relative pronouns. Be prepared to name the subject and the verb in each clause. A sentence may have more than one subordinate clause.

EXAMPLES   1. Antarctica is a continent which is almost twice the size of the United States.

1. Antarctica is a continent (which) is almost twice the size of the United States.

2. Although many early voyagers searched for this southern continent, it remained undiscovered until 1820.

2. (Although) many early voyagers searched for this southern continent, it remained undiscovered until 1820.

1. Antarctica appeared on many maps before it was actually discovered.
2. Most of the facts that we have about Antarctica were supplied by explorers of the twentieth century.
3. Richard E. Byrd is but one of the explorers who made expeditions to Antarctica.
4. As explorations progressed, many amazing facts were learned.
5. Scientists discovered several areas that contained ice layers nearly two thousand meters thick.
6. Geologists who were sent to Antarctica discovered some valuable mineral deposits which might be used when the world's supply of minerals runs low.
7. When scientists have finished their study of Antarctica's weather, they may be able to tell us a great deal about our own weather.
8. Although little plant or animal life exists there, a group of zoologists were able to study the penguin and the sea gull.
9. While the zoologists were setting up stations in Antarctica, the penguins became friendly.
10. Because Antarctica is largely covered with ice, the explorers on the expeditions faced dangers.

DIAGRAMING COMPLEX SENTENCES

The subordinate clause in the complex sentence is diagramed beneath the independent clause. A broken line is then drawn from the word that is modified in the independent clause to the verb (for an adverb clause) or the relative pronoun (for an adjective clause) in the subordinate clause. If the subordinate clause is an adverb clause, the subordinating conjunction is written on the broken line.

We had lunch in the student cafeteria when we visited the college. [complex sentence containing an adverb clause]

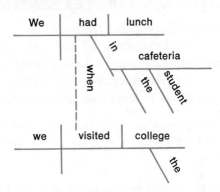

Blair has a ring which belonged to her great-grandmother. [complex sentence containing an adjective clause]

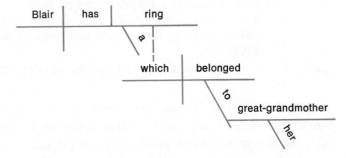

EXERCISE 6. Diagram the following complex sentences.

1. People who visit Holland in the spring see vast fields of tulips.
2. When we stood beside the Washington Monument, we felt very small.
3. The satellite will be launched if the weather remains good.
4. Aeneas was one of the few who escaped from Troy.
5. Alexander the Great, who conquered most of the known world, died at the age of thirty-three.

THE COMPOUND-COMPLEX SENTENCE

A compound-complex sentence, as the name suggests, is a combination of the compound sentence and the complex sentence. Like a compound sentence, it has at least two independent clauses; like a complex sentence, it has at least one subordinate clause.

7d. A *compound-complex sentence* has two or more independent clauses and at least one subordinate clause.

EXAMPLE   Isabel began painting only two years ago, but she has already been asked to hang one of her paintings at the art exhibit that is scheduled for next month.

Two independent clauses   Isabel began painting only two years ago, but she has already been asked to hang one of her paintings at the art exhibit

Subordinate clause   that is scheduled for next month

EXERCISE 7. The following sentences are compound-complex. Copy each clause separately, and after the clause, write *independent* or *subordinate*.

1. When we returned from camp, we were very tired, but we had many pleasant experiences to remember long afterward.
2. On our way up to the camp, which is built around a lake in the mountains, we sang songs, and some of the counselors entertained us with stories about past summers at the camp.
3. The minute that the bus stopped at the campsite, we all climbed hurriedly out, for we were anxious to see our cabins.
4. Some cabins were in the woods, and because they were shaded by many trees, they were cool.
5. We were all pleased with our accommodations, and we set to work immediately to find names for our cabins so that we would really feel at home.
6. Later in the day, a committee came around to judge the names, and from the many good ones that were tacked above the cabin doors, the committee finally chose "Linger Longer" as the best name.

REVIEW EXERCISE. Number your paper 1–20. Identify the kinds of sentences — simple, compound, complex, or compound-complex — in the following paragraphs. Use the abbreviations *S., Cd., Cx.,* and *Cd.-Cx.*

1. People who are just learning to skin dive usually begin in water that is somewhere between twenty-five and fifty feet deep. 2. At this depth there is no danger from pressure, and there is an abundance of fish and plant life. 3. After people have been diving in shallow water for several weeks or months, they may go on to deeper water. 4. Below one hundred feet there is the problem of pressure, and one must be especially careful to avoid the hazards of deep diving. 5. One of the most common hazards that threaten deep divers is caisson disease, or "the bends." 6. Nitrogen builds up in the bloodstream as the diver descends below one hundred feet. 7. If the diver is ready to

surface and ascends too quickly, then the nitrogen expands and forms bubbles in the bloodstream and body tissues. **8.** The nitrogen bubbles cause extreme pain. **9.** If the case is very severe, the diver may die, but the effects of caisson disease are not usually that serious. **10.** Fortunately, a cure was discovered in the late nineteenth century. **11.** When a diver is put back under pressure, the nitrogen bubbles dissolve, and the diver no longer feels pain. **12.** Now a decompression chamber is used for a diver who suffers from the bends.

13. Another hazard of deep diving is nitrogen narcosis. **14.** The nitrogen that the diver breathes is under pressure and consequently has a strange effect on the brain. **15.** When divers are suffering from nitrogen narcosis, they act very much like drunk people. **16.** They may do many ridiculous things. **17.** On one occasion a diver who was suffering from nitrogen narcosis began to play golf underwater. **18.** He used fish for his clubs. **19.** Luckily he did not choose a shark for one of his clubs, or the story would not be funny. **20.** Like caisson disease, nitrogen narcosis can be fatal to the unwary diver.

Usage

PART TWO

Chapter **8**

Making Subjects and Verbs Agree

Agreement in Number

Certain words in a sentence are closely related. The verb is closely related to its subject. A pronoun is closely related to the noun it stands for. Such closely related words have matching forms. When the related words are correctly matched, we say that they agree. They may agree in *number*. Rule 8a below explains the meaning of *number*.

SINGULAR AND PLURAL NUMBER

8a. When a word refers to one person, place, thing, or idea, it is *singular* in number. When it refers to more than one, it is *plural* in number.

SINGULAR   book, woman, fox, one, I, he
PLURAL   books, women, foxes, many, we, they

EXERCISE 1. Number your paper 1–20. After each number, write *S* if the word is singular and *P* if it is plural.

1. athletes
2. job
3. foods
4. patios
5. him
6. problem

7. patients	14. costume
8. feet	15. passersby
9. morning	16. us
10. beliefs	17. this
11. them	18. gases
12. each ·	19. either
13. woman	20. cities

EXERCISE 2. *Oral Drill.* Read the following expressions aloud. Tell whether each is singular or plural.

1. the lion yawns	9. they have
2. the cubs play	10. the actors rehearse
3. we listen	11. the play opens
4. no one stays	12. everyone goes
5. the refugees land	13. the curtain rises
6. she wins	14. all applaud
7. the flower blooms	15. people laugh
8. I am	

8b. A verb agrees with its subject in number.

(1) Singular subjects take singular verbs.

EXAMPLES The **candle burns** slowly.

The **car comes** to a sudden stop.

On its return trip the **plane** always **flies** at a low altitude.

[The singular subjects *candle, car,* and *plane* take the singular verbs *burns, comes,* and *flies.*]

(2) Plural subjects take plural verbs.

EXAMPLES The **candles burn** slowly.

The **prisoners walk** in the exercise yard.

Again and again the **dolphins leap** playfully.

[The plural subjects *candles, prisoners,* and *dolphins* take the plural verbs *burn, walk,* and *leap.*]

Generally, subjects ending in *s* are plural (*candles, prisoners, dolphins*) and verbs ending in *s* are singular (*burns, comes, flies*). The verb *be* is a special case.

SINGULAR	PLURAL	SINGULAR	PLURAL
I am	we are	I was	we were
you are	you are	you were	you were
he is	they are	she was	they were
Luis is	the boys are	Linda was	the girls were

EXERCISE 3. On your paper, after the proper number, write the word from the parentheses which agrees with the given subject.

1. this (costs, cost)
2. plants (grows, grow)
3. the batter (swings, swing)
4. we (considers, consider)
5. the men (was, were)
6. she (asks, ask)
7. these (needs, need)
8. those colors (seems, seem)
9. that (lasts, last)
10. days (passes, pass)

PREPOSITIONAL PHRASES BETWEEN SUBJECT AND VERB

Students often commit agreement errors because they mistake words in prepositional phrases for the subjects of verbs.

NONSTANDARD[1] The many lights on the Christmas tree makes it look very festive. [*Lights,* not *tree,* is the subject.]

STANDARD The many **lights** on the Christmas tree **make** it look very festive.

[1] For explanation of nonstandard and standard, see footnote, page 34.

8c. The number of a subject is not changed by a prepositional phrase following the subject.

Remember that a word in a prepositional phrase can never be the subject of a verb. If a sentence confuses you, imagine that the prepositional phrase is enclosed by parentheses, and go directly from the subject to the verb.

The **silence** (in the halls) **is** unusual.

EXERCISE 4. *Oral Drill.* Read each of the following sentences aloud, stressing the italicized words. Be able to tell whether the subject and verb are singular or plural.

1. Many dogwood *trees* on my street *are* in bloom.
2. Her *paper* on rare American stamps *needs* editing.
3. Your *opinion* of the candidates *gives* the pollster important information.
4. The *scientists* at Cape Canaveral *work* many extra hours during a launch.
5. Some *students* in the class *volunteer* for outside assignments.
6. *One* of the tests *shows* a flaw in the computer.
7. The *owner* of the factories *asks* for weekly reports from the managers.
8. The *chimes* in the tower *play* every hour.
9. The *temperature* inside the caverns *stays* fifty degrees all year long.
10. A good *book* on plants *costs* very little.

EXERCISE 5. Number your paper 1–10. After the proper number, write the subject and then the correct form of the verb. Remember that the subject is never in a prepositional phrase.

1. Many tourists from America (goes, go) to Holland during April or May.

2. The flowers in Holland (reaches, reach) their peak at this time of the year.
3. One of the most beautiful sights imaginable (is, are) the long expanse of flowers from Haarlem to Leiden.
4. For mile after mile a solid carpet of brilliant colors (greets, greet) the eye.
5. Strangely enough, the flowers in this section (is, are) grown for their bulbs rather than for their blossoms.
6. When the flowers are in full bloom, workers in the field (clips, clip) them.
7. Then very large garlands of brilliant blooms (is, are) made and sold to passing travelers.
8. Visitors in a Dutch city (is, are) usually amazed to find flowers everywhere.
9. Many homes in the Netherlands (is, are) filled with vases of flowers.
10. Even the cars of the Dutch often (contains, contain) little vases of flowers.

INDEFINITE PRONOUNS

Certain pronouns do not refer to a definite person, place, thing, or idea and, therefore, are called *indefinite* pronouns.

You should learn the number of all the indefinite pronouns so that you will not make an error in agreement when an indefinite pronoun is the subject of the sentence.

8d. The following common pronouns are singular and take singular verbs: *each, either, neither, one, everyone, everybody, no one, nobody, anyone, anybody, someone, somebody.*

As the examples below indicate, pronouns like *each* and *one* are frequently followed by prepositional phrases. Remember that the verb agrees with the subject of the sentence, not a word in a prepositional phrase.

EXAMPLES   **One** of the chairs **looks** comfortable.
Either of the answers **is** correct.
Everyone with passports **was** accepted.
Neither of these **satisfies** me.
Someone in the stands **has been waving** at us.

8e. The following common pronouns are plural and take plural verbs: *both, few, several, many.*

EXAMPLES   **Many** of the students **walk** to school.
Both of the pies **are** good.
Few of the guests **know** of the robbery.

8f. The words *some, any, none, all,* **and** *most* **may be either singular or plural.**

This rule is an exception to rule 8c because the number of the subjects *some, any, none, all,* and *most* is determined by a word in the prepositional phrase that follows the subject. If the word the subject refers to is singular, the subject is singular; if the word is plural, the subject is plural.

EXAMPLES   **All** of the fans **rush** home.
All of my work **is** finished.
Some of the birds **have** gone south.
Some of the glare **has** disappeared.

EXERCISE 6. Number your paper 1–15. After the proper number, write the subject and then the correct one of the verbs in parentheses.

1. All of the flags (is, are) on display.
2. Each of the flags (has, have) a special design.
3. Someone in this group (is, are) a jogger.
4. Some of our artists (uses, use) strange materials.
5. One of our modern painters (places, place) real buttons on the canvas where the buttons on clothes would be.
6. Many of them (works, work) with sawdust, nails, and sand.
7. One of Georgia O'Keeffe's paintings (shows, show) an animal's skull.
8. Several of the group (objects, object) to the increase in dues.
9. Both of the movies (looks, look) exciting.
10. Everyone in the first two rows (wins, win) a prize.
11. Several in the crowd (was, were) admitted early.
12. No one except the officials (is, are) allowed on the field.
13. Few of the lakes (freezes, freeze) in the winter.
14. Neither of us (knows, know) the way.
15. Somebody with binoculars (is, are) watching us.

REVIEW EXERCISE A. Number your paper 1–20. Read each sentence aloud. If the verb agrees with the subject, write *C* after the proper number on your paper. If the verb does not agree with the subject, write the correct form of the verb on your paper. Some sentences have more than one verb for you to consider.

EXAMPLES   1. One of the women practice medicine.
           1. *practices*
           2. Both of them work hard.
           2. *C*

1. Each of the math problems take twenty minutes to solve.
2. Some of the spectators are already leaving.
3. Neither of your arguments are very convincing.

4. All of the time-outs have been used.
5. No one on the highways are exempt from traffic rules.
6. Several of the group has taken the trip before.
7. No one without a dictionary is prepared for this assignment.
8. Most of the storm damage was reported to be along the coast.
9. Only one of the contestants are qualified.
10. Plants in good soil often live many years.
11. Several of the sparkplugs need to be replaced.
12. Few of the airlines offers a direct flight between those cities.
13. All of the trouble between the farmers and the miners were the result of a misunderstanding.
14. Many at the picnic plan to go swimming.
15. Either of those answers are correct.
16. All of the money has been spent.
17. Both of the girls in the family has red hair.
18. Some fans in the grandstand was shouting at the umpire.
19. Everybody in the stadium were amazed at the play.
20. Any one of those three routes are better than the one that goes through the city.

COMPOUND SUBJECTS

Most compound subjects which are joined by *and* name more than one person or thing; therefore, they are plural and require a plural verb.

8g. Subjects joined by *and* are plural and take a plural verb.

EXAMPLES **Antonia Brico** and **Sarah Caldwell are** famous conductors. [two are]

Last year a **library** and a **museum were** built in our town. [two things were built]

If the items in a compound subject actually refer to only one person or are thought of as one thing, the verb is singular.

EXAMPLES   The **captain** and **quarterback** of the team **is** the speaker. [One person is both the captain and the quarterback.]

Chicken and **dumplings is** a favorite Southern dish. [Chicken and dumplings is one dish.]

EXERCISE 7. Number your paper 1–10. Decide whether the subjects of the following sentences are singular or plural. Choose the correct verb form from the parentheses, and write it after the proper number.

1. March and April (is, are) windy months.
2. My mother and the mechanic (is, are) discussing the bill.
3. Virginia Wade and Tracy Austin (plays, play) today.
4. Cake and ice cream (is, are) my favorite dessert.
5. (Does, Do) Carla and Jean take dancing lessons?
6. (Is, Are) the knives and forks in the drawer?
7. Mathematics and science (requires, require) many hours of study.
8. (Here's, Here are) our star and winner of the meet.
9. Where (is, are) the bread and the honey?
10. (Does, Do) an Austrian and a German speak the same language?

8h. Singular subjects joined by *or* or *nor* take a singular verb.

EXAMPLES   A **pen or** a **pencil is** needed for this test. [either one **is**]

Neither Miami nor Jacksonville is the capital of Florida. [neither one **is**]

EXERCISE 8. Number your paper 1–10. From each pair of verbs in parentheses, choose the one that agrees with the subject.

1. Either lemonade or iced tea (tastes, taste) good on a hot day.
2. French and Italian (is, are) Romance languages.
3. Neither Lola nor Roger (has, have) ever been to California.
4. Both the mango fruit and the pistachio nut (comes, come) from trees of the sumac family.
5. The length of words (affects, affect) our ability to spell them.
6. Neither California nor Texas (is, are) as big as Alaska.
7. The French horn, the bassoon, and the oboe (is, are) wind instruments.
8. Either the captain or the cocaptain (leads, lead) the band onto the field.
9. (Does, Do) Toni or Kay know the way to the amusement park?
10. (Has, Have) the president and the vice-president of the class been chosen?

8i. When a singular subject and a plural subject are joined by *or* or *nor,* the verb agrees with the nearer subject.

EXAMPLES   Either Joan or her **friends are** mistaken. [The verb agrees with the nearer subject, *friends.*]

Neither the players nor the **director was** on time to rehearsal. [The verb agrees with the nearer subject, *director.*]

Whenever possible, avoid this kind of construction. The second sentence can be rewritten to read: *Both the players and the director were late to rehearsal.*

EXERCISE 9. Number your paper 1–10. From each pair of verbs in parentheses, choose the one that agrees with the subject.

1. Either the mayor or the city treasurer (is, are) scheduled to speak at the ceremony.
2. Teresa and her sister (has, have) a valuable record collection.
3. The Weinbergs or their cousin (owns, own) the new house on Elm Street.
4. Neither John nor Herbert (has, have) the slightest interest in table manners.
5. Neither the pitcher nor his teammates (was, were) expecting the batter to knock the ball out of the park.
6. Bread and milk (is, are) a healthful combination.
7. Either the violinists or the clarinet player (has, have) rehearsed the wrong selection.
8. The cellists and the bassoon player (is, are) waiting to find out who is mistaken.
9. The violas or the harp (is, are) out of tune.
10. Neither the audience nor the members of the orchestra (seems, seem) satisfied with the performance.

REVIEW EXERCISE B. Number your paper 1–20. Then choose from the parentheses the verb that agrees with the subject and write it on your paper.

1. Everyone in the class (wants, want) to learn more about astronomy.
2. The stars and the planets (has, have) always fascinated people.
3. A story from ancient times (says, say) that two Chinese astronomers were put to death in 2137 B.C. for failing to predict an eclipse correctly.
4. The astronomer in many cases (was, were) also skilled in astrology.

5. The court astronomer or astrologer (was, were) highly honored in Babylonia, China, Greece, and Rome.
6. Of course, one of the astronomer's main duties (was, were) to predict future events.
7. Many of their records (presents, present) interesting information about the astronomy of the time.
8. Today, almost everyone in the world (is, are) interested in space projects.
9. Yet few of us (knows, know) that in 1609 Johannes Kepler published plans for a voyage to the moon.
10. His ideas on space travel (is, are) found in a book called *Somnium*.
11. Many of the problems of space flight (is, are) suggested in Kepler's work.
12. The effects of gravity (is, are) treated at length by Kepler.
13. Kepler's voyagers in space (faces, face) an unbelievable ordeal during takeoff because they must leave the ground at a speed of 19,300 kilometers per hour.
14. The scientific problems of a moon voyage (is, are) presented by Kepler, but not the practical means for making the trip.
15. Neither he nor other astronomers of his time (was, were) familiar with rocket engines.
16. However, many attempts at flight (was, were) being made.
17. The writings of Kepler (shows, show) that he looked forward to the day when people would fly in spacecraft.
18. Few in Kepler's time (was, were) as farsighted as he.
19. Many people in those days (was, were) sure that Kepler was a sorcerer, not a scientist.
20. Today, scientists all over the world (is, are) exploring outer space with the help of manned and unmanned spacecraft.

OTHER PROBLEMS IN AGREEMENT

8j. Collective nouns may be either singular or plural.

A collective noun names a group of persons or things and is singular in form.

Common Collective Nouns

group	family	army	audience
flock	club	fleet	crowd
herd	class	troop	assembly
swarm	team	squadron	public

A collective noun takes a plural verb when the noun refers to the individual parts or members of the group. A collective noun takes a singular verb when the noun refers to the group as a unit.

EXAMPLES The **family were arguing** about where to spend the next vacation. [*Family* here refers to individuals acting separately.]

The **family was** calmed down by the grandparents. [*Family* here refers to a group considered as a unit.]

EXERCISE 10. Select five collective nouns. Use each noun as the subject of two sentences. In the first, the subject should be singular in meaning and call for a singular verb. In the second, the subject should be plural in meaning and have a plural verb.

8k. A verb agrees with its subject, not its predicate nominative.

Sometimes the subject and the predicate nominative of a sentence are of different numbers. In this case the verb agrees with the subject, not the predicate nominative. The subject usually comes *before* the linking verb and the predicate nominative *after*.

EXAMPLES   The happiest **time** of my life **was** my childhood days.

My childhood **days were** the happiest time of my life.

8l. **When the subject follows the verb as in sentences beginning with** *there* **and** *here* **and in questions, be careful to determine the subject and make sure that the verb agrees with it.**

EXAMPLES   Here **is** my **seat.**
Here **are** our **seats.**
There **is** an exciting **ride** at the fair.
There **are** exciting **rides** at the fair.
Where **are** the **programs?**

Be especially careful when you use the contractions *here's* and *there's*. These contain the verb *is* and should be used only with singular subjects.

NONSTANDARD   There's the books.
   STANDARD   There **are** the **books.**

EXERCISE 11. Number your paper 1–10. Write the correct verb for each sentence.

1. One problem of commuters (is, are) traffic jams.
2. (Here's, Here are) my biology notes.
3. The class (does, do) not agree among themselves on this issue.
4. Here (is, are) the dresses I mentioned to you.
5. (Where's, Where are) the paintings for the exhibit?
6. (Here's, Here are) the winners!
7. My present to you (is, are) these books.
8. (There's, There are) two of my favorite relatives.

9. His herd of cattle (was, were) larger than ours.
10. Here (is, are) the funniest comedians on television.

DON'T AND DOESN'T

Don't and *doesn't* (contractions of *do not* and *does not*) are often used incorrectly.

8m. *Don't* and *doesn't* **must agree with their subjects.**

Use *don't* with plural subjects and with the pronouns *I* and *you*.

EXAMPLES   These **gloves don't** fit.
    You don't speak clearly.
    I don't like that record.

Use *doesn't* with other subjects.

EXAMPLES   The **music box doesn't** play.
    She doesn't like cold weather.
    It doesn't matter.

The most frequent errors in the use of *don't* and *doesn't* are made when *don't* is incorrectly used with *he, she,* or *it*. Remember always to use *doesn't* with these singular subjects: *he doesn't, she doesn't, it doesn't.*

EXERCISE 12. *Oral Drill.* Read the following sentences aloud. By getting your ears accustomed to the correct use of *doesn't* and *don't,* you will get into the habit of using these two words correctly.

1. It doesn't look like a serious wound.
2. She doesn't call meetings often.
3. One doesn't interrupt a speaker.
4. She doesn't play records loudly.
5. Doesn't the television set work?

EXERCISE 13. Number your paper 1–10. Copy the subject of each sentence and write the correct verb (*doesn't* or *don't*).

1. She —— like rhubarb pie.
2. This —— worry him.
3. One —— get one's own way all the time.
4. Many people still —— have enough to eat.
5. My brother —— know how to paint.
6. These —— appeal to him.
7. —— everyone have a pen?
8. They —— need new watches.
9. Cold weather usually —— continue into June.
10. —— anyone in the class know about Susan B. Anthony?

REVIEW EXERCISE C. Eight of the following sentences are correct, while twelve have mistakes in agreement. If a sentence is correct, write *C* on your paper beside the proper number. If the sentence is incorrect, write the correct form of the incorrect verb.

1. Neither of our school libraries have the books I need.
2. Every one of my friends own a library card.
3. The only library in some communities is in the school.
4. Either the librarian or the assistant helps us continually.
5. Where's the books on sports?
6. The most famous library of ancient times were in Egypt.
7. Where's the list of recommended books?
8. The modern circulating library, which lends books to readers, was developed in the Middle Ages.
9. Collections of documents in a special room of a palace was probably the earliest kind of library.

10. Today there's more than fourteen thousand public libraries in this country.
11. Neither the school library nor the city libraries were open on Tuesday.
12. One of the world's great libraries are the Library of Congress.
13. A large collection of recordings are located there.
14. A shortage of money and librarians handicaps some libraries.
15. There's some books in the library that no one ever reads.
16. Many of America's prominent librarians, including Beatrice Winser, were students at the Columbia University Library School.
17. The wide sale of paperback books show that people like to read.
18. How many books of fiction is there in your library?
19. From the state library come several of the books we are using.
20. The cost of books have been rising.

Chapter 9

Correct Use of Verbs

Principal Parts of Regular and Irregular Verbs

Few errors in speaking or writing are more obvious than verb errors. The students who write *she done it, he begun, they drownded,* or *it bursted* immediately tag themselves as people who do not know the standard usages of their language.

THE PRINCIPAL PARTS OF A VERB

A verb shows the time of an action. This expression of time by the verb is called *tense.* To express different times a verb has different tenses, and the tenses are formed from four *principal parts* of the verb.

9a. The principal parts of a verb are the *infinitive,* the *present participle,* the *past,* and the *past participle.*

From these four principal parts all the tenses of our language are formed. The four principal parts of *sing* are *sing* (infinitive), *singing* (present participle), *sang* (past), and *sung* (past participle). Notice in the following sentences how the four principal parts are used to express time.

I **sing** in the school glee club.
We **are singing** at the Music Festival tonight.
Mahalia Jackson **sang** gospels at Carnegie Hall.
We **have sung** all over the state.

Here are the principal parts of two familiar verbs:

INFINITIVE	PRESENT PARTICIPLE	PAST	PAST PARTICIPLE
work	working	worked	(have) worked
eat	eating	ate	(have) eaten

Notice that the present participle always ends in –*ing*. The past participle is the form used with *has, have,* or *had.*

THE SIX TENSES

Through the use of the four principal parts of the verb and various helping verbs, you can form six tenses for the verb. When you give the forms of a verb in its six tenses, you are *conjugating* a verb.

Conjugation of Write

Principal parts: write, writing, wrote, (have) written.

Present Tense

Singular	*Plural*
I write	we write
you write	you write
she writes	they write

Past Tense

Singular	*Plural*
I wrote	we wrote
you wrote	you wrote
she wrote	they wrote

Future Tense

Singular	*Plural*
I will (shall) write	we will (shall) write
you will write	you will write
she will write	they will write

Present Perfect Tense

Singular	*Plural*
I have written	we have written
you have written	you have written
she has written	they have written

Past Perfect Tense

Singular	*Plural*
I had written	we had written
you had written	you had written
she had written	they had written

Future Perfect Tense

Singular	*Plural*
I will (shall) have written	we will (shall) have written
you will have written	you will have written
she will have written	they will have written

REGULAR VERBS

9b. A regular verb forms its past and past participle
by adding *–ed* or *–d* to the present form.

INFINITIVE	PRESENT PARTICIPLE	PAST	PAST PARTICIPLE
follow	following	followed	(have) followed
date	dating	dated	(have) dated
miss	missing	missed	(have) missed

Pay careful attention to pronunciation of the past
and past participle. Avoid nonstandard pronunciation
of these forms. Nonstandard pronunciation usually

follows two patterns: (1) adding an extra syllable—
drownded for *drowned, attackted* for *attacked;* (2) not
pronouncing the normal *–ed* ending—*ask* for *asked,*
was suppose for *was supposed.*

EXERCISE 1. *Oral Drill.* The following sentences
contain regular verbs which are often mispronounced.
Read *aloud* every sentence, stressing the pronunciation of the italicized words, especially their endings.

1. The troops *attacked* the fort.
2. Our speaker was *supposed* to arrive at six o'clock.
3. How many people have *drowned* in this lake?
4. Rosa has often *used* her knowledge of geography.
5. The accident *happened* at night.
6. The brave woman *risked* her life to save her son.
7. You *asked* me that question yesterday.
8. This shampoo has *lasted* for a long time.
9. Private detectives have sometimes *tracked*
   criminals for the police.
10. Have you *washed* the car?

EXERCISE 2. *Oral Drill.* Use the following verbs in
sentences. Put each verb in the past tense or use the
past participle and the helping verb *have* or *has.*

1. use   5. suppose   8. travel
2. experience   6. drown   9. rent
3. ask   7. attack   10. play
4. attempt

IRREGULAR VERBS

9c. An irregular verb forms its past tense in some
other way than a regular verb.

Irregular verbs form their past and past participle
in several ways:

1. by a vowel change: *drink, drank,* (have) *drunk*
2. by a consonant change: *make, made,* (have) *made*
3. by a vowel and consonant change: *bring, brought,* (have) *brought*
4. by no change: *burst, burst,* (have) *burst.*

If you do not know the principal parts of irregular verbs, you may make errors like this:

NONSTANDARD   She has drank all her milk. [*Drunk,* not *drank,* is the past participle.]

To avoid errors, memorize the principal parts of irregular verbs. Include *have* with the past participle because this helping verb is often used with the past participle.

Irregular Verbs Frequently Misused

INFINITIVE	PRESENT PARTICIPLE	PAST	PAST PARTICIPLE
1. begin	beginning	began	(have) begun
2. blow	blowing	blew	(have) blown
3. break	breaking	broke	(have) broken
4. bring	bringing	brought	(have) brought
5. burst	bursting	burst	(have) burst
6. choose	choosing	chose	(have) chosen
7. come	coming	came	(have) come
8. do	doing	did	(have) done
9. drink	drinking	drank	(have) drunk
10. drive	driving	drove	(have) driven
11. eat	eating	ate	(have) eaten
12. fall	falling	fell	(have) fallen
13. freeze	freezing	froze	(have) frozen
14. give	giving	gave	(have) given
15. go	going	went	(have) gone
16. know	knowing	knew	(have) known
17. lie	lying	lay	(have) lain

18. ride	riding	rode	(have) ridden
19. ring	ringing	rang	(have) rung
20. rise	rising	rose	(have) risen
21. run	running	ran	(have) run
22. see	seeing	saw	(have) seen
23. set	setting	set	(have) set
24. shrink	shrinking	shrank	(have) shrunk
25. sing	singing	sang	(have) sung
26. sit	sitting	sat	(have) sat
27. speak	speaking	spoke	(have) spoken
28. steal	stealing	stole	(have) stolen
29. swim	swimming	swam	(have) swum
30. take	taking	took	(have) taken
31. throw	throwing	threw	(have) thrown
32. write	writing	wrote	(have) written

Caution: Be careful not to confuse irregular verbs with regular ones. Never say *blowed, knowed, throwed,* or *bursted.*

EXERCISE 3. Your teacher or a classmate may dictate to you the infinitive form of the thirty-two irregular verbs listed earlier. Write the past and the past participle on your paper.

Merely knowing the principal parts of the irregular verbs is not enough. You should practice using them in sentence patterns. The following patterns will help you practice usage of the irregular verbs.

> Today I **bring** lunch.
> Yesterday I **brought** lunch.
> Often I **have brought** lunch.

EXERCISE 4. Number your paper 1–20. Choose the correct one of the two verbs in parentheses and write it after the corresponding number. If there are two verbs in a sentence, write them on the same line. When your paper has been corrected, read each sentence *aloud* several times, stressing the correct verb.

1. Students have often (chose, chosen) "The Devil and Daniel Webster" as their favorite short story.
2. The story was (wrote, written) by Stephen Vincent Benét.
3. Jabez Stone, a New Hampshire farmer, had (gave, given) up all hope of succeeding.
4. Everything he (did, done) turned out wrong.
5. Then one day the devil (came, come) to see Jabez Stone.
6. The devil (knowed, knew) that Jabez had (spoke, spoken) some fatal words.
7. In despair Jabez had one day (began, begun) to curse his luck.
8. He had even (went, gone) so far as to say that he would do anything to improve his lot.
9. The devil had (saw, seen) his chance and so had (came, come) to make a bargain with Jabez.
10. At first Jabez had (shrank, shrunk) from the devil's proposal.
11. Then he had (took, taken) another look at his poor farm.
12. After the devil had (spoke, spoken) to him for a short while, Jabez (did, done) what the devil asked.
13. He (throwed, threw) his soul away in exchange for good fortune.
14. Bad luck had (drove, driven) Jabez to agree to a bargain that he would soon regret.
15. For several years Jabez (drank, drunk) from the well of prosperity.
16. But all too soon the well (ran, run) dry.
17. The time (came, come) for Jabez to deliver his soul to the devil.
18. Before his time was up, though, Jabez had (rode, ridden) to see Daniel Webster, the great lawyer.
19. Luckily, Daniel Webster had (took, taken) Jabez' case.

20. You should read Benét's short story to see what Daniel Webster (did, done).

EXERCISE 5. Number your paper 1–20. After the proper number, write the past or the past participle form of the verb which completes the sentence correctly. Use the verb given at the beginning of each sentence.

1. *blow*   The girl —— air into the balloon.
2. *burst*   It finally ——.
3. *fall*   Only a few large meteorites have ever —— to earth.
4. *throw*   The umpire has —— the angry player out of the game.
5. *swim*   Marilyn Bell, a seventeen-year-old, once —— the English Channel.
6. *steal*   Lou Brock has —— more bases than any other baseball player in the history of the major leagues.
7. *ring*   Last night the bell in the deserted old tower —— for the first time in years.
8. *bring*   The same mail carrier has —— our mail for ten years.
9. *speak*   Have you —— to your classmates about the problem?
10. *choose*   The judges —— a German shepherd as the winner of the dog show.
11. *break*   Babe Didrikson Zaharias —— many track and field records.
12. *blow*   The wind has —— steadily from the north.
13. *know*   The diplomat —— that her mission was dangerous.
14. *ride*   The ambassador had —— for many miles before she found the right person.
15. *freeze*   Our milk has —— solid.

16. *see*   Have you —— all of Joanne Wood-
ward's movies?

17. *write*   The critics decided that she had ——
a masterpiece.

18. *begin* After we —— the climb, we realized that
the mountain was very steep.

19. *drink* We —— too much lemonade.

20. *burst* After she had —— out laughing, she
suddenly realized that her friend was
quite serious.

REVIEW EXERCISE A. Write two original sentences, using correctly the past and past participle forms of each verb that you missed in Exercises 4 and 5. After your sentences have been checked for accuracy, read them aloud until you feel that you have mastered the troublesome verbs.

REVIEW EXERCISE B. Number your paper 1–20. Write *C* after the number of each correct sentence. Write the correct form of the verb after the number of each incorrect sentence.

EXAMPLES 1. We drove up to the house.
            1. *C*
            2. She come upon something unusual.
            2. *came*

1. After we had rode around for a while, we stopped in front of an old house.
2. We saw that the grass had not been cut in months.
3. Many of the windows had been broke by storms.
4. We blowed our horn, but no one appeared to greet us.
5. Then we saw that a "for sale" sign in the front yard had fallen over.
6. We knowed then the house was vacant.
7. We begun to feel afraid the moment we got out of the car.

8. No one had spoken as we walked toward the house.
9. Although we had seen no one, we knocked on the door just to make sure.
10. When no one answered, we give the door a push.
11. The door burst open, and we went inside.
12. We were glad we had brought a flashlight.
13. After we had went through all the rooms downstairs, we decided to take a look upstairs.
14. Nothing at all unusual happen until we started up the stairs.
15. Suddenly we heard a noise that sounded as if a hundred balloons had bursted right in front of us.
16. We freezed in our tracks.
17. Then a loud wailing began.
18. No one ask what to do next.
19. As we run out of the house, I turned my head.
20. Coming down the stairs was a little boy who was grinning broadly at the scare he had gave to all four of us.

Sit and Set

Study the principal parts of the verbs *sit* and *set*. Notice that *sit* changes to form the past tense, but *set* remains the same in the past and the past participle.

INFINITIVE	PRESENT PARTICIPLE	PAST	PAST PARTICIPLE
sit (to rest)	sitting	sat	(have) sat
set (to place)	setting	set	(have) set

Sit and *set* are verbs which are often confused. But you will not make mistakes with these two verbs if you remember two facts about them:

(1) *Sit* means "to rest in an upright, sitting position" while *set* means "to put or place (something)."

Let's **sit** under the tree.
Let's **set** the bookcase here.

The tourists **sat** on benches.
The children **set** the dishes on the table.
We **had sat** down to eat when the telephone rang.
We **have set** the reading lamp beside the couch.

(2) *Sit* is almost never followed by an object but *set* may often be.

My aunt **sits** in the large chair. [no object]
She **sets** the chair in the corner. [Sets what? *Chair* is the object.]
The audience **sat** near the stage. [no object]
The stagehand **set** a microphone near Trini Lopez. [Set what? *Microphone* is the object.]

EXERCISE 6. *Oral Drill.* Read the following sentences aloud, paying particular attention to the meaning of *sit* and *set*. Pronounce each verb distinctly.

1. Let's sit down here.
2. Look at the dog sitting on the porch.
3. Our teacher set a deadline for our term projects.
4. Have you set the clock?
5. I have always sat in the front row.
6. Please set the carton down inside the doorway.
7. She has set a high standard for her work.
8. The woman sits by the window every day.
9. The referee is setting the ball on the fifty-yard line.
10. After I set the mop in the closet, I sat down to rest.

EXERCISE 7. Number your paper 1–10. After the proper number, write the correct one of the two words in parentheses. If the verb you choose is a form of *set*, write its object after it.

EXAMPLE   1. The movers (sat, set) our table down gently.
          1. *set, table*

1. We were (sitting, setting) outside, watching the cloud formations.
2. Peggy (sat, set) her dictionary on her desk.
3. In the summer the owners of the restaurants (sat, set) their tables outdoors.
4. Have you ever (sat, set) at a sidewalk café and watched the people go by?
5. When my grandmother needs supplies, she (sits, sets) a lantern in her window.
6. Wordsworth wrote a poem about a boy (sitting, setting) alone in a cemetery.
7. I like to (sit, set) up late, watching television.
8. The twins had not (sat, set) still for long before they were planning another trick.
9. The class had to (sit, set) still for ten minutes.
10. Where were you (sitting, setting)?

EXERCISE 8. Use correctly each of the following verbs in sentences of your own.

1. sits
2. sets
3. was sitting
4. was setting
5. sat
6. set
7. have sat
8. have set
9. will set
10. will sit

Lie and Lay

Study the principal parts of *lie* and *lay*.

INFINITIVE	PRESENT PARTICIPLE	PAST	PAST PARTICIPLE
lie (to recline)	lying	lay	(have) lain
lay (to put)	laying	laid	(have) laid

Like *sit,* lie[1] has to do with resting and it has no object. *Lay* is like *set* because it means "to put something down" and because it may have an object.

---

[1] The verb *lie* meaning "to tell a falsehood" is a different word. Its past forms are regular: lie, lying, lied, lied.

The cows **are lying** in the shade. [no object]

The workers **are laying** the foundations for the building. [*Are laying* what? *Foundations* is the object.]

The soldiers **lay** very still while the enemy passed by. [no object — *lay* here is the past tense of *lie*]

The soldiers **laid** a trap for the enemy. [*Laid* what? *Trap* is the object.]

The injured man **had lain** in the cave for weeks. [no object]

The lawyer **had laid** the newspaper next to her briefcase. [*Had laid* what? *Newspaper* is the object.]

EXERCISE 9. *Oral Drill.* Read each of the following sentences aloud several times. Be able to explain why the verb is correct.

1. The delegates laid the groundwork for future conferences.
2. She lay in bed until eleven o'clock.
3. Don't lie in the sun too long!
4. You shouldn't lay your papers on the couch.
5. The lion had been lying in wait for an hour.
6. The senator laid her notes aside after her speech on careers in politics.
7. He had lain still for a few minutes.
8. He has laid his books on his desk.
9. Our cat lies on the radiator.
10. She lays the sharp knives on the top shelf.
11. The cook laid the meat on the grill.
12. The exhausted swimmer lay helpless on the sand.
13. Lie down for a few minutes before supper.
14. She laid her pen on the edge of the desk.

EXERCISE 10. Number your paper 1–10. After the proper number, write the correct form of the proper verb (*lie–lay*) for each of these sentences.

1. My father always —— down for a few minutes before he helps prepare dinner.
2. Last night the musician —— her instrument down and joined in the dance.
3. The puppy —— very still as long as we petted it.
4. Because of the heat I have —— in the shade most of the day.
5. After she had —— the carpets in the new house, she moved in.
6. The ships were —— in the harbor.
7. The sheriff has been —— plans to catch the bank robber.
8. Have you ever —— in a hammock?
9. From where we ——, we could see the stars very clearly.
10. Whoever —— the carpet in your living room did an excellent job.

EXERCISE 11. Use correctly each of the following verbs or verb phrases in a sentence of your own.

1. lies
2. laid
3. was laying
4. has lain
5. lays
6. has been lying
7. lay (past tense of lie)
8. have laid
9. will lie
10. are lying

Rise and Raise

Study the principal parts of *rise* and *raise*.

INFINITIVE	PRESENT PARTICIPLE	PAST	PAST PARTICIPLE
rise (to go up)	rising	rose	(have) risen
raise (to lift up)	raising	raised	(have) raised

The verb *rise* means "to go up" or "to get up." *Rise* like *lie,* never has an object. *Raise,* which means "to lift up" or "to cause to rise," may, like *lay,* have an object.

My neighbors **rise** very early in the morning. [no object]

Every morning they **raise** their shades to let the sunlight in. [*Raise* what? *Shades* is the object.]

The moon **rose** slowly last night. [no object]

Last year Ana and Bill **raised** corn and tomatoes in their garden. [*Raised* what? *Corn* and *tomatoes* are the objects.]

The senators **have risen** from their seats to show respect for the Chief Justice. [no object]

The wind **has raised** a cloud of dust. [*Has raised* what? *Cloud* is the object.]

EXERCISE 12. *Oral Drill.* Repeat each of the following correct sentences aloud several times, stressing the italicized verbs and thinking of the meanings of the verbs.

1. The reporters *rise* when the President enters the room.
2. The reporters *raise* their hands to be recognized.
3. The reporter who was recognized *rose* to her feet.
4. She *has raised* an interesting question.
5. Another reporter *was rising.*
6. Several reporters *rose* at the same time.
7. Who *had risen* first?
8. He recognized the one who *rose* first.
9. Will Congress *raise* taxes this year?
10. Everyone *rises* as the President leaves.

EXERCISE 13. Number your paper 1–10. After the proper number, write the correct one of the two verbs in parentheses. If the verb you choose is a form of *raise,* write its object after it.

1. The poet Longfellow wrote "The Tide (Rises, Raises), the Tide Falls."
2. When no one paid any attention to the man, he (rose, raised) his voice.

3. The audience (rose, raised) and gave a standing ovation to the singer.
4. At the beginning of the exercise, you (rise, raise) your arms above your head.
5. The hikers (rose, raised) refreshed after a good night's rest in their warm sleeping bags.
6. The temperature has (risen, raised) to a new high for this time of the year.
7. The announcement has (risen, raised) new hope for the lives of the missing passengers.
8. Golda Meir (rose, raised) to a powerful position in the Israeli government.
9. At five o'clock our counselor shouted, "(Rise, Raise) and shine."
10. We may have (risen, raised), but we certainly did not shine.

EXERCISE 14. Number your paper 1–10. After the proper number, write the form of *rise* or *raise* that you would use in each blank in the following paragraphs.

We girls —— early to start our hike to Lookout Mountain. From our position at the foot of the mountain, it looked as though it —— straight up to the heavens.

But we had not —— at daybreak just to look at the high peak. We —— our supply packs to our backs and started the long climb up the mountain. With every step we took, the mountain seemed to —— that much higher. Finally, after several hours, we reached the summit and —— a special flag that we had brought for the occasion. When our friends at the foot of the mountain saw the flag ——, they knew that we had reached the top safely. They —— their arms and shouted.

Although we could not see them, we heard voices that seemed to —— from the valley below. Then we felt glad that we had —— early enough to climb to the top of Lookout Mountain.

REVIEW EXERCISE C. Number your paper 1–20. Choose the correct verb from the two in parentheses and write it after the proper number. If a sentence has two verbs, write both of them on the same line in the order they occur. Be prepared to explain your choices in class.

1. The great plane (rose, raised) smoothly from the runway.
2. Everyone should (sit, set) still during the performance.
3. The trail (lay, laid) in front of us.
4. After the parade the band members were glad to (sit, set) down.
5. Cooks often (lie, lay) their stirring spoons in special spoon rests.
6. The curtain (rises, raises) on a completely empty stage.
7. Key West (lies, lays) off the southwestern coast of Florida.
8. To study how solar energy works, our class (sit, set) a homemade solar panel outside the window of our classroom.
9. Legend says that when the moon (rises, raises), vampires (rise, raise) from their coffins to perform their fearful deeds.
10. While their grandmother (sat, set) in the shade, Marilyn and Ed (sat, set) the table for their picnic.
11. He would have (lain, laid) in bed all morning if we had not made him (rise, raise).
12. Smoke was (rising, raising) from the cabin's chimney as the old woman (lay, laid) her plate and cup upon the table.
13. Last night the parents carefully (lay, laid) their children's presents under the tree.

14. In Antarctica, snow (lies, lays) on the ground all year.
15. The price of gasoline has (risen, raised) in the last month.
16. We had been (sitting, setting) on the porch, watching the sun go down.
17. The stream has (risen, raised) so high that it has overflowed its banks.
18. The dignified executive (rose, raised) his eyebrows when a manager from a rival company (sat, set) down beside him.
19. Our dog (lay, laid) down in front of the door and refused to move.
20. The water level of the stream has not (risen, raised) since last summer.

CONSISTENCY OF TENSE

You should never shift tenses needlessly. When you are writing about events in the past tense, you should consistently use the past tense unless there is some reason for you to change tenses. You should not shift without reason to the present tense.

9d. Do not change needlessly from one tense to another.

NONSTANDARD   After we were comfortable, we begin to do our homework. [*Were* is past tense and *begin* is present.]

STANDARD   After we **were** comfortable, we **began** to do our homework. [Both *were* and *began* are in the past tense.]

NONSTANDARD   Suddenly the great door opened, and an uninvited guest comes into the dining hall. [*Opened* is past tense and *comes* is present.]

STANDARD   Suddenly the great door **opens,** and an uninvited guest **comes** into the dining hall. [Both *opens* and *comes* are in the present tense.]

STANDARD   Suddenly the great door **opened,** and an uninvited guest **came** into the dining hall. [Both *opened* and *came* are in the past tense.]

EXERCISE 15. Read the following paragraph, and decide what tense you should use to tell about the events. Prepare to read the paragraph aloud, making the verb tense consistent throughout.

I got back to camp somewhat later than usual last night. When I walk into my cabin, I thought something is strange. Everyone is in bed. "My roommates went to bed extremely early," I say to myself. But I soon forgot about my roommates' strange behavior and start getting ready for bed. After putting on my pajamas, I turn out the light. By this time I am ready for a good night's sleep. I think about my soft bed as I pulled back the bedspread. Then I lie down, but not for long. My soft bed had suddenly become a very hard bed. When I got up, I hear a very loud giggling from everyone in the cabin. My roommates had replaced my comfortable mattress with several hard boards.

REVIEW EXERCISE D. Number your paper 1–20. Select from each sentence the correct one of the verb forms in parentheses and write it after the corresponding number on your paper.

1. After I (saw, seen) the movie, I read the book.
2. The inner tube (bursted, burst) when I put too much air in it.
3. We always (sit, set) in the back row.
4. The people have (chose, chosen) a leader.
5. When the oxygen (run, ran) out, she was forced to surface.

6. She has (rode, ridden) the Ferris wheel five times.
7. The commander (rose, raised) a white flag over the fort.
8. The ship has (began, begun) to sink.
9. Dolphins have often (swam, swum) behind ships for many miles.
10. The mountain climbers (drank, drunk) some hot coffee.
11. His right shoulder is sore because he (lay, laid) on it all night.
12. In desperation, the quarterback (throwed, threw) a long pass.
13. No one (knowed, knew) how the feud had started.
14. Wars have always (took, taken) the lives of many people.
15. They have (broke, broken) the agreement.
16. The turtle has (shrank, shrunk) back into its shell.
17. Several skiers have (fell, fallen) on the first turn.
18. A famous jewel was (stole, stolen) last night.
19. The telephone (rang, rung), but no one answered.
20. The police officer (blowed, blew) her whistle at the speeding motorist.

REVIEW EXERCISE E. Number your paper 1–25. Write after the corresponding number the form of the verb at the left which correctly fills the blank in each sentence. In some instances you must choose the correct verb as well as the correct form.

begin 1. Snow —— to fall early this morning.
bring 2. Who —— you home last night?
eat 3. After I had —— five hamburgers, I was too full for dessert.
rise, raise 4. When prices ——, everyone complains.
come 5. My parents were asleep when I —— in.

sit, set 6. Please —— down for a while.

see   7. I —— an exhibit of his work last year.

rise, raise 8. By noon the fog had ——.

know   9. The firefighters should have —— what to do.

lie, lay 10. Bob —— the frying pan on the hot coals.

run   11. We —— into several friends at the movies last night.

give   12. They had —— away our secret.

lay   13. Yesterday we —— the new tile in the kitchen.

freeze 14. You could have —— to death.

speak 15. Has Joan —— to you about the assignment?

swim 16. When we were children, we —— there often.

write 17. At least they could have —— a postcard.

lie, lay 18. You should have —— there until help came.

throw 19. I tried to find out who had —— the winning pitch.

ring   20. The bell must have —— early.

shrink 21. My new sweater had —— when I washed it.

steal   22. The thieves had —— nothing of value.

ride   23. Unfortunately, I had never —— that horse.

take   24. She might have —— the children with her.

burst   25. As I crossed the room, my suitcase —— open.

Chapter **10**

Correct Use of Pronouns

Nominative and Objective Cases

Nouns and pronouns have case. The case of a word depends on how the word is used in the sentence. For example, a word used as a subject is in the *nominative* case; a word used as an object is in the *objective* case; and a word used to show ownership or relationship is in the *possessive* case.

The case of nouns presents no problem because a noun has the same form in the nominative and objective cases.

The **woman** [nominative] said she saw another **woman** [objective] in the park.

The possessive case of a noun usually requires only the addition of an apostrophe and an *s*.

The **woman's** friend has arrived

The case of personal pronouns, however, does present a problem because they change form in the different cases. To use these pronouns correctly, you must know their various case forms and when to use them.

THE CASE FORMS OF PERSONAL PRONOUNS

Study the following list of pronouns to see how their forms differ in the three cases.

NOMINATIVE CASE	OBJECTIVE CASE	POSSESSIVE CASE
Singular		
I	me	my, mine
you	you	your, yours
he, she, it	him, her, it	his, her, hers, its
Plural		
we	us	our, ours
you	you	your, yours
they	them	their, theirs

The pronouns *you* and *it* cause few usage problems because their forms remain unchanged in the nominative and objective cases. The possessive case forms, which show ownership or relationship, need care in spelling. (See pages 266–67.)

When *you* and *it* and the possessive pronouns are omitted from the above list, you have the following pronouns with different forms in the nominative and objective cases. Memorize the list for each case and remember which pronouns are nominative and which are objective.

NOMINATIVE CASE	OBJECTIVE CASE
I	me
he	him
she	her
we	us
they	them

The Nominative Case

10a. The subject of a verb is in the nominative case.

EXAMPLES **I** like music. [*I* is the subject of the verb *like*.]

He and **she** sold tickets. [*He* and *she* are the subjects of the verb *sold.*]

They called while **we** were away. [*They* is the subject of *called; we* is the subject of *were.*]

Pronoun usage errors occur most frequently when the subject is compound. It is very easy to say, "Lois and *me* study together" when you should say, "Lois and *I* study together." "Lois and I" is a compound subject. If you test the pronoun by itself with the verb, you can tell which form is correct.

NONSTANDARD   Me study.
   STANDARD   I study. (Lois and I study.)

Use the same test in sentences like "We girls work together" and "Us girls work together." Use the pronoun alone before the verb. "Us work together" is incorrect. "We work together" is correct, and so "We girls work together" is correct.

EXERCISE 1. *Oral Drill.* Read the following sentences aloud, stressing the italicized pronouns.

1. *He* and *she* collect seashells.
2. My grandmother and *I* are painting the boat.
3. Both *they* and *we* were frightened.
4. Did Sally or *she* answer the phone?
5. *We* girls are giving a fashion show.
6. *You* and *I* will stay behind.
7. Where are *he* and *she?*
8. My parents and *they* are good friends.
9. *She* and *I* deliver newspapers.
10. Do you and *she* like to fish?

EXERCISE 2. Number your paper 1–10. Beside the proper number, write a pronoun which will correctly

fill the blank. Use a variety of pronouns. Don't use
you or *it*.

1. She and —— are officers in the club.
2. Our friends and —— want to learn to ski.
3. Neither —— nor Cynthia is here.
4. —— and Diane have pen pals in Austria.
5. Where are —— and —— going?
6. Everyone knows that —— students are proud of
   our school.
7. No one can say that —— and —— give up easily.
8. Have you or —— ever gone deep-sea fishing?
9. Both —— and —— have entered the contest.
10. Did —— or Geraldo see the lighthouse?

10b. A predicate nominative is in the nominative case.

A predicate nominative is a noun or pronoun completing the meaning of a linking verb. A pronoun used
as a predicate nominative usually follows a form of the
verb *be: am, is, are, was, were,* and verb phrases ending in *be* or *been,* such as *will be* and *has been.*

Read the following examples aloud, stressing the
words in heavy type.

It may be **she** at the door. [*She* is a predicate
nominative following the linking verb *may be.*]
The speakers are **she** and **I.** [*She* and *I* are predicate nominatives following the linking verb *are.*]
Do you think it was **they?** [*They* is a predicate
nominative following the linking verb *was.*]

► USAGE NOTE You should understand two facts
about English usage. First, some usages are acceptable
in conversational English, but not in written English.
Second, from time to time usage changes so that expressions that were once considered nonstandard may
become standard. The application of rule 10b is an
example of both these facts. The expressions *It's me,*

That's her, It was them, etc., although they violate the rule and were once considered nonstandard, have now become acceptable spoken English. In writing, however, standard usage still follows the rule except for *It's me,* which is always acceptable and almost never appears in writing anyway.

SPOKEN   No one would believe it was her. (him, etc.)
WRITTEN   No one would believe it was she. (he, etc.)

Of course, it would be correct to use *she* in speaking, even though *her* is acceptable.

In doing the exercises in this book, base your answers on the usage of written English.

EXERCISE 3. Number your paper 1–10. Copy each linking verb and write the correct pronoun.

1. Everyone believed it was (her, she).
2. Many people think I am (she, her).
3. If it was (them, they), their parents will be angry.
4. It might have been (she, her) that he meant.
5. No one could tell that it was (we, us) students.
6. It could have been (him, he), but I doubt it.
7. Our visitors could have been (them, they).
8. I knew it was (they, them) to whom he referred.
9. If it had been (her, she), I would have known her.
10. Is that Melba or (she, her)?

The Objective Case

10c. Direct and indirect objects of a verb are in the objective case.

EXAMPLES   You surprised **us.** [*Us* is the object of the verb *surprised.*]
Our neighbor gave **her** and **me** a job. [*Her* and *me* are indirect objects; they tell *to whom* our neighbor gave a job.]

The ranger guided **us** boys to the camp. [*Us* is the object of the verb *guided*. Using the pronoun alone after the verb shows that the ranger guided *us* (not *we*) to the camp.]

Most errors in the use of the objective case occur when the object is compound. You can often avoid making an error with a compound object by trying each pronoun separately with the verb.

The representative met (she, her) and (he, him).

NONSTANDARD   The representative met she.
                The representative met he.
    STANDARD   The representative met **her.**
                The representative met **him.**
                The representative met **her** and **him.**

EXERCISE 4. *Oral Drill.* Read the following sentences aloud at least twice, stressing the italicized pronouns. When your ear becomes accustomed to the right sound of pronouns, you will be able to choose the correct forms more easily.

1. The hot chocolate burned Gail and *me.*
2. Karen showed *her* and Allen *her* houseplants.
3. The dog followed *her* and *him* to school.
4. Did you expect *us* or *them?*
5. The doctor gave *her* and *me* flu shots.
6. The president of the club called *us* girls to a special meeting.
7. Let's help Sarah and *him* with their chores.
8. Have you seen the Romanos or *them?*
9. The mayor thanked you and *him.*
10. The cook made *us* boys a special dessert.

EXERCISE 5. Number your paper 1–10. Supply correct pronouns for the blanks in these sentences; write the pronouns after the proper numbers. Be sure to use a variety of pronouns, but do not use *you* and *it*. When your answers have been checked, read aloud at least three times the corrected form of each sentence that you missed.

1. The group selected —— and —— as the king and queen of the festival.
2. We asked —— and Ms. Smith for help.
3. Lana finally found Mario and —— at the theater.
4. Do you believe Evans and ——?
5. My grandmother told —— girls what life was like when she was a girl.
6. Mother sent —— and —— for some ice cream.
7. A guide took my sister and —— through the museum.
8. Let's call Mel and ——.
9. Do you know —— or ——?
10. The storm frightened Paul and ——.

10d. The object of a preposition is in the objective case.

A prepositional phrase begins with a preposition and ends with an object, which is always a noun or pronoun. When the object is a pronoun, you must be careful to use the objective case. Below are prepositional phrases with the objects printed in heavy type.

with **me**	near **her**	except **them**
to **him**	by **us**	for **us**

Most errors in usage occur when the object of the preposition is compound. Notice that in the following prepositional phrases all pronouns are in the objective case.

about Mom and **me**	without **them** or **us**
near Carla and **her**	from Doug and **him**

EXERCISE 6. *Oral Drill.* Read each of the following sentences several times, stressing the correct, italicized pronouns.

1. The safari continued without *her* and *me.*
2. Everyone except *us* counselors had left the camp.
3. We stood beside their families and *them* during the ceremony.
4. Do you have any suggestions for Jane or *me?*
5. The clowns talked to Claire and *him.*
6. Behind *us* girls was a playful bear cub.
7. Give this to either your father or *her.*
8. With the help of Juan and *her,* we built a fire.
9. The group sat in a circle around the scouts and *them* while they danced and sang.
10. There was a spelling bee between *us* and *them.*

EXERCISE 7. Number your paper 1–10. After each number, write the prepositional phrase in the corresponding sentence, including in it a pronoun that will complete the phrase correctly. Use a variety of pronouns, but do not use *you* or *it.*

1. You can sell tickets to Roberta and ——.
2. The big day for you and —— finally came.
3. The dog was walking behind Sally and ——.
4. Everyone except —— and Deborah was resting.
5. Without you and —— we're sure to lose the game.
6. When did you last speak to Sandy and ——?
7. Our team played against both Clarkson High and ——.
8. We were near you and —— when it happened.
9. "Between you and ——" is a familiar expression in conversations.
10. Do you have news about your sister and ——?

REVIEW EXERCISE A. Number your paper 1–20. Opposite the proper number, write the pronoun in the parentheses that will make the sentence correct.

After each answer, write an abbreviation showing how the pronoun is used: *subj., p.n., d.o., i.o., obj. prep.*

EXAMPLE 1. I saw (she, her) and Amy at the circus.
1. *her   d.o.*

1. The speaker addressed (we, us) members of the graduating class.
2. Good-citizenship medals were awarded to Karen and (he, him).
3. The last performer was (she, her).
4. When will you and (I, me) meet again?
5. The dogs barked at (he, him) and Neil.
6. (We, Us) girls voted for Mary.
7. The best speller in the class is (she, her).
8. We passed Jan and (they, them) on the road.
9. The pianist at the restaurant played a special song for Jack and (she, her).
10. The guide showed the other tourists and (we, us) around the castle.
11. Catherine and (he, him) will perform next.
12. Did you give the presents to Eileen and (they, them)?
13. Ask your neighbor and (they, them) to the next meeting.
14. She sent Gloria and (I, me) beautiful scarves.
15. The one in the clown mask is (he, him).
16. The farmer gave (we, us) girls a bushel of peaches for our help.
17. The best students are John and (she, her).
18. You and (they, them) may manage the cake sale at the school bazaar.
19. I was sitting between Carmen and (she, her).
20. I wrote a theme about my grandmother and (he, him).

REVIEW EXERCISE B. Write ten original sentences, using correctly the following pronouns. After each sentence, identify the use of the pronoun or pronouns: *sub., p.n., d.o., i.o., obj. prep.*

1. you and I	6. Gail and they
2. you and me	7. us students
3. her friend and she	8. our parents and we
4. his friend and him	9. Susan and her
5. him and her	10. our teacher and us

REVIEW EXERCISE C. Number your paper 1–20. After the proper number, write the correct one of the two pronouns in parentheses.

1. Kent and (he, him) are rehearsing their parts.
2. A special report was assigned to Beth and (I, me).
3. The judges will be you and (she, her).
4. The cast of the play includes two seniors and (we, us).
5. When the curtain went up, everyone except Jim and (I, me) was on stage.
6. Have you heard from Carolyn or (she, her)?
7. She is teaching (we, us) beginners to swim.
8. It was (they, them) who called you.
9. That must have been (they, them).
10. The Jensens and (we, us) watched the elaborate display of fireworks.
11. The studio sent (she, her) and her husband to Argentina.
12. A friend painted a picture of Jan and (she, her).
13. Our neighbors lent (we, us) girls their mower.
14. Both Gina and (she, her) speak German.
15. The collection of toy elephants belongs to Fran and (he, him).
16. The two girls in white are (they, them).
17. Do you remember Ginny and (I, me)?
18. Harold and (I, me) are visiting our grandparents.
19. It's only (we, us) girls.
20. Don't leave without (she, her) and Tracy.

Chapter **11**

Correct Use
of Modifiers

Choice, Comparison, Placement

You know from your study of Chapters 2 and 3 that adjectives and adverbs are called modifiers. A modifier describes or makes more definite the meaning of another word. The adjective modifies a noun or a pronoun, and the adverb modifies a verb, an adjective, or another adverb. You also know from your study of Chapters 4 and 5 that phrases and clauses, as well as individual words, may be used as modifiers. This chapter will help you learn to use modifiers correctly and effectively.

GOOD AND *WELL*

11a. Distinguish between *good* and *well* as modifiers.

Use *good* to modify a noun or a pronoun. Never use *good* to modify a verb. Use *well* to modify a verb.

NONSTANDARD	Doris bowls good.
STANDARD	Doris bowls **well.**
NONSTANDARD	The orchestra played very good.
STANDARD	The orchestra played very **well.**

In the following examples, *good* is correct because it is a predicate adjective modifying the subject. Like all predicate adjectives, it follows a linking verb.

STANDARD   The pie tastes especially **good.** [good pie]

STANDARD   Over the microphone her voice sounds **good.** [good voice]

Well can also be used as an adjective when it refers to a person's health or appearance.

EXAMPLES   Doug feels **well** today. [*Well* is a predicate adjective modifying the subject *Doug.*]

You look **well** in red. [*Well* is a predicate adjective modifying the subject *you.*]

EXERCISE 1. *Oral Drill.* Read aloud each of the following sentences, stressing the italicized words. This exercise will train your ear and check your tendency to use *good* as the modifier of a verb.

1. Everyone did *well* on the test.
2. We work *well* together.
3. Do you sing as *well* as your sister does?
4. I can't water-ski very *well.*
5. How *well* can you write?
6. The pilot landed the plane *well.*
7. All went *well* until the actor forgot his lines.
8. Our class pictures turned out *well.*
9. The second-string quarterback can pass as *well* as the starting quarterback.
10. The plans for the square dance are working out quite *well.*

EXERCISE 2. Number your paper 1–10. If *good* or *well* is correctly used in a sentence, write + after the corresponding number. If *good* or *well* is not correctly used, write 0.

1. Georgette did not bowl as good as usual last night.
2. The plans sound good to me.
3. How good can she kick a soccer ball?

4. I don't know the new neighbors very well.
5. Although he has been sick, he looks well now.
6. I explained the situation as well as I could.
7. The team played very good.
8. Freshly baked bread smells good.
9. The work did not go so good as we had hoped.
10. How good the cake looks!

COMPARISON OF MODIFIERS

Adjectives and adverbs may be used in comparing two or more things.

> Richard is **heavier** than Bob.
> This is the **heaviest** box of the three.
> Maria spoke **more clearly** than Alicia.
> Of all the speakers, Hazel spoke **most clearly.**

When adjectives and adverbs are used to express comparison, they show degrees of comparison. They show the degree to which one word has a quality compared to another word having the same quality.

> This building is **tall.**
> This building is **taller** than that one.
> This building is the **tallest** one in the world.

> I ski **frequently.**
> I ski **more frequently** than she does.
> Of the three of us, I ski **most frequently.**

11b. There are three degrees of comparison of modifiers: *positive, comparative,* and *superlative.*

POSITIVE	COMPARATIVE	SUPERLATIVE
weak	weaker	weakest
ancient	more ancient	most ancient
loud	louder	loudest
loudly	more loudly	most loudly
good	better	best
bad	worse	worst

There are two regular ways to compare modifiers. To form the comparative degree, the letters *er* may be added to the word, or the word *more* may precede it. To form the superlative, the letters *est* may be added to the word, or the word *most* may precede it.

(1) Most one-syllable modifiers form their comparative and superlative degrees by adding *er* and *est*.

POSITIVE	COMPARATIVE	SUPERLATIVE
near	nearer	nearest
meek	meeker	meekest

(2) Some two-syllable modifiers form their comparative and superlative degrees by adding *er* and *est*, but most two-syllable modifiers form their comparative and superlative degrees by means of *more* and *most*.

POSITIVE	COMPARATIVE	SUPERLATIVE
simple	simpler	simplest
drowsy	drowsier	drowsiest
modern	more modern	most modern
pleasant	more pleasant	most pleasant

When you are in doubt about which way an adjective is compared, consult a dictionary.

(3) Modifiers of three or more syllables form their comparative and superlative degrees by means of *more* and *most*.

POSITIVE	COMPARATIVE	SUPERLATIVE
ignorant	more ignorant	most ignorant
happily	more happily	most happily

EXERCISE 3. Write the forms for the comparative and superlative degrees of the following modifiers.

1. late
2. careful
3. gracefully
4. agile

5. interesting
6. low
7. merry
8. nervous
9. efficiently
10. soft

(4) Comparison to indicate *less* and *least* of a quality is accomplished by using the words *less* and *least* before the modifier.

POSITIVE	COMPARATIVE	SUPERLATIVE
skillful	less skillful	least skillful
delicate	less delicate	least delicate

Irregular Comparison

When adjectives and adverbs do not follow the regular methods of forming their comparative and superlative degrees, they are said to be compared irregularly. You should learn the comparative and superlative degrees of the five modifiers below.

POSITIVE	COMPARATIVE	SUPERLATIVE
bad	worse	worst
good	better	best
well	better	best
many	more	most
much	more	most

REVIEW EXERCISE A. Write the comparative and superlative degrees of the following modifiers. When in doubt about the words of two syllables, consult a dictionary.

1. foolish
2. quickly
3. many
4. simply
5. polite
6. short
7. dreary
8. frequently
9. good
10. cold
11. well
12. unexpectedly
13. curious
14. much
15. near
16. enthusiastic
17. easily
18. tasty
19. bad
20. courteous

Use of Comparative and Superlative Forms

11c. Use the *comparative* degree when comparing two things; use the *superlative* when comparing three or more.

Comparing two things:

> The second problem is **harder** than the first.
> She is **more studious** than her sister.
> This book is **more carefully** written than that one.

Comparing three or more things:

> This road is the **narrowest** of the three we've traveled.
> Of all the performers, she was the **best.**
> This is the **simplest** recipe for fudge that I've seen.

Most mistakes in the use of modifiers are made when two things are being compared. Remember that the comparative degree should be used when two things are compared.

NONSTANDARD   Of the two cakes, this is the best one.
STANDARD   Of the two cakes, this is the **better** one.
NONSTANDARD   Marie is the youngest of the two girls.
STANDARD   Marie is the **younger** of the two girls.

When comparing one thing with a group of which it is a part, do not omit the word *other.*

NONSTANDARD   She is faster than any girl on her team. [She is a member of her team, and she obviously cannot be faster than herself.]

STANDARD She is faster than any **other** girl on her team.

11d. Avoid the double comparison.

A person uses a double comparison when adding *er* or *est* to the modifier and, at the same time, preceding the modifier with *more* or *most*. Words are compared in one of two ways; you should never use both ways at the same time.

NONSTANDARD Our dog is more smaller than yours.
STANDARD Our dog is **smaller** than yours.
NONSTANDARD It was the most beautifulest waterfall I had ever seen.
STANDARD It was the **most beautiful** waterfall I had ever seen.

EXERCISE 4. Number your paper 1–10. Write a *C* after the number of each correct sentence. After the number of each incorrect sentence, rewrite the sentence correcting the error.

1. The noise of band practice is getting more louder every day.
2. Helen, the star of the play, is better than any member of the cast.
3. The dog's eyes are the most saddest that I've ever seen.
4. After looking at the two hats carefully, Rodney bought the largest one.
5. In the seventh grade, work was more easier than it is now.
6. The patient looks worser today.
7. The wallpaper in the kitchen is more interesting than that in the living room.
8. New York is larger than any city in the United States.

9. "I am feeling more better," I replied.
10. She is the most agreeable person in our class.

EXERCISE 5. Use the first five words as modifiers in sentences comparing two things. Use the second five in sentences comparing three or more things.

1. bad	6. murky
2. happy	7. skillfully
3. practical	8. often
4. young	9. stubborn
5. unusual	10. damp

THE DOUBLE NEGATIVE

Words like the following are called negatives: *no, not, none, never, no one, nothing, hardly, scarcely.* (Notice that many negatives begin with the letter *n*.) When such a word is used in a sentence, it makes an important change in the meaning.

> I have found the wallet that I lost.
> I have **never** found the wallet that I lost.

11e. Avoid the use of double negatives.

We often make negative statements such as, "I never ran in a race." Negative statements in standard English require only one negative word. Use of more than one word is called a *double negative.* For example, the sentence, "I never ran in no race," contains a double negative. Double negatives are considered nonstandard English.

NONSTANDARD We don't have no extra chairs.
STANDARD We have **no** extra chairs.
STANDARD We don't have any extra chairs.
NONSTANDARD He couldn't hardly talk.
STANDARD He **could hardly** talk.

EXERCISE 6. Revise the following sentences, eliminating the double negatives.

1. Karen hasn't never been to Florida.
2. Because of the fog we couldn't scarcely see the road.
3. He never has no trouble with spelling.
4. The runners don't hardly have time to rest between races.
5. Don't use no double negatives in sentences.
6. I reached into my pocket for some change and found I didn't have none.
7. I can't hardly believe the report.
8. This doesn't make no difference to me.
9. Don't never use *not* and *hardly* together.
10. The goalie hasn't no excuse.

REVIEW EXERCISE B. Rewrite the incorrect sentences in the exercise below, eliminating the errors in the use of modifiers. You should have thirteen revised sentences.

1. Art is the most tallest boy on the team.
2. Which do you like best — apples or pears?
3. Gail works harder than any other student on the debating team.
4. Suddenly the troops marched more faster.
5. I can't hardly communicate with her.
6. Fran and Mark get along good together.
7. Don was the more careful driver of the two.
8. Laura feels worse today than she did yesterday.
9. Heidi is the best looking of the twins.
10. They can't do nothing about it.
11. Pedro did so well on the exam that the college was glad to admit him.
12. Of the two candidates, Rita is the best qualified.
13. Which is the heavier load — yours or mine?
14. Kelley doesn't want none of your advice.
15. The violinist plays extremely well.
16. Which of the four motors is the oldest?

17. Africa is much more larger than Europe.
18. Which of the two television sets costs most?
19. Every time I see her she looks more pretty.
20. Thad is more stronger than Don.

PLACEMENT OF MODIFIERS

Notice how the meaning of the following sentence changes when the modifying phrase *from Canada* is moved about in the sentence.

The professor **from Canada** gave a televised lecture on famous writers.
The professor gave a televised lecture on famous writers **from Canada.**
From Canada the professor gave a televised lecture on famous writers.

The first of the three sentences above says that the *professor* was from Canada; the second sentence, that the *famous writers* were from Canada; the third, that the *televised lecture* came from Canada. As you can see, shifting the position of the modifying phrase has resulted in important changes in meaning.

11f. Place modifying phrases and clauses so that they clearly and sensibly modify a word in the sentence.

Prepositional Phrases

You know that prepositional phrases are used as adjectives and adverbs. To make a sentence clear and sensible, you should place a prepositional phrase near the word modified.

► NOTE   As was said on page 82, adverb phrases are more flexible than adjective phrases and do not have to come immediately after the modified word.

However, to avoid confusion, an adverb phrase should be placed near the modified word. Often, as in the second standard sentence below, it can come before the modified word.

NONSTANDARD   The vase was set in the middle of the table with flowers. [*With flowers* should go with *vase,* not *table.*]

STANDARD   The vase **with flowers** was set in the middle of the table.

NONSTANDARD   I read about the lost puppy that was found in today's newspaper. [The puppy was not found in the newspaper.]

STANDARD   **In today's newspaper** I read about the lost puppy that was found.

Be careful to avoid having a prepositional phrase come between two words that it might modify. Instead, place it next to the *one* word that you intend it to modify.

UNCLEAR   She said in the morning she was going to Chicago.

CLEAR   She said she was going to Chicago **in the morning.**

CLEAR   **In the morning** she said she was going to Chicago.

EXERCISE 7. The meaning of each of the following sentences is not clear and sensible because the modifying phrase is in the wrong place. Decide where the phrase belongs; then rewrite the sentence.

1. The famous explorer told us about running into a family of baboons in today's assembly.
2. Inside the cage I watched a large, melancholy gorilla.
3. The fashion display attracted an enormous crowd in the department-store window.

4. A large crowd was watching a jet plane in the park.
5. The teacher required three articles from magazines on Pike's Peak.
6. My neighbor promised on Sunday she would take me fishing.
7. We have only one sprinter who can also high jump on the track team.
8. The hockey player broke his stick with the red cap.
9. The woman was reading a mystery story in a yellow dress.
10. We saw a meteor falling through a large telescope.

Participial Phrases

A participial phrase, like an adjective, modifies a noun or a pronoun. When a participial phrase begins the sentence, it modifies the noun or pronoun immediately following it. Notice that the participial phrases below are separated from the other parts of the sentences by commas. (Review participles, see pages 86–88.)

EXAMPLES **Screaming wildly,** the bandits chased the stagecoach.

Arriving after the others, we waited until intermission to be seated.

When you begin a sentence with a participial phrase, you should be sure that it modifies the noun or pronoun immediately following; otherwise your sentence will have a *dangling participle.*

DANGLING Coming in for a landing, the tower contacted the plane. [The participial phrase dangles because the *tower* was not coming in for a landing.]

CORRECTED	**Coming in for a landing,** the plane was contacted by the tower.
CORRECTED	The tower contacted the plane **coming in for a landing.**
DANGLING	Broken in many pieces, I saw my watch lying on the floor. [The participial phrase dangles because *I* was not broken in many pieces.]
CORRECTED	**Broken in many pieces,** my watch was lying on the floor.

EXERCISE 8. All of the sentences below contain participial phrases. Some of the sentences are nonsensical or awkward because the participial phrases dangle. If a sentence is correct, write *C* after the proper number. Rewrite all incorrect sentences so that the participial phrases modify the right words. (You may have to supply words.) A participial phrase beginning a sentence should be followed by a comma.

1. Standing on the corner, an accident happened right in front of us.
2. Exploring the cave, Carol and Marisa found a new entrance.
3. Having pulled the blanket over our heads, the cold, wet air never bothered us.
4. Damaged in an accident, we got our car repaired.
5. Confused by the questions, a period of rest was allowed the prisoner.
6. Stumbling on the curve, the race could no longer be won by the favored horse.
7. After studying for several hours, our lessons were finally finished.
8. Laid aside for cold weather, the heavy sweater was a lifesaver during the unexpected snowstorm.
9. Risking his life, the firefighter rescued the small child from the burning house.
10. Tired from the long walk, food and rest were what we wanted.

EXERCISE 9. Use correctly the following introductory participial phrases in sentences of your own.

1. Parked on a side street, ...
2. Lying on the beach, ...
3. Waiting for a telegram from her husband, ...
4. Almost destroyed by the storm, ...
5. Leading the way, ...
6. Fishing from the pier, ...
7. Not expecting a party, ...
8. Doomed to roam the sea forever, ...
9. Listening to the special bulletin, ...
10. Encouraged by the good news, ...

Clauses

Like modifying phrases, adjective and adverb clauses should be placed as near as possible to the words they modify. Notice in the following examples how the confusion resulting from misplaced clauses is cleared up when the clauses are placed near the words they modify.

MISPLACED My parents traded an old television for a new cassette recorder that they no longer wanted. [The parents no longer wanted the new cassette recorder?]

CORRECTED My parents traded an old television **that they no longer wanted** for a new cassette recorder.

MISPLACED The book was about insects that we read. [Did you read the insects?]

CORRECTED The book **that we read** was about insects.

EXERCISE 10. Read each of the following sentences. Decide what word the misplaced clause should modify; then rewrite the sentence, placing the clause near the right word.

1. The men were not far from their homes who had volunteered for the mission.
2. We waded through the water in our bare feet which was ankle deep.
3. The car ran on solar energy that can travel from Houston to Miami without recharging.
4. Several gospel songs were presented at yesterday's assembly that were often sung by Mary Lou Williams.
5. The clean-up campaign was endorsed by Mayor Tibbetts that was sponsored by the Garden Club.
6. The test was postponed by the teachers that was scheduled for Friday.
7. A strange knight entered King Arthur's hall with a message who was dressed entirely in green.
8. When I worked for Western Union, I delivered a telegram to an executive that was several pages long.
9. My cousin Myra visited me who lives in a town near Detroit.
10. A movie is being made in a Maine fishing village which is based on a best-selling novel.

REVIEW EXERCISE C. In each of the following sentences, a modifier is used incorrectly. The mistake may result from (1) a confusion between *good* and *well,* (2) incorrect comparison, (3) the use of a double negative, or (4) a dangling or misplaced modifier. Rewrite the sentences, correcting the mistakes.

1. During World War II, many installations were protected from being bombed by decoys.
2. You can't hardly imagine how effective these decoys were.
3. Trying to prevent the bombing of Berlin, a decoy city was built by the Germans.
4. Inflated rubber decoys of ships and tanks also worked very good.

5. Decoy construction became one of the most biggest activities of the war.
6. Sometimes a decoy airstrip was constructed near the real one which was made by painting the ground white.
7. The enemy bombardiers couldn't hardly tell the difference between the decoy airfield and the real one.
8. Lighting up a decoy airfield, many British bombardiers were fooled by the Germans.
9. When the British began to suspect the trick, German experts thought up new tricks who were highly skilled at decoy operations.
10. Sometimes the real field would be the most brightly lighted of the two.
11. Warned about highly lighted areas, the darker airfield would be chosen by the bombardiers.
12. No one could never know whether the real field or the decoy field would be lighted.
13. One of the most cleverest decoy operations of the war was used by the Allies just before D-day.
14. In full view, the Allies placed decoy ships in a harbor where German planes could see them.
15. The decoy ships were planted in other harbors after they were deflated.
16. Seeing many ships in many different harbors, the size of the Allied fleet was overestimated by the Germans.
17. The decoys, among other devices, caused Hitler to make one of the most costliest mistakes of the war.
18. Convinced that the big invasion was coming at Calais, many of the German divisions were ordered there by Hitler.
19. Hitler's miscalculation worked out good for the Allies.
20. Certainly, decoys played a more larger role in the war than most people realize.

Mechanics

PART THREE

Chapter 12

Capital Letters

Rules for Capitalizing

Capital letters indicate important words — the beginnings of sentences and quotations, titles, and other words that warrant attention. Most rules for capitalization you have already mastered. Perhaps there are others that you find troublesome. This chapter will help you to use capital letters correctly.

12a. Capitalize the first word in every sentence.

In order to capitalize the first word in a sentence, you must be able to identify the beginning of a sentence. If you are not sure of your ability to do this, the section on run-on sentences (pages 286–87) will help you.

INCORRECT   More and more people are discovering the benefits of exercise daily workouts at the gymnasium, on the running track, or on the tennis court strengthen the heart these workouts also control weight.

CORRECT   More and more people are discovering the benefits of exercise. Daily workouts at the gymnasium, on the running track, or on the tennis court strengthen the heart. These workouts also control weight.

The first word of a direct quotation is capitalized, even though it may fall within a sentence. For example: *Elinor shouted, "We did it!"* For a fuller explanation of this rule, see the section on writing quotations, pages 254–56.

► **NOTE** Traditionally, the first word in a line of poetry is capitalized, whether or not the word begins a sentence.

EXAMPLE   When I am dead, my dearest,
Sing no sad songs for me . . .

Some modern poets do not follow this style. If you are copying a poem, be sure to follow the capitalization the poet used.

12b. Capitalize the pronoun *I*.

EXAMPLES   Recently **I** have begun to enjoy music.
May **I** help you?

12c. Capitalize the interjection *O*.

The interjection *O* is most often used on solemn or formal occasions. Notice that it is most often used with a word in direct address and that no mark of punctuation follows it.

EXAMPLES   Hear our prayer, **O** Lord.
Protect us in the battle, **O** great Athena!

The interjection *oh* requires a capital letter only at the beginning of a sentence. It is usually followed by a comma.

EXAMPLES   **Oh**, wait till you see tomorrow's assignment.
We haven't seen her for some time — **oh,** perhaps two or three months.

12d. Capitalize proper nouns.

The proper noun, which you studied on page 31, names a particular person, place, or thing. It is always capitalized. The common noun is capitalized only when it begins a sentence or is part of a title.

PROPER NOUNS	COMMON NOUNS
Cicely Tyson	actress
February	month
Tennessee	state

(1) Capitalize the names of persons.

EXAMPLES James Baldwin is my favorite writer.
Is Alice coming, too?
According to Mrs. Sandoz, Annie Sullivan is a good subject for a biography.

(2) Capitalize geographical names.

Cities, Towns Jamestown, San Diego, Akron
States Georgia, Idaho, Hawaii
Countries Ghana, Nicaragua, Thailand
Sections of the Country the Midwest, the North

▶ NOTE Do *not* capitalize *east, west, north, south,* or any combination like *southwest* when these words indicate direction; do capitalize them when they indicate a region.

EXAMPLES Walk south for three blocks and turn left. [direction]
Jean Toomer's famous book, *Cane,* deals with the South. [region]
The fireplace never draws well when there is a strong wind from the east. [direction]
Living in the East, he had never before seen mountains as high as the Rockies. [region]

Islands   Isle of Wight, Molokai, Wake Island, Attu

Bodies of Water   Danville Reservoir, Tennessee River, Lake Erie, Niagara Falls, Tampa Bay, Indian Ocean, Puget Sound, Bering Sea

Streets, Highways   Cherry Lane, Taconic Avenue, Crescent Circle, West Ninety-fourth Street, Route 44, Skyline Drive

► NOTE   In a hyphenated street number, the second word begins with a small letter.

EXAMPLES   East Seventy-eighth Street, South Forty-third Place

Parks   Estes Park, White Mountain National Forest

Mountains   Big Horn Mountains, Mount Washington, Sawtooth Range, Pikes Peak, Great Smokies

Continents   North America, Europe, Africa, Asia

(3) Capitalize names of organizations, business firms, institutions, and government bodies.

EXAMPLES   Debating Club
Air National Guard
García's Hardware Store
United Tool and Die Corporation
Cary Memorial Hospital
Hillcrest School
Antioch College
Department of Agriculture
Governor's Council

► NOTE   Do *not* capitalize words like *school, circus, restaurant, club* unless they are part of a proper name.

Irving Junior High School	a junior high school
Ringling Brothers' Circus	a huge circus
Milbank Bridge Club	a bridge club

(4) Capitalize special events and calendar items.

EXAMPLES   World Series
National Chess Tournament
Rockland Lobster Festival
Fourth of July
Labor Day
Friday
October

▶ **NOTE**   Do *not* capitalize the names of seasons.

We go on fishing trips in spring and fall.

(5) Capitalize historical events and periods.

EXAMPLES   Ice Age, Revolutionary War, Battle of Bunker Hill, Middle Ages, Renaissance, Crusades

(6) Capitalize the names of nationalities, races, and religions.

EXAMPLES   Spanish, Egyptian, Caucasian, Moslem, Lutheran, Protestant

(7) Capitalize the brand names of business products.

EXAMPLES   Cannon towels, Buick sedan, Ivory soap [Notice that only the brand name is capitalized; the common noun following it begins with a small letter.]

(8) Capitalize the names of ships, planets, monuments, awards, and any other particular places, things, or events.

EXAMPLES   U.S.S. *Maine* [ship]   Hoover Dam
Tiros [satellite]   Pulitzer Prize

EXERCISE 1. Number your paper 1–20. For each proper noun, write a corresponding common noun. For each common noun, write a proper noun.

EXAMPLES 1. Chien Shiung Wu
 1. *physicist*
 2. country
 2. *France*

1. baseball team
2. New Year's Day
3. school
4. ocean
5. *Kidnapped*
6. Super Bowl
7. historical event
8. Rosalynn Carter
9. Age of Reason
10. lake
11. Atlanta
12. Asia
13. Lincoln Memorial
14. music group
15. business firm
16. story
17. cereal
18. soda
19. Daytona 500
20. Buddhism

EXERCISE 2. Copy these expressions, using capital letters where needed. Do not capitalize the first word unless it requires a capital.

1. labor day weekend
2. congress of the united states
3. mountains of virginia
4. eleanor roosevelt park
5. member of the peace corps
6. hoover dam
7. student at columbia university
8. federal bureau of investigation
9. united states supreme court
10. navajos of the southwest
11. member of the u.s. olympic team
12. rocky mountain national park
13. enid bagnold
14. exercises held on memorial day
15. continental can company

16. two blocks north of st. paul's cathedral
17. 36 east fifty-seventh street
18. aetna life insurance company
19. a book about the vietnam war
20. many islands of the pacific
21. the great lakes
22. a methodist
23. heinz's ketchup
24. friday, october 22
25. the battle of bull run

EXERCISE 3. Number your paper 1–10. After each number, copy and capitalize all words in the sentence that need capital letters.

1. it took two months for the *mayflower* to cross the atlantic, but it takes only four hours for a supersonic jet to go from new york to paris.
2. ethel waters spent most of her childhood in chester, pennsylvania.
3. I plan to see as many home games of the detroit tigers as i can this summer.
4. the battle of gettysburg was fought in 1863.
5. I am sure our halloween party will be hilarious.
6. new westinghouse air conditioners are being installed in the apartments.
7. the new charitable organization is jointly supported by protestants, catholics, and jews.
8. it would be fun to be at cape canaveral, florida, when a satellite is launched.
9. betty furness examined the zenith radio.
10. in the eighth grade we study the spanish-american war.

12e. Capitalize proper adjectives.

A proper adjective, which is formed from a proper noun, is always capitalized.

PROPER NOUN	PROPER ADJECTIVE
China	Chinese doctor
Egypt	Egyptian cotton
Ireland	Irish wolfhound
Middle East	Middle Eastern tour
Brazil	Brazilian artist

EXERCISE 4. Number your paper 1–10. After each number, copy and capitalize all proper nouns and adjectives in the corresponding sentence.

1. The television program presented an interesting discussion of the new african nations.
2. A belgian farmer and an english miner, both of whom once lived in africa, made the session lively.
3. She thinks copenhagen is the most beautiful of all european capitals.
4. A finnish architect, eliel saarinen, designed a number of buildings in the detroit area.
5. In our study of american literature, we read many works of the new england poets.
6. Speaking in german, the lutheran missionary gave an interesting lecture.
7. Much of our salmon comes from alaskan canneries.
8. We hope to see a shakespearean play this winter.
9. Carmen is learning to play the french horn.
10. The south american llama is a cousin of the arabian camel.

12f. Do *not* capitalize the names of school subjects, except languages and course names followed by a number.

EXAMPLES   I have tests in English, science, and math.
You must pass History II before taking History III.
Next year we will have algebra and Latin.

EXERCISE 5. Copy these phrases, inserting capitals where needed.

1. the study of russian
2. a member of an art class
3. project for science I
4. teacher of english and social studies
5. importance of french and spanish
6. problems in mathematics and ancient history
7. new interest in astronomy
8. courses in physics, civics I, and modern history
9. laboratory period for science II
10. studying history, latin, chemistry, and government II

12g. Capitalize titles.

(1) Capitalize the title of a person when it comes before a name.

EXAMPLES   There will be a short address of welcome by Governor Halsey.

Report to Lieutenant Engstrom, please.

Did you know that Dr. Politi has a new associate, a Ms. Tam?

This is the church in which the Reverend Henry Ward Beecher preached.

How many terms did President Cleveland serve?

Does Queen Sofia live in the Netherlands or Spain?

(2) Capitalize a title used alone or following a person's name only if it refers to a high official or to someone to whom you wish to show special respect.

EXAMPLES   The Secretary of Labor will hold a news conference this afternoon. [*Secretary of Labor* is a high government office.]

Since 1800 the White House has been the official residence of the President. [The word *President* is ordinarily capitalized when it refers to the President of the United States.]

Ella Grasso, Governor of Connecticut, was reelected to her office on November 7, 1978. [Although it follows the person's name, the title is that of a high office.]

The treasurer of our Scout troop has the measles. [This title is not that of a very high office.]

Ellen Rafferty, chairwoman of the program committee, reported on plans for the Winter Carnival. [The office is not high enough to warrant capitalization.]

▶ NOTE When a title is used instead of a name in direct address, it is usually capitalized.

EXAMPLES How long must I stay in bed, Doctor?
Can you tell me, Officer, how to find the new high school building?

(3) Capitalize words showing family relationship when used with a person's name but *not* when preceded by a possessive.

EXAMPLES Aunt Christine, Grandfather Smith
Maria's mother, our brother, her aunt

EXCEPTION When family-relationship words are *usually* used before a name, so that they are considered a part of the name, they are capitalized even when preceded by a possessive.

EXAMPLE Kim's Aunt Betty

When family-relationship words are used in place of a person's name, they may or may not be capitalized.

EXAMPLE Ask Mother, *or* Ask mother. [Either way is correct.]

(4) Capitalize the first word and all important words in titles of books, magazines, newspapers, poems, stories, movies, paintings, and other works of art.

Unimportant words in a title are *a, an, the,* and prepositions and conjunctions of fewer than five letters. Such words should be capitalized only if they come first or last in the title.

EXAMPLES My sister asked me to read Denise Levertov's poem, "With Eyes at the Back of Our Heads."

Katharine Hepburn and Humphrey Bogart star in *The African Queen.*

Curtain Going Up! is a biography of Katharine Cornell.

EXCEPTION When you write the names of newspapers and magazines within a sentence, do not capitalize the word *the* before the name.

EXAMPLES May I borrow your copy of the *Reader's Digest?*

Is that the late edition of the *New York Times?*

(5) Capitalize words referring to the Deity.

EXAMPLES Lord, our Father, the Creator, Son of God

► NOTE The word *god* is not capitalized when referring to the gods of ancient mythology.

EXAMPLE The Roman god of war was Mars.

EXERCISE 6. Number your paper 1–10. After the proper number, copy and capitalize the words requiring capitals.

1. Most students will enjoy reading *the call of the wild.* [a book]
2. Do you subscribe to the *baltimore sun?*
3. Franklin D. Roosevelt died during his fourth term as president of the united states.
4. We will visit uncle John and aunt Susan this summer.
5. Not every individual worships god in the same way.
6. We saw Audrey Hepburn in *roman holiday.*
7. Isabel is president of the arlington debate club.
8. The mayor announced that both the governor of Illinois and the secretary of the interior would speak at the political rally.
9. Yes, dr. Carey is a member of the hospital staff, and she is highly respected by the other doctors at the hospital.
10. How is my mother, doctor?

EXERCISE 7. Number your paper 1–10. After the proper number, copy and capitalize the words requiring capitals.

1. The audience rose as the president of the united states entered.
2. I am going to consult the *readers' guide to periodical literature.*
3. We are visiting my aunt Kay.
4. Ancient babylonian families put clay statues of their household gods on shelves.
5. We heard an address by governor Martin.
6. The vice-president and the secretary of state spoke to the reporters about South America.
7. Jack Brown, captain of our basketball team, is a senior.
8. Lillian Hellman wrote *watch on the rhine.*
9. My uncle usually brings home a copy of the *st. louis post-dispatch.*
10. Yes, judge Collins is more sympathetic than the other judge.

SUMMARY STYLE SHEET

This list gives examples of the rules of capitalization studied in this chapter. Use it as a review by studying each item below and justifying the use of each capital or small letter. The list will also be convenient for quick reference.

1. Johnson City	a city in Tennessee
2. Aztec Motel	a motel in Miami
3. Second Street	a street in Pasadena
4. Milton Pond	a pond in Milton
5. the Northeast	a northeast gale
6. North Dakota	north of South Dakota
7. the Music Club	a club for musicians
8. Slater Woolen Company	a woolen company
9. Topeka High School	a high school in Topeka
10. the Korean War	a war in Korea
11. the John Hancock Building	an insurance building
12. Washington's Birthday	Christine's birthday
13. the Industrial Revolution	a revolution in manufacturing
14. God, our Father	the gods of Greek mythology
15. the Winter Prom	a prom in the winter
16. the Sophomore Class	a class of sophomores
17. French, English, Russian	mathematics, music, geography
18. Science II	a lesson in science
19. Principal Harris	Ms. Harris, the principal
20. the President of the United States	the president of the company
21. Will you call Mother (or mother)?	My mother is here.
22. Aunt Marie	her aunt
23. the American Girl	a monthly magazine
24. the Dallas Times Herald	a newspaper
25. The War of the Worlds	an exciting book
26. customs of the Japanese	national customs
27. an Episcopalian	a sermon in church
28. Canadian bacon	bacon and eggs
29. Ford truck	a pickup truck

REVIEW EXERCISE A. Number your paper 1–10. After the proper number, copy and capitalize the words requiring capitals.

1. alice yen, the secretary of our club, could not be at the meeting.
2. admiral edward smith will speak this june at the graduation ceremonies of the united states naval academy at annapolis, maryland.
3. she studied spanish and ancient history at yale university.
4. will you tell your mother to meet me at the davidson building?
5. one volume of anne morrow lindbergh's diaries and letters is *hour of gold, hour of lead.*
6. when you go to the store, aunt myra, will you get me a package of wrigley's spearmint gum?
7. john has a summer job as a lifeguard at the beach in harrison park.
8. yesterday principal edwards conducted a meeting of the student body.
9. mr. arroyo is a vice-president of the logan trucking company.
10. if you want to find third street, go south for three blocks.

REVIEW EXERCISE B. Number your paper 1–10. After the proper number, copy and capitalize the words requiring capitals.

1. My friend barbara harris went to nigeria as an exchange student.
2. What a thrilling time nina had on grandfather morse's ranch in wyoming!
3. Do you plan to study latin and french, together with mathematics and civics II, next year?
4. The fifth day of the week, thursday, gets its name from thor, the norse god of thunder.

5. One of our most important american holidays is thanksgiving.
6. Hawaii, which joined the united states in 1959, is a group of islands in the pacific ocean 3,200 kilometers west of california.
7. A forum of young people representing the jewish, catholic, and protestant faiths met last evening at central high school on main street.
8. Our sunday group discusses the bible, and each member of the group shares a strong belief in god.
9. The swedish writer, selma lagerlöf, is the author of *the story of gösta berling* and the children's classic, *the wonderful adventures of nils.*
10. At the hampton supermarket there is a window display of kleenex napkins, kellogg's cereals, and campbell's soups.

REVIEW EXERCISE C. Write ten short sentences, using one of the items in the following list in each sentence. Use capital letters correctly, according to the rules you have studied.

1. name of a magazine
2. a business
3. a range of mountains
4. title of a person
5. title of a book
6. geographical section of country
7. a street
8. a language and two other school subjects
9. an historical event
10. a continent

REVIEW EXERCISE D. Number your paper 1–20. For each sentence, write the words that should be capitalized, capitalizing them, and the words that are incorrectly capitalized, omitting the capitals.

1. The president's news conferences in the state department auditorium were very popular.
2. In science class we are studying about such Scientists as virginia trimble, dorothy crowfoot hodgkin, and mary shorb.
3. the languages in which i'm most interested are french, spanish, and russian.
4. In sutherland junior high school we have classes in English and Mathematics.
5. Members of Morse Junior High hiking club climbed mt. chicorua.
6. The prudential building in Boston, Massachusetts, is fifty-two stories high.
7. Someday you should visit the shakespeare festival in Stratford, Ontario.
8. The 1980 winter olympics were held in lake placid, new york, a small town in the adirondack mountains.
9. The rio grande flows along the Southern border of texas; it is one of the most famous rivers on the north american continent.
10. dr. elizabeth blackwell founded a hospital in New York City.
11. The names of african and asian countries are becoming more familiar to us.
12. John Stacey, President of our Club, has received an appointment to the u.s. naval academy at annapolis.
13. Are you familiar with my favorite magazine, the *atlantic monthly?*
14. our journey this summer will take us through the northwest.
15. We are anxious to see the great Fir trees of Oregon.
16. our new High School is being built on pleasant street.
17. Over two million people are stockholders in the american telephone and telegraph company.
18. Recently, our Junior High School was visited by

indian and african teachers who are studying in this country.

19. The st. lawrence seaway, built by the Governments of canada and the united states, provides a channel from Montreal to lake ontario for sea-going vessels.

20. Many students have enjoyed reading Laura Ingall Wilder's *little house on the prairie.*

Chapter 13

Punctuation

End Marks and Commas

In spoken language the voice indicates the pauses and the stops, but in written language punctuation does the work. While English might seem easier to write without periods or commas or other marks of punctuation, it would be very difficult to read. This chapter and the next one will help you to master punctuation so that your writing will be clear and easier to read.

END MARKS

13a. A statement is followed by a period.

EXAMPLES　The lens is the most important part of a camera.
One of the greatest figure skaters was a woman named Sonja Henie.

13b. A question is followed by a question mark.

EXAMPLES　Have you watched Barbara Walters?
Is photography a science or an art?

13c. An exclamation is followed by an exclamation point.

EXAMPLES   What a good time we had!
             Wow! What a view!

13d. An imperative sentence is followed by either a period or an exclamation point.

EXAMPLES   Please give me the scissors. [making a request]
             Give me the scissors! [showing strong feeling]

EXERCISE 1. In the following paragraphs, sentences have been run together without end marks. Copy the last word of every sentence and the first word of the next sentence, inserting the proper end mark. There are twenty end marks to supply.

Have you ever visited New Salem Park in Illinois There you will find a reproduction of the little village of New Salem, just as it was when Abraham Lincoln lived there If you do visit this village, you will find that life in Lincoln's time was much harder than it is today

What tiny, crude cabins the people lived in The twenty-three cabins include ten shops, a school, and a sawmill There is also a carding mill, where wool fibers were cleaned and straightened before they were spun into cloth

The cabin of the Onstats is not a reproduction but the original cabin where Lincoln spent many hours In that living room, on that very floor, young Abe Lincoln studied with Isaac Onstat The rest of the Onstat family was also there It was the cabin's only room

Across the way a big kettle hangs under a porch This is the original kettle used by Mr. Waddell for boiling wool Mr. Waddell, the hatter of the village, made hats of wool and fur

If you looked into the various cabins, you would see rough floors and walls and uncomfortable-looking furniture You might wonder how you would enjoy living in such a home In almost every cabin there is a ladder running up to the loft where some of the family slept How cold it was up there in winter and how hot in summer

Do any of you feel you would like to go back to those days What endurance those people must have had Could we manage to live as they did

13e. An abbreviation is followed by a period.

EXAMPLES	min.	minute	Neb.	Nebraska
	St.	Street	in.	inch
	Dr.	Doctor	Mr.	Mister
	Aug.	August	Co.	Company

Note that *Miss* preceding a woman's name is not an abbreviation and is not followed by a period. Similar titles—*Mr., Mrs., Ms.*—are abbreviations. Initials used with a name are abbreviations of names and should be followed by periods.

EXAMPLES   Miss Ellsworth
A. B. Guthrie
Ms. Angstrom

COMMAS

A comma does not indicate a full stop, as a period does, but divides a sentence into readable parts by indicating pauses. If you master the use of the comma, your written work will improve in clarity. One word of warning: don't use commas carelessly. Have a reason for every comma you put into a sentence.

Items in Series

13f. Use commas to separate items in a series.

Words, phrases, and clauses in a series should be separated by commas so that they will be clear to a reader.

(1) Use commas to separate words in series.

EXAMPLES We have read poems by Longfellow, Teasdale, and Dickinson this week.

Tobacco, hammock, canoe, and *barbecue* are four of the many words that English-speaking people owe to Mexicans.

In the early morning, the lake looked cold, gray, and uninviting.

► **NOTE** You should form the habit of using a comma before the *and* joining the last two items in a series. Although many writers omit this comma, it is sometimes necessary to make your meaning clear.

UNCLEAR Next year we will study algebra, civics, French and American history. [No comma used; are we to study the French language or French history?]

CLEAR Next year we will study algebra, civics, French, and American history.

CLEAR Next year we will study algebra, civics, French history, and American history.

(2) Use commas to separate phrases in series.

EXAMPLES We found seaweed in the water, on the sand, under the rocks, and even in our shoes.

It makes no difference whether that hamster is in a cage, on a string, or under a net—it always escapes.

(3) Use commas to separate subordinate clauses and short independent clauses in a series.

EXAMPLES   Everyone wondered who had been in the house, what he had wanted, and where he had gone.

We worked, we played, and we rested.

(4) If all items in a series are joined by *and* or *or*, do not use commas to separate them.

EXAMPLE   Have you read *Huckleberry Finn* or *Tom Sawyer* or *A Connecticut Yankee in King Arthur's Court?*

EXERCISE 2. Number your paper 1–10. After the proper number, show where commas are needed in each sentence by copying the words before a necessary comma and adding the comma. Two sentences do not require commas.

1. We had lessons in swimming canoeing archery and handicrafts.
2. Mary and Frances and Ted dashed out of the car down the beach and into the water.
3. Our school has organized clubs for music art radio and chess.
4. One representative on the Student Council should be the class president or the secretary or the treasurer.
5. The school band includes clarinets saxophones trumpets trombones tubas flutes piccolos and drums.
6. I've planted seedlings fertilized them carefully and watered them each day.
7. The children played happily on the swings on the slides and in the pool.
8. Science and history and algebra are all included in next year's course of study.
9. Do you know anything about how to pitch a tent how to build a campfire or how to cook in the wilderness?

10. I enjoy swimming boating and surfing more than skiing sledding or skating.

EXERCISE 3. Number your paper 1–10. After the proper number, show where commas are needed in each sentence by copying the words before a necessary comma and adding the comma.

1. Find out who is going to the picnic what we must take and when we have to leave.
2. Sylvia Porter's financial column explains the workings of the stock market the need to make investments wisely and the dangers of careless speculation.
3. This morning Rita will wash the car Mary will pack the lunch and then we'll go on a picnic.
4. In spite of bad weather predictions, the fog lifted the sun shone and everyone was happy.
5. *The Red Badge of Courage The Wizard of Earthsea The Virginian* and *A Wrinkle in Time* are all good books for junior high students.
6. Thelma and Lynn are eager to water-ski to learn to sail and to do some skin diving.
7. Science teaches us how to conserve our forests how to prevent erosion of our land and how to control our water supplies.
8. Iron copper aluminum lumber coal and oil are some of our natural resources.
9. I would like to visit England France Spain and Norway, the Land of the Midnight Sun.
10. Soccer basketball and football are all strenuous games.

13g. Use a comma to separate two or more adjectives preceding a noun.

EXAMPLES   An Arabian stallion is a fast, beautiful horse.
The early rancher often depended on the small, tough, sure-footed mustang.

When the final adjective is so closely connected to the noun that the words seem to form one expression, do not use a comma before the final adjective.

EXAMPLE   Training a frisky colt to become a gentle, dependable riding horse takes great patience. [No comma is used between *dependable* and *riding* because the words *riding horse* are closely connected in meaning and may be taken as one term.]

A comma should never be used between an adjective and the noun immediately following it.

INCORRECT   Mary O'Hara has written a tender, suspenseful, story about a young boy and his colt.

CORRECT   Mary O'Hara has written a tender, suspenseful story about a young boy and his colt.

EXERCISE 4. Copy the following sentences, inserting commas where needed.

1. Carlos was the popular efficient president of the class.
2. The cold dry northern air is very exhilarating.
3. We loved running barefoot over the cool wet sand.
4. What a stern dignified manner that soldier has!
5. The dark dingy musty attic seemed spooky.
6. The noisy carefree spectators cheered when they saw the bright new uniforms and instruments of the marching band.
7. Have you read about the strong courageous women who fought the cold hard prairies of Iowa?
8. An alert businesslike and popular leader is needed.
9. A squat dark cooking stove stood in one corner of the old kitchen.
10. May Swenson fascinates us with her clever tantalizing poems.

Compound Sentences

13h. Use a comma before *and, but, or, nor, for,* and *yet* when they join independent clauses.

EXAMPLES The musical comedy originated in America, and it has retained a distinctly American flavor.

Grand opera is a popular form of entertainment in Europe, but few Americans have an opportunity to see live productions of operas.

Singers must devote many years to training and practice, for a musical career is a demanding one.

If the clauses in a compound sentence are very short, the comma before the conjunction may be omitted.

EXAMPLE Hammerstein wrote the words and Rodgers wrote the music.

To follow comma rule 13h, you must be able to distinguish a compound sentence from a simple sentence with a compound verb.

COMPOUND SENTENCE Margo likes tennis and golf, but she doesn't enjoy archery. [comma between independent clauses joined by a conjunction]

SIMPLE SENTENCE WITH COMPOUND VERB Margo likes tennis and golf but doesn't enjoy archery. [no comma between parts of compound verb joined by a conjunction]

EXERCISE 5. Number your paper 1–10. After the proper number, copy the words in the sentence that should be followed by commas. Add the commas. Several sentences do not require commas.

1. Homing pigeons are famous for their sense of direction but no one can explain why these birds never get lost.
2. Scientists studied these birds and the results of the studies were published.
3. Do homing pigeons get their direction from the sun or can they find their way even in darkness?
4. These birds travel equally well during the day or night but they have more difficulty when it is cloudy.
5. Blindfolded pigeons tried to fly but were unable to get off the ground.
6. Some of the pigeons landed miles from their destination and then walked the rest of the way!
7. The scientists fitted the birds with magnets and hoped to discover whether the birds used the earth's magnetic field for direction.
8. The birds all flew off in the wrong direction yet they later corrected their error and returned to their home.
9. Many other kinds of birds migrate hundreds of miles each year but how these birds stay on course is a mystery.
10. An arctic tern, for example, migrates from the Arctic Circle to Antarctica and it covers this distance in only five months.

Phrases and Clauses

Participial phrases, as you learned on page 200, act as adjectives to modify nouns or pronouns. Subordinate clauses may also act as adjectives (see page 98).

In some sentences, the participial phrase or adjective clause is essential to the thought. It cannot be removed without destroying the meaning.

EXAMPLES All farmers **growing hybrid corn** owe a debt to an Austrian monk named

Gregor Mendel. [The participial phrase in heavy type tells which farmers. It is essential to the meaning of the sentence.] Mendel made the discoveries **that have become the basis of modern genetics.** [The adjective clause modifies *discoveries*. It cannot be removed without destroying the meaning.]

In other sentences, the participial phrase or adjective clause is *not* essential to the thought. Such a phrase or clause can be removed without changing the basic meaning.

EXAMPLES   Sometimes seeds and nuts, **forgotten by the squirrels that hid them,** germinate far away from their parent plants. [The participial phrase can be removed without changing the basic meaning of the sentence: *Sometimes seeds and nuts germinate far away from their parent plants.*]

Migrating birds, **which often fly hundreds or thousands of miles,** are one of the main carriers of seeds. [The adjective clause can be removed without changing the basic meaning of the sentence: *Migrating birds are one of the main carriers of seeds.*]

13i. Use commas to set off participial phrases and adjective clauses that are not essential to the basic meaning of the sentence. Do not use commas with phrases or clauses that are essential to the meaning.

To *set off* with commas means to separate from the rest of the sentence. If the phrase or clause comes in the middle of the sentence, a comma is needed before and after it. If the phrase or clause comes at the end, a comma is needed before it; if the phrase or clause comes at the beginning of the sentence, a comma is needed after it.

EXAMPLES   A new spider web**, shining in the morning light,** is an impressive example of engineering. [nonessential participial phrase; commas needed]

Anyone **who finishes early** may start on tomorrow's assignment. [essential adjective clause; no commas needed]

If a participial phrase or adjective clause is preceded by a proper noun, a comma is ordinarily needed to separate it from the noun.

EXAMPLE   Cybill reported on *Insects and Plants,* which was written by Elizabeth Cooper.

EXERCISE 6. Number your paper 1–20. Write *C* after the numbers of sentences that are correctly punctuated. After the numbers of other sentences, write the words that should be followed by commas and add the commas.

1. Ynes Mexia hoping to find new kinds of plants explored the dense jungles of Brazil.
2. The plants which she collected were carefully dried and preserved.
3. Traveling and working alone for many months she found a tremendous variety of new and unusual plants.
4. Mrs. Nina Floy who was an assistant to Ynes Mexia kept detailed records of her jungle discoveries.
5. Ynes Mexia who spent a year in search of unknown plants on the South American continent collected nearly one thousand new varieties of plants on her expedition.
6. Louis Pasteur striving to save a child from

death by rabies used the vaccine which conquered that dread disease.

7. The scientists who discovered radium were Pierre and Marie Curie.

8. Marie Sklodowska Curie who was born in Poland discovered both polonium and radium.

9. Marie Curie devoting her life to her work was twice awarded the Nobel Prize.

10. Lake Superior which covers an area of 30,000 square miles is the largest of the Great Lakes.

11. Autumn which is New England's most colorful season is enjoyed by many tourists.

12. The man who became the world's most famous promoter was named Phineas Taylor Barnum.

13. P. T. Barnum promoting some of the most out-standing attractions of all time developed a method of advertising called *ballyhoo*.

14. This form of publicity relying on a quick and forceful appeal to the audience has been widely used by business and industry.

15. A midget whom Barnum named General Tom Thumb entertained the Queen of England in 1844.

16. Barnum also purchased a giant elephant which was named Jumbo.

17. The word *jumbo* meaning anything of great size soon became a part of the English language.

18. Do you know any other terms which originated in the circus and became common words in our language?

19. In 1871 Barnum opened his circus which was titled *The Greatest Show on Earth*.

20. Later becoming active in politics Barnum was elected twice to the Connecticut legislature and served one term as mayor of Bridgeport, Con-necticut.

13j. Use a comma after a participial phrase or an ad-verb clause that begins a sentence.

Forced onto the sidelines by a torn liga-ment, Harris was restless and unhappy. [intro-ductory participial phrase]

When March came, the huge ice pack began to melt and break up.

An adverb clause that comes at the end of a sentence does not usually need a comma.

The huge ice pack began to melt and break up **when March came.**

EXERCISE 7. Number your paper 1–10. If a comma is needed in a sentence, supply it by copying the word before it and adding the comma. If no comma is needed, write *C* after the number.

1. Orbiting around the sun nine planets make up our solar system.
2. Because the weight of the sun is 700 times greater than the combined weight of the planets the sun holds each planet in orbit.
3. Our solar system appears quite large when we think of it in terms of familiar distances.
4. Measuring about 6.5 billion kilometers in diameter the orbit of Pluto marks the outer boundary of our solar system.
5. Compared with Earth's distance from the stars Pluto is actually a close neighbor.
6. We can reach the nearest star outside our solar system if we travel 40 trillion kilometers.
7. Being a star itself our sun is one of 100 billion stars bound together into a galaxy.
8. When we view the sky through a telescope on a clear night we can see more than 10 million of these stars.
9. Seeming to be so close together the stars in our galaxy are actually trillions of kilometers apart.
10. Although our galaxy is very large there are other larger galaxies within the universe.

Interrupters

When an expression like *of course* or *well* or a person's name interrupts a sentence, commas are needed to set off the interrupter. If the interrupting expression comes in the middle of the sentence, two commas are needed. If it comes first or last, only one comma is needed.

13k. Use a comma after a word such as *well, yes, no, why,* when it begins a sentence.

EXAMPLES   Why, you really should know about Sarah Winnemucca!
               Yes, she helped her Piute people.
               Well, she opened a school in Nevada.

▶ NOTE   Such words are not followed by a comma if they do not interrupt the sentence; that is, if no pause follows them.

EXAMPLES   Why is Rebecca early?
               Well along in the second game, there was a double play.

13l. Use commas to set off an expression that interrupts a sentence.

(1) Appositives and appositive phrases are usually set off by commas.

An *appositive* is a word which means the same thing as the noun it follows; usually it explains or identifies the noun. An appositive phrase is an appositive plus the words that go with it.

EXAMPLES   Have you ever been in Texas, **the Lone Star State**? [*The Lone Star State* is an appositive meaning the same thing as *Texas.*]

The Rio Grande, **one of the major rivers of North America,** forms part of the border between Texas and Mexico. [*One of the major rivers of North America* is an appositive phrase meaning the same thing as the *Rio Grande.*]

▶ NOTE When an appositive is closely related to the word it follows, no comma is needed. Such appositives are usually one word.

EXAMPLES my sister Odelite
the writer Cather

EXERCISE 8. Copy the sentences which require commas. Insert the commas.

1. Katy Jurado the actress has appeared in many fine motion pictures.
2. The composer Beethoven became completely deaf and still wrote several symphonies.
3. Carolyn Keene the writer of the Nancy Drew stories is a popular writer.
4. Have your heard of "Go" the Japanese board game that is played with black and white markers?
5. Science my favorite subject gets more fascinating each year.
6. Atoms the building blocks of nature combine to form molecules.
7. Elizabeth Bowen the English novelist was born in Ireland and moved to England early in her childhood.
8. Thousands of pilgrims journey each year to the shrine of Thomas à Becket the martyred saint of Canterbury.
9. Only two animals a horse and a cow were saved from the fire.
10. A black funnel-shaped cloud the sign of a tornado sent everyone running for shelter.

(2) Words used in direct address are set off by commas.

When someone speaks directly to another person, using that person's name, commas precede and follow the name.[1]

EXAMPLES   Would you rather go to Africa or South America, **Hazel?**

Mrs. **Clarkson,** I just want to get to the beach this weekend.

Can you tell me, **sir,** when the next bus is due?

EXERCISE 9. Number your paper 1–10. After the proper number, copy the words in the sentence that should be followed by a comma and add the comma.

1. Ms. Tseng may I ask the speaker a question?
2. Are you leaving tomorrow for your vacation John?
3. Can you tell us Ramona where we can find the information we need?
4. You need more practice Jan if you are to become a good diver.
5. Helen and Marie come here at once if you want to go with us.
6. You scoundrel what do you mean by trying to cheat your friends?
7. May we go now Mother or must we wait for the others?
8. Be sure to dress warmly girls; the weather is really cold.
9. Let's get out of here Sue; it's too spooky for me.
10. Boys are you ever going to be ready to leave on time?

[1] For rules governing the use of commas in dialogue, see page 257.

(3) Parenthetical expressions are set off by commas.

Occasionally a sentence is interrupted by an expression like *to tell the truth, in my opinion, in fact.* Such expressions are called *parenthetical* because, like words enclosed in parentheses, the expressions are not grammatically related to the rest of the sentence. These expressions are set off by commas.

EXAMPLES The President said, **off the record,** that he was deeply disappointed.

To be honest, I thought the movie was fairly good.

It wasn't very good, **in my opinion.**

These expressions are often used parenthetically:

in fact	however
mind you	for example
as I was saying	to tell the truth
of course	nevertheless
on the contrary	I suppose (*or* know
for instance	*or* believe *or* hope)
in my opinion	if you ask me

► NOTE Such expressions are not always parenthetical. Be careful to use commas only if they are needed.

What, **in her opinion,** is the best closing hour? [a parenthetical expression set off by commas]

I have no faith **in her opinion.** [not a parenthetical expression; no commas needed]

Traveling by boat may take longer, **however.** [a parenthetical expression, preceded by a comma]

However you go, it will be a delightful trip. [*however* not used parenthetically; no commas needed]

EXERCISE 10. Number your paper 1–10. After the proper number, copy the words in the sentence that should be followed by commas and add the commas.

1. Well we should get started by six o'clock.
2. You too can learn to play golf if you are willing to practice.
3. The story in my opinion is much too long and complicated.
4. Yes Mary Wells Lawrence has been extremely successful in advertising.
5. Modern turnpikes for example are marvelous feats of engineering.
6. You will stay I hope as long as you possibly can.
7. No you will not enjoy that book unless you like mysteries.
8. Mathematics I'm afraid is my hardest subject.
9. The weather to tell the truth was much too hot.
10. Why what a surprise this is!

13m. Use a comma in certain conventional situations.

The conventions of English usage require that commas be used in dates, in addresses, and after the salutations and closings of letters.

(1) Use a comma to separate items in dates and addresses.

EXAMPLES The delegates to the Constitutional Convention signed the Constitution on September 17, 1787, in Philadelphia, Pennsylvania.

The Passover holiday begins on Wednesday, April 14, this year.

My friend has just moved to 6448 Higgins Road, Chicago, Illinois.

The zip code number should be written several spaces after the state (unless you are writing it in a sentence). No comma should come before it.

Jackson Heights, New York 11372

► **NOTE** If a preposition is used between items of an address, a comma is not necessary: He lives at 144 Smith Street *in* Moline, Illinois.

(2) Use a comma after the salutation of a friendly letter and after the closing of any letter.

EXAMPLES   Dear Aunt Margaret,
Sincerely yours,
Yours truly,

EXERCISE 11. Copy the following items on your paper, inserting commas wherever needed.

1. 443 North University Avenue Ann Arbor Michigan   48103
2. 1900 Lower Road Linden New Jersey   07036
3. Monday August 4 1980
4. after January 1 1981
5. 379 Scott Avenue Salt Lake City Utah   84115
6. Michigan Avenue at Twelfth Street Chicago Illinois
7. Thanksgiving Day 1982
8. from June 23 1981 to January 2 1982
9. either Tuesday September 3 or Saturday September 7
10. Box 147F Wisconsin Dells Wisconsin   25367
11. the building on the corner of Market Street and Highland Avenue in Akron Ohio
12. Sincerely yours
13. Dear Jean
14. Friday July 9 in Roanoke Virginia
15. Sunday June 19 at 24-20 Loring Place Yorktown Heights New York

REVIEW EXERCISE A. Number your paper 1–20. If a comma is needed in a sentence, supply it by copying the word before it and adding the comma. If a sentence is correctly punctuated, write a *C* after its number.

1. Since Susan's visit was to be a short one we wanted to do something special each day.
2. A beach party was planned for the first day but the weather was bad.
3. Disappointed we went to the movies instead.
4. At the movies we met Mary Tom Jane and Harry.
5. Since no one had plans for the evening, we arranged to have a party in our playroom.
6. Our parents helped us get food and drinks together, and everyone brought records for dancing.
7. Susan who was a very appreciative guest said she had never had so much fun.
8. On Saturday July 18 we all went to the beach together.
9. Yes we swam rode surfboards and played ball on the sand.
10. After enjoying a long afternoon of play, everyone tired and hungry ate an enormous supper.
11. Completely exhausted by our day out-of-doors we were very happy to tumble into our beds at an early hour.
12. Susan lived on a farm, and she invited us to visit her on another weekend.
13. Although we had seen many farms, visiting one was a new experience.
14. It was great fun in my opinion to see all the cows, horses, pigs, and chickens.
15. When the roosters began to crow at dawn the farm seemed to come to life.
16. Breakfast was very early so that we could get to the barn to see the milking machine help feed the pigs and scatter grain for the chickens.
17. Dinner was at noon and we had never seen such heaping platters of mashed potatoes fried chicken fresh peas and homemade blueberry biscuits.

18. After we had eaten our dessert of apple pie and homemade ice cream, we stretched out under a big tree and went to sleep.
19. Since it was a warm humid afternoon we were glad later that we had the chance to go down to the river for a cool refreshing swim.
20. Getting ready for bed that night we decided that the farm which we were visiting was a perfect place for a vacation.

REVIEW EXERCISE B. Number your paper 1–20. After the proper number, supply commas and end marks in the following sentences by copying the word before a mark of punctuation and adding the comma or end mark.

1. Yes Mary you and Alice may go with us
2. If the weather permits we will leave Saturday morning September 7 at six o'clock
3. You should take your bathing suits girls as the weather will still be warm
4. Since she's done such good work Lisa will certainly go along Joe
5. Dad will drive Alice will take charge of maps and Joe will help make sandwiches
6. What a wide smooth highway this is
7. If one is not in a hurry the quiet tree-lined roads are very inviting
8. However the turnpikes help us get to our destination quickly
9. Do you prefer fresh water or salt water for swimming Carol
10. Well we may get a chance to try both lakes and ocean
11. We are not sure when we'll stop or just how long we'll stay
12. What great fun we will have
13. If we plan well we need take only a few clothes on the trip

14. The temptation I know is to take too much
15. If we took everything we thought we needed what a crowded uncomfortable car we'd have
16. My parents much to my surprise do not plan to do any fishing
17. However they do plan to play golf and they will take their clubs
18. Planning our route getting together the things we need and packing carefully will take some time
19. Our parents who have so much to do for us will be busy
20. No this is not our first long trip

REVIEW EXERCISE C. Number your paper 1–20. After the proper number, supply commas and end marks in the following sentences by copying the word before a mark of punctuation and adding the comma or end mark.

1. Totaling one third of the land area of the earth Asia is the world's largest continent
2. If both North and South America were fitted into Asia there would be a little space left over
3. Asia contains some of the coldest the hottest the wettest and the driest areas of the world
4. The Himalayas the highest mountains in the world are covered with mighty glaciers
5. Asia however also contains one of the world's most unusual bodies of water the Dead Sea
6. Mt. Everest is 8,848 meters above sea level and the Dead Sea is 395 meters below sea level
7. What a wonderful view one must have from the high peaks
8. On May 29 1953 a New Zealand mountain climber Sir Edmund Hillary stood on the summit of Mt. Everest highest point on the earth's surface
9. Then on May 22 1963 Jim Whittaker became the first American to reach this point

10. Junko Tabei one of a team of Japanese women reached the summit in 1975

11. Probably many young people who love climbing have been inspired by these feats

12. Isn't it interesting to read about other countries and other people

13. Because you live in America your life is different from that of a boy or girl who lives in Burma or India

14. The geography of a country whether we enjoy studying it or not greatly affects the life of the people

15. Now that we can travel from one country to another so quickly we need to understand all we can about one another

16. We should know how other people live what their homes are like and what kinds of problems they may have

17. We study French Spanish German Russian and I'm sure other languages

18. There is a Peruvian woman living at 122 Main Street Ashburnham just a few miles from the regional school we all attend

19. No she has no difficulty with the language but she does laugh at our slang.

20. When we know people from different countries how thrilling our study of geography is

REVIEW EXERCISE D. Number your paper 1–20. If a sentence has been punctuated correctly, write *C* after the proper number. Supply commas and end marks in the other sentences by copying the word before a mark of punctuation and adding the comma or end mark.

1. Unless I notify you otherwise please send your letters to my summer address 15 Cedar Avenue Plymouth New Hampshire.

2. Sally, are you ever going to visit us?

3. Peggy Guggenheim the art collector owned a beautiful palace in Venice.
4. We enjoyed, too, meeting the many young people who were there.
5. What a perfect day we have had
6. No Melba you may not stay any longer.
7. Our vacation extends from Friday June 22 to Thursday September 5
8. We will soon learn what is to be done, how long it will take, and how best to accomplish the job.
9. The book which you are reading is considered a classic.
10. Guadalupe, who is the leader of the group, has been ill.
11. We don't know in fact just how many young people will be here.
12. Running hurriedly down the stairs, Marie caught the heel of her shoe in the carpet and fell.
13. William Lauren Jerry and Jennifer the teacher wants to see you all after school
14. Determined to win the prize Helen practiced for many hours
15. The girl who is determined to win must work very hard.
16. The storm our first real hurricane came suddenly.
17. Why Jane what do you intend to do with that
18. The snowstorm is over, the wind has died down, and we are going out to shovel the walk.
19. Well, what a good job you've done, boys!
20. Do you know that Naomi Sims has her own line of cosmetics, Sharon?

Chapter 14

Punctuation

Semicolons, Colons, Italics, Quotation
Marks, Apostrophes, Hyphens

Just as we use different facial expressions,
gestures, and intonations to convey meaning when we
speak, we need several different marks of punctuation
to make clear the meaning of our written language. In
this chapter you will study the use of six marks of
punctuation.

SEMICOLONS

The semicolon, as you can tell from its appearance,
is part period and part comma. It signals a pause
stronger than a comma but not so strong as a period.

14a. Use a semicolon between independent clauses
in a sentence if they are not joined by *and, but, or, nor,
for, yet.*

EXAMPLES   On our first trip to Houston I wanted to
see the Astrodome; my little brother
wanted to visit the Johnson Space Center.

Our parents settled the argument for us;
they took us to see a rodeo in a nearby
town.

A period (and capital) between the independent
clauses would change these examples into two sen-

tences. This would be correct, but it would not show how closely related the ideas are.

► NOTE Very short independent clauses without conjunctions may be separated by commas.

EXAMPLE The leaves whispered, the brook gurgled, the sun beamed benignly.

14b. Use a semicolon between independent clauses joined by such words as *for example, for instance, that is, besides, accordingly, moreover, nevertheless, furthermore, otherwise, therefore, however, consequently, instead, hence.*

EXAMPLES Shirley Hufstedler became Secretary of Education in 1979; moreover, she was the first person to hold this cabinet position.

Mary Ishikawa decided not to stay at home; instead, she went to the game.

Certain animals combine surprising characteristics; for example, the duck-billed platypus is a mammal with a ducklike beak, dense fur, and a wide, flat tail.

The early Christians refused to worship the Roman emperor as a god; therefore, they were persecuted by the Romans.

English was Louise's most difficult subject; accordingly, she gave it more time than any other subject.

14c. A semicolon (rather than a comma) may be needed to separate the independent clauses of a compound sentence if there are commas within the clauses.

The mark of punctuation that is ordinarily used to indicate a separation between independent clauses is a comma. But if commas are used within the clauses,

it may be difficult to distinguish between these commas and a comma indicating the end of a clause. In
such a case, a different, more emphatic signal – the
semicolon – is needed.

EXAMPLE   A tall, svelte woman entered the large,
           drafty room; and a short, slight, blond
           woman followed her.

EXERCISE 1. Number your paper 1–10. After the
proper number, indicate that the sentence requires a
semicolon by writing the words before and after the
semicolon and inserting the mark of punctuation. If
the sentence does not require a semicolon, write *C*
after the proper number. Seven of the following sentences require a semicolon.

 1. Map makers have explored almost all areas of the
    earth, they are now exploring the floors of the
    oceans.
 2. Some scientists predict the development of under-
    sea cities, but this prediction seems at least
    questionable.
 3. In the future, perhaps, people will choose to live
    in a city in space, or they may prefer to have an
    apartment in an undersea city.
 4. Roger Maris hit his sixty-first home run during
    the last game of the 1961 baseball season, until
    then Babe Ruth had held the record for the most
    home runs in a season.
 5. Some reptiles like a dry climate, but others prefer
    a wet climate.
 6. Many of today's office buildings look like glass
    boxes, they appear to be made entirely of
    windows.
 7. In April 1912, a new "unsinkable" ocean liner,
    the *Titanic,* struck an iceberg in the North
    Atlantic, as a result, 1,493 persons lost their lives.
 8. The *Titanic* carried nearly 2,200 passengers and

crew, however, it had only enough lifeboats to accommodate 950.

9. The tragedy brought stricter safety regulations for ships, for example, the new laws required more lifeboats and better training of crews.

10. Today's shipwrecks produce a different kind of tragedy, for instance, if a large oil tanker is wrecked, the loss of life may be small, but the spilled oil damages beaches, birds, and fish.

COLONS

The colon says, in effect, "Note what follows."

14d. Use a colon before a list of items, especially after expressions like *as follows* or *the following*.

EXAMPLES   Minimum equipment for camping is as follows: bedroll, utensils for cooking and eating, warm clothing, sturdy shoes, jack-knife, coil of rope, and flashlight.

This is what I have to do on Saturday: clean my room, shop for a birthday present for my sister, baby-sit for Mrs. Magill for two hours, do my Spanish homework, and make a cake for dinner.

14e. Use a colon in certain conventional situations.

(1) Use a colon between the hour and the minute when you write the time.

EXAMPLES   11:30 P.M.
                  4:08 A.M.

(2) Use a colon after the salutation of a business letter.

EXAMPLES   Gentlemen:
                  Dear Ms. Gonzalez:
                  Dear Sir:

► NOTE   The friendly letter requires a comma, not a colon, after the salutation.

EXERCISE 2. Number your paper 1–10. Supply necessary semicolons, colons, and commas by copying the word before a mark of punctuation and adding the punctuation.

1. Spectators were arriving early at the stadium already eager vendors were hawking their wares up and down the aisles.
2. Some of the music was lively some was somber.
3. We have seen the following birds this summer blue jays robins cedar waxwings Baltimore orioles chickadees and nuthatches.
4. Mother knows a great deal about baseball she is an avid fan of the game.
5. Anyone arriving late will not be admitted.
6. The gym is on the ground floor the classrooms are above it.
7. Next year we will study these subjects French algebra science history and English.
8. The first day at camp June was homesick but sports and crafts and new friends soon cured her of feeling lonely.
9. The following schedule will be observed breakfast at 7 30 A.M. classes from 8 30 A.M. until 12 00 noon lunch at 12 30 and the rest of the day free for recreation.
10. Children like to read about dinosaurs most adults do too.

UNDERLINING (ITALICS)

Italics are printed letters that lean to the right, *like this.* In handwritten or typewritten work, italics are indicated by underlining. If your composition were to be set in type, the typesetter would use italics for underlined words. For example, if you wrote—

Born Free is the story of a lioness who became a pet.

the printed version would look like this:

Born Free is the story of a lioness who became a pet.

14f. Use underlining (italics) for titles of books, periodicals, works of art, movies, ships, and so on.

EXAMPLES   *Big Red* is a book about an Irish setter.
Carson McCullers' *Member of the Wedding* became a fine play.
The *Philadelphia Inquirer* has won many of the nation's top journalism awards.
Did you see the most recent copy of *Popular Mechanics?*
Star Wars was one of the most popular movies ever made.

► NOTE   When writing the title of a newspaper or a magazine within a sentence, underline the title. Do not underline or capitalize the word *the* with the name of a newspaper or magazine within a sentence. The name of a city in a newspaper title is usually, but not necessarily, underlined.

EXAMPLE   My parents subscribe to two newspapers published in other cities: the St. Louis Post-Dispatch and the San Francisco Chronicle.

EXERCISE 3. Number your paper 1–10. After the proper number, copy and underline the words in the sentence that should be in italics.

1. Popular Science, Popular Mechanics, and Popular Photography are all very popular magazines.

2. We always read the Sunday edition of the New York Times.
3. Are you familiar with George Gershwin's Rhapsody in Blue?
4. Edna Ferber, one of our most prolific writers about American life, wrote Giant, Show Boat, and American Beauty.
5. Guernica is a famous painting by Picasso.
6. Katharine Graham, the publisher of the Washington Post, is one of this year's commencement speakers.
7. Peter and the Wolf is a musical composition that tells a story.
8. Olivia Newton-John starred in the movie Grease.
9. Betty Comden and Adolph Green have often collaborated in writing Broadway shows such as Bells Are Ringing and Fade Out, Fade In.
10. Our family subscribes to the Atlantic, the National Review, Newsweek, the National Geographic, and the Christian Science Monitor.

WRITING QUOTATIONS

Quotations are words spoken or written by someone and reported directly. In your writing you will often find it necessary to tell what someone has said, whether you are describing a true happening or writing an imaginary story. You will need to know several rules of punctuation in order to write quotations in a standard form that can be easily read by others.

14g. Use quotation marks to enclose a direct quotation—a person's exact words.

Quotation marks before and after a person's words show exactly what was said.

EXAMPLES "Has anyone in the class swum in the

Great Salt Lake?" asked Ms. Estrada.
[Ms. Estrada's exact words]
"I did last summer," said June. [June's
exact words]

Do not confuse a person's exact words with a re-
wording of the person's speech. If you tell what
someone said without repeating the exact words, you
are using an *indirect* quotation. No quotation marks
are needed for an indirect quotation.

INDIRECT   Pauline asked for **my interpretation of
the poem.** [not Pauline's exact words; no
quotation marks needed]
DIRECT   Pauline asked, **"What is your interpretation of the poem?"** [Pauline's exact
words; quotation marks needed]
INDIRECT   I told her that **I thought the poet was
expressing awe at the power of nature.**
DIRECT   **"I think the poet is expressing awe
at the power of nature,"** I said.

14h. A direct quotation begins with a capital letter.

EXAMPLES   Jimmy shouted, "A parade will be held
here tomorrow in honor of our governor!"
"Is it true?" asked Sandra.
Carla groaned, "And I won't be able to
be there!

14i. When a quoted *sentence* is divided into two parts
by an interrupting expression such as *he said* or
Mother asked, the second part begins with a small
letter.

EXAMPLES   "What are some of the things," asked
Mrs. Perkins, "that the astronauts who
walked on the moon discovered?"
"They found out," answered Gwen, "that

the moon is covered by a layer of dust."
"I had no idea," George added, "that
my room at home was so much like the
moon!"

If the second part of an interrupted quotation
starts a new sentence or if it begins with a word that
ordinarily requires a capital, it should start with a
capital letter, of course.

EXAMPLES "Anything that is dangerous is exciting,
too," remarked Mrs. Perkins. "Space
travel is no exception." [The second
part begins with a capital because it is a
new sentence.]

"In my opinion," Tony said, "Mars
is more fascinating than the moon."
[The second part begins with a capital,
because Mars, a proper noun, is always
capitalized.]

EXERCISE 4. Copy the following sentences, supplying whatever capitals and marks of punctuation are
needed. Two sentences require no changes and should
not be copied.

1. how long will it be, asked Laura, before you are
   ready to go?
2. if it can be arranged, the teacher announced, we
   will visit the United Nations next Thursday.
3. read this book, said Nilda you'll enjoy it.
4. we must hurry to the beach, said Ed, for the tide
   will be high in an hour.
5. Mrs. Isoye, our science teacher, says she has
   a new telescope that we may use tonight.
6. that will be fun, said Jim I've never used a telescope.
7. maybe we can see more of the surface of the
   moon Alice suggested it's very strange-looking.

8. yes, Jim answered, but I would rather travel to the moon for an even closer look.
9. Alice replied that looking at the moon through a telescope would be enough for her.
10. Some people, answered Jim, just don't have the adventurous spirit.

14j. A direct quotation is set off from the rest of the sentence by commas or by a question mark or exclamation point.

EXAMPLES "I've just finished reading a book about Narcissa Whitman," Ellen said.
"Was she one of the early settlers in the Northwest?" asked Janet.
"What an adventure!" exclaimed Carol.

14k. A period or a comma following a quotation should be placed inside the closing quotation marks.

EXAMPLES Ramón said, "Hank Aaron was better than Babe Ruth because he hit more home runs in his career."
"But Hank Aaron never hit sixty in one year," countered Paula.

14l. A question mark or an exclamation point should be placed inside the closing quotation marks if the quotation is a question or exclamation. Otherwise it should be placed outside.

EXAMPLES "What is the time difference between California and Chicago?" asked Ken. [The quotation is a question.]
Linda exclaimed, "I thought everyone knew that!" [The quotation is an exclamation.]
Is the right answer "two hours"? [The

whole sentence is a question, but the
quotation is not.]

If a sentence contains two questions, you still use
only one question mark: Who said, "What's in a
name?"

EXERCISE 5. Copy the following sentences, supplying whatever marks of punctuation and capitals are
needed.

1. Mother may we go to the movies this afternoon
   asked Mary Ann
2. Yes Mary Ann replied Mother if you will come
   directly home after the show
3. Please lend me some money John said Frank I've
   spent my allowance
4. Did you say I'm out of stamps
5. What a fine lesson we've had today exclaimed the
   teacher
6. Play ball shouted the umpire
7. John's question was What is helium
8. Did Selma answer A gaseous element
9. Fire Fire cried the boys the whole kitchen is
   on fire
10. Christine called her sister Mother wants you
    right away

14m. When you write dialogue (two or more persons
having a conversation), begin a new paragraph each
time you change speakers.

EXAMPLE   "What did you think of that movie
about Japan?" Sara asked Ron as they
left the school building.

"I was surprised at the scenes in
Tokyo. I didn't know it was so much like
Chicago or New York."

"I guess a lot of the young people

don't wear traditional Japanese clothes nowadays," Sara said. "I hope the kimono doesn't disappear completely—it's so pretty."

"How would you like to wear one to school tomorrow?" asked Ron. "You'd be the center of attention."

14n. When a quotation consists of several sentences, put quotation marks only at the beginning and at the end of the whole quotation, not around each sentence in the quotation.

INCORRECT   "Memorize all your lines for Monday." "Have someone at home give you your cues." "Enjoy your weekend!" said Ms. Goodwin, knowing very well we would not.

CORRECT   "Memorize all your lines for Monday. Have someone at home give you your cues. Enjoy your weekend!" said Ms. Goodwin, knowing very well we would not.

EXERCISE 6. Rewrite the following dialogue, punctuating and paragraphing correctly.

Well Lola how did you enjoy reading *Treasure Island* asked Miss Cranston I thought it was great Miss Cranston Fine Lola Can you tell us one or two things you liked especially There was plenty of excitement Lola replied and I guess I like lots of that Anything else Well Jim seemed to be real and it's fun to read about adventures like his even though you know they just couldn't happen What chapter did you think was most important The chapter where Benn Gunn came into the story it was very important to the plot Good Lola you've really thought about the story Now let's hear from someone else

14o. Use single quotation marks to enclose a quotation within a quotation.

EXAMPLES   "I said, 'The quiz will cover Unit 2 and your special reports,' " repeated Mr. Allyn.

"What poem begins with the line, 'I'm going out to clean the pasture spring'?" Carol asked.

14p. Use quotation marks to enclose titles of chapters, articles, short stories, poems, songs, and other *parts* of books or magazines.[1]

EXAMPLES   Irwin Shaw's "Strawberry Ice-Cream Soda" is a story of an older and a younger brother.

Our assignment for tomorrow is the first part of Chapter 11, "Americans Create New States out of the Wilderness."

Helen can still recite several stanzas of "Paul Revere's Ride," which she memorized last year.

The poetry of Elizabeth Madox Roberts is the subject of an article called "A Tent of Green" in the *Horn Book Magazine*.

EXERCISE 7. Copy the following sentences, inserting punctuation marks and quotation marks where needed and underlining words that should be in italics.

1. Today we are studying the chapter Settlers Move into the West.
2. Doris says that she read a magazine article entitled Along the Oregon Trail.

[1] For the use of italics for titles, see rule 14f on page 253.

3. Do you know the poem All Day on the Prairie?
4. Who wrote the story To Build a Fire asked the teacher.
5. I know said Sara. It's from a book called Lost Faces, by Jack London.
6. Do you know who said We have nothing to fear but fear itself asked Ellen.
7. The magazine American Heritage has thrilling stories from American history.
8. How many trips to the moon did the U.S. astronauts make asked Beth.
9. Did you read asked Ms. White the article Space Shuttle Problems in the Miami Herald.
10. My lunch hour has been changed Dick said. Now I don't have lunch until 12 30.

REVIEW EXERCISE A. If a sentence is punctuated correctly, write *C* after its number on your paper. Copy the incorrect sentences and make all necessary corrections.

1. Mother warned us "Be sure to have these things with you a first-aid kit a compass plenty of matches and a can opener.
2. "Are you going away now," Alice said, "we haven't had dinner yet."
3. "Why, Jim," cried Sam, "you've cut your finger badly!"
4. There's a spider on my shirt yelled Bill
5. The girls asked if we really knew how to handle a boat.
6. "Mona, do you know who said Give me liberty or give me death" asked the teacher.
7. We should get started by 10 30 A.M. it will take us at least two hours to get there
8. "Come on in," shouted Diane. "The water's fine!"
9. Let us get our work done now I suggested. It will seem much harder if we leave it.
10. "What a job this has been!" exclaimed Marta.

11. Oh dear sighed Cheryl isn't the umpire ever going to say Play ball

12. Laura asked, which team are you cheering for Cheryl

13. Father asked if we wanted to go to the movies.

14. Mary said she and Sally would be over this evening, but it's raining so hard that they may not come.

15. These are the things you'll need on the picnic sandwiches lemonade pickles cookies fruit and anything else edible.

16. I don't know where Jane can be, Gladys She distinctly said I'll meet you here in an hour.

17. Arna Bontemps' The Day-Breakers is a good poem for anyone to know.

18. "That was a lot of homework, Mrs. Ames. It took two hours," said Marsha.

19. "What a fine rider James is!" exclaimed the instructor.

20. "Come, come, Dick," said Miss Sanchez, you can do better than that."

REVIEW EXERCISE B. Write a brief dialogue between two classmates. Show that you understand the use of quotation marks and the paragraphing of dialogue.

APOSTROPHES

The *apostrophe* has two uses: to show ownership or relationship, and to show where letters have been omitted in a contraction.

The Possessive Case

The possessive case of a word shows ownership or relationship.

EXAMPLES Sandra's boat

> Mother's job
> a book's title
> an hour's time

▶ **NOTE** Personal pronouns in the possessive case require no apostrophe: Is this bat *ours, yours,* or *theirs?*

14q. To form the possessive case of a singular noun, add an apostrophe and an *s*.

EXAMPLES a dog's collar
a country's natural resources
a moment's thought
one cent's worth
Charles's typewriter

EXCEPTION A proper name ending in *s* may add only an apostrophe under the following conditions:

1. The name consists of two or more syllables.
2. Adding *'s* would make the name awkward to pronounce.

EXAMPLES Mr. and Mrs. Rogers' house
Marjorie Kinnan Rawlings' novels
Hercules' feats

EXERCISE 8. Number your paper 1–10. After the proper number, copy from each sentence the nouns that are in the possessive case and supply the necessary apostrophes.

1. The dogs leash is too short.
2. That cars tires are badly worn.
3. Davids homework is on the table.
4. I was surprised at Vickys answer.
5. The roar of one planes engines was deafening.
6. Anns greatest desire was to have a bicycle like her sisters ten-speed.

7. You may be able to borrow Henrys book for the review.
8. Have you seen my mothers hat?
9. A pilots life must be exciting.
10. Put your mothers briefcase and Alices bag in the car, please.

14r. To form the possessive case of a plural noun ending in *s*, add only the apostrophe.

EXAMPLES   friends' invitations
citizens' committee
pupils' records

The few plural nouns that do not end in *s* form the possessive just as singular nouns do, by adding an apostrophe and an *s*.

EXAMPLES   men's suits
mice's tracks
children's voices

▶ NOTE Do not use an apostrophe to form the *plural* of a noun. The apostrophe shows ownership or relationship, not number.

INCORRECT The new car's are sporty this year.
CORRECT The new cars are sporty this year. [plural]
CORRECT The new car's styling is sporty. [possessive]

A noun in the possessive case (shown by an apostrophe) is usually followed by a noun.

EXAMPLES   car's styling
book's cover
women's group
Jean's friends

EXERCISE 9. Ten plural expressions are listed below. On your paper, write the possessive for each one.

EXAMPLE   1. artists paintings
          1. *artists' paintings*

1. boys   hats
2. women   magazines
3. neighbors   houses
4. girls   friends
5. three weeks   losses
6. Joneses   car
7. men   clothing
8. children   toys
9. cities   slums
10. oxen   pens

EXERCISE 10. Draw lines, making three columns on your paper. Label the columns *Singular Possessive, Plural,* and *Plural Possessive.* In each column, write the form of the noun which the column calls for.

1. house
2. baby
3. pilot
4. enemy
5. calf
6. valley
7. mouse
8. child
9. citizen
10. student
11. wolf
12. piano
13. customer
14. decoy
15. goose

Contractions

14s. Use an apostrophe to show where letters have been omitted in a contraction.

A contraction is a word made by combining or shortening two or three words. An apostrophe takes the place of the letters that are omitted.

EXAMPLES   Where is the exit?
          Where's the exit?
          We will have gone by then.
          We'll have gone by then.
          She might have let us know.
          She might've let us know.

The word *not* is contracted to *n't*. This is often added to a verb to form a contraction. Usually the spelling of the verb is unchanged.

is not	isn't
are not	aren't
does not	doesn't
do not	don't
was not	wasn't
were not	weren't
has not	hasn't
have not	haven't
had not	hadn't
should not	shouldn't
would not	wouldn't
could not	couldn't

But:

shall not	shan't
will not	won't
cannot	can't

Contractions may also be formed with nouns or pronouns and verbs:

I am	I'm
you are	you're
she would	she'd
you will	you'll
they are	they're
Ann is	Ann's

Its and *It's*

The word *its* is a pronoun in the possessive case. It does not have an apostrophe.

The word *it's* is a contraction of *it is* or *it has* and requires an apostrophe.

EXAMPLES   **Its** right front tire is flat. [*Its* is a possessive pronoun.]

It's wet paint. [*It's* means *it is.*]
It's been a long time. [*It's* means *it has.*]

Whose and Who's

The word *whose* is a pronoun in the possessive case. It does not have an apostrophe.

The word *who's* means *who is* or *who has*. Being a contraction, it requires an apostrophe.

EXAMPLES   **Whose** idea was it? [*Whose* is a possessive pronoun.]
Who's next in line? [*Who's* means *who is.*]
Who's been in my room? [*Who's* means *who has.*]

Your and You're

The word *your* is a possessive pronoun. It does not have an apostrophe.

You're is a contraction of *you are*. It requires an apostrophe to show where the letter is omitted.

EXAMPLES   **Your** paper shows great improvement, Leon. [*Your* is a pronoun in the possessive case.]
You're going to get a better mark this term. [*You're* means *you are.*]

In Plurals

14t. Use an apostrophe and *s* to form the plural of letters, numbers, and signs, and of words referred to as words.

EXAMPLES   Doesn't he know the *ABC*'s?
Your *2*'s look like *5*'s.
Don't use &'s in place of *and*'s.

EXERCISE 11. Number your paper 1–10. Copy from the following sentences the items that require an apostrophe. Supply the apostrophes.

1. The girls wont say where theyll be.
2. Lets go watch the baseball game.
3. Jill gets all *A*s and *B*s on her report card.
4. It is incorrect to use &s in a theme.
5. Everything depended on the number of 10s and 20s we had.
6. Get your books; theyre in the library.
7. Do you know what youre doing?
8. Whos going skiing tomorrow?
9. Dont forget to put in your +s and −s.
10. Always cross your *t*s and dot your *i*s.

EXERCISE 12. Write six sentences in which you use the following words correctly: *its, it's; whose, who's; your, you're.*

HYPHENS

14u. Use a hyphen to divide a word at the end of a line.

Often when you write, you find there is not enough space for a whole word at the end of the line. When this happens, you may divide the word, using a hyphen to indicate the division.

EXAMPLES How long has the building been under construction?
  If you want to know, look it up in the almanac.

Be careful to divide words only between syllables. For the rules on dividing words, see page 326.

14v. Use a hyphen with compound numbers from

twenty-one to ninety-nine and with fractions used as adjectives.

EXAMPLES   There were twenty•one ducks in that flock.

A two•thirds majority will decide the issue, and the other one third will have to abide by the decision. [In the first use, *two-thirds* is a compound adjective modifying *majority;* in the second use, *third* is a noun modified by the single adjective *one.*]

EXERCISE 13. Number your paper 1–10. After the proper number, write the words from the following expressions which require hyphens. Supply hyphens.

1. a three fourths majority
2. one half of the room
3. one hundred twenty five people
4. ninety eight
5. Fifty ninth Street
6. twenty four eggs
7. one third of a game
8. three fourths of the population
9. one and nine tenths centimeters
10. one quarter of the distance

REVIEW EXERCISE C. Form contractions from the following groups of words:

1. will not	8. should not	15. we are
2. there is	9. let us	16. I am
3. who will	10. cannot	17. was not
4. they are	11. you are	18. she is
5. who is	12. does not	19. you will
6. is not	13. he will	20. would not
7. it is	14. shall not	

REVIEW EXERCISE D. Number your paper 1–20. After the proper number, copy the words in the following sentences that require apostrophes or hyphens. Supply these apostrophes and hyphens.

1. Heres where we get off.
2. Whose coat is that on the chair, Cindys or Nancys?
3. Wholl get the tickets for tonights game?
4. The Blaine sisters Irish setter won first prize at the dog show.
5. I wonder if theyre ready; we have forty three miles to drive.
6. Two fifths of Joans allowance will be deducted until she has paid for the broken window.
7. Shouldnt you inquire about directions for getting there?
8. Standing on the corner of Seventy ninth Street and Walker Avenue, I saw thirty two tall women walking small pets.
9. He just cant seem to understand.
10. Ive seen Andys project, but wheres yours?
11. Youve no idea how hard weve worked!
12. Twenty five students (almost four fifths of the class) raised their hands to show that theyd taken long trips during their vacation.
13. If Mary wants the job, shed better come now!
14. The measure received the two thirds majority necessary to pass.
15. When questioned, the couple claimed that they hadnt planned their neighbors surprise party.
16. Harveys going away tomorrow, but Im remaining at home.
17. Its appearance is nice, but its not useful.
18. Please see whos at the door.
19. Lets find out whats happening at your house.
20. My ancestors first settled in this state ninety eight years ago.

REVIEW EXERCISE E. Copy the following sentences,

supplying semicolons, colons, italics, quotation marks, apostrophes, and hyphens where needed.

1. Ill meet you promptly at 7 20 at Fifty eighth Street and Regal Court, said Leah, so be sure youre there on time.
2. The Lafayette Chronicle, the Smiths home town newspaper, has an article about them its very informative.
3. The following students scored over ninety five on last weeks test Linda, Tom, Ken, and Priscilla.
4. I dont think said Irene that youve read The Telltale Heart. [a short story]
5. When I asked the time, did you say 5 40 or 5 45?
6. Jo said that her parents owned two thirds of the company while the Wards had a one fifth share.
7. Tony said he would attend the meeting however, Felicia announced, I won't go.
8. My favorite sculpture is Augusta Savage's Lift Every Voice and Sing.
9. Hogans face shone as he announced Ive found the deers tracks moreover Ive caught sight of the deer.
10. She listed the planets nearest the sun as follows Mercury, Venus, Earth, and Mars.

Sentence
Structure

PART FOUR

Chapter 15

Learning "Sentence Sense"

Fragments and Run-on Sentences

When you speak, you signal the end of a sentence by making your voice rise or fall and by pausing between sentences. When you write, the signals you use are end marks: periods, question marks, and exclamation points. If you use these marks incorrectly, you give your reader the wrong signals. Using written signals requires more attention than using spoken ones, but the two kinds are related. You can eliminate many of your punctuation problems by reading aloud what you have written and listening for the signals your voice makes.

Two frequent errors that occur in written composition are the *sentence fragment* and the *run-on sentence.* When you put a period, question mark, or exclamation point after a group of words that is not a complete sentence, you have made the error of writing a sentence fragment. When you omit end marks between two or more separate sentences, you are writing a run-on sentence. To avoid these errors, apply the "sentence sense" you use when you speak.

FRAGMENTS

A sentence expresses a complete thought. When only a part of a sentence is written as a complete sentence, the resulting error is a sentence fragment. A fragment almost always belongs with the sentence that precedes it.

15a. A *fragment* is a separated sentence part that does not express a complete thought.

To decide whether or not a group of words is a sentence, ask yourself these two questions: (1) Does it have a verb and its subject? (2) Does it express a complete thought? If the answer to either question is "no," the group of words is not a sentence but a fragment of a sentence.

In each example below, a sentence is followed by a fragment printed in italics. Note that all the fragments, except the one in the third example, do not contain verbs and their subjects. The third one, which is a subordinate clause, has a verb and its subject, but it does not express a complete thought.

> The newspaper staff worked late. *Putting out a special edition.* [The fragment contains no main verb or subject.]
>
> We looked forward to meeting Ms. Case. *Our new physics teacher.* [The fragment contains no verb or subject.]
>
> *As the horses neared the gate.* The excitement increased. [The fragment contains a verb and a subject, but it does not express a complete thought. It leaves the reader wondering what happened "as the horses neared the gate."]

Since these fragments all belong to the sentences they precede or follow, you can correct them by joining them to these sentences.

The newspaper staff worked late **putting out a special edition.**

We looked forward to meeting Ms. Case, **our new physics teacher.**

As the horses neared the gate, the excitement increased.

EXERCISE 1. Seven of the italicized groups of words below are fragments, while three are complete sentences. Indicate a complete sentence by placing a *C* after the proper number. Correct each fragment by copying the entire item and making the fragment part of the sentence.

EXAMPLES 1. Dolphins are intelligent animals. *That are being closely studied today.*

1. *Dolphins are intelligent animals that are being closely studied today.*

2. The study of this aquatic mammal may have surprising results. *The dolphin may eventually be trained as a diver's sea-going partner.*

2. *C*

1. The man who has done the most research on the dolphin is Dr. John C. Lily. *Who is attempting to devise a method of communication between humans and dolphins.*

2. *By putting a partially paralyzed dolphin into a tank with other dolphins.* Dr. Lily discovered the dolphin's distress call.

3. The disabled dolphin emitted its distress call. *When it began to sink.*

4. It was immediately assisted by two other dolphins. *They lifted it to the surface for air.*

5. Dolphins usually stay together in groups. *Helping each other out in times of trouble.*

6. A baby dolphin is looked after by two adults. *Its mother and an assistant mother serve as nurses.*

7. Even the deadly shark is no match for two angry mother dolphins. *Circling and striking at their foe with their hard, beaklike noses.*
8. *In addition to having unusual ability to mimic the human voice.* The dolphin is of extreme interest because of its streamlined body structure and its amazing built-in sonar system.
9. Nuclear-powered submarines have been designed in the same general shape as the dolphin. *It is the most perfectly streamlined animal known.*
10. The dolphin possesses a built-in sonar apparatus. *Which is as accurate as sonar equipment used by scientists.*

EXERCISE 2. Copy the following paragraph, joining fragments to the sentences to which they belong. You might have to leave out several words as you rewrite a sentence to correct the fragment.

Everyone is interested in the pony express. Which operated for eighteen months and during that time lost only one saddlebag. There were 308 runs made by the pony express. One of the fastest runs that was made by the riders. It was made in 1861. When Lincoln's first inaugural address was carried across the country. The trip covered 1,966 miles. And required seven days and seventeen hours for the riders to go from St. Joseph, Missouri, to Sacramento, California. Do you think postal rates are high today? Compare our rates today with those of the pony express. Which first charged five dollars per half-ounce of mail but later reduced its rate to one dollar per half-ounce.

Three Kinds of Fragments

The *subordinate clause,* the *verb phrase,* and the *appositive phrase* are three kinds of fragments that often appear in student writing. Once you recognize that these three word groups cannot stand alone as complete sentences, you will have gone a long way toward eliminating fragments from your writing.

The Subordinate Clause

15b. **A subordinate clause must not be written as a sentence.**

As you learned on page 94, a subordinate clause has a verb and its subject but does not express a complete thought. It cannot stand by itself but must always be attached to an independent clause. *As she turned the corner* is a subordinate clause. If you read this word group aloud, you will hear at once that it is not a complete sentence. Read the following subordinate clauses aloud. Do they sound like complete sentences? Then notice the difference when they are joined to independent clauses.

When it rains during a football game [What happens then?]
Who directed us to our seats [If a question is intended, then the word group is a sentence. If not, it is a fragment.]
When it rains during a football game, the stadium looks like a patchwork quilt of umbrellas.
We gave our tickets to an usher **who directed us to our seats.**

Remember that relative pronouns (*who, whom, whose, which, that*) or subordinating conjunctions (see the list on page 104) introduce subordinate clauses. These are very important words, for they can change a sentence into a fragment.

SENTENCE It rains during a football game.
FRAGMENT When it rains during a football game
SENTENCE An usher directed us to our seats.
FRAGMENT An usher who directed us to our seats

EXERCISE 3. The following paragraphs contain ten fragments. Each fragment is a subordinate clause incorrectly written as a sentence. Copy the paragraphs, attaching the fragments to the related independent clauses.

Fifteen very young dinosaurs were waiting in a nest. While their mother went looking for food. Before the adult dinosaur could return to its young. Disaster struck. The small prehistoric creatures all perished. When a volcano buried the nest in debris.

Scientists recently uncovered the fossils of these small dinosaurs. Which lived 70 million years ago. After they studied the remaining fragments of bones. Scientists reconstructed the appearance of the dinosaurs. The name given to these extinct lizards was *hadrosaur*. Which means "duck-billed." Adult *hadrosaurs* were plant eaters. That could scoop up vegetation from watery swamps.

The discovery of these small fossils was important. Because it shed light on one of the great mysteries about dinosaurs. Before this recent discovery was made. Scientists debated whether dinosaurs were coldblooded or warmblooded animals. Fossil evidence shows these tiny hadrosaurs were living in a nest. They must have been warmblooded. Because coldblooded animals are neither fed by their parents nor protected in nests.

EXERCISE 4. Make each of the following fragments into a complete sentence by adding an independent clause to go with the subordinate clause. Write each sentence on your paper.

EXAMPLE   1. Because I missed the bus by seconds.
                 1. *I was twenty minutes late to school because I missed the bus by seconds.*

 1. who broke her glasses

2. because the lights on the stage went out during the performance
3. while Jolene was rehearsing her part
4. after the fish got away
5. who is president of the Student Council
6. that are working on a clean-up campaign for the school
7. if you want to own a pet
8. which were racing across the lake
9. because the library closes at six o'clock
10. whom I met at your party

The Verbal Phrase

15c. A verbal phrase must not be written as a sentence.

A verbal is a word formed from a verb but used as another part of speech. One kind of verbal, the participle, is often mistaken for a verb, particularly when it begins a phrase. *Reading comic books all the time* is such a phrase. It is not a complete sentence, as you can tell by reading it aloud. Although the participle *reading* is a verb form, it is not a verb since it cannot be used with a subject: *I reading, she reading.* Only when accompanied by a helping verb is a participle used as a verb: *I am reading, she is reading.*

As you know from the –*ing* ending, *reading* is a present participle. Similarly, a past participle cannot be used as a verb unless it is accompanied by a helping verb.

PHRASE   built of bamboo

SENTENCE   A house **built of bamboo** cannot withstand a heavy wind. [*Built* begins a participial phrase.]

SENTENCE   The house **was built** of bamboo. [*Built* is accompanied by a helping verb; it is part of a verb phrase.]

Notice how the fragments below, which are verbal phrases, are corrected by the addition of independent clauses.

FRAGMENTS   Lying lazily on the beach
              Written by Virginia Hamilton

SENTENCES **Lying lazily on the beach,** I completely forgot to notice the time.
           The Planet of Junior Brown is a delightful novel **written by Virginia Hamilton.**

EXERCISE 5. Below are verbal phrases incorrectly written as sentences. Write ten complete sentences by adding an independent clause to each of the verbal phrases. Underline the participle in each sentence.

1. Standing alone.
2. Seeing the exit sign.
3. Expecting guests.
4. Waiting for the bus.
5. Painted bright colors.
6. Sparkling in the sunlight.
7. Firing the rockets.
8. Chosen as the captain of the debating team.
9. Walking on the hot pavement.
10. Working on the project for weeks.

EXERCISE 6. The following paragraphs contain ten verbal phrases incorrectly used as sentences. Rewrite the paragraphs, joining the fragments to the proper independent clauses.

Alice's Adventures in Wonderland is a literary classic. Read by college students as well as elementary school students. Every child enjoys this story. Missing some of the fun but laughing at many of the comic incidents. When children grow up, they read the story again. Finding more humor in it this time.

In one of the most famous episodes in the book, Alice goes to a tea party. Given by the Hatter. The Hatter and his companions, the March Hare and the Dormouse, have allowed dirty dishes to pile up everywhere. Being very lazy. Alice finds herself at no ordinary tea party. The Dormouse tells a long story. Falling asleep in the middle. The March Hare offers her wine. Alice is told that there is no wine. After accepting the offer. For a while the three creatures ask her riddles. Having no answers. Then they ignore her completely. Carrying on a ridiculous conversation among themselves. Finally, Alice manages to escape from her strange companions. Thoroughly exhausted.

The Appositive Phrase

15d. **An appositive phrase must not be written as a sentence.**

An appositive phrase, an appositive with its modifiers, identifies or explains the noun or pronoun it follows (see page 237). Neither an appositive nor an appositive phrase can stand alone as a sentence; it should be set off from the rest of the sentence by a comma or commas.

FRAGMENT   The eighteen sailors rowed 3,618 miles to Timor. An island near Java.

SENTENCE   The eighteen sailors rowed 3,618 miles to Timor, **an island near Java.** [*An island near Java* is an appositive phrase explaining *Timor* and should be joined to the rest of the sentence.]

FRAGMENT   We had dinner at the Banana Tree. An interesting restaurant near Key West.

SENTENCE   We had dinner at the Banana Tree, **an interesting restaurant near Key West.** [*An interesting restaurant near Key West* is an appositive phrase explaining *Banana Tree.*]

EXERCISE 7. Rewrite the following expressions, attaching the appositive phrases to the independent clauses from which they have been separated. Change punctuation and capital letters wherever necessary. Some of the appositive phrases belong in the middle of sentences.

1. Rachel and I enjoy playing Parcheesi. A game from India.
2. The entrance to the Mediterranean is guarded by Gibraltar. A rocklike peninsula.
3. Astronomers have long been intrigued by Saturn. The planet with rings.
4. Thursday was named for Thor. The Norse god of thunder.
5. We saw two movies. A science fiction thriller and a western.
6. In 1818 Mary Wollstonecraft Shelley wrote *Frankenstein.* The famous horror novel.
7. The Battle of Marathon was won by the Greeks. One of the most famous battles in the history of the world.
8. Coretta King has become as well known as her husband for the advocacy of civil rights. The widow of Martin Luther King, Jr.
9. The world's largest cactus plants often reach a height of fifty feet and live for seventy-five years. The huge saguaros in Arizona.
10. Pumpkins were a staple of the Native American diet and still appear in the supermarkets every fall. Members of the squash family.

REVIEW EXERCISE A. Rewrite the following items, eliminating fragments by attaching them to independent clauses. Then write whether each fragment is a *subordinate clause, verbal phrase,* or *appositive phrase.*

1. As I was driving home. I saw a turtle in the middle of the highway.
2. It had been rolled over on its back by a car. While trying to cross the road.
3. Now it was lying there in the middle of the highway. Helplessly moving its feet back and forth.
4. Because I remembered that a turtle cannot get off its back on a smooth surface. I stopped the car and picked the animal up.
5. It immediately drew its feet and head under its shell. So that I could see no more than two eyes. Staring at me from inside the shell.
6. The turtle that I had found was a box turtle. A very shy land dweller.
7. I took it to Tall Oaks. My parents' cottage in the mountains. Since I wanted to observe it for a while.
8. Arriving there, I put the turtle down on a rug. Which covers most of the living room floor.
9. The turtle slowly began to stick its feet and head out from its shell. After being still for almost ten minutes.
10. As soon as it felt safe, it crawled very awkwardly but quickly across the rug. Heading for a corner of the room.

REVIEW EXERCISE B. Some of the following groups of words are sentences; others are subordinate clauses, verbal phrases, or appositive phrases incorrectly written as sentences. Number your paper 1–25. Write *S* after the corresponding number of each complete sentence. Write *F* after the corresponding number of each fragment. Be prepared to tell how you would correct each fragment by making it a part of a related sentence.

1. Almost every book on art includes a reproduction of the *Mona Lisa*. 2. One of the most famous paintings in the world. 3. The *Mona Lisa* was painted by Leonardo da Vinci. 4. Who worked on it for four years (1503–06). 5. The painting was never quite finished. 6. After working for several hours. 7. Leonardo would sit down in front of the *Mona Lisa* to quiet his nerves. 8. Some people say that Leonardo did not finish the painting. 9. Because he wanted an excuse to keep it with him.

10. There is a mysterious smile on the face of the woman in the painting. 11. Which has intrigued people for centuries. 12. Although no one knows the true explanation of the smile. 13. Several different legends have grown up about it. 14. One story says that the woman was smiling sadly when she sat for the portrait. 15. Because her child had died. 16. Another story, however, goes on to say that Leonardo hired musicians to play during the sittings. 17. Flutists and violin players. 18. So that he could capture the young woman's rapt expression.

19. When Leonardo left Italy and moved to France. 20. He took the painting with him. 21. The French king persuaded him to sell the painting. 22. Which now hangs in the Louvre. 23. An art museum in Paris.

24. The *Mona Lisa* has been exhibited in several countries. 25. So that many people can have a chance to see the woman with the mysterious smile.

RUN-ON SENTENCES

Another common writing fault that you can avoid by using your sentence sense is the *run-on sentence*.

Run-on sentences occur when the writer fails to recognize the end of a sentence and runs on into the next sentence without proper punctuation or, sometimes, without any punctuation at all.

15e. A *run-on sentence* consists of two or more sentences separated only by a comma or by no mark of punctuation.

RUN-ON	Romare Bearden is a prominent artist his collage is in the museum.
CORRECTED	Romare Bearden is a prominent artist. His collage is in the museum.
RUN-ON	Lee Trevino was playing in the golf tournament, I hoped I could go.
CORRECTED	Lee Trevino was playing in the golf tournament. I hoped I could go.

Remember that a comma marks a break in a sentence, not the end of the sentence. Thus a comma should not be used between two sentences.

EXERCISE 8. Correct the following run-ons. Number your paper 1–10. After the proper number, write the last word in the first sentence and place a period after it; then write the first word of the next sentence, beginning it with a capital letter.

EXAMPLE 1. Virgin Islands' weather is perfect, daytime temperatures are in the 80's year around.
      1. *perfect. Daytime*

1. In nineteenth-century England there were two types of English pepper moths one type was all black and the other had gray and white speckles.
2. The black variety was extremely rare, most people had only seen speckled pepper moths.

3. The moths lived on the bark of surrounding trees, most trees in England had a gray moss covering them.
4. The speckled moths blended into this background the birds who ate pepper moths could not see them against the gray moss.
5. The black moths could be easily seen they were frequently killed by birds.
6. The Industrial Revolution in England produced many factories, when the smoke and soot created by the factories filled the air, it covered the neighboring trees.
7. The amount of soot, two tons per square mile, was enough to color the trees black, the speckled moths could now be easily seen by birds searching for food.
8. The black moths blended into the background of the black trees, the birds began to dine on the speckled variety.
9. Within fifty years, the black variety outnumbered the speckled moths 99 to 1, the advantage of a particular color for protection had completely reversed.
10. Other animals use protective coloration certain kinds of fish have the same color as their surroundings and can blend with the background to escape enemies.

EXERCISE 9. Each of the following passages contains several run-on sentences. You will find the passages hard to read because run-on sentences always interfere with the clear expression of ideas. After you have decided where each sentence should end, write the last word of each complete sentence on your paper. Place the appropriate end mark after the word; then write the first word of the next sentence, beginning it with a capital letter.

EXAMPLE 1. *Jest* once had a different meaning than it does today, in medieval times the English used the word to refer to a brave act or the story of such a deed, by the sixteenth century it meant "to jeer or mock" now, of course, a *jest* is a joke.

1. *today. In*
   deed. By
   mock." Now,

1. Our word *humor* has an interesting history, it comes from the Latin word for "liquid," in the Middle Ages people believed that four liquids in the body made up one's character, thus a person with too much of one humor might be quite odd or eccentric.

2. Our word *paper* comes from the French word *papier,* this word can be traced back to the Greek *papyros,* which is the name of an Egyptian plant, part of this plant was sliced into strips and then soaked in water, finally it was pressed and pasted into a writing material that was used by the Egyptians, Greeks, and Romans.

3. The comma can be traced back to the Greek language, our word *comma* comes from the Greek word *komma,* which means "a piece cut off" when you use a comma, you cut off an expression from the rest of the sentence.

4. The word *rigmarole* came from a group of documents called *ragman roll* written in 1291, Scottish lords signed these documents to prove their loyalty to King Edward I of England since many of the documents were so full of signatures that they were confusing and hard to read, the word *rigmarole* came into our language it means "a series of confused or foolish statements."

5. Have you ever wondered about the origin of the word *sandwich*, it came into use during the eighteenth century, John Montagu, the Earl of Sandwich, was addicted to gambling, so addicted that he often would not stop for his meals, during one of his twenty-four-hour gambling sessions, he instructed someone to bring him slices of bread with roast beef inserted between them because the Earl of Sandwich did not want to stop gambling long enough to go to dinner, the world gained the sandwich.

EXERCISE 10. Of the following sentences, five are correct and five are run-ons. After the proper number, copy only the run-ons, making whatever corrections are necessary.

1. The Amazon is the second longest river in the world, it flows through South America for 3,900 miles.
2. When the runner broke the school's record, everyone in the stadium stood up to cheer him.
3. There is an old belief that birds begin to choose their mates on February 14 perhaps this legend is responsible for our association of romance with Valentine's Day.
4. Have you ever heard of Six Mile that's a strange name for a town.
5. Hank Aaron was born in Mobile, Alabama, which is the birthplace of several other former major league stars.
6. My grandfather says that we will have six more weeks of winter because the groundhog saw its shadow on February 2.
7. The winner of the World Cup of soccer is decided every four years, hundreds of millions of people watch the tournament on television.
8. Before the airplane was invented, many people made wings, but they did not succeed in flying.

9. Aladdin had a magic lamp, and when he rubbed it, two jinn appeared to do his bidding.
10. "The albatross is a bird which is popular in legend and literature," our teacher explained, "it is the largest of the seabirds."

REVIEW EXERCISE C. Some of the following expressions are sentences. Others are fragments or run-ons. Number your paper 1–10. After the proper number, write *S* (sentence), *F* (fragment), or *R* (run-on). Be prepared to tell how you would correct the fragments and run-ons.

1. All cats are able to climb trees, some spend most of their time in trees.
2. Others prefer to spend more time on the ground.
3. All cats have the ability to draw back their claws and shield them.
4. When the claws are not in use.
5. A notable feature of the cat family.
6. Most cats have long tails.
7. That they use for balance.
8. Many cats are tailless, their hind legs are longer than their forelegs.
9. All cats have good vision and excellent hearing.
10. Few cats catch their prey by outrunning it, they stalk their victims patiently and silently.

REVIEW EXERCISE D. Some of the following expressions are sentences. Others are fragments or run-ons. Number your paper 1–20. After the proper number, write *S* (sentence), *F* (fragment), or *R* (run-on). Be prepared to tell how you would correct the fragments and run-ons.

1. Medusa and her two sisters were three horrible monsters who, at one time, had been beautiful women.
2. Medusa, the most beautiful of the three, was very

    proud, she boasted that she was even more beautiful than the goddess Athena.

3. Because of her pride, she and her two sisters were turned into monsters.
4. Who had hissing serpents for hair.
5. No one dared look upon Medusa and her sisters.
6. Because anyone who did turned to stone.
7. Lying all about them were stones that had once been men.
8. Medusa and her two sisters menaced the land for years finally they were challenged by Perseus.
9. A young, handsome warrior.
10. Having been given magic weapons by the gods.
11. Perseus set out to kill Medusa.
12. The only mortal one of the three sisters.
13. When he approached the area in which the monsters lived.
14. Perseus put on a magic cap which made him invisible, he held up a shield that had been given to him by Athena.
15. Studying the reflection of Medusa and her sisters in his shield.
16. Perseus slowly approached the monsters.
17. Luckily, they were sleeping.
18. Still using the shield as a mirror, he cut off Medusa's head with a single stroke he put the head into a special pouch.
19. Which had also been given to him by Athena.
20. The other sisters awoke but could not see him, therefore he escaped with the head of Medusa.

REVIEW EXERCISE E.　Pretend that you are writing to a person who has never seen a comic strip. Write a paragraph in which you describe one of the main characters in your favorite comic strip. After you have finished writing the paragraph, read each sentence orally, one by one, to be sure that you have not carelessly written a fragment or a run-on. Make the necessary corrections on your paper.

16

Sentence Combining and Revising

Correcting Choppy and Monotonous Styles of Writing

As you continue in school and your writing assignments become more demanding, you should develop the habit of writing at least two drafts of a composition. In the first draft, express what you have to say. In the revised draft, concentrate on writing clearly and well and on eliminating any faults in style. Watch especially for groups of choppy, abrupt sentences and for rambling sentences held together by a string of conjunctions. Such sentences, while occasionally effective, become monotonous and tiresome if used too often.

This chapter will show you how to recognize such poorly written sentences and how to revise them.

CORRECTING A CHOPPY STYLE BY COMBINING SENTENCES

Short sentences are often effective in a composition, but a long series of short sentences tends to irritate readers. They slow the reader down and make it difficult to focus on what is being said. Such choppy sentences are often similar in construction and thus are monotonous in their effect. The following passage of choppy sentences would irritate most readers:

> Victor visited Williamsburg, Virginia. Marsha also went. The visit took place during the summer. They both visited for the first time. They toured the buildings together. Marsha was studying the antiques collection. Victor was examining the architecture. They began to share each other's interest. The architecture was from the colonial period. The antiques were from the colonial period.

This passage is very choppy. By combining sentences that are closely related, the passage could be rewritten as follows:

> During the summer, Victor and Marsha visited Williamsburg, Virginia, for the first time. As they toured the buildings together, Marsha was studying the antiques collection, but Victor was examining the architecture. They began to share each other's interest because both the architecture and the antiques were from the colonial period.

Several methods have been used in revising the passage. For example, the first four sentences in the original version have been combined into one sentence containing a compound subject and two prepositional phrases. To improve your writing style, you should be familiar with each of the ways to combine short, related sentences.

16a. Combine short, related sentences by inserting adjectives, adverbs, or prepositional phrases.

> WEAK   At half time, the coach gave the players confidence in themselves.
> The players had been discouraged.
> BETTER   At half time, the coach gave the discouraged players confidence in themselves.
> [The adjective *discouraged* in the second sentence is inserted into the first sentence.]

WEAK	In the second half, the team improved. They improved rapidly.
BETTER	In the second half, the team improved rapidly. [The adverb *rapidly* in the second sentence is inserted into the first sentence.]
WEAK	The solar-energy panels were installed yesterday. They are on the garage roof.
BETTER	The solar-energy panels were installed yesterday on the garage roof. [The prepositional phrase *on the garage roof* in the second sentence is inserted into the first sentence.]

When you join short sentences by inserting adjectives, adverbs, or prepositional phrases, be sure the new sentence reads smoothly. (Review the rule concerning commas separating adjectives, on page 229.)

EXERCISE 1. Combine each group of short, related sentences into one sentence by inserting adjectives, adverbs, or prepositional phrases. There may be more than one correct way to combine the sentences. Add commas where they are necessary.

EXAMPLE 1. The bird sings in the cage.
The bird is yellow.
It sings sweetly.
The cage is by the window.
1. *The yellow bird sings sweetly in the cage by the window.*

1. Melissa chains her bike to a post.
The post is steel.
2. The sky descended into the horizon.
The sky was blue.
The horizon was hazy.
3. The fans filed into the rows.
They filed noisily.

4. The guitarist tuned her instrument.
   She was on the stage.

5. The two parties argued their cases.
   The parties were angry.
   They argued in front of the judge.

6. Conservation laws protect wildlife.
   The laws are strong.
   They protect wildlife inside state parks.

7. We will make the decorations.
   We will do this shortly.
   The decorations are for Flag Day.

8. Miguel wrote his letter.
   He wrote it on Saturday.
   It was a letter to the mayor.
   He wrote it carefully.

9. Poland has the tallest structure.
   It is the tallest structure on earth.
   Poland is in eastern Europe.

10. The tallest structure is an antenna.
    It is a very thin antenna.
    It is a radio-station antenna.

16b. Combine closely related sentences by using participial phrases.

A participial phrase (see page 88) is a group of related words that contains a participle and that acts as an adjective, modifying a noun or a pronoun. In the following examples, all the words in heavy type are part of the participial phrase.

Grinning from ear to ear, Michelle trotted off the stage. (*grinning* is a present participle)

Battered by the high seas, the small ship limped into port. (*battered* is a past participle)

Two closely related sentences can be combined by making one of the sentences a participial phrase.

EXAMPLE   The librarian answered our question.
He was whispering in low tones.

Whispering in low tones, the librarian
answered our question.

A participial phrase must be placed close to the noun
or pronoun it modifies. Otherwise the phrase might
confuse the reader.

MISPLACED   Caught in the chicken coop, the farmer
cornered the fox.

IMPROVED   The farmer cornered the fox caught in
the chicken coop.

► NOTE   Use a comma after a participial phrase that
begins a sentence.

EXAMPLE   Embarrassed by our loss **,** our team sat in
the locker room.

EXERCISE 2.   Combine   each   of   the   following
groups of sentences into one sentence by using a
participial phrase. Make sure that the participial
phrase is not misplaced. There may be more than one
correct way to combine the sentences. Add commas
where they are necessary.

EXAMPLE   1. The class worked quickly.
They divided up the job.
1. *Dividing up the job, the class worked
quickly.* or *Working quickly, the class
divided up the job.*

1. The referee signaled a score.
She was standing beneath the basket.
2. The secretary called a meeting.
He was troubled by the press reports.
3. The audience roared their applause.
They were interrupting the singer.

4. Betty captured the flag.
   She ruined the other team's late comeback.
5. Ellis wrote a thank-you note.
   It expressed his joy over the visit.
6. The students voted yesterday.
   They were electing a class president.
7. The elderly woman crossed the street.
   She was helped by two pedestrians.
8. The town is safe and secure.
   It nestles beneath two mountains.
9. I was puzzled by the rules of the game.
   I decided not to play.
10. The team on the passing bus started to sing.
    They drowned out the teacher's voice.

Another method of combining short, related sentences is to join the subjects to make a compound subject or to join the verbs to make a compound verb.

16c. Combine short, related sentences by using compound subjects.

A compound subject (see page 15) consists of two or more simple subjects joined by a conjunction such as *and* or *or* and having the same verb. In the following example, the compound subject is printed in heavy type.

EXAMPLE   This **table** and that **chair** are ready for the movers.

Often two short sentences may contain similar verbs but different subjects.

EXAMPLE   The radio report predicted rain.
          The television news also predicted it.

You can combine these short sentences by writing a single sentence with a compound subject.

> **Both the radio report and the tele-**
> **vision news** predicted rain.

Words that connect a compound subject are *and, or,*
both — and, either — or, and *neither — nor.* The choice
of the conjunction depends upon the meaning of the
sentence.

Compound subjects must agree with the verb in the
sentence.

EXAMPLES   Paul has missed the bus.
His sister has missed it also.
Paul and his sister have missed the bus.
[Subjects joined by *and* and *both — and*
take a plural verb.]

An almanac gives the answer.
An atlas gives the answer.
Either an almanac or an atlas gives the
answer.
[Singular subjects joined by *or, either — or,*
and *neither — nor* take a singular verb.]

EXERCISE 3. Combine each pair of sentences by
writing one sentence with a compound subject. Be
sure the subject and the verb agree in number.

EXAMPLE   1. Arlene will not be at the party tomorrow.
Margery will not be there either.
1. *Neither Arlene nor Margery will be at*
the party tomorrow.

1. Rugby is played in England.
Soccer is played there also.
2. Soda is not allowed in the stands.
Popcorn is not allowed either.
3. My sister went to the zoo.
I went there with her.
4. The sun is a reliable source of energy.

Coal is another reliable source.
5. Engineering might be Teng's career choice.
   Medicine might be his career choice instead.
6. Tracy Austin will play in the tournament.
   Björn Borg will play also.
7. Listening to music is one of my favorite pastimes.
   Reading is another of my favorites.
8. The treasurer could be responsible for the minutes.
   The secretary could be responsible instead.
9. Maples grow well in this area.
   Birches grow well too.
10. Chewing gum is not allowed in class.
    Whispering is not allowed either.

16d. Combine short, related sentences by using compound verbs.

A compound verb (see page 17) consists of two or more verbs that have the same subject and are joined by a conjunction. In the following example, the compound verb is printed in heavy type.

EXAMPLE   The senator **voted** for the conservation law but **lost** the election.

You can combine two sentences by writing one sentence with a compound verb.

EXAMPLE   He backed the car down the driveway.
           He lurched to a stop in the street.

           He backed the car down the driveway and lurched to a stop in the street.

The connecting words used most frequently to join compound verbs are *and, but, or, either – or, neither – nor,* and *both – and.* The choice of the conjunction depends upon the meaning of the sentence.

EXERCISE 4. Combine each pair of short sentences into a single sentence with a compound verb. Use connecting words that clearly state the relation between sentences.

EXAMPLE   1. In February Teresa visited her grandparents in Puerto Rico.
She also toured Everglades Park in Florida.
            1. *In February Teresa both visited her grandparents in Puerto Rico and toured Everglades Park in Florida.*

1. He repaired the bicycle yesterday.
He raced with it today.
2. Ruth had a better plan.
She proposed it during class.
3. Elgin finished dinner before everyone else.
He stayed at the table anyway.
4. I had heard of polecats.
I had never seen one before.
5. The guard did not hear the car approaching.
She was taken completely by surprise.
6. This worthless timetable may be misprinted.
It may be out-of-date.
7. The train was late leaving the station.
It still arrived on time.
8. Mr. Verris slowly and casually crossed the hall.
He entered the room quietly and handed out the tests.
9. The giant wave swamped the boats in the harbor.
It also toppled the lighthouse.
10. She will announce the field trip soon.
She will wait another week, instead.

REVIEW EXERCISE A. The following passage contains several short, related sentences. Rewrite the passage, combining the sentences by the methods you have learned thus far. Your new passage should not change the meaning of the original. Add commas where they are necessary.

The Majestic River runs between the mountains. It is a deep river. It runs swiftly. The mountains are high. Lush, green vegetation crowds the river's shores. The vegetation also grows up the mountain slopes. Campers fish in the river's pools. Day hikers also fish there. The pools are clear. The pools are beneath the rapids. Canoes can navigate the river. Rafts can also do this. The rafts are rubber. They can navigate the river from High Falls to Bolt's Landing.

16e. Combine short, related sentences by making them into a compound sentence.

A compound sentence (see page 128) is really two or more simple sentences joined together. When simple sentences are joined together in a compound sentence, they are called independent clauses. The following sentence has two independent clauses.

EXAMPLE Tractor drivers bulldozed a barrier around the forest fire, and helicopter crews drenched the fire with chemicals.

Two simple sentences closely related in meaning may be joined into one compound sentence.

EXAMPLE The quarterback threw a long pass.
A defender intercepted the ball.

The quarterback threw a long pass, but a defender intercepted the ball.

The conjunctions used to join the parts of a compound sentence are usually *and, but, or,* or *nor.* The choice of the conjunction depends upon the meaning of the sentence.

Be sure that the ideas you connect in the compound sentence are closely related and equal in importance. If you attempt to correct a choppy passage by connecting unrelated ideas, the result will be even worse than the original, choppy version.

UNRELATED IDEAS	I read the entire television schedule.
	I like to watch news documentaries.
RELATED IDEAS	I read the entire television schedule.
	I could not find even one interesting program.
UNEQUAL IDEAS	Lynn was elected class president. Cara didn't vote.
EQUAL IDEAS	Lynn was elected class president. Peter became secretary.

► NOTE Do not forget to put a comma before *and, but, or,* or *nor* when they join independent clauses (see page 231).

EXAMPLE Alice brought her new water skis, and Tina borrowed her parents' ski boat.

EXERCISE 5. Most of the following items consist of two or more closely related ideas. Combine these ideas into a single compound sentence, using *and, but,* or *or* as the connecting word. Add commas where they are necessary. A few items contain unrelated or unequal ideas. In such cases, write *U* after the appropriate number on your paper to show that the ideas are better expressed in two separate sentences.

1. Other nations use the metric system for weights and measures.
   The United States has decided to use the same system.

2. International trade depends upon a uniform system of weights and measures.
   The United States leads the world in scientific research.
3. The United States is slowly converting to the metric system.
   This process is called metrification.
4. We can resist the change until the last possible moment.
   We can learn to use the metric system now.
5. The metric system is actually very easy to use.
   A decimeter is one-tenth of a meter.
6. Metric weights are based on the kilogram.
   Metric lengths use the meter as the basic unit.
7. Many citizens still use the old system of measurement.
   Many professions and corporations have switched to the metric system.
8. All metric measurements are based on the number ten.
   Some baseball parks measure their distances in meters.
9. Counting by tens is second nature to most people.
   The metric system still seems complicated to many.
10. Metrification will be a difficult process.
    Careful planning will help.

Compound sentences can combine equal ideas from two separate sentences. When combining unequal ideas, however, it is best to use complex sentences.

16f. Combine short, choppy sentences into a complex sentence. Put one idea into a subordinate clause.

A complex sentence (see page 132) has an independent clause and at least one subordinate clause.

(1) Use an adjective clause to combine sentences.

An adjective clause (see page 98) is a subordinate clause which, like an adjective, modifies a noun or pronoun. In the following example, the adjective clause is in heavy type.

EXAMPLE   The girl **who just waved to me** is my first cousin. [The adjective clause modifies *girl.*]

Adjective clauses begin with one of the relative pronouns — *who, whom, whose, which,* or *that* (see page 98). Study the following examples of the relative pronoun used in a sentence.

EXAMPLES   Mr. Allen praised Tom, **who** had written an excellent paper.

Mr. Bingley gave a slide show **which** the entire class enjoyed.

The answer **that** she gave was an abrupt and definite "No."

When two sentences are closely related, the second sentence may help to modify a noun, pronoun, or adjective in the first sentence.

EXAMPLE   Nora played her favorite record.
I had given it to her. [This sentence modifies *record* in the first sentence.]

You can combine these two sentences by turning the second sentence into an adjective clause and inserting it into the first sentence.

Nora played her favorite record, **which I had given to her.**

► NOTE   Use commas to set off adjective clauses that are not essential to the basic meaning of the sentence. Do not use commas with clauses that are essential to the meaning. (See page 233.)

EXAMPLES   This is my favorite coin, which I bought four years ago. [nonessential clause]
This is the coin that I told you about. [essential clause]

EXERCISE 6. Combine each of the following groups of sentences into a single sentence by putting one of the ideas into an adjective clause. Use commas where they are necessary.

EXAMPLE   1. Wendy Quon won the championship.
She is a great athlete.
1. *Wendy Quon, who is a great athlete, won the championship.*

1. The girl spoke to me.
I did not know her.
2. The motion was passed by the Student Council.
I had offered it.
3. Mr. Bellack is our new minister.
He finished divinity school last year.
4. Julie dived in to help Jan.
Julie is the best swimmer in our crowd.
5. I helped with the campaign of Senator Blake.
She is the best candidate for the office.
6. Peter was the best dancer at the party.
He studies ballet.
7. Mrs. Morrison swims all year.
She does not look like an athlete.
8. "The Tell-Tale Heart" is my favorite story.
It was written by Edgar Allan Poe.
9. She gave us some advice.
It hindered more than it helped.
10. This statue is the most expensive item in the store.
It is made of pure gold.

Another type of subordinate clause is the adverb clause.

(2) Use an adverb clause to combine sentences.

An adverb clause (see page 102) is a subordinate clause which, like an adverb, modifies a verb, adjective, or adverb.

EXAMPLE   She sings **whenever she is alone.**

Adverb clauses, like adverbs, may tell *how, when, where, why, to what extent,* or *under what condition* an action is done. They begin with a subordinating conjunction. In the preceding example, *whenever* is a subordinating conjunction.

Study the following list:

Subordinating Conjunctions

after	before	than	whenever
although	if	unless	where
as	since	until	wherever
because	so that	when	while

Examine these two sentences:

The conductor stopped the orchestra.
The violins were not in tune.

You can combine these two sentences by turning the second sentence into an adverb clause and inserting it into the first sentence.

The conductor stopped the orchestra because the violins were not in tune.

When you combine two short sentences by turning one of them into an adverb clause, be careful to choose the correct subordinating conjunction. (The common subordinating conjunctions are *because, although, since, if, unless, when, before, after.*) Because a subordinating conjunction shows the relationship between clauses, a poorly chosen conjunction will show a false or meaningless relationship. For example, a number of subordinating conjunctions could be used to join the following two sentences, but not all of them would show a relationship that makes sense.

EXAMPLE   Mario is industrious.
            He receives high grades.

UNCLEAR   Unless Mario is industrious, he receives high grades.

CLEAR   **Since** Mario is industrious, he receives high grades.

► NOTE   A comma is used after an adverb clause placed at the beginning of a sentence.

EXAMPLE   Although her head ached, she continued dancing.

EXERCISE 7. Combine each of the following groups of sentences into a single complex sentence by putting one idea into an adverb clause. Refer to the list of subordinating conjunctions on page 307.

EXAMPLE   1. Rosa saw the fox near the tree.
            She photographed it.
           1. *When Rosa saw the fox near the tree, she photographed it.*

1. Her ankle pained her sharply.
   She kept on playing.
2. Doris did not go to the movie.
   She had a headache.
3. He saw the truck rolling down the hill toward him.
   He jumped onto the curb.
4. The temperature dropped sharply.
   We kept right on skating.
5. Jane's mother motioned to us.
   We walked across the street.

6. The baby threw the plate on the floor.
   Sam rushed to the kitchen.
7. Mrs. White was just about to start the test.
   We ran into the room.
8. My eyes were growing tired.
   I did not stop studying.
9. Cathy held the tent up straight.
   Jeannette hammered down the stakes.
10. Norm forgot the time of the party.
    We were late.

REVIEW EXERCISE B.   Combine each of the following groups of sentences into one sentence, using the sentence-combining techniques you've learned. Do not change the meaning of the sentences you combine. Add commas where they are necessary.

EXAMPLE   1. The jury returned its verdict.
             The prisoner was set free.
             The real criminal was arrested.
          1. *When the jury returned its verdict, the prisoner was set free, and the real criminal was arrested.*

1. The umpire called a strike.
   The batter left the plate.
   The fans protested.
   The fans were angry.
   They protested with loud screams.
2. One of the crew grabbed the rope.
   She pulled in the sail.
   The captain held the tiller.
   She held it tightly.
3. The day was over.
   It was a hard day.
   The Brimwells sat together.
   They sat by the fire.
   They told stories.

The stories were about their ancestors.
4. Federal Bank sponsors a refresher course.
   The course is in mathematics.
   The course is open to every student.
5. The President wants to fight inflation.
   He gave a speech on television.
   He did this last night.
   The people want action, not words.

REVIEW EXERCISE C. Combine each of the following groups of sentences into one smooth, clear sentence by using the sentence-combining techniques you have learned. Do not change the meaning of the sentences you combine. Add commas where they are necessary.

1. No one has ever solved the mystery.
   It is the mystery of the ship *Mary Celeste*.
   It set sail in 1872 bound for Europe.
   It set sail from New York.
2. The ship was found.
   It was floating in the Atlantic Ocean.
   It was found without a crew.
3. The crew may have been murdered.
   The crew may have deserted.
   No sign of a struggle was found.
   There was no reason to desert.
4. A child's toys lay undisturbed.
   They lay on the bed.
   It was the captain's bed.
   The toys suggest that the child left suddenly.
5. People still look for clues.
   These people are curious.
   The clues explain the crew's disappearance.

REVIEW EXERCISE D. The following paragraph contains choppy sentences. Revise the paragraph by combining sentences to create clear, varied sentences, but be careful not to change the meaning of the original paragraph. Use the sentence-combining methods you have learned. Add commas where they are necessary.

Wayne felt nervous asking questions in class. He had helpful questions to ask. He had interesting questions to ask. Today Wayne took a chance. He raised his hand. He asked the question calmly. He didn't feel nervous. The class session finished. Wayne got up. He turned to his friend, Boyd. He said, "That wasn't so bad, after all."

REVIEW EXERCISE E. Revise the following paragraph to eliminate choppy sentences, but be careful not to change the meaning of the original paragraph. Use the sentence-combining methods you have learned. Add commas where they are necessary.

Robert Frost wrote many poems. Frost grew up in New England. The poems are about the countryside in winter. One poem has been popular with students. It is titled "Stopping by Woods on a Snowy Evening." In this poem a traveler pauses on a journey. The traveler pauses for a moment. The journey is by horse. The traveler watches the snow. It is falling in the woods. The woods are far from the nearest village. People disagree about the poem's meaning. They enjoy it immensely. It seems to touch on a deep truth about life. It describes a common, everyday experience.

CORRECTING A MONOTONOUS STYLE

If you look at the first passage on page 294, you will notice that each sentence in the paragraph begins in the same way, a subject followed by a verb. In the rewritten version, however, each sentence begins differently. The first sentence begins with a prepositional phrase, the second sentence begins with a subordinate clause, and so on. This was done to avoid a monotonous style.

16g. Correct a monotonous style by varying the beginnings of sentences.

A series of sentences that begin in the same way produces a monotonous style. Young writers often write a paragraph of sentences all of which begin with the subject. To avoid such monotony, you can rewrite some sentences to begin with a modifier: an adverb, an adverb clause, a prepositional phrase, or a participial phrase. You will not need to revise them all, however. If all the sentences were changed to begin with an adverb, for example, the passage would be as monotonous as before. Moreover, you should not write an unclear or awkward sentence merely for the sake of variety. If a sentence sounds best with the subject first, you should leave it that way and try to revise some of the sentences near it, if necessary.

(1) Vary sentences by beginning them with adverbs.

EXAMPLES   She paid her debts willingly.
Willingly she paid her debts.
She said sorrowfully, "We're leaving."
Sorrowfully she said, "We're leaving."

(2) Vary sentences by beginning them with adverb clauses.

EXAMPLES   The pain eased after the tooth was pulled.
After the tooth was pulled, the pain eased.

He was not afraid to fight, although he was small.

Although he was small, he was not afraid to fight.

EXERCISE 8. Revise the following sentences by beginning them with either an adverb or an adverb clause.

1. She agreed to his proposal reluctantly.
2. The puppy started whining instantly.
3. We went fishing whenever work permitted.
4. He carefully sharpened the carving knife.
5. She lived in Mexico before she moved here.
6. Tim was polite although they had angered him.
7. She will wash the car if you wish.
8. She wisely pretended not to hear.
9. He will go to college if he gets a scholarship.
10. She gave him a tip although she had little money.

(3) Vary sentences by beginning them with prepositional phrases.[1]

EXAMPLES   A portrait of our mother hung on the wall.
     On the wall hung a portrait of our mother.
     A police officer sat in the car.
     In the car sat a police officer.

Sometimes when you move a prepositional phrase, you will need to change the position of the verb also.

EXAMPLE   A kettle hung above the fire.
     Above the fire hung a kettle.

(4) Vary sentences by beginning them with participial phrases.[2]

A participial phrase is usually separated from the rest of the sentence by a comma.

EXAMPLES   She sang for the crowd, **accompanying herself on the piano.**
     Accompanying herself on the piano, she sang for the crowd.

---

[1] If you need to review the prepositional phrase, turn to pages 76–77.
[2] If you need to review the participial phrase, turn to page 88.

The fielder, **running back,** leaped high to catch the ball.

Running back, the fielder leaped high to catch the ball.

They stared at each other in bewilderment, **stunned by the news.**

Stunned by the news, they stared at each other in bewilderment.

EXERCISE 9. All of the following sentences begin with the subject. For the sake of variety, rewrite them with an adverb, a phrase, or a clause at the beginning.

1. Alice practices the piano after she finishes her homework.
2. Sandy ate the whole bag of popcorn as she sat through the movie.
3. The rainmaker, jumping from his chair, smiled with satisfaction as he pointed at the dark clouds massing overhead.
4. The mechanic will repair your car if you tell him what you want done.
5. Tom stared in wordless wonder at the box of mechanic's tools.
6. The general wore a Medal of Honor on his coat lapel.
7. The scouts were singing loudly and happily as they were hiking back to camp.
8. She kept score, watching the players on the field intently.
9. Her parents said, finally, that she could go hiking on Saturday afternoon if she finished painting the fence.
10. Aunt Martha took the twins to the new swimming pool on the very next day.

EXERCISE 10. Use the following adverbs and adverb clauses to begin sentences of your own.

1. Carefully
2. Proudly
3. Happily
4. Unwillingly
5. As soon as Carmen heard the news,
6. Because he felt tired,
7. As if we had plenty of money,
8. Suddenly
9. After she thought it over,
10. Whenever my grandparents visit us,

EXERCISE 11. Use the following prepositional and participial phrases to begin sentences of your own.

1. On her day off
2. Resisting temptation,
3. Strolling around the zoo,
4. In shocked surprise
5. Wrapped around his arm,
6. Inside the old valise
7. At the bottom of the well,
8. Delighted with the new coat,
9. Picking up the cards,
10. Turning toward the class,

REVIEW EXERCISE F. Revise choppy and monotonous sentences in the paragraphs below by using the following methods:

1. Combine short sentences into longer sentences.
2. Vary the beginnings of sentences.

It may not be necessary to revise every sentence. Your aim should be a series of sentences that are clear and show variety, and thus are pleasing to read.

A lens is different from an ordinary pane of glass. A pane of glass has a flat surface. A lens is curved. Rays of light go through a pane of glass without much change. Rays of light are bent, or refracted, in a lens. This refraction may change both the shape and the size of an image. The curve of the lens determines the size of the image. A concave lens curves inward. It is called a reducing glass. A convex lens curves outward. It is a magnifying glass. Lenses often combine the qualities of a concave and convex lens. Lenses may be concave on one side and convex on the other. A lens may also have one flat surface. A planoconcave lens is flat on one side and concave on the other, for example.

An optical lens must be made from glass of high quality. It must be manufactured by highly trained experts. Optical glass is first tested for flaws. It is then molded into disks. A disk is first ground roughly, then precisely, to give it the correct shape. It is finally polished with ferric oxide. This substance is called "rouge" by glassmakers.

Two or more lenses are combined in a microscope so that we can see very small objects. One lens is called the objective. It produces the primary image. The second lens is the eyepiece, or ocular. It magnifies the primary image. A microscope is judged not only by its magnifying power. It is also judged by its resolving power. This is its power to show separation between things that are very close together.

CORRECTING RAMBLING SENTENCES

Sometimes you may try to avoid a choppy style by stringing many short sentences together, using the conjunctions *and, but,* and *so* to join them. Such rambling sentences are just as irritating and monotonous to read as short, choppy sentences. Learn to avoid them in your writing.

16h. Correct rambling sentences by combining ideas and avoiding the overuse of *and, but,* and *so.*

Since rambling sentences are usually choppy sentences joined by conjunctions, the methods of correcting choppy sentences may also be applied to rambling sentences. Think of a rambling sentence as a series of choppy sentences as you revise it. Combine some of the clauses as compound or complex sentences. Vary the beginnings of other sentences. Study the following rambling sentence to see how it was revised.

RAMBLING   I saw a television program last night, and it was about invaders from another planet and my younger brother Ted became frightened so my mother calmed him down and informed him that there is little evidence of life on other planets but there may be life on Mars but it is probably at a very primitive stage of development.

REVISED   Last night I saw a television program which was about invaders from another planet. When my younger brother Ted became frightened, my mother calmed him down. She informed Ted that there is little evidence of life on other planets. There may be life on Mars, but it is probably at a primitive stage of development.

As with choppy sentences, the first step in revising a rambling sentence is to recognize it as bad writing. When you revise your compositions, watch for long sentences in which the conjunctions *and, but,* or *so* are used a great deal. Usually you will find that the independent clauses are not very closely related. These clauses should be rewritten to show a closer relationship, or, sometimes, they should be allowed to stand as complete sentences. The final step in revising rambling (or choppy) sentences is to read aloud what you have written. If the passage does not sound right, you have more revising to do.

EXERCISE 12. Revise the rambling style of the following passages. Break the sentences down into clauses, and combine some clauses into compound or complex sentences. Let other clauses stand as complete sentences. To avoid a monotonous style, vary the beginnings of some sentences. Then read the passages aloud to see if they flow smoothly and have sentence variety.

1. Paul bought some skis, and he decided he must learn to ski systematically, and so he asked himself what to do first. The answer was to consult an instructor, and the instructor pointed out that it was dangerous to ski if you didn't know how to fall down properly, and so Paul thanked her, and he went home, and he dressed in his new ski clothes, and he went out on the slopes and practiced falling down all day. He sprained his wrist at three o'clock, and he twisted his leg at 4:36, and he left the slopes at 4:38, and now the skis are mine. I bought them from Paul for a song, and so tomorrow I plan to take my first fall at 9:30 sharp.

2. Joan thinks she can speak French, but she made a funny mistake the other day when Lisa came limping into class with a bandage on her ankle, and she had sprained it while playing hockey, so Joan thought she would show off her French. She meant to say *c'est dommage,* and it means "that's too bad," but she said *c'est fromage* instead, and it means "that's cheese," but Joan was quite proud of herself until Mrs. Stevens pointed out her mistake.

REVIEW EXERCISE G. There are both choppy and rambling sentences in the following passage. Revise it so that the sentences are clear, well written, and varied. Read your revised version aloud to see if it flows smoothly.

The dam is not a modern invention. It was used in ancient times. It was used very early in Egypt. It was used to dam the Nile River. The first dam recorded in history was built about 2600 B.C. It was a large stone dam. It was located about eighteen miles south of Memphis. This dam was an engineering failure. Other Egyptian kings built other dams to store water. Their dams created Lake Moeris.

The Babylonians also built dams to control the Tigris and Euphrates Rivers, and the Romans built dams, and the dams lasted for centuries. The Emperor Nero directed the building of a dam, and it lasted for 1,300 years, but the Arabians built a dam that lasted over a thousand years, and it was two miles long and 120 feet high so it was the greatest dam ever built.

Two of the largest dams in the world today are in the United States. One is the Hoover Dam, and it is near Las Vegas, Nevada. The other is the Grand Coulee Dam, and it is in the state of Washington. Each dam is an important source of electrical power. They serve American cities. They produce over 10,000 megawatts of power each year.

Composition

PART FIVE

Chapter **17**

Manuscript Form

Standards for Written Work

A manuscript is any typewritten or hand-written composition, as distinguished from a printed document. In your schoolwork this year and during the years ahead, you will be writing more and more manuscripts. You should learn standard form for your written work now and follow it in all your papers.

17a. Follow accepted standards in preparing manuscripts.

Your teacher will find it easier to read and evaluate your papers if they are properly prepared. There is no single correct way to prepare a paper, but the rules below are widely used and accepted. Follow them unless your teacher requests you to do otherwise.

1. Unless you typewrite your compositions, write them on standard size ($8\frac{1}{2} \times 11$ inches) lined paper. For typewritten papers, use standard size white typing paper.

2. Follow the school policy concerning use of both sides of the paper. In general, it is preferable to write on only one side of the sheet.

3. Write in blue or black ink or use a typewriter. If you type, double-space the lines.

4. Leave a margin of about two inches at the top of the page and margins of about one inch at the sides and bottom. The left-hand margin should be straight. The right-hand margin should be as straight as you can make it.

5. Indent the first line of each paragraph about one-half inch from the left.

6. Write your name, the class, and the date on the first page. Follow your teacher's instructions on the placement of these items. You may put them on three separate lines in the upper right-hand corner of the sheet, or write them in one line across the top of the page. Either way, they should begin about one inch down from the top of the page.

7. If your paper has a title, write it in the center of the first line. Skip a line between the title and the first line of your composition.

8. If the paper is more than one page in length, number the pages after the first, placing the number in the center, about one-half inch down from the top.

9. Write legibly and neatly. If you are using un-lined paper, try to keep the lines straight. Form your letters carefully, so that *n*'s do not look like *u*'s, *a*'s like *o*'s, and so on. Dot the *i*'s and cross the *t*'s. If you have to erase, do it neatly.

17b. Learn the rules for using abbreviations.

In your writing, you should spell out most words rather than abbreviate them. A few abbreviations, however, are commonly used and are considered acceptable in written work.

The following abbreviations are acceptable when used with a name: *Mr., Mrs., Ms., Dr., Jr.,* and *Sr.* If they do not accompany a name, spell out the words instead of using the abbreviations.

EXAMPLES   Mr. Arroyo   Dr. Doris Yen
           Mrs. Galzone   Charles Grant, Jr.
           Have you met the doctor?
           Rosa is a junior partner of the firm.

The abbreviations A.M. (*ante meridiem* — before noon), P.M. (*post meridiem* — after noon), A.D. (*anno Domini* — in the year of the Lord), and B.C. (before Christ) are acceptable when they are used with numbers.

EXAMPLES   The meeting is called for 3:30 P.M.
           Augustus Caesar lived from 63 B.C. to
           A.D. 14. [Notice that the abbreviation
           A.D. precedes the number, but B.C.
           follows it.]

Abbreviations for organizations are acceptable if they are generally known.

EXAMPLE   That woman is an agent for the FBI. [Ab-
           breviations for government agencies are
           usually written without periods.]

17c. Learn the rules for writing numbers.

Numbers of more than two words should be written in numerals, not words. If, however, you are writing several numbers, some of them one word and some more than one, write them all the same way. Always spell out a number that begins a sentence.

EXAMPLES   Dana and I used **twenty-three** rolls
           of film this week.
           From San Mateo take Route **280**.
           Karen started with **120** baby chicks, but
           now she has only **90**.
           Two hundred and fifty-seven people
           were staying at the hotel during the week
           of the convention.

Write out numbers like *seventh, fifty-third,* and so on. If they represent the day of the month, however, it is customary to use numerals only.

EXAMPLES I was the **first** [not 1st] customer at the bank this morning.

Flag Day is **June 14.**

17d. Learn the rules for dividing words at the end of a line.

Dividing a word at the end of a line in order to keep an even margin should generally be avoided, but sometimes it must be done.

1. Divide a word between syllables (pronounceable parts) only. If you are in doubt about the syllables in a word, look it up in the dictionary. Never divide a one-syllable word.

INCORRECT	screa- med	(*Screamed* is a one-sylla- ble word.)
INCORRECT	buil- ding	(The syllables of *building* are *build* and *ing*.)
CORRECT	build- ing	
INCORRECT	bewitch- ed	(We do not pronounce the word bewitch-ED.)
CORRECT	be- witched	

2. Do not divide a word so that only one letter is left on a line.

INCORRECT	. . . man- y . . .	. . . i- magine . . .

17e. Learn the standard correction symbols.

In marking your papers, your teacher may use some or all of the symbols given below. If you memorize these symbols, you will understand at once what is wrong in your paper. If you are not sure how to correct your error, use the index of your book to find the section that you need to review.

ms error in manuscript form or neatness
cap error in use of capital letters
p error in punctuation
sp error in spelling
frag sentence fragment
ss error in sentence structure
k awkward sentence
nc not clear
rs run-on sentence
gr error in grammar
w error in word choice
¶ You should have begun a new paragraph here.
t error in tense
∧ You have omitted something.

Instead of doing exercises for this chapter, apply what you have learned here to every paper that you write. Remember that the appearance of your written work makes an impression on the reader. If your papers show evidence of orderly care, your teachers will give you credit for it and will be better able to evaluate the content of your writing.

Chapter 18

Writing Narratives

Planning a Story; Using Vivid Details, Dialogue, and Description

Have you ever heard anyone described as a "natural storyteller"? Do you know someone who can hold everyone's attention when relating a personal experience? Such persons use gestures, facial expressions, and tone of voice to make their stories vivid and interesting, but they are also careful to organize their stories. They make sure that their stories lead somewhere and end with a definite point, and that what they say is clear to their listeners. They are skilled in the art of *narration*.

Not all of them, however, can write a story as well as they can tell it. They may not be as skilled in using words as they are in using gestures and facial expressions. Someone writing a story does not have personal contact with the audience and must rely on words to make contact. Yet, as you know from your reading, written stories can be as interesting, as funny, or as thrilling, as a story that is told.

Over the years, fine writers have made us aware of how much can be done with words alone. They have shown that even the simplest story must have a plan behind it, and they have used many effective devices in writing their stories. In this chapter, you will learn the basic principles of planning a story and some of the devices which make a story vivid and interesting.

PLANNING A STORY

What do you write about in a letter to a friend? Mostly, you tell about the things that have been happening to you: about coming down with the measles just before you were to start an exciting trip, about the new dress you accidentally ripped on the first day you wore it, about the fun you had in summer camp — after getting over poison oak. Such incidents can be the basis of many interesting stories. But you must plan such a story more carefully than a letter to a friend. A friend knows much about you, but the reader of your story may be a complete stranger. You must be sure to give all necessary information.

18a. Plan your story before writing it.

Before writing a story of a personal experience, work out a rough plan to guide your thinking and to help you to include all the necessary details.

Such a plan should list the necessary information. If you list the information under the categories of *When, Where, What happened,* and *How you felt,* you will usually find that you have included all the important information, as in the following story plan.

1. *When:* I was five years old.
2. *Where:* I was alone in my aunt's car.
3. *What happened:* I tried to drive the car. I released the brake. Car rolled. Hit a fence, a tree, smashed into a house.
4. *How you felt:* Very surprised.

A story about a personal experience need not end with an explicit statement of how you felt about the events described. Often your story will be more effective if you merely suggest your feelings rather than state them. You will find it helpful, however, to include such a statement in your story plan.

EXERCISE 1. Read the following personal experience narrative. Write a story plan for the story, listing information under the headings *When, Where, What happened,* and *How the writer felt.* Follow the form of the story plan at the bottom of page 329.

Model Personal Experience Narrative

A neighbor who lived at the other end of the block, across from the orchard, came to our cottage in distress. There was a sick person at their house and help was needed. It was a situation in which I would clearly be in the way. My mother did something unusual; she decided to leave me alone in the cottage. . . .

While the twilight lasted I had no problems. I sat by the back door facing the orchard, thinking of many things, alert for the footsteps of Doña Henriqueta. But as night fell and the darkness deepened, I decided that since I was taking care of the house I might as well be inside of it. . . .

My mother had said that if I felt sleepy I was to get into bed. That would have been very well if she had been there and it was still light outside. Now it was certainly the wrong thing to do. The back door would be open and I might be caught asleep on top of the bed by a ghost or a kidnapper.

I crawled under the bed wrapped in my sarape and wedged myself on the floor as close to the door as possible. I intended to stay awake and crawl out as soon as my mother was home.

I was awakened by voices in the room. By the candlelight I could see feet shuffling by me. People were calling my name. I heard my mother say, "The well. Please look in the well again."

I wormed my way from under the bed, stuck out my head, and said, "Here I am."

I could not understand why a mother should not be overjoyed to find that her son had not fallen into the well and drowned but had only been asleep under the bed. She wanted to know since when I had forgotten that I was to answer instantly when I was called.[1]

18b. Learn the basic parts of a story.

Most good stories include five basic story elements. It will help to remember these elements as you write.

1. Interesting start
2. Beginning explanation
3. Action
4. Climax
5. Ending

Read the following model of a personal experience narrative and the explanation that follows it.

Model Personal Experience Narrative

Some years ago my friend Sandy and I tried to go to the moon, but some apples and pears got in our way. Both Sandy and I had seen a television program about reaching the moon. When we talked about the program, we agreed that the important thing was to get up enough speed to overcome the earth's gravity. The rest would be easy. We decided to make an experiment. There was a long block in our neighbor-

[1] From *Barrio Boy* by Ernesto Galarza. Copyright 1971, University of Notre Dame Press, Notre Dame, Indiana 46556. Reprinted by permission of the publisher.

hood that ran downhill and then uphill. If we took Sandy's wagon and got up enough speed going downhill, we might be able to leave the earth going uphill.

The next morning we got up very early. We wanted to reach the block before people started coming out of their apartment houses to go to work. I sat in the front of the wagon. Sandy gave a push and jumped on behind me. The wagon went faster and faster. Sandy and I cheered. We were sure that we would leave the earth's gravity and would be on our way to the moon. I began to daydream about newspaper headlines and being interviewed on television.

Suddenly Sandy yelled, "Watch out!" Going uphill had made our wagon change direction. We were headed straight for Mrs. Clark's fruit stand. I grabbed the handle of the wagon to steer, but it was too late. We crashed into the fruit stand and almost hit Mrs. Clark. Mrs. Clark shouted. The fruit spilled in all directions.

The story has a sad ending. Out of our allowances we paid $3.40 for the fresh fruit that Mrs. Clark lost. Sandy's wagon had a big dent in it. I was spanked for sneaking out of the house in the early morning. Sandy and I postponed our plans for the next moonshot indefinitely.

This narrative contains the five basic elements of a story. The first sentence is the *interesting start*. It tells the reader what the story is about in such a way that the reader's curiosity is aroused. The rest of the paragraph is the *beginning explanation*. Notice that the paragraph does not supply *unnecessary* information. It does not tell how Sandy and the writer became friends, nor does it give all the details of their talk about the program. It tells only enough to show why they decided to make the trip.

Furthermore, this paragraph avoids a common error in story writing: beginning in the wrong place.

The real beginning of the story is the decision of Sandy and the writer to make the trip. The story should not begin with getting up that morning or going to school or even with Sandy meeting the writer. Similarly, a story about an actor forgetting lines in a school play should begin with the particular incident that makes the actor nervous, not with the drama club deciding to put on the play.

The step-by-step events that happen after the beginning explanation of a story make up the developing *action*. In the story about the trip to the moon, the second paragraph gives such a step-by-step account. It tells very specifically what happened the morning of the attempted trip to the moon.

The *climax* is the high point of a story. In this story the climax, in the third paragraph, is the wagon crashing into Mrs. Clark's fruit stand. The way in which this climax is made vivid by the use of specific details and effective verbs will be discussed later in this chapter.

The *ending* of a story ties up the loose ends. In this story, the ending tells what happened after the wagon hit the fruit stand. The ending may state in so many words how the writer felt about the events of the story, or the writer's feelings may merely be suggested. Although we are not told directly, the details about the spanking, the dented wagon, and paying for the damaged fruit give us a good idea how Sandy and the writer must have felt. We are not surprised that they did not plan another trip to the moon for a while.

Sometimes a story may not contain all these elements. An interest-arousing opening and a strong climax are, of course, assets to a story, but they are not necessities. Many good stories lack them. But keeping the five basic elements in mind as you write will help you to organize your story.

EXERCISE 2. As a small child, did you ever try to imitate somebody you admired? Do you know anyone who did? Write, in 100 to 150 words, the story of such a personal experience. Make a plan first. If you do not remember such an incident, an item in the following list may suggest an experience that you can write about.

1. You tried using your mother's cosmetics.
2. You used your big brother's razor.
3. You tried a backflip off a high diving board.
4. You tried a stunt on a bicycle or trapeze.
5. You tried to press pleats in a skirt.
6. You tried to use a sewing machine.
7. You tried to diaper your baby sister.
8. You tried to fix your hair in a grown-up style.
9. You tried to milk a cow.
10. You tried to ice-skate for the first time.

EXERCISE 3. Write a story of about 150 words on the topic "The First Money I Ever Earned." Prepare a story plan first. If you cannot think of an incident, the following list may help you to invent one.

1. Not crying when the barber cut my hair
2. Running an errand
3. Mowing a lawn
4. Picking berries or fruit
5. Baby-sitting
6. Cleaning up the yard or courtyard
7. Walking a dog
8. Making tacos
9. Washing windows or a car
10. Pulling weeds or clipping a hedge
11. Delivering papers, groceries, packages
12. Selling tin foil, bottles, magazine subscriptions
13. Raising and selling chickens or rabbits
14. Helping paint a fence or a barn
15. Serving and dishwashing for a party

EXERCISE 4. Write a story of 150 to 200 words about a personal experience which embarrassed you at the time it happened, but which you can laugh about now. Before you write the story, make a preliminary plan. (See pages 329–30.) Include the five basic story elements in your story.

WRITING VIVID STORIES

Vivid means "clearly seen and lively." A reader responds to a vivid story because the writer's skill has made the story come alive. Your story may not be as clear and lively as one by a professional writer, but you can learn certain principles that will improve your stories.

Choosing Details

18c. Choose details to make the action vivid.

Reread the model narrative (pages 331–32). Notice how the second and third paragraphs tell exactly what happened. Suppose the following paragraph were substituted. Would the story be as effective?

> The next morning we got in the wagon and went downhill. Then the wagon got out of control, and we ran into a fruit stand. Some of the fruit was spilled.

The use of effective details makes a story vivid. If such details are missing, the reader will lose interest in the story.

(1) Choose specific details.

Compare the following two paragraphs. Which is the more interesting?

When the canoe touched the river bank, I told John to push us away with his paddle. Instead he panicked. He got up and tried to climb to the shore. In his efforts, he overturned the canoe. I fell into the water.

The canoe glided toward the river bank. I felt a bump as it touched land. "Use your paddle. Push us away," I told John. He put his hand on the side of the canoe and pushed himself to his feet. I yelled at him to sit down, but he wasn't listening. His hands trembled. Awkwardly he teetered on one foot as he reached out to grab a branch that was hanging over the bank. The canoe began to rock. "Sit down!" I yelled. The canoe rocked violently. Suddenly I was thrown from my seat and hit the water with a splash.

Most readers would agree that the second paragraph is the more effective. The first paragraph gives only general information about what happened. The second paragraph tells how John used his hand to push himself up and how he looked (teetering awkwardly) as he tried to leave the canoe. Instead of the general statement *I fell into the water,* the second paragraph gives two specific details: being thrown from the seat and the splash of hitting the water. Also, the second paragraph does more than tell what happened; it *shows* what happened. There is no direct statement about John panicking. A detail, the trembling of John's hands, shows that he was too nervous to follow instructions correctly.

To sum up, the second paragraph is superior in two ways: (1) It gives specific details to make the action vivid; (2) it avoids general statements and lets the readers draw their own conclusions from the details.

EXERCISE 5. Rewrite one of the following paragraphs. Use specific details to make your readers feel that they are participating in or witnessing the action.

1

There was one minute to go in the last quarter. I caught the pass and ran sixty yards for a touchdown. The crowd cheered.

2

There was a very long line in front of the ticket office as I arrived. I was impatient at first. Then I began to think about something else. When the man behind the window asked me how many tickets I wanted, I was very much surprised.

3

When the leader called on me, I was very nervous. I grew calmer as I explained why our club should donate to the Community Fund. At the end of my speech, the members applauded.

4

The two boys clenched their fists and threatened each other. Each of them wanted to appear brave but did not really want to fight. After the crowd watching them had gone, each muttered a final insult and left.

EXERCISE 6. Write a paragraph of 50 to 75 words about one of the following situations. Assume that your paragraph is to be part of a longer narrative. Before you begin to write, think of as many details as possible that would be appropriate for the situation. Select the most vivid ones for your paragraph.

1. Sliding on the ice and bumping into a woman carrying packages
2. Hitting a long, high ball that you think is a home run until the center fielder catches it
3. Being caught in a hailstorm

4. Winning (or losing) a three-legged race at a picnic
5. After riding for twenty minutes, discovering you are on the wrong bus
6. Trying to keep a little boy from crossing the street against the traffic light
7. Helping move furniture during spring cleaning
8. Saving someone from drowning
9. Making a report to the class
10. Working with your block association

(2) Use specific verbs.

Some verbs describe actions more specifically than others. The verb *walk*, for example, gives a general idea of an action; the verbs *amble, stroll, swagger,* and *shuffle* give a more specific impression. When used appropriately, such verbs can help the reader form a clear picture of the action. Of course, you should not try to use a vivid verb in every possible situation. If you are simply telling how you get to school in the morning, it would be better to use *walk* than *stroll* or *amble*. If the point is *how* you walk, a more specific verb may be the thing.

EXERCISE 7. Some of the verbs in the following paragraph are specific and some are not. List the specific verbs, and be prepared to explain how these verbs make the action vivid.

The circus was a blend of movement, color, and noise. In the center ring, a bareback rider performed. As her horse pranced around the ring, the rider tensed, whirled in the air, and landed neatly on the horse. In another ring, a seal held a large ball in its flippers. A clown dressed in orange, green, and purple tiptoed up and reached out for the ball. The seal yelped. The clown staggered back, threw up his hands, and flopped to the sawdust floor. Above the crowd, aerialists performed their dangerous work. A man swung out on a trapeze, holding a woman by the wrists. Suddenly he released her. As she plunged into space, a third aerialist swooped down just in time and caught her by the wrists.

(3) Omit unnecessary details.

As you write, you may think of many details to include in your story, but not all of them may belong. Consider each detail before you make the final copy. Ask yourself: Does this detail, interesting as it may be, give information that is unnecessary to understanding the story? Does it detract attention from what is happening in the story? If the answer to these questions is *yes*, eliminate the detail.

The following story contains one unnecessary sentence. It is in heavy type.

> Last August I went to an auction with my friend Leslie. She hoped to get a large Rookwood vase for a low bid. However, there were several antique dealers sitting behind us. Just before the bidding started, we heard the dealers whispering excitedly. They would stop at nothing if they wanted the vase, which Maria Nichols probably had designed.
>
> The auctioneer began calling for bids. Leslie opened with twenty dollars. The dealers raised the bid to thirty. Quickly the bidding reached seventy-five. **I noticed Sarah Horne, my art teacher, come in at that point.**
>
> One of the dealers said, "Eighty-five."
>
> Leslie called out, "One hundred dollars."
>
> My heart was beating rapidly as the auctioneer cried, "Going, going, gone!" Leslie had bought the vase.

The detail about the teacher gets in the way of the story's action. At this point the reader is eager to find out what happened, not learn who was present. The only persons really necessary to the story are Leslie, the antique dealers, and the writer. The teacher plays no important part in the action, and mentioning her only distracts and confuses the reader.

In your own stories, be careful to stick to the point. Suppose you are writing a story about the last few minutes of a basketball game in which you scored the winning points. You may think of many incidents that happened during the game, but some of them have little to do with your story. For example, one of the players may have collided with the referee and knocked him down. Unless this incident is closely related to your triumph, you should not include it in your story.

EXERCISE 8. In the following story there are five sentences containing unnecessary details. Copy these sentences on your paper.

The day of the Halloween party, Marilyn Freeman told me she was sure that she would win the prize for the best costume. She was coming as Marie Antoinette, and her mother had bought her an authentic eighteenth-century costume, including a wig. Marilyn's father is a dentist. "What are you coming as?" she asked.

I said, "Oh, you'll see." I didn't have much chance of winning the prize, but I didn't want Marilyn to know that. All I had was a ghost costume that my mother and I had made out of a sheet. Janet Goodrich was coming as a pirate.

That evening we had lamb chops for dinner. At the dinner table, my mother asked me why I looked so gloomy. I told her about Marilyn's costume. "We'll have to do something about that," said Mother.

First she got some of Father's medals and pinned them on the sheet. Then she pasted on some gold stars. After I put on the costume, she got my brother Billy's western outfit, took off the holster, and put the cartridge belt around my waist. Billy can be nice, but he is usually a pest. Finally, Mother took a black crayon and drew a beard on the sheet.

Rita, Tony, Joyce, Jennifer, and Greg were at the Halloween party. To Marilyn's surprise and my own, I won the prize for the best costume – as the ghost of a dead general!

EXERCISE 9. Write a story of about 200 words. Use good details and specific verbs to make the action vivid. Before writing the final copy of your story, reread it and remove unnecessary details. If you cannot think of a topic on your own, use one of the following suggestions.

1. An unexpected gift
2. A quarrel with your best friend
3. Meeting relatives you never knew you had
4. An illness that spoiled a trip
5. An accident that you saw happen
6. How you became friends with a person you had disliked at the start
7. How you learned to swim (or skate or dance, etc.)
8. How you helped somebody in trouble
9. How you got unexpected help when you needed it
10. How you learned a lesson from an older person

DIALOGUE

Conversations in stories are called *dialogue.* Using dialogue is one method of making a story vivid.

18d. Use dialogue to make your stories lively and convincing.

If you present the direct speech of people, your writing will be livelier and more realistic than if you merely describe their thoughts and feelings indirectly. Direct speech can vividly reveal the personalities of the speakers. Conversation makes a story seem more lifelike and exciting.

In the following passage, the characters are engaged in conversation, but what they say is described — it is not reported directly. The result is a dull, uninteresting paragraph.

> My friends Sue and Edie went abalone fishing at Hondo Beach. When I met them, I asked where they had been. They told me. I asked what an abalone was. Sue said it was a shellfish. I asked how they caught abalone. Sue said they waded out into the water and pried them off the rocks. Edie said the water was very cold, and that the abalone were hard to pry off the rocks. I wanted to know if the abalone were good to eat. Sue said yes, if properly cooked; but Edie said they were awfully tough.

In the following paragraphs, the conversation is written as dialogue. Notice how much more interesting this second version is. Notice also that it is much more convincing. The dialogue not only adds liveliness; it also indicates the personalities of the speakers. Sue and Edie sound like real people, each with a distinct personality, and the dialogue shows their personalities.

> I ran into Sue and Edie on the street.
> "Where'd you go yesterday?" I asked them.
> "Abalone fishing at Hondo Beach," Sue said.
> "What's abalone?" I wanted to know.

"A shellfish."

"Like oysters?"

"No more like oysters," Edie snorted, "than a wheelbarrow is like a motorcycle."

Sue explained, "An abalone has just one top shell, like a snail. It's open at the bottom."

"You fish for 'em with hook and line?"

"Gosh, are you ignorant!" Edie said.

"They stick to the rocks, under water," Sue said, "and you wade out—"

"In water that's so cold you turn blue," Edie interrupted.

"—and you pry them off the rocks. It's easy."

"Yes, sure," Edie said, "as easy as prying names off plaques."

"What do you do with them?" I asked.

"Eat them," Sue said.

"If you're crazy enough," Edie said. "By rights, you should use them for shoe soles."

"They're not tough if you remember to tenderize them by pounding before you fry them."

"Personally," Edie insisted, "I prefer slabs of old automobile tire fried in axle grease."

One of the problems in writing conversation is to keep the reader aware of who is talking. There are many ways to do this. How many different ways of revealing who is speaking are shown in the passage above? Notice where the speaker is identified—at the beginning, at the end, or in the middle of his speech. With several speeches, there is no identification, yet the reader knows easily who the speaker is because the author has been careful to make it clear.

Before you write a story with conversation in it, review the rules for punctuation of dialogue on pages 254–60. Remember these three rules:

1. Place quotation marks before and after words that anyone speaks.

2. Use commas to separate a person's speech from the rest of the sentence.

3. Start a new paragraph to indicate a change of speaker.

EXERCISE 10. The following story is told without direct quotations. Rewrite it, putting the appropriate lines into direct quotations.

A mean, bullying man borrowed a plow from his meek neighbor and failed to return it. Finally the owner of the plow asked for it. The big man said sorrowfully that he could not return it; rats had eaten it up. When the little man left without his plow, the big man laughed and laughed.

Some days later, the big man found that the buzz saw he used to cut up logs had been ruined by somebody. Furious, he went to his little neighbor and shouted that someone had knocked big chunks out of his fine new saw. The little man suggested that the damage must have been done by cats. Wildly, the big man protested that it couldn't have been cats, that it would take mighty tough cats to bite pieces out of a buzz saw. This was so, the little man agreed; in a country where the rats feed on iron, the cats have to be tough.

EXERCISE 11. Select two of the following situations and write a short conversation to fit each of them. Let the dialogue show the personalities of the speakers.

1. Two motorists have had a collision; each is saying that the accident is the other's fault.
2. Two small boys are bragging about their dogs.
3. Two friends argue about a baseball hero.
4. A girl insists to her parents that she is old enough and capable enough to have a part-time job.
5. A girl tries to persuade her mother to let her skip piano practice that day.

6. Two girls try to persuade a third girl to invite two particular boys to a party she is giving.

7. A girl tries to make her parents see why it is impossible for her to go to a boy cousin's party.

8. A boy tries to convince his parents that his allowance must be increased.

9. A girl is helping a boy with his algebra, but he would rather talk about sports.

10. An uncle treats his nephew like a baby; the boy tries to convince his uncle that he has grown up.

DESCRIPTION

18e. Use description to make your stories vivid and convincing.

A good description makes the reader see, hear, or otherwise experience something. You have already learned how good details and specific verbs can make the description of action vivid. Description can also improve a story in other ways. A description of a scene can make a reader feel present at the scene. A description of a person may almost make a reader familiar with that person. Properly used, description can convince the reader that what is happening in a story is real because the details seem real.

The longer your story, the more description you will probably employ. There is no place for a long description of a person or scene in a very short story, but even here a sentence or two of vivid detail can make the story more effective. In this part of the chapter, you will learn how to use description to improve your stories.

(1) Use details that appeal to the senses.

Before you can write a good description, you must learn to be a good observer. Notice the things around you, and make a mental list of them. For example, what might you observe in the halls when classes are passing at your school? First, you would *see* the students on their way to their classes. Next, you would *hear* them talking with each other or shouting to students across the hall. Finally, you would *feel* some of them jostling you as you passed them.

Just as you learn about life around you through your senses, so you can make a story lifelike by using details that appeal to the senses. The senses you will use most often are *sight* and *hearing,* but many times you will also use *touch, taste,* and *smell.* The more senses you appeal to, the more convincing your description will be.

Read the following model description. How many of the five senses do the details appeal to?

Model Description

I pushed up the high steps and into the aisle of the bus. The shrill screaming, shouting, and laughing were like a wall of noise in front of me. Because we had been waiting in the rain, the air in the bus was steamy and smelled of wet wool and rubber raincoats. As I tried to squeeze past the boy ahead of me in the aisle, my books began to slide out of my arms. When I grabbed for them, my right hand struck a hockey stick and was twisted backward painfully. The books slipped away. I saw that every seat was taken, but nobody seemed to be sitting down. The aisle was jammed. Everywhere arms were waving and pushing.

EXERCISE 12. Test your powers of observation on your way home from school. How many details can you observe? To which senses do they appeal? List at least ten details.

EXERCISE 13. Write a description of about 150 words based on the list you made for Exercise 12.

EXERCISE 14. The following paragraphs might belong to stories in which long descriptions would be out of place. The addition of several vivid sentences would improve the stories. Rewrite two of the three paragraphs, following the directions in parentheses.

1

At the end of the debate an elderly man stood up. "I've attended many town meetings," he said, "and I've never heard such nonsense as I've heard tonight." Angrily he tore the meeting's agenda into pieces. (Insert several sentences to follow the first. Describe how the elderly man looked and spoke.)

2

My sister had worked on the model boat for months. It had occupied most of her spare time. Lovingly she had carved, sanded, and painted it. Now she held it proudly in her hand, displaying it before us. (Write two or three sentences about the boat.)

3

It was a very unpleasant trip. I was relieved when the plane finally arrived at the San Francisco airport. (Insert several sentences after the first. Show how the trip was unpleasant. Appeal to at least three of the senses.)

(2) Select adjectives and adverbs carefully, and use them sparingly.

As you remember, an adjective describes a noun or a pronoun and tells *What kind, Which one, How many.*

An adverb describes a verb, an adjective, or another adverb and tells *When, Where,* or *How.*

Lazy writers will not try to find the adjective or adverb that gives an exact description. They will rely on dull, tired words that have already been used too often. For example, they may write:

> We had a swell time, because the speaker was very interesting. He made some tremendously good remarks. After he finished, the applause was absolutely fabulous. We all agreed that he was a terrific speaker.

The writer of this passage indicated that the speaker was *interesting* and *terrific,* but these tired words tell little about the speaker or his speech. Was he *stimulating? thought-provoking? witty? persuasive?* Similarly, the applause is described as *absolutely fabulous,* a phrase which has almost no meaning. Was the applause *enthusiastic? deafening?*

Get into the habit of avoiding such words as *swell, terrible,* and *terrific.* When you encounter these words in your own writing, cross them out and find adjectives and adverbs that are more interesting and more exact in meaning.

Some vague, dull, and overused adjectives and adverbs are

nice	grand	tremendous
swell	terrible	really
horrible	cute	wonderful
neat	fabulous	great
cool	awful	very
funny	absolutely	terrific

EXERCISE 15. Number your paper 1–10. After the proper number, replace the overused adjectives and adverbs in italics with words that you think are fresher and more exact. Use your dictionary, if you need to.

EXAMPLES 1. After Geraldo sprained his ankle, he walked in a *funny* way.
1. *peculiar*
2. Since Marsha was elected secretary of the club, she has become *terribly* efficient.
2. *extremely*

1. Harriet, your birthday party was *nice*.
2. I had an *absolutely terrible* time at the dentist's.
3. It is a *cute* little puppy that often does *cute* tricks.
4. Jane Brady has recorded a *terrific* new song.
5. Just as we ran out of ideas, Lois Keller made a *neat* suggestion.
6. Fran gave a *swell* performance in the class play.
7. Margie's hair looks *horrible* this morning.
8. The homework Mr. Rubin assigned is *really* difficult.
9. Frank plays the clarinet *awfully* well.
10. We had an *awfully wonderful* weekend at your home.

EXERCISE 16. Write the following sentences. For the first five, fill in each blank with as fresh and exact an adjective as you can. Supply fresh and exact adverbs for the second five sentences. Use the dictionary if you need to.

1. She refused to give him a(n) —— answer.
2. In spite of his —— suit, he looked shabby.
3. They ate an enormously —— dinner.
4. The actress wore a strikingly —— evening gown.
5. The general handled his troops with —— skill.
6. A frightened child —— asked a question.
7. My new sweater is —— scarlet.
8. After cleaning house, I flopped —— on my bed.
9. The wind was whistling outside, but the Hernandez family sat —— around the fire.
10. Breathing ——, I began to unwrap the presents.

Adjectives and adverbs are like spices in food. They are necessary for seasoning, but too many of them will spoil the dish. Do you feel that the following passage is overseasoned?

The cute, reddish-brown, friendly dog sagged mournfully and wearily at its generous owner's feet. The huge man with the long, massive legs had hunted tirelessly and eagerly all that clear, sunny day. Now he had fallen blissfully asleep in the soft, comfortable easy chair.

This passage would be more effective if some of the modifiers were eliminated:

The reddish-brown dog sagged at its owner's feet. The huge man had hunted eagerly all day. Now he had fallen asleep in the soft easy chair.

Sometimes you may be tempted to include a great many adjectives and adverbs in your own stories in the hope that such a practice will make your writing more vivid. Using too many modifiers, however, will weaken your description. Choose your modifiers carefully. Look over your description to see if you have used two or more words with similar meaning to describe something.

Cut out repetitious modifiers that do not contribute much to a description. In the passage about the hunter and the dog, the elimination of unnecessary adjectives and adverbs resulted in a stronger description.

Another method is to use comparisons. Sometimes a comparison is the most vivid and exact way to describe a person or an object. Good writers do not merely describe a task as difficult. They write that the task "was like completing a jigsaw puzzle while blindfolded." Other writers might compare a group to "a military procession with a brass band, the way they always set the pace for their companions." Comparisons are often effective, but readers may tire of them even sooner than they will tire of modifiers. Use comparisons sparingly and save them for important moments in your stories.

A third method is to rewrite some sentences so that nouns and verbs do the work of describing. The sentence *He was a joyous, smiling boy* can be changed to *His smile showed his joy.* In the second sentence, the adjectives *smiling* and *joyous* have been changed to nouns. Verbs with descriptive adverbs may be replaced by more exact verbs. The sentence *Suddenly he ran forward and quickly pulled the letter from her hand* can be changed to *He darted forward and jerked the letter from her hand.* The verb *darted* replaces *suddenly ran,* and the verb *jerked* replaces *quickly pulled.*

EXERCISE 17. The passage below has too many adjectives and adverbs. Rewrite it according to the following directions:

1. Eliminate unnecessary modifiers from the first two sentences.

2. Use a comparison in the third sentence (perhaps to a little dog cautiously approaching a big dog).

3. Rewrite the last sentence so that an exact verb will replace a verb and an adverb.

The shabby, pathetic-looking little man shuffled timidly and fearfully along the dingy, cracked, uneven sidewalk. His old, battered hat jiggled precariously on his head. When he saw Mr. Abercrombie, the banker, coming up the street, he cautiously sidled up to him. Mr. Abercrombie walked haughtily past.

EXERCISE 18. Write a story about a time you enjoyed a big success. If you prefer, invent such a story.

Be sure to plan before you write, bearing in mind the basic parts of a story. Try to use fresh and exact adjectives and adverbs. The following list of ideas may help you think of a story.

1. You won a merit badge.
2. You won a contest and got a prize.
3. You pitched a winning game.
4. You took a prize-winning photograph.
5. You were in a talent show.
6. You built a radio set that worked.
7. You won the lead in a class play.
8. You found something of value: money, jewelry, etc.
9. You scored a winning goal.
10. You caught a big fish.
11. You won an election for patrol leader, class president, cheerleader, etc.
12. You made a patchwork quilt.

(3) Use description to make characters and setting vivid.

The persons in a story are called the *characters,* and the place where a story happens is called the *setting.* A story gains conviction if the reader knows something about the characters and setting. If a character is to play an important role in a story, a description will focus attention on that character. For example, at the beginning of *Treasure Island,* the author Robert Louis Stevenson focuses attention on one important character in the story:

> I remember him as if it were yesterday, as he came plodding to the inn door, his sea chest following behind him in a handbarrow; a tall, strong, heavy, nut-brown man; his tarry pigtail falling over the shoulders of his soiled blue coat; his hands ragged and scarred, with black, broken

nails; and the saber cut across one cheek, a dirty, livid white.

Setting may also play an important role in a story. If you were writing about a night spent in a supposedly haunted house, the house itself would be an important factor and a description of it would make your story more effective. Eudora Welty begins *Losing Battles,* a novel which tells of one day in the life of a large rural family, with a beautiful description of dawn in the country. Notice her use of comparisons.

> When the rooster crowed, the moon had still not left the world but was going down on flushed cheek, one day short of the full. A long thin cloud crossed it slowly, drawing itself out like a name being called. The air changed, as if a mile or so away a wooden door had swung open, and a smell, more of warmth than wet, from a river at low stage, moved upward into the clay hills that stood in darkness.
>
> Then a house appeared on its ridge, like an old man's silver watch pulled once more out of its pocket. A dog leaped up from where he'd lain like a stone and began barking for today as if he meant never to stop.[1]

EXERCISE 19. Pretend one of the following persons is a character in a story, and write a description of 75 to 100 words. Let physical details show the personality of the character. You might also show the character performing some typical action.

1. An aunt or uncle
2. A police officer
3. The president of your class
4. Your best friend

[1] From *Losing Battles* by Eudora Welty. Copyright © 1970 by Eudora Welty. Reprinted by permission of Random House, Inc.

5. A public official you have seen on television
6. The librarian at your local library
7. Your older brother or sister
8. A salesperson in a department store
9. A waiter
10. A character you invented

EXERCISE 20. Write a description of a setting (no longer than 100 words) which might be used in a story. Perhaps you can make your setting suggest a feeling or mood; mystery, dreariness, brilliance, gaiety, fear, and so on.

REVIEW EXERCISE. Write a story of about 400 words. Use dialogue if it is appropriate.

Chapter 19

The Paragraph

Developing and Writing Paragraphs

In your reading, you almost always encounter paragraphs as small parts of a longer piece of writing. However, compositions only one paragraph long can be useful and interesting. In this chapter, you will learn to write good one-paragraph compositions. This will be excellent preparation for planning and writing longer papers later. Both short and long papers require the same writing skills, and short papers are usually easier to write just because they are short.

THE STRUCTURE OF A PARAGRAPH

19a. **A paragraph is a series of sentences developing one topic.**

The main idea or topic in the following paragraph is stated in the first sentence. The rest of the paragraph consists of a series of sentences that give details to support this idea.

The term *white elephant,* which means "a possession that is expensive to maintain and is of little use," originated in ancient Siam. To punish a disobedient noble, the King of Siam gave this person a white elephant, an animal that was considered sacred. The noble had to buy expensive jeweled coverings for the sacred animal and feed it huge quantities of the finest food. Often, the noble had to hire a special caretaker to look after the animal. Because of the enormous costs of caring for the white elephant, the noble eventually went broke.

All the details in this paragraph are about the origin of the term *white elephant.* In contrast to this well-structured paragraph, the following paragraph is poorly structured. As you read it, notice that it does not develop the topic, which is stated in the first sentence. Shifting from the king, to elephants, to nobles, the paragraph does not give the information in a logical sequence. The sentences do not hang together. After you have read the paragraph, you may wonder just what the writer was trying to say.

The term *white elephant,* which means "a possession that is expensive to maintain and is of little use," originated in ancient Siam. The king gave a white elephant to a noble. White elephants were sacred. The noble eventually went broke. Food was expensive and so was the elephant's decoration. The king punished a noble this way. The elephant often had a special caretaker who would look after it.

The Topic Sentence

19b. The topic of a paragraph is stated in one sentence. This sentence is called the *topic sentence.*

If a paragraph has one main idea, it should be possible to state that idea in a sentence. Such a sentence is called the *topic sentence*. In the following paragraphs the topic sentence is in heavy type.

1

Hot water ruined the rich silver mines of the old Comstock Lode in Nevada. The tunnels and shafts were so hot and damp from the steaming water which seeped into them from underground sulphur springs that miners had to work stripped to the waist and take frequent rests. Occasionally streams of boiling water shot into the tunnels, forcing men to run for their lives. This water collected in sumps, and men who fell into them died in agony. The hot water accumulated, gradually filling the tunnels and bringing all mining to a halt.

2

Wise consumers have learned to recognize deceptive sales practices. Some store owners, for example, may offer merchandise at "thirty percent off" but may have raised the original prices beforehand. Another deception is that of "bait and switch." A store will advertise an item at a truly low price (the bait). A customer asking for this item will be told that it is inferior in quality to another brand that costs more (the switch).

In these paragraphs, the topic sentence is the first sentence. This is its usual position, and often its most effective position. At the beginning it tells the reader what the paragraph is going to be about. Knowing this, the reader is able to follow the writer's idea easily.

However, the topic sentence may come elsewhere in the paragraph. In the following paragraph the topic sentence comes last and summarizes the preceding sentences.

In the old days, coal miners worked with pick and shovel and hand drill. Today, hand tools are replaced by power cutters, drilling machines, mechanical loaders, timbering machines, and roof bolters. Electric locomotives, replacing mules, pull larger cars that carry heavier loads. Belt conveyors, too, move coal in a continuous flow through mine tunnels to the cleaning, washing, and loading machines. **In every way, mechanization has vastly increased the efficiency of coal mining.**

EXERCISE 1. Find the topic sentence in the following paragraphs. Number your paper 1–5 and copy the topic sentence of each paragraph.

1

Playfulness is a characteristic of most animals. Kittens wrestle and spar with each other. Puppies chase their tails, and bear cubs slide down mud banks. Sailors know that porpoises often race with vessels.

2

Ursula Le Guin won both the Hugo and Nebula awards for her novels. She also received a Newbery Medal and a National Book Award for the second and third parts of her *Earthsea Trilogy*. On several other occasions she received Hugo awards for her short stories. Ursula Le Guin has won just about every prize available for her works of science fiction.

3

A number of place-names taken from Native American tongues are usually difficult to spell. The names that have undergone changes present few spelling problems. Mauwauwaming has become, and is easily spelled, Wyoming. Machihiganing has been changed to Michigan. Rarenawok and Asingsing are now Roanoke and Sing Sing. But the spelling of other names, which seeks to reproduce the sound of the original words, must present travelers with a few uneasy moments. Consider, for example, the modern tourist who is spending several weeks in Maine and must write home about having seen Lake Magaguadavic and Lake Mooselookmeguntic and about passing through the towns of Oquossoc, Passadumkeag, Mattawamkeag, and Wytopitlock.

4

For the first time in generations our forests are growing more wood each year than we are cutting. This does not mean that fewer trees are cut; on the contrary, each year more logs are hauled out of the forests than were removed during the preceding year. It is the rate of growth of new wood that is rising annually. This increase is due to wise forest management. Trees that are mature or diseased are cut out to allow room for growth of healthy or younger trees. Loggers leave seed trees to make sure that new growth gets started, or they plant seedlings where there are not enough seed trees.

5

Many people think that the rocket is a recent invention. Although the rocket has received its greatest development within the last fifty years, it was used as a primitive weapon many centuries ago. The Chinese had rockets in the thirteenth century and called them "arrows of fire." In the fifteenth century, the Italians used rockets which traveled over the ground on rollers and were made in the shapes of animals. Neither the Chinese nor the Italian rockets were probably very destructive. They were designed to frighten enemies, not to kill them.

The Concluding, or Clincher, Sentence

Sometimes a paragraph may be long and complicated or may include details that the writer wants to emphasize. Such a paragraph may end with a concluding sentence. This sentence clinches the point made in the paragraph.

The concluding sentence restates the idea of the topic sentence, summarizes details in the paragraph, or does both. It is helpful at the end of a long paragraph but usually seems out of place in a short paragraph. Do not use the concluding sentence unless it really contributes to a paragraph's effectiveness. The concluding sentence in the following paragraph appears in heavy type. Notice how this sentence restates the idea of the topic sentence.

> There is still some good outdoor cooking going on in this country, but none of it needs machinery. The first meal that comes to mind is a clambake last summer in Maine. Here is the authentic recipe for a clambake: dig a big hole in a beach. If you have a Maine beach to dig your hole in, so much the better, but any beach will do. Line the hole with rocks. Build a big fire on the rocks and take a swim. When the fire is all gone, cover the hot rocks with seaweed. Add some potatoes just as they came from the ground; some corn just as it came from the stalk; then lobsters, then clams, then another layer of seaweed. Cover the whole thing with a tarp and go for another swim. Dinner will be ready in an hour. It will make you very happy. **No machine can make a clambake.**[1]

[1] From "The Great American Barbe-Queue" by Charles Kuralt in *Saturday Review*. © Saturday Review 1976. All rights reserved. Reprinted by permission of the publisher.

DEVELOPMENT OF A PARAGRAPH

19c. Plan your paragraph before you write it.

Your teacher may assign a paragraph topic, or you may be asked to decide on a topic yourself. Finding a topic is easy if you keep certain things in mind.

Finding a Topic to Write About

You can find a good topic for a paragraph by thinking about your own interests and experience. Consider the ideas and information you know firsthand that would make good material for a composition. Jot down a number of possible subjects as they occur to you. Start by listing general categories that interest you, such as sports, school, hobbies, teachers, family, food, camping, pets, games. Then, from these general categories, choose the one category you would like to write about.

Narrowing the Topic

A general category, however, is too big for treatment in one paragraph. Therefore, you must narrow it down to a smaller topic. For example, if you decide to write about sports, narrower topics might be the sports you know best: tennis, soccer, swimming, hockey. But none of these could be handled in a single paragraph. You will have to narrow the subject even further. Tennis can be broken down into the various strokes: serve, forehand, backhand, volley, smash. Any one of these could be a good topic for a one-paragraph composition. If, for example, you choose to write about how to hit a forehand drive, you could explain the position of the feet, the way to grip the racket, how to start the stroke, and how to finish it. Two or three sentences on each of these skills should produce a solid paragraph.

Writing a Topic Sentence

Having decided what you are going to write about, you need to write a topic sentence to introduce your paragraph. This sentence should make clear what the paragraph is to be about and be interesting enough to make someone want to read the paragraph.

EXERCISE 2.   Select from the following five topic sentences the one you think would be most effective. Prepare to explain why you think this sentence is best.

1. After mastering the four steps to a good forehand drive, a tennis player can easily win more games.
2. To perfect a forehand drive, a tennis player must learn four things.
3. In tennis, a dependable, fast, and accurate forehand drive will do more than anything else to discourage your opponents.
4. You can improve your tennis by learning a few facts about how to hit a forehand drive.
5. Any tennis player can develop a strong forehand drive.

EXERCISE 3.   Make your own list of topics to write about in a one-paragraph composition. From your list, select three topics. Plan what you will say about each of them, and write a clear topic sentence for a paragraph on each. Select one of the topic sentences and, using it as your opening sentence, write a paragraph of approximately 100 words.

A Paragraph Plan

The topic sentence states the general idea of a paragraph, but other sentences are needed to develop and support the topic sentence. To be sure that these other sentences provide effective support, plan your paragraph in advance. Write your topic sentence. Then make a list of the supporting ideas that will develop this sentence. Discard those that are not related to the main idea of the paragraph.

Notice that the writer of the following paragraph made a plan before writing the paragraph.

TOPIC SENTENCE   Prospecting for oil in California in the early days was often a strange and risky business.

SUPPORTING IDEAS   1. telltale explosion
2. prospecting by nose
3. the oilcloth test

Prospecting for oil in California in the early days was often a strange and risky business. Oil seekers got a wonderful clue one day when a cowhand lit a match and accidentally tossed it to the ground. It fell into a ground-squirrel burrow—and an explosion resulted that stampeded the cowhand's stock. The burning match had fallen into a hole full of natural gas which was the vapor from a petroleum seep. Prospectors began to look for other such telltale signs. They would sniff at holes in the ground to detect the odor of petroleum gas, and, if they caught a whiff, would drop a match into the hole. If a loud bang resulted, an oil seep had been located. The test was refined to detect fainter accumulations of gas: the prospector would erect a six-foot tent of oilcloth over a hole and stick a goose quill in the top of the tent. A few days later a match would be applied to the quill.

If a flame burned, it proved that gas from an oil seep was present, and the prospector would file a mineral claim on the land.

EXERCISE 4. Choose one of the following topic sentences. By answering the questions that follow it, find supporting ideas that develop the topic sentence. Make a plan for your paragraph and then write it.

1. The helicopter is a workhorse of the air. (What can a helicopter do that a fixed-wing plane cannot? How can these abilities be used in farming? rescue work? fighting forest fires? traffic control? inspecting power lines and pipelines?)
2. Vacationing at the seashore is fun. (What sports and activities can you participate in at the beach? What can you do if you just feel like loafing?)
3. A young person can earn money after school. (Have you ever mowed lawns? delivered for a department store or grocery? gardened? baby-sat? clerked?)
4. It is important to learn to be a good loser. (Can anybody win all the time? What are the harmful results of fretting and fuming about defeat? What are the advantages of taking a loss good-naturedly?)
5. Bike touring is an excellent way to travel. (Is it less expensive than train travel? Are the routes safe and clearly marked? What kinds of sights can one enjoy? What are the health benefits? Is it a popular sport?)
6. Baking a pie is a simple process. (What are the ingredients? What are the necessary steps? What mistakes should one avoid?)
7. My first airplane ride is still a vivid memory. (What was the destination? With whom did you go? What impressed you most about the plane? Was the take-off smooth? Were you frightened at any point?)

8. A best friend must have certain qualities. (What about loyalty? a sense of humor? the ability to sympathize when you are in trouble? What is the most important quality in a best friend?)

19d. Develop a paragraph by giving details or examples to support the main idea.

The topic sentence of a paragraph is always a general statement. It must be supported by a number of more specific statements which give additional information to make the main idea more meaningful. This information may be facts, examples, incidents, or reasons.

If your topic sentence were *The Mexicans who lived in the Southwest taught the settlers from the East many things,* you would need specific supporting examples. You could mention that the *vaqueros* showed the settlers how to handle cattle and to train horses. You might add that the Mexicans introduced high-horned saddles and *sombreros* to the new ranchers. In the following example about the American Revolution, numbers have been added to help you see the supporting details.

Most of the young soldiers had — topic sentence
very little schooling. They wrote
the way they talked, and it is amusing
today to see how they spelled. They
wrote ¹bums for bombs; ²warter for   (1–10) Support-
water; ³git for get; ⁴sartin for cer-   ing details
tain; ⁵arams for arms; ⁶Dullerway
for Delaware; ⁷cateridges for car-
tridges; ⁸Salletoga for Saratoga; and
⁹jest or jist for just. The names of

French officers must have been responsible for many troubled moments. We can almost see the young soldier scratching his head as he tries to figure out how to write the name of the Marquis de Lafayette. [10] In at least one instance, this puzzler came out as <u>Markis Delefit</u>.[1]

Examples are often used to support a topic sentence. In the following paragraph, the writer uses three examples to develop the topic sentence. Notice that each of these examples is developed more fully than any of the details in the paragraph above.

You'll see a block and tackle being used especially where heavy weights must be lifted or moved. — topic sentence

[1] Cranes, power shovels, and hoists make use of the block and tackle because it reduces the force that the engine must develop. (1) cranes and power shovels

[2] Of course, on sailing ships pulleys and block and tackle have been used for thousands of years for hoisting the sails and "trimming" them — pulling them into the right position. Perhaps the movable pulley was invented by a sailor! (2) on sailing ships

[1] From *Story of the American Nation* by Edward L. Biller, et al., published by Harcourt Brace Jovanovich, Inc. Reprinted by permission of the publisher.

[3] You may see painters or bricklayers (3) scaffolds
at work, standing on a scaffold that
is hung by a block and tackle at each
end. When they want to raise their
platform a bit higher, a small force
put into the block and tackle at each
end allows them to raise themselves,
the platform, and their equipment.[1]

EXERCISE 5. Develop one of the following topic
sentences and its supporting facts or examples into a
paragraph. You may add facts and examples if you
wish. If you prefer and your teacher approves, you
may make up a topic sentence of your own, find your
own facts or examples to support the topic sentence,
and then write a paragraph.

1. We remember and honor great events in our
   history by having national holidays.
   a. Memorial Day
   b. Fourth of July
   c. Labor Day
   d. Veteran's Day
2. Children are protected by safety regulations from
   the dangers of fast-moving traffic.
   a. crossing guards
   b. traffic signals and stop signs at pedestrian
      crossings
   c. rules against jaywalking
   d. speed laws

[1] From *You and Your Resources,* by Paul F. Brandwein, et al., published
by Harcourt Brace Jovanovich, Inc. Reprinted by permission of the
publisher.

3. The American public is deeply interested in sports events.
   a. sports sections in newspapers
   b. some popular magazines dealing solely with sports
   c. television and radio broadcasts of regular and special sports events
   d. crowded baseball parks and football stadiums
4. Thomas Alva Edison, who patented over a thousand inventions, provided us with many of our daily conveniences and pleasures.
   a. the electric light bulb
   b. the phonograph
   c. telephone improvements
   d. the moving-picture camera and projector
5. Our country has many kinds of climates.
   a. hot desert of Death Valley
   b. snow peaks of the Rockies
   c. warm beaches of Florida
   d. cool forests of Maine
6. Home accidents are often caused by children's carelessness.
   a. dropping pins or needles on the floor to be stepped on by bare feet
   b. pushing fingers or hairpins into electric outlets or television sets
   c. leaving skates on stairways
   d. playing with matches
7. We take for granted today many conveniences which were unknown fifty years ago.
   a. television
   b. automatic washers
   c. the speed of air travel
   d. no-iron fabrics
8. Many skills contribute to a winning football team.
   a. accurate passing
   b. speed and evasiveness
   c. determined blocking
   d. quick thinking

9. Through the centuries, people have found a number of ways to preserve food for long periods of time.
   a. pickling and preserving with spices
   b. curing and smoking meats
   c. canning a wide variety of foods
   d. freezing fresh fruits and vegetables
10. People living in a city have many places to visit in their leisure time.
    a. public parks
    b. libraries
    c. theaters
    d. museums

EXERCISE 6.   Write a paragraph of about 100 words in which you use one or more examples to explain or support the idea of the topic sentence. If you cannot think of a topic, here are some suggestions.

1. Unusual events can happen suddenly
2. Some jobs are more enjoyable than others
3. The treasures that money cannot buy
4. The ways a rainy day can be enjoyable
5. The reward of constant and consistent effort (Use an athlete's daily training as an example.)
6. How wood may be used in different ways

19e. Develop a paragraph by telling an incident.

Sometimes an incident or an anecdote can make the idea of the topic sentence more memorable to the reader. An incident follows the pattern of a story, but it is very brief and presents only the important details. If the incident is too long and too full of narrative details, then it may distract the reader from the topic being illustrated.

Notice, in the following paragraph about the Roman emperor Julius Caesar, how the incident gives the reader a lasting impression of Caesar's courage.

All his life, Julius Caesar was a proud and fearless soldier. As a youth, he was captured by pirates. When he learned that they demanded twenty talents [units of money] for his release, he jeered at them for underestimating the value of their prisoner and set the ransom at fifty talents. During his stay on the pirates' island, he treated his captors as servants. He joined in their games and read poems and speeches, which he composed, to them. When they failed to appreciate his work, he called them savages and threatened to have them hanged. After the ransom was paid, Caesar organized a force of men, sailed against the pirates, and captured them on their island. True to his promise, he executed them all.

— topic sentence

incident

EXERCISE 7. Select one of the following topic sentences to develop into a paragraph. Prove the point it makes with a good incident or anecdote. Make up your own topic sentence if you prefer.

1. My dog is a smart animal.
2. Some television programs teach you to expect good in people.
3. Unexpected company can be embarrassing.
4. Sometimes promises are hard to keep.
5. Mistakes are worthwhile if you learn from them.

6. Occasionally you make friends in unexpected ways.
7. Sometimes I am very lucky.
8. It is a mistake to lose your temper.
9. Cooking isn't as simple as it looks.
10. The first day at a new school can be unhappy.
11. Postponing one's homework is not a good idea.
12. A good friend is a help when you are in trouble.

19f. Develop a paragraph by giving reasons to support your main idea.

When your topic sentence states an opinion, give reasons to support the opinion. Persuading others that your opinion is correct depends a great deal on how convincing your reasons are. Suppose your topic sentence were *Our neighborhood needs a new swimming pool.* A reason like *I'm tired of going to the old swimming pool* would convince few people, if any. But if you pointed out that the neighborhood had grown and that the old pool was too small to accommodate everyone who wished to use it, then you would stand a good chance of persuading others.

The following paragraph begins with an opinion. Not everyone would agree with it, but the writer has given some persuasive reasons to support it.

There are several reasons for including a large portion of vegetables in one's daily diet. [1] Farm produce such as broccoli, celery, or squash is rich in the minerals and vitamins that a body needs for good health. [2] Vegetables are very low in calories and, therefore, are

topic sentence
reasons (1–4)
supporting
topic sentence

nonfattening. ³Cooking vegetables can be an enjoyable task because of the variety of recipes available in any vegetarian cookbook. ⁴In a time of rising food prices, the cost of fresh vegetables at the local supermarket is low when compared to the cost of meat products or processed foods.

EXERCISE 8. Develop one of the following topic sentences and its supporting reasons into a paragraph. If you prefer and your teacher approves, make up a topic sentence of your own and write a paragraph, developing the topic by giving reasons.

1. Young people should be given a regular weekly allowance.
   a. self-respect
   b. amount of allowance sets limit on spending
   c. permits planning and saving
   d. removes need of coaxing
2. All students should learn cooking in school.
   a. useful when camping
   b. to help out at home
   c. when grown, to help prepare meals for family
   d. to appreciate cooking more intelligently
3. Baby-sitting is a job that requires training.
   a. ability to treat cuts and bruises
   b. change and bathe a baby
   c. amuse a young child
   d. soothe a frightened child
   e. handle occasional emergencies
4. Young people should be responsible for a pet.
   a. to learn about needs, habits, character of some other living thing
   b. to develop concern for another's comfort

   c. to enjoy the love and companionship of a pet
5. A person my age should have a paying job.
   a. to earn spending money
   b. to develop self-confidence
   c. to develop a sense of responsibility and worth
   d. to learn a little about some line of work
   e. to contribute a little to the family living costs
6. Doing volunteer work in a local hospital is a step toward a career.
   a. helps develop concern for others
   b. helps develop ideals of behavior
   c. helps develop self-reliance
   d. helps acquire useful knowledge

EXERCISE 9. Write three topic sentences and make a plan for each. (See page 363.) The first plan, or outline, should develop the topic sentence by giving details or examples; the second should develop the topic sentence by telling an incident; the third, by giving reasons.

EXERCISE 10. Choose one of the plans you made for Exercise 9 and write a paragraph based on it.

UNITY IN PARAGRAPHS

19g. Every sentence in a paragraph should support the main idea expressed in the topic sentence.

All sentences in a paragraph should develop, explain, or prove the paragraph's main idea. A sentence that departs from the main idea contributes nothing to the paragraph. Furthermore, by wandering from the central topic, it confuses the reader.

   Each of the following paragraphs contains a sentence, in heavy type, that wanders from the central topic.

1

A device has recently been developed to enable a blind person to detect objects by sound. Many blind people use canes to probe for obstacles; this device uses a beam of sound instead. The blind person wears a transmitter, which sends out the beam, and a receiver, which gives a signal. If there is no obstacle in front, the blind person hears only a steady hum. If the beam of sound hits an obstacle, the hum grows louder. If the obstacle is very near, the hum becomes a screech, warning the blind person to stop or turn aside. **Books printed in braille also help blind people to overcome their handicap.**

2

The mamba, a huge African snake that can reach a length of fourteen feet, is one of the deadliest reptiles on earth. It hunts aggressively, preying on small animals. Afraid of nothing, the mamba will attack whatever or whoever crosses its path. **I came face to face with one of these fierce snakes at the Washington Zoo last summer.** The bite of a mamba is usually fatal unless the victim receives antiserum.

EXERCISE 11. In each of the following paragraphs there is a sentence that wanders from the main idea. Write the number of the paragraph. Then copy the unnecessary sentence.

1

The miners of Panamint faced the problem of how to prevent the silver bullion they shipped out on the stagecoaches from being seized by highwaymen. How, the miners debated, could they stop these holdups? It was impossible to send an army of guards along with each coach. Bill Stewart worked out a cheap, simple answer to the problem. Bill had made his first fortune in the Comstock mines. He sent his bullion out in an open wagon attended only by the driver, who carried no weapons of any kind. The plan worked. Thieves disgustedly let the bullion pass. For what could men on horseback do with silver bullion that had been melted and formed into a huge ball so heavy that they could not lift it?

2

The problem of water supplies, a concern all over the world, is related to the problem of food supplies. Millions and millions of acres that could produce crops to feed people and animals lie idle for lack of moisture. Millions of people go to bed hungry every night. Yet millions of gallons of water flow unused to the sea every second. Fast-flowing water deepens and widens riverbeds; slow-flowing water drops silt to fill the channels. The United States spends billions of dollars a year on soil and water projects. Other nations, too, must spend money and energy to bring water to unused land if the problem of growing enough food for their people is to be solved.

3

Many people consider the computer to be the most revolutionary invention of modern times. It can make calculations with dizzying speed, performing, in a matter of seconds, feats that would normally take a lifetime of human labor. A computer can sort through the mountains of data used in business or government and provide instantaneous, accurate answers to the most minute questions. The abacus, an ancient invention, is like a tiny computer. As new advances in computer design are made, a computer will become as common a household feature as television.

4

One of the dangers that a crew must guard against when drilling an oil well is a "blowout"—a sudden explosive rush of oil and gas up the drill pipe. Blowouts can hurl the heavy drilling tools out of the ground as if shot from a mile-long cannon, smashing the derrick, killing workers, and starting oil-well fires that may burn for months and waste much precious oil. The Lakeview #1, a famous California gusher, fortunately did not catch fire. To prevent blowouts, a device called a "blowout protector" is installed at the top of the drill hole. At the first warning rumble in the drill pipe, the crew can quickly shut the drill pipe at the top, sealing the oil and gas within the hole and protecting machinery and workers.

COHERENCE IN PARAGRAPHS

A paragraph is hard to read if the sentences do not follow each other in logical order. Each individual sentence may be good, and all the sentences may be directly related to the paragraph's main idea. But unless the sentences are arranged according to a logical plan, the reader will have no clear idea of what the paragraph is about. Paragraphs with a logical plan have the quality of *coherence*.

Arrangement of Ideas

19h. Arrange the ideas in a paragraph according to a definite plan.

There are a number of ways of arranging the ideas in a paragraph. Three of the most useful plans are *chronological order, spatial order,* and *order of importance.*

(1) Ideas in a paragraph may be arranged *chronologically.*

Chronological order—the order of time—is used most frequently in stories, where events are told in the order they happened. But chronological order is also useful in other kinds of writing. A paragraph explaining how to sew a hem or build a model plane will divide the explanation into steps and give these steps in the order they should be done. In the following paragraph, notice how the underlined words help you to follow the chronological steps in order.

> The fundamental technique for easy cycling is called ankling. The foot pivots at the ankle with each revolution of the crank. ¹Start at the top of the stroke (12 o'clock) with the heel slightly lower than the toes. ²Push with the ball of the foot and simultaneously pivot at the ankle on the downstroke so that the foot levels out, and continue this motion so that at the bottom of the stroke the toes are lower than the heel. ³With toe clips, pull up on the upstroke as well. The main thing to strive for is smoothness and steady, even pressure. ⁴Practice this slowly, in a high gear, and away from traffic so that you can concentrate on watching your feet.[1]

topic sentence

steps (1–4) arranged in order of time

(2) Ideas in a paragraph may be arranged *spatially.*

When you describe objects, the most useful plan is to deal with the objects in terms of their position. In

---

[1] From *Richard's Bicycle Book* by Richard Ballantine. Copyright © 1972 by Richard Ballantine. Reprinted by permission of Ballantine Books, a division of Random House, Inc.

describing a room, you might begin with the objects nearest you – the lamp, the sofa – and finally describe the objects farthest from you – the painting on the wall, the plants on the windowsill. If you were describing the parts of an object, you would also deal with them in terms of position. For example, a description of a car might begin with the front bumper, headlights, and fenders, pass on to the dashboard and seats, and conclude with the taillights, trunk, and rear bumper. When you arrange your sentences according to the position of the objects, you are using *spatial order*.

The following description of the earth's composition proceeds from the outer layers of the earth to the inner layers.

Earth scientists have discovered that the earth is composed of a number of layers. ¹The outside layer, called the crust, is hard rock, which varies in thickness. In many places it is twenty or thirty miles thick, but beneath some parts of the sea it has a thickness of only three miles. ²Inside the crust, there is a layer about 1,800 miles deep called the mantle, which is composed of flowing rock. ³Beneath the mantle is the outer core, a layer about 1,300 miles thick and thought to be liquid iron. ⁴Finally, there is the inner core, which is a ball of hot, solid metal.

topic sentence

details (1–4) arranged in order of position (spatially)

(3) Ideas in a paragraph may be arranged in *order of importance*.

Items in a paragraph that do not involve time or position can often be arranged in order of importance. This plan is especially useful when the topic sentence is a statement of opinion and the other sentences present supporting reasons. You may use the order of least important to most important or of most important to least important. Either plan helps your reader to see the connection between sentences and so to understand your paragraph.

The following paragraph uses the order of least important to most important.

> Our class needs a student news- — topic sentence
> paper. [1]A newspaper can entertain   reasons (1–4)
> the class by printing interesting   in order of
> news about students. [2]It can an-   increasing
>   importance
> nounce important events like a
> basketball game or Halloween party.
> [3]The money raised from sales can
> be donated to a worthy cause or
> used to buy a gift for the school.
> [4]Most important, a student news-
> paper can provide valuable training
> for students by letting them write for
> readers their own age.

EXERCISE 12. Choose three of the following topics and write a topic sentence and paragraph plan for each. Your first plan should use chronological order; your second plan should use spatial order; and your third plan should use order of importance.

1. A typical morning at your house
2. How to iron a dress
3. Why an after-school job is a valuable experience
4. The appearance of your assembly hall
5. The thrilling conclusion of a basketball (or baseball or football) game
6. Raising a farm animal
7. The importance of physical fitness
8. How a particular bicycle looks (your own or a friend's)
9. The advantages of living on a farm (or in a big city)
10. Your reasons for choosing a particular career

Transitional Words and Expressions

19i. Use transitional expressions to make clear the organization of a paragraph.

Well-planned sentences follow one another naturally in a paragraph. Sometimes, however, it is wise to provide clues that help the reader to follow your train of thought more easily. Words that show the relation of one sentence to another within the paragraph are called *transitional expressions.* The underlined words in the paragraphs on pages 377, 378, and 379 are examples.

Transitional expressions can be classified according to the kind of relationship they show.

CHRONOLOGICAL

first	later	formerly
then	soon	after
meanwhile	now	finally

SPATIAL

outside	near	above
inside	behind	to the right (left)
beyond	ahead	in the distance

BETWEEN IDEAS

furthermore	in fact	therefore
moreover	in conclusion	on the other hand
similarly	however	as a result
in addition	consequently	on the contrary

The transitional expressions in the following paragraph are printed in heavy type. Notice how they help the reader understand the plan behind the paragraph and the relationship between the sentences.

The first plastic was invented as the result of a contest. After the War Between the States, the game of billiards became very popular, and a great demand arose for billiard balls, which had always been made of ivory. Now there was not nearly enough ivory to meet the demand. **Consequently,** one firm offered a prize of ten thousand dollars for a good substitute. A young printer, John Wesley Hyatt, mixed cellulose, nitric acid, and camphor, and produced a substance which was called "celluloid." This new substance did not prove to be suitable for billiard balls, and Hyatt did not win the prize. **However,** the invention turned out to be worth a great deal more than ten thousand dollars. **Soon** many articles were being made from this plastic. **As a result,** Hyatt became wealthy.

EXERCISE 13. Write a paragraph based on one of the paragraph plans you prepared for Exercise 12. Underline the transitional expressions you use.

REVIEW EXERCISE. Write a paragraph of 100 words or more on a topic from the list below or on some other topic of your choice. Follow a definite plan of organization—chronological, spatial, or order of importance, whichever is appropriate. Be sure that you have a good topic sentence and that you support it with sufficient details or examples, with an incident, or with reasons.

1. A sport I would rather watch than play
2. If I could travel anywhere I wished
3. Baking an angel food cake
4. A person I admire
5. How to make a bird feeder, bookends, magazine rack, etc.
6. How to tune a guitar
7. The layout of the front page of a newspaper
8. What I dislike (or like) about television commercials
9. The fictional character I would most like to be
10. My favorite holiday

TYPES OF PARAGRAPHS

The Narrative Paragraph

As you know, a narrative is a story. A narrative paragraph, then, is a paragraph-length story. It may be a story about you or something that has happened to you. Or it may be a story in which you are not directly involved.

A narrative paragraph begins with a general statement—like a topic sentence—which tells the reader what the story will be about. For example, the following sentence could introduce a narrative paragraph: "One day when I was nine years old, I learned the dangers of telling a lie." This sentence leads into the story of what happened to the writer as a result of telling a lie.

Notice three things about the following model of a narrative paragraph:

1. The paragraph begins with an introductory statement which arouses the reader's interest.

2. The order of details is chronological — the order in which the events happened.
3. The writer uses description and narrative details to make her story vivid.

Model Narrative Paragraph

It was when I was fifteen that I had a curious experience which made a lasting impression on me. I was walking with our gamekeeper on his afternoon round. We had seen a fair number of deer before we sat down to rest on the edge of a forest glade. Soon a roebuck appeared and made his way to the side of a little brook, nibbling as he went. The light was waning and the stillness of the forest seemed to enhance the beauty of the animal as it moved toward us. I remember that I was actually reflecting on the senselessness of shooting such a perfect creature when the keeper handed me his rifle, telling me to shoot the roebuck because its antlers were malformed. I aimed, shot, and killed. What had I done? How could I think so lovingly of the deer and a moment later kill it? Would I ever be able to trust myself again? Then, before we strung the buck on a pole, the keeper proudly presented me with a twig of pine dipped in the animal's blood. At dinner the twig was still in my buttonhole and my uncle, who was a keen sportsman, congratulated me on getting my first buck, but I felt like a murderess and vowed never again to shoot for sport.[1]

In the model, Joy Adamson writes about a memorable experience that happened to her. She, the writer, is the main character in her own story. This narrative model is called a *first-person narrative* because the

[1] From *The Searching Spirit* by Joy Adamson. Published in the United States by Harcourt Brace Jovanovich, Inc. and in Great Britain by William Collins Sons & Co. Ltd. Reprinted by permission of the publishers.

writer (I) is involved in the action of the story. In another kind of narrative, the *third-person narrative,* the writer is not involved in the action. The following model is an example.

Model Narrative Paragraph

The cat saw he would not find another home, and he moved off, nosing and feeling his way from one garden to another, through empty houses, finally into an old churchyard. This graveyard already had a couple of stray cats in it, and he joined them. It was the beginning of a community of stray cats going wild. They killed birds and field mice that lived among the grasses, and they drank from puddles. Before winter had ended, the cats had had a hard time of it from thirst, during the two long spells when the ground froze and there was snow and no puddles. Birds were hard to catch because the cats were so easy to see against the clean white. But on the whole they managed quite well. One of the cats was female, and soon there were a swarm of wild cats, as wild as if they did not live in the middle of a city surrounded by streets and houses.[1]

Before beginning a narrative paragraph, always decide whether you, the writer, will be involved in the action of the story. Do not mix first- and third-person narrative in a story.

EXERCISE 14. Search your memory for something that you think would make an interesting narrative paragraph. Write an introductory sentence and tell the story in one paragraph, approximately 100–150 words.

[1] From "An Old Woman and Her Cat" by Doris Lessing. Copyright © 1963, 64, 68, 69, 71, 72 by Doris Lessing. Reprinted by permission of the Author and her Agents, James Brown Associates, Inc. and Curtis Brown.

The following topics may suggest an idea for a story.

1. Are animals able to think?
2. A great day for the team
3. An experiment that didn't work
4. A good time regretted by all
5. A big surprise
6. Lost!
7. A bad mistake
8. Minding the store
9. A secret well kept
10. A chore that turned out to be fun

The Descriptive Paragraph

A descriptive paragraph is one that gives a picture in words. It may picture a place (a park, a street, a house, a lake), a person (a character in a story, a TV personality, a friend), a happening (a picnic, a family gathering, school recess), or an object (a piece of furniture, a car, a musical instrument). A descriptive paragraph is frequently part of a story. Its purpose is to describe people and places so that the reader can experience the story fully.

A descriptive paragraph need not be long, but it should be vivid. Action verbs, adjectives that describe size, shape, and color, and adverbs that describe actions must be carefully chosen to make a clear picture. Never be satisfied with the first descriptive word or phrase that occurs to you; hunt for the best. If possible, use words that appeal to the senses — sight, sound, smell, touch, and taste.

The opening sentence of a descriptive paragraph tells the reader what is going to be described. The rest of the paragraph supplies the necessary details.

The following model paragraph describes a walk in a tropical rain forest. The writer makes the experience vivid by giving details that appeal to our senses. As you read, notice which senses are included.

Model Descriptive Paragraph

I remember my first walk in a Nigerian rain forest. It is moist and the air is soft, a comforting warm smell actually made by the fungi underfoot. The trunks of the great trees rise straight up and tall, set out like pillars along the nave of a great Gothic cathedral. Clouds float between the branches, drifting patches of vapor that come and go. The trees branch out at about a hundred feet. Where there is a break in the canopy, light streams through against the rising mist in rays that you can see. I remember how an ugly dead growth on the branch of one tree suddenly opened in at the middle and said, "Gronk." It was a giant yellow casque hornbill. I remember, too, how the silence that made me place my feet so carefully was broken as frogs began to sing, then more frogs and more until the song swept into the distance and stopped as suddenly as it had begun.[1]

The Order of Details in a Description

When you write a description, you should pay special attention to the order in which you mention the details. In a description in which the author remains more or less stationary, the details are arranged spatially. In other words, they are so arranged that the location of each part of the picture is clear. Review rule (2), page 377. Spatial arrangement is used in the following model paragraph about a quilt.

---

[1] From "Remembrances of a Rain Forest" by Paul Colinvaux in *The Nature Conservancy News,* July/August, 1979. Reprinted by permission of the publisher.

Model Descriptive Paragraph

A quilt is a simple project. It consists usually of a bottom lining, a stuffing of cotton or wool, a top lining, and the top itself. But there the simplicity stops. The top is made of a number of separate squares joined either side to side, or separated from each other by cloth borders. Thus a quilt that measures sixty by eighty inches might take forty-eight 10-inch squares, sixteen 13-inch ones [plus separating borders], or any of a number of other combinations. Each square is usually identical in pattern but distinctive in color.[1]

This paragraph first describes the layers of a quilt. Then it discusses the arrangement and dimensions of the squares that make up the top layer. It ends with the mention of the pattern and color that make up each square.

Another method for arranging details is chronological order. The author of the model about the rain forest, for example, gives details about the forest in the order in which he comes upon them during his walk.

EXERCISE 15. Search your memory for a place, a person, a happening, a scene, or an object that you can describe in a brief paragraph—approximately 75 words. Fashion a clear and interesting introductory sentence. Write the paragraph so that your reader will see clearly what you are describing. If you need suggestions, you may find the following helpful.

[1] From *The Foxfire Book* by Eliot Wigginton. Copyright © 1968, 1969, 1970, 1971, 1972 by The Foxfire Fund, Inc. Reprinted by permission of Doubleday & Company, Inc.

1. Your favorite house, room, store, view, road
2. Your favorite friend, relative, neighbor, actor, singer, entertainer, athlete, teacher
3. Your favorite church, theater, museum, monument
4. Your favorite possession

The Expository Paragraph

An expository paragraph gives information about a single topic or explains a single topic for the reader. You may often find paragraphs that inform in a daily newspaper. An article about a warehouse fire, for example, may contain paragraphs that give information on the size of the fire, the location of the warehouse, the efforts of the firefighters, and so on. You can find paragraphs that explain in any textbook or reference book. These paragraphs may tell you how to study maps, how to fix a leaky faucet, or how to grow a small cactus. Explanatory paragraphs can also tell why something happens: for example, why leap years occur, why the tides rise and fall, or why we protect bald eagles. Expository paragraphs are usually developed by facts or reasons.

The purpose of the following model is to give information about the ocean. The paragraph is developed by facts that relate to the size and depth of the world's oceans.

Model Expository Paragraph

The ocean covers 71 percent of the Earth's surface. But what we see is, of course, only the top of it. On the average, the ocean is 2.3 miles (3.7 kilometers) deep. The total volume of the ocean is about 300 million cubic miles (1,200 million cubic kilometers). That means if you built a square tank 36 miles (58 kilometers) on each side and poured all the ocean water into it, you would have to build the walls as high as the Moon in order to hold it all.[1]

The following model is explanatory. Its purpose is to explain why most lightning victims in the past were church-bell ringers.

Model Expository Paragraph

In past centuries, most lightning victims were bell ringers in churches. More than a hundred of them died in Germany between 1753 and 1783, because of the practice of sounding the bells during storms. The custom dates to the time of Charlemagne, and is variously explained as a storm warning system, a way to drive off evil spirits, or an attempt at breaking the continuity of the lightning path with the bell sounds. Martin Uman of the University of Florida, author of *Understanding Lightning,* writes that medieval church bells were often inscribed "Fulgura fango," or "I break the lightning." But it was the bell ringer who got broken, attached as he was by his rope to the metal bell in the tallest part of the spire, in a building set apart from all the rest.[2]

The order of details in an expository paragraph depends on the kind of exposition involved. In an informational paragraph, the facts may be stated in any order that is clear. If you are writing about an event, you may give the facts in chronological, or time order. If you are simply listing a number of facts about a subject, you may consider putting the most important fact last as a kind of climax. In an explanation of how to do or how to make something, the details

---

[1] From "The Ocean" in *Asimov On Numbers* by Isaac Asimov. Copyright © 1977 by Isaac Asimov. Reprinted by permission of the author.

[2] From "Jove's Thunderbolt" by Dava Sobel in *Harvard* Magazine. Copyright © 1979, Harvard Magazine, Inc. Reprinted by permission of the publisher.

are almost always arranged chronologically because a process is being explained step by step.

EXERCISE 16. By thinking for a while, you may discover that you know the material for some subjects about which you can write an expository paragraph, either informational or explanatory. For example, you know enough about the school you attend to write an informational paragraph about it, and you know enough about your community to do the same. Other subjects may be suggested by the items in the following list.

Informational
  Equipment and supplies needed for an overnight hike
  My typical day's schedule
  Characteristics I like in a teacher
  The work of an airport traffic controller
  The language of teen-agers
  Some interesting places to visit in this community
Explanatory
  How to load a camera
  How to make cookies
  How to clean a room
  How to change a tire
  How to perform on the parallel bars
  How to save money when shopping
  How to plan a party
  Why I like (do not like) to travel with my family
  Why I will vote for ——
  Why an accident occurred

Chapter 20

The Composition

Planning and Writing an Expository Composition

Although compositions may be of varying lengths – some no longer than a paragraph – the word *composition* usually means a piece of writing of at least 250 to 300 words that is divided into several paragraphs. Of course, the right length for any particular composition depends on the subject and the amount of information presented about it. The minimum of 250 to 300 words is intended only to give you a general idea.

The *expository* composition, like the expository paragraph (see pages 388–90), presents a certain amount of information about a subject. All writing presents some information; a narrative about a family incident may well contain some facts about your house or neighborhood, the members of your family, and so on. In expository writing, however, the information is the main thing. The object is to tell the readers something they may not know and to tell them in a way that they will understand. You can see that exposition is a very important kind of writing. Most things we know we learn from other people, and a great many of these things we learn through reading. In your lifetime you have accumulated a great deal of information that will be interesting or helpful to others. To present it clearly and well, you will need the skills that are discussed in this chapter.

SELECTING A SUBJECT

Some of the compositions you write this year will be on subjects assigned by your teacher. For these, you will simply have to be sure that you understand the assignment and know how to find the information that you will need. At other times, you will probably be able to choose a subject of your own. Such a choice may be the most important decision you make in planning and writing your composition. It requires careful thought.

20a. Choose a subject that you know something about.

The best subject is one that you know well. Nuclear submarines and rocket engines are interesting, but the chances are that you are not an expert on either. On the other hand, you may know a lot about stamp or coin collecting—how to start a collection, where to obtain specimens, what pleasures and advantages this hobby offers. Such a subject, which you can write about from your own experience, is an excellent possibility for a composition. If you stop to think about it, there are a number of things that you know about. Your whole experience is raw material for compositions.

A good composition, of course, need not always be about things you have done yourself. Much of what you know has come to you secondhand from books and other sources. If you have done considerable reading about the War Between the States, the Pony Express, the Gold Rush, or the early days of aviation, you have information that could be the basis of a good composition. As a rule, however, such a subject should be one that you know already, not one that you have to read up on extensively before you write.

EXERCISE 1. Think of two subjects from your own experience that you could use for compositions and two more that you know about mainly from books, magazine articles, or other sources. List the four subjects, indicating which are from your experience and which are from other sources. Choose your subjects carefully. You will be working with one or more of them in later exercises.

20b. Limit your topic.

If you have to write 300 words or more, you may think that a broad, general subject will do better than a smaller one. It is true of course that there is more to say about "The History of Aviation" than about "The Wright Brothers' First Flight." The trouble is, there is too much that *has* to be said about a large subject. Whole books have been written about the history of aviation. All that a short composition on this subject can do is make a number of general statements without the supporting details that would make such statements meaningful. Exposition calls for precise, detailed information. The larger the topic, the more details you have to deal with.

Your composition will not succeed unless its subject is well chosen and well developed for the reader. When you have thought of a subject, therefore, it is essential that you consider whether it is manageable in the number of words you have in mind. For example, stamp collecting may provide you with an idea for a composition, but the whole subject is too large. On the other hand, a composition telling how to get started with a stamp collection is a limited topic just right for a 300-word composition.

EXERCISE 2. Five of the subjects listed below are too general to make good composition topics. Five are limited enough to be suitable. Write *S* after the number of each suitable topic. For the broad general topics, write a smaller but related topic that would do for a short composition.

EXAMPLES   1. Spring cleaning at our house
                      1. *S*
                      2. Sports
                      2. *Our neighborhood baseball team*

1. The youth of an American President
2. Preparing for an overnight hike
3. Mystery stories
4. Agriculture in Africa
5. Profile of a local disc jockey
6. Pioneer life
7. Air pollution
8. Starting a vegetable garden
9. Hunting for snakes
10. The civil rights movement

20c. Remember the purpose of your composition.

In general, all expository compositions make explanations. However, the specific purpose you have in mind should guide you first in limiting your topic and then in selecting details and planning the composition. Suppose you have decided to write about fish. If your purpose is to show that fish are an essential part of anyone's diet, you will limit your topic in one way. If it is to show how to catch a trout, you will limit the topic in another way. Before you settle on a definite topic to write about, be sure that you can state your purpose.

EXERCISE 3. Write a statement of purpose for each of the topics that you listed in Exercise 1. You may revise the original topics if you wish.

EXAMPLE   1. *Keeping goldfish as pets* [topic]
To explain the proper methods of feeding and caring for goldfish [statement of purpose]

EXERCISE 4. Write a composition of 250–300 words on one of the topics from Exercise 1. Include, at the top of your paper, the statement of purpose that you worked out for Exercise 3 above. As you write, keep this purpose in mind and consider whether what you are saying really carries it out.

PLANNING A COMPOSITION

20d. Plan your composition before writing.

You have already had some practice in making a plan for a paragraph. Since a composition is usually longer and more complicated than a paragraph, there is even more need for a careful plan. The final result of the planning you do for a composition will be a topic outline (see pages 403–04), but there are several important steps that come first.

(1) Make a list of ideas.

Once you have chosen a topic, jot down ideas as they occur to you. At this stage, do not try to organize the ideas. Simply list any details or ideas that may be related to your topic.

When you have completed your list, eliminate any ideas that are not closely related to the topic. In exposition, as in most other kinds of writing, what you leave out can be as important as what you put in. By crossing a poorly related idea from your list, you can often improve your paper greatly.

TOPIC   Beginning a stamp collection
PURPOSE To explain how to collect and display stamps

educational value
family mail
hobby stores
removing stamps from envelopes
fun of watching collection grow
learning locations of countries
appreciating beauty of stamps
history of postage stamps [eliminated because it does not contribute to purpose of composition]

learning about people and customs of foreign lands
mounting stamps in album
supplies: tongs, hinges, album
post office
stamp packets
approval sheets
valuable stamps [eliminated because a beginning collector would not ordinarily try to acquire valuable stamps]

EXERCISE 5. The following list contains several unnecessary ideas. Copy them on your paper. Be prepared to give reasons for your choices.

TOPIC   Repairing a bicycle
PURPOSE To show how to make simple repairs on a bicycle

adjusting the handlebars
long-distance bicycling
streets vs. dirt roads
removing the chain
locating a tire puncture

safety helmets
selecting a bicycle
locking the bicycle
measuring the height of the seat

EXERCISE 6. Prepare a list of about ten ideas on a topic of your own choice. You may use one of the topics from Exercise 2, if you wish. At the top of your list, write a title and statement of purpose. Later on you will be asked to write a composition on this subject.

(2) Group your ideas under headings.

Now that you have listed your ideas and eliminated the unsuitable ones, you are ready to begin grouping closely related ideas together. To do this, you must consider whether two or more ideas have something in common — whether there is a larger idea that includes them. For example, here are six of the ideas from "Beginning a Stamp Collection" (page 396):

1. fun of watching collection grow
2. removing stamps from envelopes
3. learning about people and customs of foreign lands
4. appreciating beauty of stamps
5. learning locations of countries
6. educational value

A quick glance tells us that some of these ideas are related and some are not. There is an obvious connection between numbers 1 and 4, both of which involve pleasure or enjoyment. A similar connection exists between 3, 5, and 6, all of which have something to do with the educational aspect of collecting stamps. Only 2 does not combine with a related idea.

Once you have grouped your ideas by finding a larger idea that they have in common, it is an easy step to give each group a heading. You simply express the central idea of the group in a word or phrase. For example, we grouped the following items together since they both dealt with pleasure, or enjoyment:

1. fun of watching collection grow
4. appreciating beauty of stamps

We need only choose between *pleasure* and *enjoyment*, and we have a heading for the group. Suppose we choose pleasure:

Pleasure
    fun of watching collection grow
    appreciating beauty of stamps

It will be easier to find a heading for the group including 3, 5, and 6:

    3. learning about people and customs of foreign lands
    5. learning locations of countries
    6. educational value

Obviously, 3 and 5 describe specific educational values of collecting. Therefore, the heading for this group is supplied by one of the ideas from the list itself:

Educational value
    learning about people and customs of foreign lands
    learning locations of countries

By following the same general process of grouping ideas and adding heads, the complete list of ideas for the composition on stamp collecting would look like this:

Pleasure   heading
    fun of watching collection grow ⎫
    appreciating beauty of stamps   ⎬ related ideas
Educational value   heading
    learning about people
        and customs of foreign lands ⎫
    learning locations of countries ⎬ related ideas

Sources of stamps   heading
   family mail   }
   hobby stores | related
   post office   } ideas
   stamp dealers }
Displaying stamps   heading
   removing stamps from envelopes }
   supplies: tongs, hinges, album } related ideas
   mounting stamps in album }

Perhaps the process of grouping is not quite finished. Our first two headings have more similarity than we noticed at first—they are, in fact, the reasons for collecting stamps. Therefore we can combine our first two groups into one:

Reasons for collecting stamps   heading
   Pleasure   subheading
      fun of watching collection grow }
      appreciating beauty of stamps } related ideas
   Educational value   subheading
      learning about people and customs }
        of foreign lands } related ideas
      learning locations of countries }

Notice that indention is used to show that ideas are grouped under headings.

EXERCISE 7. The ideas for each of the following topics can be organized under two separate headings. First write the topic as a title. Then supply appropriate headings and list related ideas under each heading.

EXAMPLE   1. Baking a cake
              Mixing ingredients; flour; shortening; rolling dough; setting oven; sugar; eggs

1. *How to Bake a Cake*

Ingredients	*Procedure*
flour	*mixing*
shortening	*ingredients*
sugar	*rolling dough*
eggs	*setting oven*

1. School activities
   Glee club; football; baseball; science club; drama club
2. Model planes
   Balsa wood; sharp knife; cutting out parts; gluing parts together; blueprints; paint; painting; glue
3. Encyclopedias
   Using the index to find information on a topic; gaining additional information from maps and charts; finding topic alphabetically by title; skimming to find needed facts; taking notes on the article

20e. Make an outline.

An outline has the same relation to the composition you will be writing as an architect's blueprint has to the finished building. You have already limited your topic and listed supporting details, crossing out those that have no real bearing on the purpose of your composition. You have grouped related ideas under suitable headings.

The purpose of your outline is to show all of the ideas and headings that will go into the composition in the order you will take them up and in the relation they have to each other. It is possible that you may find a reason for changing your plan slightly once you have started writing. In that case, revise your outline accordingly. Preparing an outline is not just an extra job. It will make the writing much easier.

There is a conventional form for outlines which you should learn to use. The main ideas in the composition are indicated by Roman numerals (I, II, etc.). These will usually be the heads under which you grouped related ideas earlier (see page 398). In the outline for a composition on "Beginning a Stamp Collection," for example, the first Roman numeral head might be

    I. Reasons for collecting stamps

Notice that the heading itself begins with a capital and that it is not a complete sentence. This will be true of all of the heads in the kind of outline (*topic outline*) you are working with.

The idea expressed in the first head indicates that several reasons will be given. If each of the reasons is taken up separately, each will become a subheading under the main heading. These divisions of the main idea are indicated on an outline with capital letters:

    I. Reasons for collecting stamps
       A. Pleasure
       B. Educational value

Notice that the subheadings are indented to show that they are divisions of the idea marked with the Roman numeral. Since the subheadings are divisions, there must obviously be at least two of them. An outline should never have just one subhead under a main head. The reason for this is that subheads are used to divide the main heads into smaller parts, and whenever you divide *anything,* you must end up with at least two parts.

IMPROPER   I. Reasons for collecting stamps
             A. Pleasure
         II. Sources for the collector

If the only reason for starting a collection is

pleasure, then the Roman numeral heading should be revised and the isolated subheading eliminated:

BETTER   I. The pleasure of collecting stamps
            II. Sources for the collector
            etc.

If either or both of the subheadings can be further divided, a further indention is made and the new and smaller ideas are marked with Arabic numerals (1, 2, etc.):

  I. Reasons for collecting stamps
     A. Pleasure
        1. Fun of watching collection grow
        2. Appreciating beauty of stamps
     B. Educational value
        1. Learning about people and customs of for-
           eign lands
        2. Learning locations of countries
 II. etc.

For most short papers, these levels of headings and subheadings will be sufficient. If you wish to make still smaller divisions, the following skeleton outline shows how it is done:

  I.
    A.
      1.
      2.
        a.
        b.
    B.
 II. etc.

Arranging groups of related ideas in outline form will help you to find a clear and logical order of presentation. Often the ideas themselves suggest the proper method of arrangement. For example, the topics in an outline for a composition about producing a play might follow the order of time: choosing the play, casting the play, rehearsing the play. A composition on "Our Obligations," on the other hand, might call for topics arranged from the most general to the most specific: obligations to our country, obligations to our community, obligations to our family.

The major topics for "Beginning a Stamp Collection" may be arranged in order of time. Certainly the idea of "acquiring stamps" belongs before that of "displaying stamps," and "reasons for collecting stamps" comes before either. The complete topic outline on this subject would look something like this:

TITLE   Beginning a Stamp Collection [title not part of outline]

PURPOSE   To give reasons for collecting stamps and to show how to get started

   I. Reasons for collecting stamps
     A. Pleasure
       1. Fun of watching collection grow
       2. Appreciating beauty of stamps
     B. Educational value
       1. Learning about people and customs of foreign lands
       2. Learning locations of countries
  II. Sources for the collector
     A. Family mail
     B. Post office
     C. Hobby stores
     D. Stamp dealers
       1. Packets
       2. Approval sheets
 III. Stamp display
     A. Supplies
       1. Album
       2. Hinges
       3. Tongs

    B. Procedure
      1. Removing from envelopes
      2. Mounting in album
IV. Specialization

Notice that a fourth main idea has been added to provide a conclusion for the composition. The writer has told how to start a collection; he wants to end by giving the reader some idea of a more advanced kind of collecting. The problems of writing a conclusion are discussed later in this chapter.

EXERCISE 8. Copy the incomplete outline at the left. Then fill in the blanks with the topics given at the right.

OUR SCIENCE CLUB

PURPOSE   To explain how our science club began and to show its activities

I. Formation of club	Holding elections
A.	Tours of laboratories
B.	Recruiting members
C.	Discussions of current
1. Campaigning	scientific developments
for office	Raising an ant colony
2.	Choosing a name
D. Writing the club	Industrial laboratories
constitution	Electing officers
II.	Club activities
A.	Studying a bacterial
1. Government	mold
laboratories	
2.	
B. Projects	
1.	
2.	
C. Talks by eminent speakers	
D.	

EXERCISE 9.   Arrange the following ideas and details into an outline. Include a statement of purpose. Your outline, like the one on pages 403–04, should have three levels.

TAKING A CAMPING TRIP

Major ideas
      Camp health and safety
      Planning
      Setting up camp

Supporting ideas and details

Selecting equipment	Dry ground
Making a fire	Safety when hiking
Safety tips	Arranging the wood
Setting up tents	Tents
Presence of fuel	Purifying water
Knives, hatchets, and axes	Safety in the water
Chopping wood	Choosing a campground
Selecting clothing	Bedding
Personal health	Food, pans, plates, spoons, etc.

EXERCISE 10.   Convert the list of ideas which you made for Exercise 6 into an outline. Include a title, a statement of purpose, at least two main headings, and supporting ideas for each main heading. Later you will use this outline to write a composition.

WRITING THE COMPOSITION

20f. Learn the basic parts of a composition: introduction, body, conclusion.

An expository composition has three basic parts. The *introduction* should prepare the reader by indicating the general purpose and subject of the composition. Notice that the sample composition on pages 407–09 begins, "Stamp collecting is a very popular hobby for several reasons." This sentence not only gives the basic idea of the paragraph, it also leads to the basic purpose of the composition—to tell how to begin a stamp collection.

The *body* is the longest part of a composition and contains most of the information. It carries out the purpose indicated by the introduction. In the sample composition, the body consists of the second, third, fourth, fifth, and sixth paragraphs, which develop ideas given in parts II and III of the sample outline.

The *conclusion* brings the composition to a definite close, and should not be long or complicated. One way of ending a composition is to sum up some of the points made earlier. Notice that the last sentence of the sample composition restates the main idea of the first paragraph.

In a short composition, the introduction and the conclusion need not be longer than one or two sentences.

20g. Use transitional expressions to connect paragraphs.

In Chapter 19, you studied one use of transitional expressions—connecting sentences within a paragraph. Transitional expressions are also used to make a smooth connection between successive paragraphs in a composition. As the following list indicates, most transitional words can join paragraphs as well as separate sentences.

first	furthermore	besides
then	moreover	thus
next	therefore	for example
in addition	nevertheless	in fact
even more	on the other hand	finally

BEGINNING A STAMP COLLECTION

Stamp collecting is a very popular hobby for several reasons. Collectors gain pleasure from the varied colors and designs of the stamps, while they enjoy the fun of watching their collections grow. In addition, stamp collecting has educational value. Stamps often tell the collector much about a country's important customs, events, and famous citizens. Furthermore, collectors soon learn to find out the exact location of a country. Often they are interested enough to find out other important facts about that country.

Beginning collectors can start with family mail. A variety of stamps can be collected from the letters and packages the average family receives. If a relative or family friend happens to be living overseas, another valuable source is available.

In addition, the collector can get domestic stamps at the post office. Some large post offices have special windows for new stamps, but all post offices have the new stamps. Foreign stamps can often be bought in hobby stores or ordered from stamp dealers.

introduction

(reasons for collecting stamps—I, A–B in outline)

body

(acquiring stamps—II, A in outline)

(II, B–C in outline)

(II, D in outline)

In fact, stamp dealers who advertise in magazines (often in magazines popular with young people) are an important source of stamps for all collectors. Most dealers offer beginners a packet of assorted stamps at a low price. After collectors have acquired many common stamps, they may be interested in dealers' approval sheets. Stamps on an approval sheet are usually less common than those in the packets; each is mounted and priced separately. Collectors keep any stamp they want and send their money and the remaining stamps back to the dealer.

(displaying stamps—III, A in outline)

Most collectors display their stamps in albums. Albums for beginners usually have sections for the different countries and pictures of some of the stamps. Besides an album, a collector needs stamp tongs —a sort of tweezers—and hinges, small bits of gummed paper that connect the stamp to the album page.

(outline III, B)

Stamps taken from the family mail, as well as many included in the packets that come from dealers, have to be removed from the part of the envelope to which they are still sticking. To remove the stamp, the collector first places it face down on a blotter and moistens the envelope paper with warm water. After the paper is thoroughly soaked, the stamp can usually be easily removed. By working slowly and carefully with the tongs, the collector can avoid tearing or otherwise damaging the stamp. To mount the stamp in an album, the collector allows it to dry, then folds a hinge with the gummed side out, moistens it, and attaches the stamp to the page.

After beginners have had a taste of the pleasure of collecting, they are likely to want to specialize. For example, they may wish to concentrate on stamps of a particular country, or on those that have ships or certain animals on them. Whether they specialize or not, however, they are certain to gain much enjoyment and knowledge from their hobby.

conclusion
(specializing —
IV in outline)

20h. Revise your composition.

When you have completed the first draft of your composition, take the time to read and revise your paper carefully. You will be looking for omitted words, grammatical errors, and mistakes in spelling, of course; however, you should also be looking for ideas that are not as clearly expressed as they could be, sentences that have an awkward sound, paragraphs that do not adequately develop their topic sentences, and so on. Be sure to read the composition aloud and to listen for sentence completeness and variety.

The following checklist will serve as a guide to revision:

REVISION CHECKLIST

1. Rewrite confusing sentences and paragraphs.
2. Omit unnecessary details.
3. Omit unnecessary words and phrases.
4. Check all punctuation.
5. Look for common spelling errors.

EXERCISE 11. Write a composition based on the outline you made for Exercise 10. If you have second thoughts about the subject for your composition, you may revise your outline now. Use the checklist above as a guide to revision before you hand in your composition.

SUMMARY

1. Choose a subject you know, either from personal experience or reading.

2. Limit your topic and decide the purpose of your composition.

3. Jot down ideas.

4. Organize these ideas in an outline.

5. Write the first draft.

6. Revise carefully.

Chapter **21**

Writing Summaries and Reports

Gathering and Organizing Information

All through school and in your later life as well, you will be called upon to find information and report on it in your own words. No skill that you study this year will be more useful—not just in English classes, but in all of your other courses as well. Skill in gathering information and reporting on it is not difficult to acquire if you keep a few simple steps in mind.

SUMMARIES

The simplest kind of report is the *summary,* an account in your own words of a longer piece of writing.

21a. In writing a summary, give in your own words the main ideas of the original article.

The main point of a summary is to provide a short, handy account of a longer piece of writing. To be useful, a summary should be no longer than one third the length of the original.

To write a summary, first read the article or other piece of writing carefully. Then go through it again, this time jotting down the main ideas. Now write your summary, restating the main ideas briefly. Be sure to state the ideas in your own words. At the end give the source of the original article.

ORIGINAL ARTICLE

Halley's comet is a brilliant comet named for the English astronomer Edmund Halley. Historical records show that Halley's comet was seen as long ago as 240 B.C. It reappears every 76 to 79 years.

From the earth, Halley's comet can be seen only as it nears the sun. It was last near the sun on April 24, 1910, approaching as close as 55 million miles (89 million kilometers). Scientists at Helwan Observatory, in Egypt, photographed it in August, 1909. It was then about 300 million miles (480 million kilometers) from the sun. It became brighter as it approached the sun and the earth. In early May, 1910, the comet's head was as brilliant as the brightest stars. Its great tail stretched about two thirds the distance from the horizon to directly overhead. Halley's comet came as close to the earth as 14 million miles (23 million kilometers) on May 20, 1910. On the next day, the earth is believed to have passed through the comet's tail. Halley's comet was last observed with a camera on July 1, 1911. Halley's comet will return and reach its closest point to the sun on February 9, 1986.[1]

SUMMARY

Halley's comet, named for the English astronomer Edmund Halley, can be seen every 76 to 79 years. When it last appeared in 1910, the comet looked like a brilliant star and its tail stretched high above the

[1] From *The World Book Encyclopedia.* © 1980 World Book-Childcraft International, Inc. Reprinted by permission of the publisher.

horizon. In the same year, the earth may have passed through the comet's great tail. Halley's comet will come into view again in 1986.

Notice that the article is 195 words long while the summary is only 61 words, less than a third as long. Notice also that the summary omits details about exact distances and exact days. Instead it concentrates on what the comet looks like and in what years the comet approaches the earth.

EXERCISE 1. Write a summary of the following article. Read the entire article before beginning your summary. Try to limit the summary to less than 100 words.

UNLOCKING EARTH'S TREASURE OF IRON

America's great industrial output is based upon a plentiful supply of steel made from our rich resources of iron. Many years ago, however, industry faced a limit to its production: lack of iron ore. Enough ore for only a dozen years or so remained.

Our deposits of rich ore were almost gone. We had, however, enormous deposits of lean iron ore — enough to last us for centuries. Unfortunately, this lean ore, called *taconite,* was held in rock so hard that it could not be mined. Even when this taconite was broken up by great effort, the particles of iron could not be separated from the very hard rock which held them. The iron we needed so urgently was locked so tightly into the ground that we could not free it.

Then a key was found! Engineers developed a machine called a *jet-piercer.* This machine is an enormous blowtorch that spurts oxygen and kerosene and a jet of water. The tremendous flame causes the water to explode into steam. The combination of shooting fire and steam tears a hole in the hard ore, into which explosives can be lowered to blast the taconite apart.

Another problem still remained. How could the tiny particles of iron be separated from the hard rock? Researchers ground the iron very fine, as fine as sugar or face powder. Then they ran a huge magnet over the ore. The iron particles were lifted out of the powder and they clung to the magnet! In this way the iron was separated from the waste rock.

Still the iron powder could not be used to make steel. The powder was so fine that, if dumped into a blast furnace, it would simply be blown out. The researchers finally solved this problem by putting the powder into a slanting drum, adding water, and revolving the drum. The motion caused damp particles of iron to cling together and to form into balls the size of marbles. These marbles, given a heat treatment to harden them, could be used in blast furnaces. The treasure of iron had finally been unlocked from the earth by a key of flame.

EXERCISE 2. Write a summary of the following paragraphs, bringing out the main points. The paragraphs have a total of 465 words. Your summary should be no more than a third as long.

American English is one of the most standardized languages in the world today. There are differences in words and expressions, and there are differences in pronunciation from one locality to another, but few of them are such as to cause us any real trouble in understanding one another. A person who lives in a place as far in the extreme southeast of the nation as Key West, Florida, can move to a city as far in the extreme northwest as Seattle, Washington, and not have the least bit of trouble talking to new neighbors or understanding and being understood by them. In the same manner a person who lives as far in the northeast as Portland, Maine, can transfer to a new home, job, or school in a city as far southwest as Los Angeles, and not have any real language difficulties. We are so used to this fact and take it so much for granted that we hardly ever stop to think about it or appreciate it. And yet we should, because it is very important to us all, personally and as a nation.

Few other nations have so uniform a language. Even in England, for instance, where English was born and where it had been growing and developing for at least a thousand years before it came to America, you will find many dialects, which are sublanguages, or little languages within the big language, and these dialects differ so much from one another in the way words are pronounced or used that very often people speaking these different dialects cannot understand one another. This can happen in England, and it can also happen in almost any other country. Great national languages, like French, Italian, German, Russian, Chinese, are broken up into so many different dialects on their home soil that traveling around from one part of the country to another can be almost as difficult for the people who live there as it would be traveling in a foreign country whose language they didn't know at all.

But this does not happen in the United States. You can drive across the nation, you can move your home, your activities, your entire life to any part of the country that you want to without having any real language problems to face in doing so. It means that Americans as a nation are able to work together and play together; they are able to exchange ideas, and to share the same ideals; it has bound us more closely as Americans, and it helps us to have and build a strong, united nation.[1]

EXERCISE 3. Summarize one of the following.

1. A magazine article related to material your social studies class is studying
2. An encyclopedia article
3. A newspaper article
4. A chapter in a science book
5. A magazine profile of a historical figure or a celebrity in the news
6. An editorial that gives reasons for supporting or opposing an important local issue

LONGER REPORTS

A more challenging kind of report, which you will often be asked to write, requires you to gather and organize information from a number of different sources. In writing this kind of report, there are three basic steps:

1. Gathering information
2. Organizing the information
3. Writing and revising the report

Before you begin to search for information, however, you should have a good idea of what kinds of information to include and what not to include.

21b. Know your assignment.

Sometimes you will be asked to choose your own topic for a report. Then you face the same problems as in writing other kinds of compositions: finding a

[1] From *Our Language: The Story of the Words We Use* by Eloise Lambert. Copyright © 1955 by Lothrop, Lee & Shepard Co., Inc. Reprinted by permission of the publisher.

topic and limiting it. (See pages 392–93.) The best kind of topic to choose is one in which you are already interested and about which you wish to learn more.

Often your teacher will assign you a topic. Be sure you understand the assignment and know how long your report is to be. In a report, as in other kinds of writing, it is important to omit unnecessary details. Knowing your assignment will help you judge which details are necessary and which unnecessary.

For example, if you were asked to write a report on the duties and responsibilities of the governor of your state, you might tell how the governor supervises the work of various state institutions and departments and administers the laws passed by the state legislature. You would not describe how a candidate for governor campaigns for election, recount stories about past governors, or tell about the duties of other public officials such as mayors or members of Congress.

Gathering Information

21c. Find sources of information about your topic.

Usually, the reference section of your library is the best place to begin gathering information. An encyclopedia or other general reference work will usually provide you with a good introduction to your subject. Depending on your subject, you may find additional information in more specialized reference books. (For a more detailed discussion of reference books, see pages 487–94.)

Reference books usually provide a more or less general introduction to a subject. For more detail, you must find books and magazine articles about it. To find books on your subject, you will be making use of the card catalogue (described on pages 484–86). Unless your subject is a broad one, it may be treated in *parts* of several books but not be the subject of a whole book itself. In this case, you will need to use the indexes of some of the books the card catalogue directs you to in order to find the information you need.

To find what has been written about your subject in magazines, consult the *Readers' Guide to Periodical Literature* (described in detail on pages 492–93).

EXERCISE 4. Choose one of the following topics, and look up four sources of information about it. At least one source should be an article in an encyclopedia or other reference book; at least one should be a book (or part of a book) on the subject. Write your topic on a sheet of paper and list the four sources below it. For each, give title, author (if given), and number of pages devoted to the subject. If one of the sources is a periodical, give the name and date of the publication, as well as title and author of the article.

1. How the Declaration of Independence was written
2. The national park system
3. The history of Esperanto
4. The debate over the Equal Rights Amendment
5. Jane Addams' contributions to social work
6. The early days of aviation
7. The invention of television
8. Asteroids
9. The Egyptian pyramids
10. Renewable energy sources

21d. Take notes on your reading.

You cannot hope to remember all the details of information that you collect without taking notes.

The most efficient way to take notes is to write them on cards or slips of paper, using a different card for each note. Early in your reading, you will find that the subject matter of your report falls into a number of general divisions or topics. As soon as you have three or four of these, you can use them as headings for your note cards. When you find information that would come under one of these headings, you write the heading at the top of the note card and write the notes under it. When you find useful material that does not fit under one of the headings, make up a new heading. The list of headings will form a working outline of your report. As you read and take notes, you will be continually revising the working outline. Every note card must have a heading showing the general subject. Following the notes, give the source: the title, author, and page number of a book; the name, date, article title and author, and page number of a magazine article.

Write notes in your own words. Occasionally you may need to quote the exact words used in the source, but it is much better to rephrase the information in your own words. If you do use an exact quotation, be sure to put quotation marks around it. Copying a writer's words without using quotation marks is completely unacceptable in a report or in any other writing.

Taking notes on cards or slips has a great advantage: when you come to write your final outline, you can arrange the cards in the order in which you plan to use them.

Suppose you are preparing a report on the importance of seafood. You have consulted an encyclopedia (see sample note card next page) and the card catalogue, where you found books that deal with your subject: *Conserving Natural Resources* by Shirley W. Allen, *World Sea Fisheries* by Robert Morgan, *The*

Seafood resources
    The food resources of the sea seem limitless. However, some species of fish must be protected from extinction.
    Compton's Encyclopedia
    Volume 5 p.116

Sample Note Card

Sun, the Sea, and Tomorrow by F. G. Walton Smith and Henry Chapin, and *The Sea Against Hunger* by C. P. Idyll. After reading the encyclopedia article, which gives an overall view of the subject, you decide that you will deal with the following three main topics in your report:

    I. Need for seafood
    II. Kinds of seafood
    III. Utilizing our seafood resources

These topics are the beginning of a working outline.

On page 10 of *The Sea Against Hunger,* you find this information:

> "Fish is approximately 70–75 percent water, 19 percent protein, 5 percent fat, 3 percent nitrogen, and 1 percent phosphorus. . . . The nutritional value of fish protein is equal to that of protein from beef, veal, lamb, or pork . . . ."[1]

[1] From *The Sea Against Hunger* by C. P. Idyll. Published by Thomas Y. Crowell. Copyright © 1970 by C. P. Idyll. Reprinted by permission of Harper & Row, Publishers, Inc.

> Need for seafood
>   Fish, which is almost 20 percent
> protein, offers the same protein value
> as most types of meat.
>   The Sea Against Hunger
>   by C.P. Idyll
>   p. 10

This information deals with the first of the topics in your working outline—*Need for seafood*. On a note card you jot down this topic as a heading. Below it you record in your own words the information you want. Finally, you write the source of your information.

In another book you find other useful information as follows:

"Tunny. (Tuna.) A group of large and voracious species frequenting warm water, the largest of which (the bluefin tuna: *Thunnus thynnus*) reaches a length of 10 feet and a weight of over half a ton. . . .

"Tuna are caught in large quantities by the U.S.A. and Japan and in fairly large quantities by France and Spain."[1]

This information deals with the second of the topics in your working outline—*Kinds of seafood*. Since you will have additional cards dealing with other kinds of seafood, you will make the heading on your note card read "Kinds of seafood—tuna."

[1] From *World Sea Fisheries* by Robert Morgan, published by Pitman Publishing Co.

> *Kinds of seafood - tuna*
>
> *Individual bluefin tuna grow as long as 3 meters with a weight of over half a metric ton.*
>
> *Japan and the U.S.A. catch the most tuna.*
>
> <u>*World Sea Fisheries*</u>
> *by Robert Morgan*
> *p. 41*

As you continue taking notes, you will follow the same procedure: (1) Write the heading at the top of the note card. (2) Write the information in your own words. (3) Write the source at the bottom.

EXERCISE 5. Choose a topic for a report which you will later write. Be sure the topic is not too large to cover in one report. If necessary, review the material in the previous chapter on limiting your topic. (See pages 393–94.)

Find information about your topic in at least four different sources (including reference books), and take notes on cards or slips of paper. Prepare at least ten note cards on your topic. Each note should include a heading, the notes, and the source of information, including the page number. (If your teacher asks you to hand in your notes, prepare an additional card giving your name and the name of your topic and place it in front of the other cards.)

If you have difficulty in finding a topic, here are some suggestions. Some of these topics are too broad to cover in a short report and must be limited before you begin to take notes.

1. Ways in which an electromagnet is used
2. The sinking of the *Titanic*
3. Balloon racing
4. The preparation and use of cosmetics
5. Women in federal and state government
6. The story of silkworms
7. The cause and cure of air pollution
8. New kinds of aircraft and what they do
9. The history of devices for telling time
10. Plant life in the desert
11. Pioneer photographers
12. Rain-making
13. The differences between a bird's eye and the human eye
14. The history of a game that interests you
15. The need for flood control
16. A particular fashion in women's clothing
17. The work of a landscape architect
18. An endangered species
19. Research in space medicine
20. Animals of the Arctic
21. How a play is produced
22. The Equal Rights Amendment
23. The discovery of penicillin
24. The research of Marie Curie
25. The work of Martin Luther King, Jr.

Organizing the Report

21e. Organize your notes according to their headings.

Now that you have made notes for your report, you must prepare them for use. You may discover that some information is duplicated or that some facts do not fit your topic as you have limited it. Eliminate such notes. Next organize your notes by sorting the cards in piles according to their headings. You will then have in one pile all the information on one heading, or topic. If you follow these steps, your final out-

line will take shape, and you will have organized all
the information for your report.

21f. Make a final outline based on your notes.

Study this final outline for the report on seafood.

FOOD FROM THE SEA

   I. Need for seafood
      A. Lack of sufficient meat for much of the
         world's population
      B. Fish as an abundant source of food
  II. Kinds of seafood
      A. Fish
        1. Herring
        2. Salmon
        3. Tuna
        4. Halibut
        5. Cod
      B. Shellfish
        1. Oysters
        2. Clams
        3. Scallops
 III. Utilizing our sea resources
      A. The sea as a potential food source
      B. Need to protect individual species of fish

EXERCISE 6. Prepare a complete outline for your
own report based on the notes written for Exercise 5.
(To review outlining, see pages 400–04.)

Writing the Report

21g. Using your final outline and your notes, write
your report.

You have gathered information, and you have organized your material in the form of an outline. As
you write, observe the following suggestions.

1. Be sure you understand all the terms you use. If uncertain, look up the words in the dictionary.

2. As you write, keep in mind the basic parts of a composition: *introduction, body, conclusion.* (See pages 405–06.) Make your introduction interesting. It is important to catch your reader's attention at the outset.

3. Use your own words in writing the report. It is tempting to copy a passage from a book, but copying is not writing. Introduce quotations only when they are particularly apt or striking.

4. Put every necessary detail into your report, but omit unnecessary items. Stick to your subject.

5. Give details in their proper order, using your outline as a guide.

6. At the end of the report, list the sources from which you got your information.

EXERCISE 7. Write a first draft of your report. Be sure the report is in your own words and that it has an introduction, a body, and a conclusion.

REVISION CHECKLIST

Content
1. Does the report contain enough information?
2. Are all the facts accurate?

Construction and Style
3. Does your report have an introduction and a con-clusion?
4. Do the title and opening paragraph arouse the reader's interest?
5. Is each paragraph constructed around one idea?
6. Are your sentences complete? Have you avoided sentence fragments and run-on sentences?
7. Are your sentences varied to avoid monotony?

Form

8. Does your paper have a heading—name, class, and date?
9. Is there a title? Is it capitalized properly?
10. Are there one-inch margins at the left and right?
11. Is your name on each page of the report? Are the pages numbered?
12. Is the first line of each paragraph indented?
13. Are your sources listed at the end of the report?
14. Is the penmanship legible? Is the paper neat?

Revising Your Report

The first draft of any writing assignment is rarely free of errors. It is always wise to go over a piece of writing to locate any errors and correct them. Since a report may contain errors of fact as well as writing errors, you should be especially careful in revising it. In making your revisions, use the checklist above.

Here is the final copy of the report on seafood. Notice that the opening paragraphs provide an introduction and the final paragraph a conclusion to the report. The body of the report is concerned with the different kinds of seafood available.

THE SEA'S HARVEST

The world does not raise enough cattle, sheep, and other meat animals to provide food for all its people. As a result, much of the world's population is underfed. According to the United Nations Food and Agricultural Organization, meat production would have to increase enormously each year to deliver enough food—especially protein—for every person. This just cannot be done.

Fortunately, seafood, which is equal in protein value to most kinds of meat, is in abundant supply. Feeding an increasing world population will be possible if more and more food is taken from the sea.

Fish such as herring, salmon, tuna, halibut, and cod provide most of the world's seafood. They offer both nourishment and variety at dinner tables.

Herring are small yet make a large contribution to the world's diet. Types of this fish are especially important to countries such as Norway, Japan, and the United States. A very nutritious fish, herring can be served fresh or preserved in various ways.

Salmon and tuna are also important seafoods, particularly in canned form. Alaska, which is a major producer of salmon in the United States, packs and ships this fish to countries around the world. Most of the world's supply of tuna is caught by fishing crews from the United States and Japan. The tuna, unlike the herring, is usually a very large fish. A single bluefin tuna can grow as long as 3 meters and weigh over half a metric ton.

Most halibut come from waters off the coast of the United States and Canada. Like tuna, halibut are large fish, growing up to 2 meters long and weighing as much as 135 kilograms. Millions of cod, another important food fish, are taken each year from the Atlantic. Cod-liver oil is one major product of this catch.

Shellfish also contribute to the world's food supply. Oysters, clams, scallops, lobsters, and shrimp are highly prized seafoods and are enjoyed in many places around the world. In the United States, millions of kilograms of oysters are consumed each year. Although the United States harvests more oysters annually than any other country, Japan, Canada, and New Zealand also produce large catches. The United States is a major source as well of the world's supply of scallops and clams.

Seafood totaling billions of kilograms is harvested each year, but this amount is only a small portion of the available food resources in the sea. The world can thus increase its food supply by taking more food from the sea, where the resources seem unlimited. Great care, however, must be taken against overfishing any single species. Some varieties of sardines and salmon have already nearly vanished from the oceans. As more and more seafood is caught, rules must protect species threatened by extinction.

Sources   *Compton's Encyclopedia,* Vol. 5
           Conserving Natural Resources by Shirley W. Allen
           The Sea Against Hunger by C. P. Idyll
           The Sun, the Sea, and Tomorrow by F. G. Walton Smith and Henry Chapin
           World Sea Fisheries by Robert Morgan

EXERCISE 8. Write the final draft of your report. If your teacher says so, hand in your outline and first draft with it.

BOOK REPORTS

A book report gives two kinds of information: what the book is about and what you thought of it.

The first and usually longer part of a book report tells what the book is about. This should include only the book's highlights. If you are reporting on a novel, indicate the background of the story — time, place, main characters. Give a general idea of what happens and mention some of the main characters. Avoid getting bogged down in details. If you are reporting on a nonfiction book, summarize the important information given. If you are reporting on a biography, indicate why the person written about is important, and mention chief incidents in that person's life.

The second part of a book report may be shorter

than the first, but it is just as important. It gives your reaction to the book and shows how perceptively and intelligently you have read it. Give specific reasons for liking or disliking the book. Tell why others might share your opinion. A statement like *I enjoyed this book because I am interested in horses* tells little about a book. The following sentence is a better beginning for a statement of opinion: *This book is clearly and vividly written and presents much interesting information about horses.*

When you write a book report, keep these guides in mind:

Guides

1. Give the title of the book and the name of the author. Underline the title when you write it.

2. When you tell what happened (or happens) in a book, decide on past or present tense and stick to it. Avoid shifting from present to past or past to present.

3. When you summarize a nonfiction book, be sure that you understand everything you describe and that your summary of complicated information is clearly written.

4. In your statement of opinion, tell how the book has influenced your thinking or ambitions. Use examples to support your ideas.

Chapter 22

Writing Letters

Friendly Letters, Social Notes, Business Letters

Receiving letters from friends is always a satisfying experience. It is interesting to learn what they have seen and done recently, what they think, and what has happened to mutual friends. However, you will not receive many letters unless you reply to them.

When you begin to write a letter, you may think: But I don't have anything to say! A moment's thought will show that this is untrue. What do you want to learn from friends' letters? What questions do you want answered? Probably they have the same kinds of questions to ask you.

FRIENDLY LETTERS

22a. In a friendly letter, write about the things that interest you and the person to whom you are writing.

Before you write a friendly letter, jot down your ideas. Include news that will interest your friend. Think of your friend's letter to you. Were there any questions or comments that need a reply? As you write, keep in mind the person who will receive your letter. You would not send the same kind of letter to a friend you met at summer camp as to your favorite uncle.

Study the following example of a friendly letter. Would you say that Bill is thinking of his friend Tom as he writes? Why? How would this letter be different if it were written to Bill's aunt?

1849 West Sixth Street
Los Angeles, California 90014
April 14, 1981

Dear Tom,

    You asked what Carl and I have been up to lately. Well, Carl is taking care of a horse for friends of his parents, but he's afraid to ride it. I said I'd ride it. You know me — no brains.

    That horse jumped suddenly high into the air and tried to throw me off. I stayed on, though, until it reared straight up and fell over backwards. Carl's dad ran over to me. He was mad, but all he said was that maybe we'd better put the horse back in the stable.

    You asked what I'm doing for the Science Fair at school. Carl and I have taken photographs of cloud formations. We are mounting these photographs for an exhibit on weather forecasting.

    How about letting me know what you're doing?

               Sincerely,
               Bill

22b. Choose stationery and ink that are appropriate for a friendly letter.

Use letter stationery. White is always appropriate, though other colors may be used. *Never use lined paper.*

Write in ink, never in pencil. (If you can type *well,* type your letters.) Avoid ink blots and erasures. Keep your writing neatly spaced and properly aligned; crowded lines that climb or stagger or droop give a bad impression. Make your margins wide; try to keep them equal on top and bottom as well as on the sides.

Try to estimate in advance how long your letter will be. A brief letter may require only one page. If you use folded stationery and the letter runs to two pages, do not write on the back of page one but skip over to page three. If the letter is longer than two pages, use the page order of a book; write the second page on the back of the first, and so on.

22c. Follow generally accepted rules for the form of a friendly letter.

The form of a friendly letter is not hard to master. Study the following instructions and example.

1. *Heading*

The *heading* tells when and where the letter was written. It consists of three lines, placed at the upper right corner of the page. The address of the writer is placed on the first two lines, and the date on which the letter was written is placed on the third. Note that a comma is used between city and state and between the date of the month and the year. The zip code num-

18 Prince Street
Houston, Texas 77008
April 14, 1981

Dear Bob,

_____

_____

_____

_____

_____

_____

Sincerely yours,
Jim

Form of a Friendly Letter

ber appears several spaces after the state and on the same line. There is no punctuation at the ends of the lines.

Two kinds of headings are appropriate in a friendly letter. The example shown on this page is in *block style*. That is, the second and third lines of the heading begin directly below the beginning of the first line.

Another style that is often used for handwritten friendly letters is *indented style,* in which the heading looks like this:

2534 Polk Place
Portland, Oregon 97235
May 6, 1982

2. *Salutation*

The *salutation* begins at the left-hand margin and is placed a short distance below the heading. In a friendly letter, it is followed by a comma.

3. *Body*

The *body* of a friendly letter is the message, what you have to say. It may begin directly below the end of the salutation, or may be indented about an inch from the left margin. The first line of each paragraph that follows must be indented the same distance.

4. *Closing*

The *closing* for a friendly letter may be *Your friend, Sincerely, Sincerely yours,* or any similar phrase you like, except *Yours truly* and *Very truly yours,* which are used only on business letters. It is placed just below the final line of the letter, beginning a little to the right of the middle of the page, and is followed by a comma. Only the first word of the closing begins with a capital.

5. *Signature*

The signature in a friendly letter need be only your first name. Center it under the closing. Always write the signature by hand, even if you have typed the rest of the letter.

EXERCISE 1. Make a list of experiences you've had in the last few days. Using this list as a basis, write a letter to a friend of your own age. Follow the instructions on the preceding pages concerning both content and form.

EXERCISE 2. Using the list you prepared for Exercise 1, write a letter to a relative or to an adult friend. As you write, keep in mind the receiver of your letter. In class, discuss how your two letters differ.

Addressing the Envelope

The envelope of a letter should be addressed with care. The letter may not be delivered if the address is carelessly written. The zip code number should always be included. There should always be a return address so that the post office may return the letter if your correspondent has moved.

Study the following instructions and example.

1. Place the return address in the upper left corner of the envelope.

2. Place the address of the person to whom the letter is going just below the middle and to the left of the center of the envelope.

3. If the letter is going to an adult, write a title before the name: *Mr., Mrs., Ms., Dr.,* and so on. Do not put a title before your name in the return address.

4. Write the state on a separate line, as in the example, or on the same line as the city. Put a comma after the city if the state is written on the same line. Place the zip code number several spaces after the state.

5. If you use *Post Office Box, Rural Free Delivery,* or *Rural Route* in the address, you may use abbreviations: *P.O. Box 351, R.F.D. 1,* or *R.R. 1.*

Susan Froelich
597 Spruce Street
Kansas City, Kansas 66143

> *Miss Astrid Addison*
> *89 Kirkland Street*
> *Cambridge*
> *Massachusetts 02127*

A Model Envelope

EXERCISE 3. Using your ruler, draw the outlines of four envelopes. Then address the "envelopes," using the following information. Use your own return address for each one.

1. miss edna a burns   16 casita way
   omaha nebraska   68138
2. mrs h b byerley   111 orchid way
   st louis missouri   63149
3. ms ellen craig   p o box 753
   butte montana   59601
4. dr n t bain   r r 8
   winamac indiana   46996

EXERCISE 4. Choose one of the following situations and write the letter it suggests. If you prefer to invent your own situation, you may do so. Address an envelope for your letter.

1. You are visiting relatives in another city, and they have taken you to see a World Series game. Write to your parents, telling them about the visit and the game.

2. A friend who lived nearby has moved some distance away. Give her recent news about your neighborhood and ask questions about her new home and neighborhood.
3. You are a CB radio operator and have been exchanging messages with a CB radio hobbyist in another town. Invite him to visit you. Describe the members of your family and tell him about the fun he will have on his visit. If you like, tell him about other CB operators you have contacted.
4. You are a 4-H Club member. At a recent 4-H convention you made friends with a member from another part of the state. Write a letter to your new friend, telling about recent club activities and the exhibit you are busily preparing for the 4-H Club county fair.
5. You have recently attended a wedding. Write to a friend or relative, describing the events of the wedding: the ceremony, the reception, the behavior of the bride and groom and their parents, your own reactions.
6. Write to a friend who is in the hospital. Tell her you are looking for a job but that you can't decide where to look first. Ask her to suggest some ideas. Describe your interests and the kinds of careers you are considering.
7. You have been elected secretary of your club. Write to a friend or relative, describing the club, its purpose, and its members.
8. Write to an older brother or sister at college. Tell about your own progress at school and ask questions about college life.

Folding the Letter

If your letter stationery consists of a folded page, fold it in half and insert it, fold first, into the envelope.

If the stationery is a single sheet of the same width as the envelope, fold the bottom third up, then the top third down, and insert it into the envelope, with the last fold first. See the illustrations on pages 446–47.

SOCIAL NOTES

22d. Write prompt, courteous social notes.

Social notes are written for a limited purpose, such as to extend or accept an invitation, or to thank someone for a gift or favor. Such notes generally follow the form of a friendly letter and are written on personal stationery. If they are brief, they may be written on correspondence cards.

Since you will have many occasions to write social notes, you should learn to write them properly.

The Thank-You Note

After receiving a gift or favor from someone whom you cannot immediately thank in person, you should write a thank-you note. Always write promptly. A delay gives the impression that you do not really appreciate the gift. A thank-you note will seem less like a duty letter if you write about something else as well, and if you give specific reasons for your gratitude.

Study the thank-you note on the opposite page. Has Tony thanked his uncle properly?

EXERCISE 5. Write a thank-you note and address an envelope for one of the following situations, or choose a situation of your own.

1. A friend, who lives in another city, has sent you a new sweater for your birthday.
2. An aunt, who owns her own company, has sent

641 Ardmore Avenue
Philadelphia, Pennsylvania 19153
June 3, 1981

Dear Uncle Harry,

Thanks ever so much for the model plane engine. I'm having a lot of fun with it. The other boys tell me that a Junior Wasp model like this is very dependable. It starts easily and runs with no trouble. I've been running it on a breaking-in block. It's surprising how much roar such a tiny engine has! I'm eager to finish building my model. I know this engine will really make it zoom.

The folks gave me some fine birthday presents too; but I suspect that I'll remember this birthday most of all because of your wonderful gift.

Your nephew,
Tony

A Thank-You Note

you a share of her company's stock for graduation.
3. Your grandmother, who lives in another town, has sent you ten dollars for your birthday.
4. An older cousin, who is with the army in Europe, has sent you a set of dolls in the native costumes of various countries.
5. A family friend, on a trip to Mexico, has sent you a fine, brilliantly colored blanket.

The Bread-and-Butter Note

Occasionally you are invited to visit friends or relatives who live out of town, and you spend several days with them. After you return home, you must write a note to your hosts — your friend's parents, or the adult or adults really responsible for your comfort — to thank them for their kindness to you. This note, commonly called a "bread-and-butter" note, should be written promptly. Tell your hosts how much you enjoyed your stay and appreciated their efforts to make your visit pleasant. Mention some of the things they did for you. Put yourself in your hosts' place: wouldn't you like to hear that the trouble you went to, in order to make sure that a guest had a good visit, is remembered with a glow of pleasure? Your hosts will be interested, too, in what kind of trip you had returning home, so it is appropriate to mention that briefly.

Study the sample bread-and-butter note. Notice that, like the thank-you note, it follows the form of a friendly letter.

EXERCISE 6. Write a bread-and-butter note expressing thanks for the hospitality you received on a recent visit, or imagine that you were in one of the following situations, and write a bread-and-butter note.

1. A friend's family has taken you with them on a canoe trip along a mountain stream.
2. While your mother was ill in a hospital, you stayed with your grandmother. She lives on a big farm.
3. An uncle has taken you to an amusement park and paid for all your rides.
4. An aunt has taken you on a trip to New York City,

34 Casa Grande Drive
Berkeley, California 94713
August 6, 1981

Dear Mr. and Mrs. De Stefano,

Ever since I got home, I've been thinking about the wonderful week I spent with your family in Yosemite Park. The park had always been a sort of picture album place to me, and now I've got my own snapshots of it! But the outdoor scenery was only part of the pleasure of camping with your family. Waking up in the morning to the smell of frying bacon and eggs, hiking up the steep trails and coming back to cool off with a swim in the river, sitting around the campfire singing and telling stories — I'll remember these things for a long time. Thanks ever so much for having me as a guest.

Please tell Helen I'll send her some of my snapshots as soon as they are ready.

Sincerely yours,
Nora Davis

A "Bread-and-Butter" Note

where you visited the Empire State Building, the United Nations Building, and the Statue of Liberty.

5. You spent your summer vacation with your older married sister and her husband. They live in a nearby town and have two small children.

BUSINESS LETTERS

You may have already written a business letter on your own. Perhaps you have ordered goods from a firm or requested information from an institution or government department. Later you will have occasion to write other business letters when you apply for a job or entrance to a school or when you request travel reservations and theater tickets. Such letters are important in our daily lives, and you should learn to write them clearly and correctly.

22e. Follow generally accepted rules for the form of a business letter.

Business firms use printed business stationery in two sizes: $8\frac{1}{2} \times 11$ inches, and (for brief letters) $5\frac{1}{2} \times 8\frac{1}{2}$ inches. You should use unruled white paper of standard typewriter size: $8\frac{1}{2} \times 11$ inches. If you type well, it is always advisable to type your business letters. If you do not type well, however, write carefully with pen and ink.

Make your letter neat and attractive. Center it on the page, leaving equal margins on the right and left sides and on top and bottom. Avoid ink blots, erasures, and crossed-out words. Write only on one side of the page.

The form of a business letter is somewhat different from that of a personal letter. One important difference is that a business letter always includes an *inside address*. Study the following instructions and example.

1. *Heading*

A business address always requires a complete heading: street address on the first line; city, state, and zip code number on the second line, with a comma between the city and state; date on the third line, with

567 Hardwood Street
San Diego, California 92128
December 10, 1981

Mr. John Anders
Acme Sporting Goods Company
33 Norton Avenue
Cleveland, Ohio 44105

Dear Mr. Anders:

_____

_____

_____

_____

_____

Very truly yours,

Donald Hayes

Donald Hayes

Form for a Business Letter

a comma between the day and the year. It is better not to abbreviate the month and the state.

Block style, not indented style, should be used in the heading of a business letter.

2. *Inside Address*

A business letter, for filing purposes, requires an inside address, which gives the name and the address of the person or the firm (sometimes both) to whom you are writing. A comma is used between the city and state, and the zip code number appears several spaces, or about one-quarter inch, after the state. Place the inside address four typewriter lines below the heading and on the other side of the page, flush with the left-hand margin.

3. *Salutation*

The salutation is placed two typewriter lines below the inside address, flush with the left-hand margin. It is followed by a colon, not a comma as in a friendly letter.

The kind of salutation you use will vary. Writing to a person whose name you have used in the inside address, it is proper to say *Dear Mr. ——:* (or *Dear Miss ——:* or *Dear Mrs. ——:* or *Dear Ms. ——:*).

EXAMPLE   Ms. S. E. Sorenson, Circulation Manager
Astronomy Magazine
67 East Eighth Street
New York, New York   10003

Dear Ms. Sorenson:

If you are writing to a person whose name you do not know, but whose official position you do know, you say *Dear Sir:* or *Dear Madam:*

EXAMPLE   Public Relations Director
State Oil Company
317 Bush Street
Dallas, Texas   75243

Dear Sir:

     or

Dear Madam:

If, however, you are writing not to a particular individual but to a group or a company, you may use an
impersonal salutation (*Customer Service:, Editors:*)
or the traditional salutation (*Gentlemen:*). When you
use the traditional salutation, it is understood that the
group you are writing to may be composed of both
men and women.

EXAMPLE   Bradley Electronics Corp.
             56 La Mesa Drive
             Lafayette, California   94549

             Mail Order Department:

4. *Body*

The first sentence of the body of a business letter
begins two typewriter lines below the salutation; that
is, the same distance that the salutation is below the
inside address. This first line may be indented about
an inch or the length of the salutation. The first lines
of all paragraphs in the body should be indented the
same distance. (If you are using a typewriter, indent
five spaces.) Keep your left-hand margin straight;
keep the right-hand margin as straight as you can.

5. *Closing*

The standard form for the closing of a business letter
is *Yours truly* or *Very truly yours* or *Sincerely yours.*
The closing should begin a little to the right of the
middle of the page. Only the first word is capitalized.
A comma follows the closing.

6. *Signature*

Directly below the closing, in line with it, sign your
full name in ink. If you are typing the letter, type your

name below your written signature. Never put a title (Mr., Mrs., Miss, etc.) before your handwritten signature.

Yours truly,
Margaret Nolan

Very truly yours,

John Anderson
John Anderson

7. *Envelope*

The return address and the address on the envelope of a business letter are written and placed exactly as they are on the envelope of a friendly letter. The "outside" address should be the same as the inside address.

8. *Folding the Letter*

If the letter is written on $8\frac{1}{2} \times 11$-inch paper, and is to be put into a long envelope, fold the sheet up a third of the way from the bottom, then fold the top

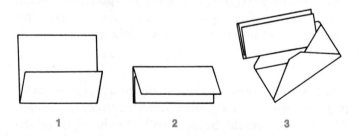

1   2   3

third down over it. If the sheet is to go into a small envelope, fold the page up from the bottom to within a quarter of an inch of the top; then fold the right side over a third of the way, and fold the left side over it. Insert the letter into the envelope with the last fold at the bottom.

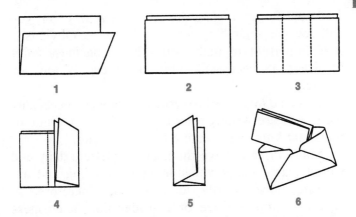

EXERCISE 7. If your teacher agrees, have the class begin a collection of business letters from home. Appoint a class committee to arrange a bulletin board display of these letters.

EXERCISE 8. The following paragraph contains all the information needed for a business letter. Write the letter in correct form and arrangement on a sheet of business stationery. Address an envelope for it.

32 Berenda drive, Flagstaff, Arizona 86001 december 2 1982 Acme outfitting company inc p.o. box 289 milwaukee wisconsin 53248 customer service department kindly send me your mail order catalogue on sporting goods and hunting and fishing equipment thank you yours truly judy muller

22f. In a business letter, be clear, courteous, and brief.

If you buy something at the corner store and find, when you return home, that you have the wrong items —size 7 shoes instead of size 8, or pink thread instead of blue—you can quickly correct the error by walking back to the store. But if you order an item by mail, and forget to state the correct size or color, you will receive something you do not want. Obviously, it is important to make sure that a business letter furnishes all necessary information clearly and accurately.

It is also important to write courteously, especially when you are writing a letter of request. A crude or impatient letter will make a bad impression.

Many firms receive thousands of letters daily and would waste many valuable hours reading and answering unnecessarily long letters. Therefore, to ensure prompt service or consideration, a business letter should be brief and to the point.

Two common kinds of business letters are the *order* letter and the *request* letter.

The Order Letter

When writing an order letter, be sure to identify the merchandise you want by its catalogue number or the place you saw it advertised and by its price. State whether you are charging the merchandise or paying for it by cash, check, money order, or C.O.D.

▶ NOTE   You will order many items of merchandise not by letter but by order blank. When you use an order blank, be sure to follow the directions carefully and fill in all the blanks. No covering letter is necessary.

EXERCISE 9.   Scan the advertisements in a catalogue, newspaper, or magazine. Select an item you would like to have, and write a letter ordering it. Exchange letters with a classmate. Examine that letter. Check to see whether (1) it follows the business letter form; (2) it identifies exactly the item wanted; (3) it states how the item is being paid for.

```
                                    89 East First Street
                                    Kankakee, Illinois 60901
                                    March 10, 1982


        Standard Equipment Company
        448 Westwood Boulevard
        St. Louis, Missouri 63107

        Mail Order Department:

             Please send me the field glasses, No. 791,
        which you advertised for $11.98, postpaid, in
        the February 17 issue of the Farm Gazette.
             I am enclosing a money order for $11.98.


                             Very truly yours,

                             Rachel Beam
                             Rachel Beam
```

Model Order Letter

EXERCISE 10. Choose one of the following situations for a business letter. Address an envelope.

1. You ordered a pair of rabbits, New Zealand Giants, from Beyer's Mail Order Mart, 88 H Street, Augusta, Georgia 30915. You received a set of "rabbit ears" antennae for a television set. Write a letter asking for a correction of the mistake.
2. You ordered a cashmere sweater from the Chic Shop, 49 Sierra Road, Philadelphia, Pennsylvania 19154. When it arrived, it was the wrong size and color.

3. You ordered a first baseman's glove from Harold's Sporting Goods, Inc., 724 Freneau Parkway South, Bangor, Maine 04401. Instead you received a catcher's mask.

4. You ordered (enclosing full payment) a pair of work gloves from Mercantile Mail Order Company, 97 West Ivy Street, Cleveland, Ohio 44153. You received twelve pairs of mittens in various sizes.

5. For your mother's birthday, you ordered an embroidered sweater from Gifts Galore, 819 West Drive, Dubuque, Iowa 52018. In your letter you enclosed a money order. Your mother's birthday is two weeks away, and the sweater has not yet arrived.

The Request Letter

Occasionally you have to write a letter to get information, to ask for a pamphlet or a catalogue or samples. In such a letter you are, of course, asking a favor; be brief, clear, and courteous.

EXERCISE 11. Write to a department of your city or state government, asking for free pamphlets or leaflets about the duties and services of the department. Address an envelope for your letter, but do not mail the letter unless you are seriously interested in the information. Remember: Your request is more likely to be granted if you are courteous in making it.

EXERCISE 12. Write a letter for one of the following situations. Address an envelope, but do not mail the letter unless you are serious about your request.

1. Your class has been studying wildlife conservation. You would like some maps showing the great "flyways" on the continent of North America used

34 Addison Place
Boise, Idaho 83742
December 2, 1982

Air-Industry, Inc.
10 West Norton Avenue
Los Angeles, California 90037

Publicity Department:

    Our eighth-grade class at Brice Junior
High School is studying the use of helicopters
in farming operations. If you have a free
brochure describing your helicopters and how
they are used on farms, we would appreciate
receiving ten copies.

                Yours truly,

                Martha Ames

                Martha Ames

Model Request Letter

by migrating birds. Write for such maps to the Fish
and Wildlife Service, United States Department of
the Interior, Washington, D.C.

2. Your group wishes to visit a famous museum
in your locality (or the Guggenheim Museum in
New York City, New York, or the Hearst Castle
in San Simeon, California). Write for information
about visiting hours and fees. Find out whether a
reduced rate is possible for your group. Inform the
management of the museum of your group's purpose in making the visit.

3. Write to the United States Government Printing Office, Washington, D.C. Ask if they have publications on a particular subject such as national monuments. Tell why you are interested in this subject.

▶ **NOTE** The United States Postal Service recommends the use of two-letter codes for states, the District of Columbia, and Puerto Rico. The service also recommends the use of nine-digit zip codes. When you use these codes, the address should look like this:

EXAMPLE   Ms. Linda Ramos
6 Northside Dr.
St. Joseph, MO   64506–1212

The two-letter code is in capital letters and is never followed by a period. The following is a list of two-letter codes for states, the District of Columbia, and Puerto Rico.

Alabama AL	Louisiana LA
Alaska AK	Maine ME
Arizona AZ	Maryland MD
Arkansas AR	Massachusetts MA
California CA	Michigan MI
Colorado CO	Minnesota MN
Connecticut CT	Mississippi MS
Delaware DE	Missouri MO
District of Columbia DC	Montana MT
Florida FL	Nebraska NE
Georgia GA	Nevada NV
Hawaii HI	New Hampshire NH
Idaho ID	New Jersey NJ
Illinois IL	New Mexico NM
Indiana IN	New York NY
Iowa IA	North Carolina NC
Kansas KS	North Dakota ND
Kentucky KY	Ohio OH

Oklahoma OK	Texas TX
Oregon OR	Utah UT
Pennsylvania PA	Vermont VT
Puerto Rico PR	Virginia VA
Rhode Island RI	Washington WA
South Carolina SC	West Virginia WV
South Dakota SD	Wisconsin WI
Tennessee TN	Wyoming WY

CHECKLIST

Friendly Letters and Social Notes

1. Jot down your ideas before you write the letter. Include news the other person might like to know. Answer any questions that may have been asked in your friend's last letter.
2. Use the correct form. Include your address and date in the heading. Place a comma after the salutation and closing.
3. Write a neat letter. Never use pencil.
4. In a note of thanks, be specific about whatever it is you are grateful for. Avoid the stiff and formal appearance of a duty letter.

Business Letters

1. Use the correct form. Use block style for the heading, not indented style. Include an inside address in the letter. Place a colon, not a comma, after the salutation.
2. Be careful to include all information necessary to understand or act upon your letter.
3. In an order letter, be brief and to the point.
4. In a request letter, make your request courteously.

REVIEW EXERCISE. Write a letter for each of the following situations. Address an envelope for your letter.

1. Write an order letter to Travis Novelty Company, 18 Meadow Street, St. Louis, Missouri 63128, for

the following merchandise: 2 giant balloons, at $.35 each; 18 pencils, with the name "Pat" printed in silver, at $.15 each; and 1 box of birthday candles, at $1.35. You are enclosing a money order to cover the total cost.

2. Write a request letter asking for the summer schedule of plays at the Beacon Summer Theater, Portsmouth, Rhode Island 02871; inform the theater that you represent a group and need information on group ticket rates.

Aids to
Good English

PART SIX

Chapter 23

The Dictionary

Arrangement and Content of Dictionaries

When using most words, you rely upon your own experience as to their meaning, pronunciation, and general appropriateness. You have been accumulating this kind of experience about words since you first learned to talk. But no matter how extensive your experience with words, there will be times when it fails to provide the specific information you need. In such situations, you should turn to your dictionary.

Dictionary makers depend upon the experience of all users of English. A good dictionary tells you what meanings a word has had, how it is usually spelled and pronounced, what its history is, and, often, the kind of situation in which it is appropriate or inappropriate. Dictionaries are intended to back up and broaden your own experience. Travelers venturing into unfamiliar territory value the maps and notes of others who were there before. A good dictionary provides you with much the same kind of information about unfamiliar words. If you are not yet making sufficient use of the dictionary, this chapter will show you how to do so.

Since dictionaries differ from one another in their methods of presenting information, a textbook can treat only the general features that dictionaries have in common. The best guide to the use of your dictionary is the introductory section that explains the arrangement of entries, the system of showing pronunciations, and special features of that particular book. If you are using one of the dictionaries specially prepared for students of your age, you will find everything you need to know carefully explained. If you use a larger dictionary, possibly at home or in the library, you will find a briefer but still adequate explanation in the front part. In either case, take the time to find out how your dictionary goes about the job of presenting information. Finding an entry will not be much help to you if you do not know how to interpret the information.

ARRANGEMENT

23a. Learn how to find a word in the dictionary.

The words in a dictionary are listed in alphabetical order. This does not mean simply that all words beginning with a particular letter are lumped together in one section. It means that words having *a* as a second letter come before those that have *b* as a second letter, and so on through all the other letters in the word. To find whether *force* or *form* comes first, you have to look at the fourth letter; to decide between *reconcile* and *reconciliation,* you have to look at the ninth. Running through the alphabet nine times is a lot of trouble. If you are still hazy whether *q* comes before *s,* or *m* before *n,* you will save yourself time and effort by getting it straight right now.

Two special problems should be kept in mind: abbreviations and entries of more than one word.

Some dictionaries explain abbreviations in a special section, but most dictionaries define them in the main part of the book right along with the other entries. In such dictionaries, abbreviations are entered according to the letters in them, *not* according to the complete words that they stand for. Thus, the abbreviation *pt.* (meaning *pint* or *part*) comes after *psychology*, even though both words that the abbreviation can stand for would come before *psychology*. In a dictionary, the abbreviation *St.* (for *saint*) comes after *squirt* and before *stab*. A name like *St. Denis*, however, would appear under the full spelling — *saint*.

Two or more words used together as a single word (*open season, prime minister*) are treated as though they were a single word. Thus *open shop* appears after *openly* because *s* comes after *l*.

EXERCISE 1. Arrange the following words, phrases, and abbreviations in alphabetical order.

watermelon	static
department	muddy
curtain	Mrs.
stateside	departmental
municipal	curtail
dept.	mudguard
st.	mt.
curvature	munificence
munificent	water wheel
water moccasin	department store

Where you open a dictionary to find a word makes a difference. You can find *municipal* if you open at the *s*'s and leaf back to the *m*'s, but it would be better to open at the *m*'s in the first place. This is how to open near the place you want.

1. *Divide the dictionary into thirds.* Think of your dictionary in three parts consisting of the following groups of letters:

abcde   fghijklmnop   qrstuvwxyz

The parts do not look equal because more words start with some letters than with others. However, if you will try these divisions, you will get three fairly equal sections. Your first object is to open to the third of the dictionary in which the word you want is to be found.

EXERCISE 2. After the appropriate number, indicate in which third of the dictionary (first, middle, last) you would find each of the following words.

1. falcon
2. recruit
3. equation
4. opportunity
5. robin
6. cryptic
7. stability
8. pensive
9. decimal
10. fable

2. *When you have found the right third, find the letter you want.* As you get used to thinking of the dictionary in thirds, you will gradually come to know in what part of each third to look for particular letters. It helps to know, for example, that more words begin with *s* than with the letters *u, v, w, x, y,* and *z* combined.

EXERCISE 3. With your dictionary closed on your desk in front of you, your teacher or another student in the class will call out a letter at random. Suppose you hear *g* called. You will then open your dictionary near the beginning of the middle third and call out the number of the first page you find that has words beginning with *g*. The winner can then call out the next letter for the class to find. If you are not clear about which letters belong in which third, it will help to have them written out in front of you.

3. *When you have found the right letter, begin looking at the guide words. Guide words* are printed in heavy type at the top of each dictionary page. The one on the left is the same as the first word defined on that page; the one on the right is the same as the last word on that page. Words that fall between guide words in the alphabet will appear on that page. A word that comes alphabetically before the first guide word will be found on a page toward the front, and one that comes after the second guide word will be found toward the back.

In using guide words, you will find it useful to have a general idea of the number of words beginning with a particular letter. If you are looking up *stanchion,* for example, and open to a page that has the guide words *size* and *skinner,* you can safely turn several pages at a time because you know that the *s*'s take up many pages. On the other hand, if you are looking up *yucca* and open to a page with the guide words *yawn* and *yet,* you had better turn one page at a time because it does not take long to get through the *y*'s. In general, look closely at the guide words on each page when you are close to the page you want, and turn several at a time when you are further from it.

EXERCISE 4. Number your paper 1–15. Suppose the guide words *needy* and *neither* appear on a particular dictionary page. After the proper number, make a plus sign if the corresponding word would appear on that page. Write *before* if it would appear on an earlier page and *after* if it would appear on a later page.

EXAMPLES   1. nefarious
           1. +
           2. navy
           2. *before*

1. negative   6. ne'er-do-well 11. negligent
2. necessary   7. newcomer   12. Neanderthal
3. needle   8. noble   13. nemesis
4. nearsighted   9. neediest   14. New Zealander
5. neophyte   10. necktie   15. negotiate

FINDING THE RIGHT MEANING

23b. Learn to find the meaning you want.

Most English words have a number of different meanings. Some common words, like *run,* for example,
have thirty or more. When you go to the dictionary,
you are usually interested in a particular meaning of a
word—one that will fit into the particular sentence or
situation in which you heard or read the word. Nevertheless, it is a good idea to scan all of the meanings
given. By doing so you will form a general impression
of the range of meanings that word may have. When
you have read them all quickly, you can focus on the
part of the entry that seems most closely related to
the meaning you need.

Each separate meaning of a word is explained in a
numbered definition. Some dictionaries use letters
within numbered definitions to distinguish between
closely related meanings. To see how this works,
examine the following dictionary entry for the word
offensive:

> ¹**of·fen·sive** \ə-'fen-siv\ *adj* **1 a** : of, relating to, or designed for
> attack ⟨*offensive* weapons⟩ **b** : being on the offense ⟨the *of-*
> *fensive* team⟩ **2** : giving unpleasant sensations ⟨*offensive*
> smells⟩ **3** : causing displeasure or resentment : INSULTING ⟨an

offensive remark⟩ — **of·fen·sive·ly** *adv* — **of·fen·sive·ness**
n
²offensive *n* **1** : the act of an attacking party ⟨on the *offensive*⟩ **2**
: ATTACK ⟨launch an *offensive*⟩

Suppose you want to find the meaning of *offensive* in the sentence: *The child was scolded for making such an offensive remark.* By recognizing that the word is used as an adjective in this sentence, you can concentrate your search on the entry which gives definitions for the adjective (*adj.*) *offensive*. Definitions 1. and 2. do not fit the context, but definition 3. does. What is more, the illustrative example for 3. provides a context very similar to the one you have in mind.

Now look back at the sample entry and notice that *offensive* is listed again, this time as a noun (*n.*). This particular dictionary gives separate entries for each part of speech. The small numeral 2 coming before the entry word shows that it is the second entry for the same word. Other dictionaries may not list parts of speech in this way. They may have all the definitions of a word in one entry, with each part of speech in its own subgroup. The following definition, taken from a different dictionary, illustrates the latter method. Notice that the definitions for the noun subgroup, marked by — *n* for *noun*, begin with the numeral *1*.

of·fen·sive |ə fĕn′sĭv| *adj.* **1.** Offending the senses; unpleasant: *an offensive smell.* **2.** Causing anger, displeasure, resentment, etc.: *offensive language.* **3.** |ô′fĕn′sĭv| *or* |ŏf′ĕn′-|. Of an attack; aggressive; attacking: *an offensive play in football.* —*n.* **1.** An aggressive action; an attack: *their third major offensive of the war.* **2.** An attitude of attack: *take the offensive.* —**of·fen′sive·ly** *adv.* —**of·fen′sive·ness** *n.*

Whichever dictionary you use, you will find meanings more rapidly if you know your parts of speech.

EXERCISE 5. Below are three groups of dictionary definitions and ten sentences using the defined words. Number your paper 1–10. After the proper number, write the number of the definition giving the correct meaning of the word as it is used in the sentence.

> **¹rough** \\'rəf\\ *adj* **1 a** : having an uneven surface : not smooth **b** : covered with or made up of coarse and often shaggy hair or bristles ⟨a *rough*-coated terrier⟩ **c** : difficult to travel over or penetrate : WILD ⟨*rough* country⟩ **2 a** : characterized by harshness, violence, or force **b** : DIFFICULT, TRYING ⟨a *rough* day at the office⟩ **3** : coarse or rugged in character or appearance: as **a** : harsh to the ear **b** : crude in style or expression **c** : marked by a lack of refinement or grace : UNCOUTH **4** : marked by incompleteness or inexactness ⟨a *rough* draft⟩ ⟨*rough* estimates⟩ [Old English *rūh*] — **rough·ly** *adv* — **rough·ness** *n*

From *Webster's School Dictionary* © 1980 by G. & C. Merriam Co., Publishers of the Merriam-Webster Dictionaries. Reprinted by permission of the publishers.

1. This morning we had a *rough* exam in science.
2. Mrs. Logan made a *rough* sketch of the model.
3. Joan's coat is made of *rough* material.

> **cred·it** |krĕd′ĭt| *n.* **1.** Belief or confidence; trust: *I placed full credit in the truthfulness of the state records.* **2.** Reputation or standing: *It is to his credit that he worked without complaining.* **3.** A source of honor or distinction: *a credit to his team.* **4.** Approval, honor, or acclaim for some act or quality; praise: *They shared the credit for the book's success.* **5.** Certification that a student has fulfilled a requirement by completing a course of study. **6.** An acknowledgment of work done, as in the production of a book, motion picture, or play. **7.** A reputation for repaying debts and being financially honest: *He has good credit at all stores.* **8. a.** A system of buying goods or services by charging the amount, with payment due at a later time: *buy on credit.* **b.** Confidence in a buyer's ability and intention to pay at some future time: *The store extended credit to him.* **c.** The period of time allowed before a debt must be paid. **9.** The amount of money in the account of a person or group, as at a bank. **10.** In accounting: **a.** The amount paid on a debt. **b.** The right-hand side

of an account, on which such payments are entered. —*modifier: a credit risk; a credit rating.* —*v.* **1.** To believe; trust: *He credited her explanation for the delay.* **2.** To give honor to (a person) for something: *They credit him with founding modern biology.* **3.** To attribute (something) to a person: *Some credit the song to Haydn.* **4.** To give academic credits to (a student). **5.** In accounting: **a.** To give credit for (a payment). **b.** To give credit to (a payer).

From *The American Heritage School Dictionary,* © 1977 Houghton Mifflin Company. Reprinted by permission of the publisher.

4. Paying your bills promptly will help you establish a good *credit* rating.

5. Oscar winners often share the *credit* with their coworkers.

6. How many *credits* do you need in social studies before you can graduate?

²**train** *vb* **1** : to direct the growth of (a plant) usually by bending, pruning, and tying **2 a** : to teach something (as a skill, profession, or trade) to ⟨was *trained* in the law⟩ **b** : to teach (an animal) to obey **3** : to make ready (as by exercise) for a test of skill **4** : to aim (as a gun) at a target **5** : to undergo instruction, discipline, or drill [Middle French *trainer* "to draw, drag"] **syn** see TEACH — **train·able** \ˈtrā-nə-bəl\ *adj* — **train·ee** \trā-ˈnē\ *n*

From *Webster's School Dictionary* © 1980 by G. & C. Merriam Co., Publishers of the Merriam-Webster Dictionaries. Reprinted by permission of the publisher.

7. On a talk show, one enthusiastic pet owner claimed that he *trains* bullfrogs to dance.

8. Astronomers will *train* their telescopes on Halley's comet.

9. I *train* the ivy to grow around the window frame.

10. Ms. McConnell *trains* every morning for the marathon race.

CONTENT

23c. Learn what different kinds of information a dictionary gives you about words.

So much information is packed into the typical dictionary definition that some of it is likely to be overlooked if you are not careful. Most of the explanations below correspond to the labels on the sample column on page 467. Consult the sample column as you study these notes so that you do not overlook any of the information your dictionary has to offer.

1. *The entry word.* The word to be defined is called the *entry word.* It appears in heavy type. You use the entry word to locate a definition, to get the correct spelling of a word, and to find out how it is divided into syllables, if it has more than one syllable. Most dictionaries also indicate words that are capitalized by beginning the entry word with a capital letter. However, capitalization may be indicated in other ways, especially in dictionaries not specially designed for high school students. If there is more than one acceptable spelling of a word, the alternative is usually listed immediately after the entry word:

moustache *or* **mustache**

In most cases the first spelling listed is the one that most people prefer to use. You will never go wrong by using the first spelling given in any dictionary.

2. *Illustration.* Sometimes the best way to indicate the meaning of a word is through an illustration. *Agouti* on page 467 is such a word. The definition tells you the meaning of this word; the illustration *shows* you the animal itself.

3. *Pronunciation.* The pronunciation of a word is usually indicated immediately after the entry word by means of special respelling, which is explained in detail on pages 477–79. The dictionary from which the sample column on page 467 was taken uses slant lines (\\) to enclose the pronunciation respelling, but many

other dictionaries use brackets to enclose the respelling. The sounds represented by the symbols in the pronunciation respelling are explained in a key that usually appears inside the front cover of your dictionary. A shorter key may appear at the bottom of each page or every other page. (For more about pronunciation, see pages 477–79.)

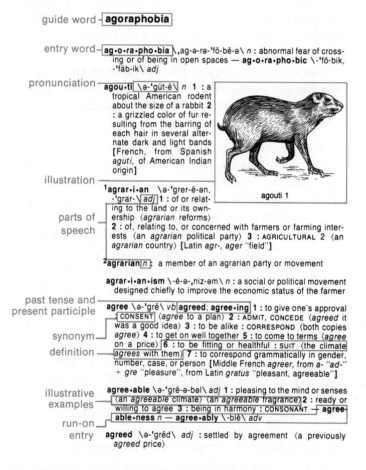

guide word — **agoraphobia**

entry word — **ag·o·ra·pho·bia** \,ag-ə-rə-'fō-bē-ə\ *n* : abnormal fear of crossing or of being in open spaces — **ag·o·ra·pho·bic** \-'fō-bik, -'fäb-ik\ *adj*

pronunciation — **agou·ti** \ə-'güt-ē\ *n* **1** : a tropical American rodent about the size of a rabbit **2** : a grizzled color of fur resulting from the barring of each hair in several alternate dark and light bands [French, from Spanish *aguti*, of American Indian origin]

illustration

agouti 1

¹agrar·i·an \ə-'grer-ē-ən, -'grar-\ *adj* **1** : of or relating to the land or its ownership ⟨*agrarian* reforms⟩

parts of speech — **2** : of, relating to, or concerned with farmers or farming interests ⟨an *agrarian* political party⟩ **3** : AGRICULTURAL 2 ⟨an *agrarian* country⟩ [Latin *agr-, ager* "field"]

²agrarian *n* : a member of an agrarian party or movement

agrar·i·an·ism \-ē-ə-,niz-əm\ *n* : a social or political movement designed chiefly to improve the economic status of the farmer

past tense and present participle — **agree** \ə-'grē\ *vb* **agreed; agree·ing 1** : to give one's approval : CONSENT ⟨*agree* to a plan⟩ **2** : ADMIT, CONCEDE ⟨*agreed* it was a good idea⟩ **3** : to be alike : CORRESPOND ⟨both copies

synonym — *agree*⟩ **4** : to get on well together **5** : to come to terms ⟨*agree* on a price⟩ **6** : to be fitting or healthful : SUIT ⟨the climate

definition — *agrees* with them⟩ **7** : to correspond grammatically in gender, number, case, or person [Middle French *agreer*, from *a-* "ad-" + *gre* "pleasure", from Latin *gratus* "pleasant, agreeable"]

illustrative examples — **agree·able** \ə-'grē-ə-bəl\ *adj* **1** : pleasing to the mind or senses ⟨an *agreeable* climate⟩ ⟨an *agreeable* fragrance⟩ **2** : ready or willing to agree **3** : being in harmony : CONSONANT — **agree·able·ness** *n* — **agree·ably** \-blē\ *adv*

run-on entry — **agreed** \ə-'grēd\ *adj* : settled by agreement ⟨a previously *agreed* price⟩

4. *Definition.* The definition gives the meaning or meanings of a word. When a word has more than one meaning, each meaning is defined separately in a numbered definition. (Some dictionaries use letters to distinguish between meanings so closely related that they are defined in a single numbered definition.)

5. *Illustrative example.* For many words, and for different meanings of the same word, sample contexts are provided to show how the word is used. Don't overlook sample contexts. They often provide essential clues to the meaning of a new word. For example, a *hoax* is a kind of trick, but you cannot say that you have taught your dog a "hoax." Illustrative examples often provide the clues that will prevent you from making mistakes in usage.

6. *Synonyms.* Synonyms are words that have similar meanings. In the sample column on page 467, for example, *consent* is given as the synonym for *agree.* (The word *consent* is printed in block letters to indicate that it is a synonym.) Words that are synonyms can be used alike in some contexts but not in others. For example, the words *deep* and *profound* are synonyms when the subject is "mystery." The words *stern* and *rear* are synonyms when one is sailing on a boat.

7. *Run-on entry.* Many English words have companion forms that are closely related to them in meaning. Dictionaries include these words at the end of an entry as *run-on entries.* At the end of the adjective *bad,* for instance, you may find the notation " − **bad′ly** *adv.* − **bad′ness** *n.*" Although often no definitions are given in a run-on entry, a part-of-speech label is provided for each companion form. Some dictionaries also give the pronunciation for the companion form. (For more about companion forms, see pages 508–10.)

8. *Part of speech.* The part of speech of a word is indicated by an italicized abbreviation:

n.	noun	*adv.*	adverb
pron.	pronoun	*prep.*	preposition
v. or *vb.*	verb[1]	*conj.*	conjunction
adj.	adjective	*interj.*	interjection

Many English words can be used as more than one part of speech. For such words, a dictionary will indicate how the definitions are related to the part-of-speech labels. In some dictionaries, all the definitions for one part of speech are grouped together after the label, as on page 467. Other dictionaries provide consecutively numbered definitions, with the part-of-speech label after each numeral. The most frequent usages are given first. The second method is used in the following entry:

> **smart** [smärt] **1** *adj.* Quick in mind; intelligent; bright; clever. **2** *adj.* Keen or shrewd. **3** *adj.* Witty and quick but not deep: *smart* remarks. **4** *adj.* Sharp and stinging: a *smart* cuff on the ear. **5** *n.* A sharp, stinging sensation. **6** *v.* To experience or cause a stinging sensation: eyes *smarting* from smog; The cut *smarts*. **7** *v.* To feel hurt, sorry, irritated, or upset: He still *smarted* over their rude remarks. **8** *adj.* Clean, neat, and trim in appearance. **9** *adj.* Fashionable; stylish: a *smart* outfit. **10** *adj.* Vigorous; brisk; lively: to move at a *smart* pace. — **smart′ly** *adv.* — **smart′ness** *n.*

From *The HBJ School Dictionary.* Copyright © 1977 by Harcourt Brace Jovanovich, Inc. Reprinted by permission of the publisher.

[1] Unabridged dictionaries and those designed for older students distinguish between verbs like *wonder* in the sentence "I wonder" and verbs that require another word to show who or what is receiving the action; for example, *hit* in "The batter hit a home run." Such dictionaries label verbs like *wonder,* in the first example, *v.i.,* and verbs like *hit,* in the second, *v.t.* The abbreviation *v.i.* stands for *intransitive verb; v.t.* stands for *transitive verb.* Transitive verbs always have to have an object—a word showing who or what was affected by the action expressed by the verb.

A dictionary also provides the following information:

Usage label. Not all words entered in a dictionary are equally acceptable in all situations. A usage label is a mild warning that people use a word (or use a particular meaning of a word) only in certain situations. For example, the label *slang* indicates a word that may be used in certain informal situations but is likely to call attention to itself when used in other situations. Another label, *archaic,* indicates that a word was once common but is now rarely used. A third label, *dialect,* indicates that a word is used in only one part of the country. The introduction to your dictionary explains the meaning of all the usage labels employed by your dictionary.

Origin. For some words, school dictionaries provide information about the history of a word, usually by indicating the language from which it was borrowed. Such information may appear near the beginning of the definition or at the end, as in the example below.

> **dex·ter·ous** [dek′strəs *or* dek′stər·əs] *adj.* **1** Skillful in using the hands or body; adroit: a *dexterous* billiard player. **2** Mentally quick; keen. — **dex′ter·ous·ly** *adv.* ◆ *Dexterous* comes from a Latin word meaning *skillful,* which in turn comes from a Latin root meaning *on the right* or *right-handed.*

From *The HBJ School Dictionary.* Copyright © 1977 by Harcourt Brace Jovanovich, Inc. Reprinted by permission of the publisher.

Encyclopedic information. A small number of dictionary entries deal with people and places. There are better places to find out about important people and places than in a dictionary—these are described in Chapter 24. However, if all you need is a general identification or location, the dictionary will usually provide it, as in the following entry.

Pierce (pirs), **Franklin** 1804–69; 14th president of the U.S. (1853–57)

EXERCISE 6. Number your paper 1–10. Write a synonym for each of the words below. If necessary, use the dictionary.

1. coax
2. development
3. distinct
4. diversity
5. final
6. find
7. happy
8. melancholy
9. perhaps
10. plain

EXERCISE 7. Copy from your dictionary the usage labels for five of these words. Be prepared to explain what the labels tell you and how they would affect your use of the words.

1. afeared
2. corny
3. davenport
4. gabby
5. loco
6. lorry
7. ope
8. petrol
9. pone
10. raspberry

EXERCISE 8. Copy from your dictionary a run-on entry for each of the following words.

1. celebrate
2. cold
3. fair
4. foolish
5. liquidate
6. mobilize
7. negative
8. rapid
9. reform
10. smooth
11. suppress
12. thin
13. turgid
14. water
15. weigh

EXERCISE 9. Copy from your dictionary two definitions for each of the following words, each definition to be for a different part of speech. Following the definitions, indicate the parts of speech by using part-of-speech labels.

EXAMPLE   1. flower   a. The part of a plant that normally bears the seed, *n*.
b. To blossom; to bloom, *v*.

1. back	6. match
2. chance	7. net
3. holiday	8. range
4. Chinese	9. register
5. maneuver	10. tag

EXERCISE 10. Look up the following persons and places in your dictionary. Be able to tell what information the dictionary provides about them.

1. Ruth	6. Orinoco
2. Helen of Troy	7. New Delhi
3. Emily Brontë	8. Maria Montessori
4. Port Said	9. Sequoya
5. Majorca	10. Tierra del Fuego

SPELLING

23d. Learn to use your dictionary for spelling and capitalization.

If you are not sure about the spelling of a word, you should look it up in the dictionary. Occasionally, it may be difficult to find. If you did not know the initial letters of *gnaw, knife,* and *pneumonia,* you might look for these words under *n.* Fortunately, most words in the dictionary are easier to find. The spelling of the initial sound of a word is much more regular in English than the spelling of sounds in the middle or at the ends of words. To find how most words are spelled, simply follow the principles of alphabetical order and let the guide words help you.

Variant Spellings

A dictionary occasionally gives two spellings for a word; *abridgment* and *abridgement, coconut* and *cocoanut, partisan* and *partizan.* Both spellings are correct, but usually a dictionary indicates which spelling is more usual by listing it first. Thus, *abridgment,* listed before *abridgement,* is given as the more common spelling in several dictionaries.

EXERCISE 11. Copy from your dictionary a variant spelling for five of the following words. Be able to tell whether one spelling is preferred.

1. cantaloupe
2. demon
3. fantasy
4. frowsy
5. honor
6. judgment
7. likeable
8. mold
9. rickshaw
10. salable
11. savior
12. sulfur

Unusual Plurals

If the plural of a noun is formed in an unusual way, a dictionary will give the plural form with the abbreviation *pl.* preceding it. For example, the plural of *datum* is given as *data.* Some dictionaries list plurals that are formed in the regular way if there is a chance that the plural will be misspelled. The plural of *valley* might be given (*valleys*) so that no one will make the mistake of ending the plural in *-ies.* Always read the entire entry of a word to be sure of knowing its correct plural form.

Unusual Verb Forms

When a verb forms its past tense, its past participle, or its present participle in an unusual way, a dictionary will list these irregular forms. On page 467, the past tense and present participle forms of *agree* are given. The past participle form is not provided since this is the same as the past tense form. In the entry for *freeze*, a dictionary lists all three forms: *froze, frozen, freezing*.

Comparatives and Superlatives

When the comparative and superlative forms of an adjective are spelled in an unusual way, a dictionary provides these forms either near the beginning or end of an entry. Sometimes the abbreviations *compar.* and *superl.* are used.

> **love·ly** [luv′lē] *adj.* **love·li·er, love·li·est**
> **1** Having qualities that make people love one: a *lovely* child. **2** Beautiful: a *lovely* rose. **3** *informal* Enjoyable; pleasant: to have a *lovely* time at a party. **— love′li·ness** *n.*

From *The HBJ School Dictionary.* Copyright © 1977 by Harcourt Brace Jovanovich, Inc. Reprinted by permission of the publisher.

EXERCISE 12. Copy from your dictionary the unusual spelling forms (if any) for the following words. After the forms, write (*1*) if they are unusual plurals, (*2*) if they are unusual verb forms, or (*3*) if they are unusual comparatives and superlatives.

EXAMPLE   1. swim
            1. *swam, swum, swimming* (2)

1. city
2. choose
3. defy
4. good
5. index
6. individuality
7. mad
8. needy
9. rise
10. rob

CAPITALIZATION

In English, proper nouns are capitalized while common nouns are not. You should be familiar with the rules for capitalization given in Chapter 12. If you are not sure about capitalizing a certain word, the dictionary might help you by printing the word either with or without a capital or stating whether or not the word is usually capitalized.

Sometimes a word should be capitalized in one sense but not capitalized in another. In such a case, the dictionary indicates which meaning requires a capital. For example, some dictionaries print *Mass,* meaning a religious ceremony, with a capital; but *mass,* meaning a large amount or number, appears uncapitalized. *Pole,* meaning a native of Poland, is printed with a capital; *pole,* meaning a slender piece of wood, is not capitalized.

EXERCISE 13. Look up the following words in a dictionary to see when they are capitalized. Be able to explain why they are or are not capitalized in each usage. Your dictionary may not give capitalized uses for all the words.

1. cupid
2. democrat
3. devil
4. episcopal
5. japan
6. calliope
7. nativity
8. pope
9. senate
10. west

SYLLABLE DIVISION

A dictionary divides all words into syllables. *Agreeable* on page 467 is divided into three syllables. Knowing the syllables of a word may help you spell the word. In addition, if you have to divide a word at the end of a line when you are writing, you must know the syllables to divide correctly. (See page 326.)

If your dictionary uses small dots or dashes between the syllables of a word as on page 467, be careful not to confuse these marks with a hyphen. Look up a hyphenated word like *mezzo-soprano* or *open-minded* to be sure you can tell the difference.

EXERCISE 14. Copy the following words, dividing them into syllables. Use the same method to indicate syllable division that your dictionary uses.

1. absolution
2. comma
3. endurance
4. extra
5. flexible
6. junior
7. penetrating
8. severity
9. socialize
10. underdog

PRONUNCIATION

23e. Learn to use your dictionary for pronunciation.

One of the most important pieces of information given in a dictionary is the pronunciation of a word. This information usually comes immediately after the entry word and is enclosed within slant bars (as on page 467) or within parentheses. Be careful not to confuse the pronunciation indication with the spelling of a word.

The Accent Mark

In words of two or more syllables, one syllable is always pronounced with greater force than the others. A dictionary indicates which syllable needs emphasis by using an *accent mark*. Most dictionaries use one of two kinds of accent marks: either the mark ' appearing before the syllable or the mark ' placed after the syllable. Both marks appear well above the center of a letter. Look at the pronunciation indication for *agree* on page 467. Which of the two accent marks is used?

In a word of three or more syllables, a dictionary usually indicates two accent marks, one primary, the other secondary. The word *elevator* has a primary accent on the syllable *el* and a weaker accent on *vat*. Dictionaries generally show the secondary accent in one of three ways. When the mark (′) is used to indicate primary accent, the secondary accent is indicated by a weaker mark (′) or by two marks (″). When the primary accent (ˈ) is used, the secondary accent is a similar mark placed at the bottom of a syllable (ˌ). In the word *agoraphobia* (page 467), where does the secondary accent mark occur?

EXERCISE 15. Copy the following words, dividing them into syllables, and indicate the accented syllables. Use the kind of accent marks that are used in your dictionary.

1. aristocrat
2. detrimental
3. distribution
4. frugal
5. hornpipe
6. masquerade
7. Olympian
8. revolt
9. sarcasm
10. similarity

Pronunciation Symbols

A dictionary uses pronunciation symbols to indicate the pronunciation of a word. Most symbols are regular letters of the alphabet, but they are used more strictly than in ordinary writing. For example, the letter *c* can have several different pronunciations, as in the words *city, control,* and *cello.* A dictionary would indicate the beginning sounds of these words as *s, k,* and *ch.* To show the pronunciation of vowels, which is harder to indicate than the pronunciation of consonants, a dictionary uses *diacritical* marks — special symbols placed above the letters.

Indicating pronunciation is among the dictionary maker's most difficult tasks; and thus it is not surprising that dictionaries should vary in their use of symbols. In order to use the pronunciations given in your dictionary, you must become familiar with the symbols it uses. A key to these symbols usually appears inside the front cover and sometimes on each page as well. In addition, your dictionary probably includes a thorough explanation of its pronunciation symbols in the introduction. Study this explanation carefully.

In this chapter you will study several diacritical marks that are used by most dictionaries.

Long Vowels

To indicate a long vowel, a dictionary generally uses a diacritical mark called a *macron*—a long straight mark over the vowel. When a macron is used, the long vowel is said to have the sound of its own name.

EXAMPLES   main   \mān\
                  mean   \mēn\
                  mine   \mīn\
                  moan   \mōn\
                  immune \imūn\

Notice the use of the macron in the pronunciations of *agoraphobia* and *agree* on page 467.

Short Vowels

The vowels in the words *mat, head, bid, dot, could,* and *cut* are called short vowels. Dictionaries differ in their methods of showing the sound of short vowels.

One method uses a symbol called a *breve* (pronounced *brēv*) over the vowel. Another method is to leave short vowels unmarked.

EXAMPLES   mat   (măt) or \mat\
           head (hĕd) or \hed\
           bid   (bĭd) or \bid\

Sometimes, when all that we say in an unaccented syllable is the sound of the consonant, the pronunciation indication in certain dictionaries may omit the short vowel altogether.

The Schwa

Most recent dictionaries use an upside-down *e* as a symbol to represent the blurred, unclear sound of "uh." This sound occurs in the phrase *the pen* (thə pen) and in the following words:

minute (min′ət)
Karen (Kar′ən)
permit (pər mit′)
police (pə lēs′)
busily (biz′ə lē)

Most dictionaries use the schwa for the "uh" sound only when it occurs in unaccented syllables, but several dictionaries use this symbol when the sound occurs in accented syllables and in one-syllable words. Consult your dictionary to see how it uses the schwa sound.

EXERCISE 16. Copy from your dictionary the pronunciation of the following words. Follow the practice of your dictionary in using parentheses or slant lines to enclose the pronunciation. Be able to explain all the diacritical marks used.

1. diet
2. erase
3. bumblebee
4. matriarchy
5. nation
6. poverty
7. puny
8. revolve
9. seldom
10. sidesaddle

EXERCISE 17. Follow the directions in Exercise 16.

1. appetite	6. heritage
2. collection	7. major
3. debatable	8. Manila
4. fraternal	9. radiator
5. gelatinous	10. slippery

REVIEW EXERCISE. Use complete sentences in writing the answers to the following questions. If necessary, look the information up in the chapter.

1. Define
   a. synonym   c. guide word
   b. macron   d. schwa

2. Name three kinds of information about spelling that a dictionary provides.

3. After which of the following words would *mother-in-law* occur in a dictionary?
   motherly   motherhood
   mother   motherland

4. What kind of information is given by the following terms: *slang, informal, archaic?*

Chapter 24

The Library

The Dewey Decimal System, the Card Catalogue, Reference Books

You can carry about in your head only a limited amount of information, but you can find out almost anything you want to know if you know where to look for it. Your best place to look for information is a library, whether it is your school library or a public library. To use a library efficiently, you must understand its system of arranging the books, magazines, pamphlets, and other materials it contains so that you can find what you want easily and quickly.

THE ARRANGEMENT OF A LIBRARY

Fiction

24a. Learn to locate books of fiction.

In most libraries all books of fiction are located together in one section. The books are arranged on the shelves in alphabetical order according to authors' last names. For example, if you were looking for *The Good Earth* by Pearl S. Buck, you would go to the fiction section and find the books by authors whose last names begin with *B*. Among these, you could easily locate books by Buck. You might find a number of these and have to look along the shelf to find *The Good Earth*. To help you do this, the library arranges books by the same author also in alphabetical order according to the first word in the title, unless that word is *a, an,* or *the.* If the first word is *a, an,* or *the,* the second word of the title is used for alphabetizing. *The Good Earth* would come then in the *G* position.

▶ **NOTE** Books by authors whose names begin with *Mc* (like McDonald) are arranged as though the name were spelled *Mac; St.* is arranged as though spelled *Saint.*

EXERCISE 1. Number your paper 1–10. After these numbers, write the authors and titles of the following books of fiction in the order in which they would be arranged in the library.

1. *The Light in the Forest* by Conrad Richter
2. *Curtain* by Agatha Christie
3. *Jane Eyre* by Charlotte Brontë
4. *Dirt Track Summer* by William Campbell Gault
5. *Crooked House* by Agatha Christie
6. *The Incredible Journey* by Sheila Burnford
7. *The Friendly Persuasion* by Jessamyn West
8. *Wuthering Heights* by Emily Brontë
9. *The Tamarack Tree* by Betty Underwood
10. *The Martian Chronicles* by Ray Bradbury

Nonfiction

24b. Learn the Dewey decimal system of arranging nonfiction.

The Dewey decimal system is named after Melvil Dewey, the American librarian who developed it. Under this system, books are classified under ten headings, and each heading has a number. Books having the same number are placed together in the library. The numbers and headings are as follows:

000–099	General works (encyclopedias and other reference materials)
100–199	Philosophy
200–299	Religion
300–399	Social Sciences (economics, government, etc.)
400–499	Language
500–599	Science
600–699	Technology (engineering, aviation, inventions, etc.)
700–799	The Arts (architecture, music, sports, etc.)
800–899	Literature
900–999	History (including geography, travel books, and biography)

The number given to a book is known as the book's call number. To see how the Dewey system works, take as an example Arthur Zaidenberg's *How to Draw Cartoons*. Since the book is about art, its number will be in the 700's. Within this broad category, the numbers 740–749 are used for books on drawing and decorative arts. Books on freehand drawing are given the number 741. By means of a decimal the classification is narrowed further. The number 741.5 is given to books about drawing cartoons, and 741.5–Z is the call number for the book *How to Draw Cartoons*.

Biographies are arranged in alphabetical order according to the names of the persons written about, not according to the names of the persons who wrote the biographies. For example, *The Helen Keller Story* by Catherine Owens Peare will appear among the K's. The call number may consist of B, for biography, with K, for Keller, under it — $\frac{B}{K}$, or it may consist of 92 with K under it — $\frac{92}{K}$. Some librarians use the B; others use the 92, which is a short form of the Dewey number for biography — 920; still others use 921.

EXERCISE 2. Number your paper 1–10. Within which number range in the Dewey decimal system would you find each of the following?

EXAMPLE   1. A book on modeling in clay
1. *700–799*

1. A book about Greek philosophy
2. A book about travels in Africa
3. A book about the development of the French language
4. A book about the Presidency
5. A collection of biographies of pioneer men and women
6. A book about baseball
7. A book about the Bible
8. A history of Portugal
9. A book about English poetry of the eighteenth century
10. A book about organic chemistry

THE CARD CATALOGUE

You can find out the call number of any book in the library by looking the book up in the card catalogue.

24c. Learn to use the card catalogue.

The card catalogue is a cabinet with small drawers which contain file cards arranged in alphabetical order. These cards represent the books in the library — fiction and nonfiction. For each book of fiction there are at least two cards, an *author card* and a *title card*. For each book of nonfiction, there are usually three cards, an *author card,* a *title card,* and a *subject card.* If the book is by two or more authors, there is an author card for each name.

Each card provides a different means of finding a book. If you are looking for a book by a particular author, you would look for the *author card.* If you know the title of the book but not the name of the author, you would look for the *title card.* If you need information about a particular subject (rockets and rocketry, for instance) but do not have a specific book or author in mind, you would look for a *subject card;* that is, you would look for cards with the word *ROCKETS* at the top.

Study the sample cards and explanation below.

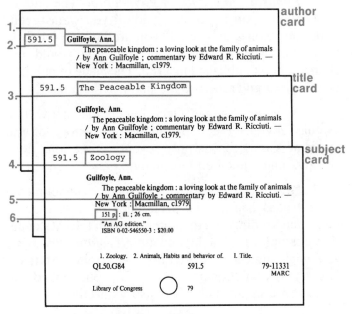

Principal Items of Information on a Card

1. *Name of author.* This information appears first on author cards, which are filed alphabetically under the author's last name. All books by one author are then arranged in the alphabetical order of titles. An author's birth date is often given after the name.

2. *Call number.* This Dewey decimal number tells you where to find the book in the nonfiction section of the library.

3. *Title of book.* On title cards this information appears first. Title cards are filed alphabetically in the card catalogue according to the first word of the title, not counting the words *a, an,* or *the.*

4. *Subject.* The subject of a book appears first on subject cards. Like author cards and title cards, they are arranged alphabetically in the card catalogue.

5. *Publisher and date of publication.* The date of publication is an important guide if you want recent information on a subject. If you are looking for facts about last year's baseball season, you would not choose a book published in 1980. The place of publication is often given before the publisher's name.

6. *Number of pages.* Occasionally this fact will be useful. Obviously a book about the history of the Supreme Court that is only seventy pages long does not give much detailed information.

7. *"See" and "see also" references.* Sometimes a subject card has a "see" reference or a "see also" reference sending you to another card in the catalogue. For example, if you looked up *Revolutionary War,* you might find a card saying, "See United States — History — Revolutionary War." If you looked up *Diving,* you might find, "See also Skin Diving."

EXERCISE 3. Using the card catalogue, list the call number, title, author, and date of publication of one book on each of five of the following topics.

1. French Impressionist painters
2. Lasers
3. Birds of Europe
4. Baseball
5. Florence Nightingale
6. South America
7. American poets and poetry
8. Computer games
9. Japanese Americans
10. Scientists

REFERENCE BOOKS

24d. Learn to use the reference books available in the library.

The section devoted to reference books is one of the most important parts of a library. These books contain information on a great many subjects or tell where such information can be found. Once you become familiar with the different reference books in your library, they will prove a valuable aid to your studies.

Encyclopedias

An encyclopedia contains articles on a wide range of subjects. These articles are written by experts and present information not only through words but through pictures, charts, and maps. Many articles, especially articles about cities, states, and countries, contain lists of facts and tables of figures. When you are writing a report, an encyclopedia article will give you a good overall view of the subject and may also suggest more detailed sources of information.

Three encyclopedias for persons of your age are

Compton's Pictured Encyclopedia
World Book Encyclopedia
Collier's Encyclopedia

All these encyclopedias consist of many volumes and arrange their articles alphabetically by subject. The guide letter or letters on the spine of each volume will help you to find information about a particular subject. Guide words at the top of each page will help you to find a specific article. Use them as you would use guide words in a dictionary. (See pages 460–61.) If you cannot find an article under a particular subject, look for similar subjects or for a larger subject that includes yours. For example, information on *super-sonic flight* can probably be found in an article on *aviation.*

You can also find information in an encyclopedia by using the index. Most encyclopedias have indexes, but the indexes are not always located in the same place. For example, the index of *Collier's Encyclo-pedia* is the last volume, while the index in *Compton's Encyclopedia* is at the end of each volume. You can use the index to locate maps, charts, tables, and il-lustrations, as well as articles about a particular subject. Usually there is a guide to using the index at the beginning of the index itself.

The index in the last volume of the *World Book Encyclopedia* is in somewhat different form. It is a "Reading and Study Guide," which is arranged by subjects. Each subject is divided into a series of smaller subjects for which a list of articles available in the encyclopedia is given.

EXERCISE 4. Look up two of the topics below in an encyclopedia and take half a page of notes on each of them. Below each group of notes, write the title of the article, the name of the encyclopedia, the volume number, and the number of the page on which you found the information.

EXAMPLE 1. The tourist industry in Hawaii
      1. *3,000,000 tourists visit Hawaii annu-ally. Busiest months are July and August. The Hawaii Visitors Bureau, founded in 1903 and supported by the government and by business people, holds advertising campaigns to attract tourists. "Hawaii" World Book En-cyclopedia, volume 9, page 102*

 1. Soft-coal mining in the United States

2. The paintings of Mary Cassatt
3. Famous volcanoes
4. Dinosaurs
5. The Battle of Hastings
6. The origin of bowling
7. Penguins
8. The native tribes of Australia
9. The rules and strategy of backgammon
10. The invention of the Diesel engine
11. The statues on Easter Island
12. How to care for a pet
13. Ambergris, its origins and uses
14. The electron microscope
15. The population and industries of Maine
16. The building of the Appian Way
17. The ruins at Angkor Wat
18. Mesmerism
19. Stonehenge
20. Electronic music

Atlases

Atlases are reference books made up mainly of maps. Often they contain much other information, such as the population figures for cities, states, and countries; principal crops; natural resources; and major industries.

Atlases are of several kinds. Some contain maps for all the countries of the world. Others contain maps for a particular country only. Historical atlases show how countries have changed through the years, while economic atlases show such things as trade routes and natural resources. Several of the common atlases are

The Encyclopaedia Britannica Atlas
Hammond Contemporary World Atlas
National Geographic World Atlas
Rand McNally Popular World Atlas

Atlases will prove valuable in your history and geography courses. You should learn about the different kinds of information that atlases provide and become thoroughly familiar with at least one atlas.

EXERCISE 5. Consult a world atlas and write answers to two of the following questions.

1. Name three national parks in California.
2. List three important geographical features (mountains, rivers, plains, deserts, lakes, etc.) of each of the following countries:
   a. Brazil   b. Algeria   c. England
3. List the countries which border on each of the following:
   a. Switzerland   b. Venezuela   c. Turkey
4. List four major products of each of the following countries:
   a. Bolivia   b. Ethiopia   c. Pakistan   d. Iraq
5. In which country is each of the following cities situated?
   a. Volgograd   b. Riyadh   c. Jena   d. Sapporo
6. List the following states in order of population beginning with the highest:
   a. Illinois   c. Virginia   e. Maine
   b. Alaska   d. Ohio   f. California

Almanacs

An almanac consists in large part of lists of miscellaneous information, including sports statistics, names of government officials, population figures, and birth and death rates. In addition, an almanac is a good place to find much recent information, since almanacs are published annually and give many facts about the preceding year. For instance, if you want a review of the important events of last year, you should consult this year's almanac.

Three useful almanacs are *The World Almanac and Book of Facts,* the *Information Please Almanac,* and *The CBS News Almanac.* The various kinds of information in an almanac are not organized alphabetically or according to any other kind of logical, systematic arrangement. The best way to find information in an almanac is to use the index. In *The World Almanac* the index is at the front of the book, while in the other almanacs it is at the back.

EXERCISE 6. Consult one of the almanacs mentioned above and write answers to two of the following questions.

1. Give the birth dates and birthplaces of the following persons: (Look up "Personalities, noted" or "Celebrated persons.")
    a. Eudora Welty   d. Robert Redford
    b. Mike Nichols   e. Jesse Jackson
    c. Billie Jean King
2. Give the names of the Secretaries of State during the administrations of the following Presidents:
    a. John Quincy Adams   d. William Taft
    b. William Harrison   e. Warren Harding
    c. Abraham Lincoln
3. Who won the Nobel Prize for physics in 1923? 1938? 1946? 1970? 1976?
4. Give the name of the author and novel that won the Pulitzer Prize for fiction in each of the following years:
    a. 1926   c. 1947   e. 1959
    b. 1928   d. 1955   f. 1980

Biographical Reference Books

A biographical reference book contains short biographies of famous persons. The following are among the most useful of these books. Find out whether they are in your library.

Who's Who, and Who's Who in America — useful for principal biographical facts about living persons only.

Webster's Biographical Dictionary — very short biographies of famous persons, modern and historical.

Contemporary Authors and Contemporary Authors: First Revision — interesting profiles of modern writers.

Current Biography — lives of persons currently prominent in the news. Published monthly.

THE READERS' GUIDE

To find a magazine article on any subject, you use a very valuable reference book called the Readers' Guide to Periodical Literature. Published twice a month (once a month in July and August), the Readers' Guide indexes articles in more than one hundred magazines. Every two years the issues are collected and published in a large volume. You can look up an article by its subject (like Tutenkhamun) or by its author. To save space, the listings use abbreviations. If you are in doubt about the meaning of the abbreviations, you should consult the keys in the front of the Readers' Guide.

Study the excerpts (on the following page) from an issue of the Readers' Guide. The marginal notes will make clear the information given.

Suppose you are writing an article about ancient Egypt and wish to include some information about King Tut's tomb. The Reader's Guide (see the opposite page) would lead you first to the subject Tutenkhamun, then to the subdivision Tomb, and finally

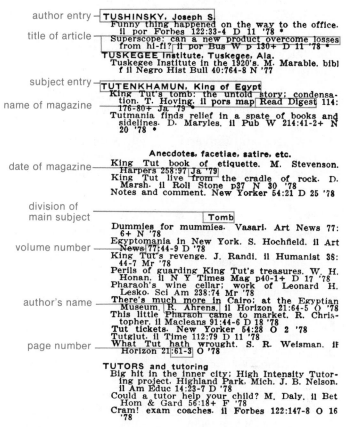

author entry — TUSHINSKY, Joseph S.
Funny thing happened on the way to the office.
il por Forbes 122:33-4 D 11 '78 •
title of article — Superscope: can a new product overcome losses
from hi-fi? il por Bus W p 130+ D 11 '78 •
TUSKEGEE Institute, Tuskegee, Ala.
Tuskegee Institute in the 1920's. M. Marable. bibl
f il Negro Hist Bull 40:764-8 N '77

subject entry — TUTENKHAMUN, King of Egypt
King Tut's tomb: the untold story; condensa-
name of magazine — tion. T. Hoving. il pors map Read Digest 114:
176-80+ Ja '79 •
Tutmania finds relief in a spate of books and
sidelines. D. Maryles. il Pub W 214:41-2+ N
20 '78 •

Anecdotes, facetiae, satire, etc.
date of magazine — King Tut book of etiquette. M. Stevenson.
Harpers 258:97 Ja '79
King Tut live from the cradle of rock. D.
Marsh. il Roll Stone p37 N 30 '78
Notes and comment. New Yorker 54:21 D 25 '78

division of
main subject — Tomb
Dummies for mummies. Vasari. Art News 77:
6+ N '78
Egyptomania in New York. S. Hochfield. il Art
volume number — News 77:44-9 D '78
King Tut's revenge. J. Randi. il Humanist 38:
44-7 Mr '78
Perils of guarding King Tut's treasures. W. H.
Honan. il N Y Times Mag p40-1+ D 17 '78
Pharaoh's wine cellar; work of Leonard H.
Lesko. Sci Am 238:74 Mr '78
author's name — There's much more in Cairo; at the Egyptian
Museum. R. Ahrens. il Horizon 21:64-5 () '78
This little Pharaoh came to market. R. Chris-
topher. il Macleans 91:44-6 D 18 '78
Tut tickets. New Yorker 54:28 O 2 '78
Tutglut. il Time 112:79 D 11 '78
page number — What Tut hath wrought. S. R. Weisman. il
Horizon 21:61-3 O '78

TUTORS and tutoring
Big hit in the inner city; High Intensity Tutor-
ing project, Highland Park, Mich. J. B. Nelson.
il Am Educ 14:23-7 D '78
Could a tutor help your child? M. Daly. il Bet
Hom & Gard 56:18+ F '78
Cram! exam coaches. il Forbes 122:147-8 O 16
'78

to an article by W. H. Honan in the *New York Times Magazine* of December 17, 1978. The entry for this article gives the following information:

An article about King Tut's tomb titled "Perils of Guarding King Tut's Treasures" by W. H. Honan can be found in the *New York Times Magazine.* The article, which is illustrated (il), begins on page 40 and is continued on later pages (p40–1+) of the December 17, 1978, issue (D 17 '78).

EXERCISE 7. In the *Readers' Guide,* find an article listed under any five of the following subjects. Copy the entry for the article. Be ready to explain the information for the entry.

1. Scandinavia
2. Phonograph records
3. Lakes
4. Colleges and universities
5. Personnel management

6. Space probes
7. Elephants
8. Coal
9. Submarine boats, atomic powered
10. Washington, D.C.

SUMMARY LIST OF LIBRARY REFERENCE TOOLS

The card catalogue
Reference books
   Encyclopedias
   Atlases
   Almanacs
   Biographical reference books
      Who's Who
      Who's Who in America
      Webster's Biographical Dictionary
      Contemporary Authors
      Contemporary Authors: First Revision
      Current Biography
   Readers' Guide to Periodical Literature

REVIEW EXERCISE. Number your paper 1–20. Write the reference tool from the preceding list to which you would turn first to get information on the corresponding subject in the list below.

1. Latest developments in cancer research
2. History of the Nobel Prize
3. Source of the Mississippi River
4. Antarctica—climate, terrain, etc.
5. Motion Picture Academy Award winners in 1980

6. Title and author of a library book on outer space
7. Diplomatic career of James Russell Lowell, the American poet
8. Origins of jazz music
9. Titles of novels by Joy Adamson (1910–1980), a writer
10. Population of Naples, Italy
11. Natural resources of the Rhineland in Germany
12. A list of magazine articles on a recent international crisis
13. The work of Grant Wood, American artist
14. Winners of the World Series since 1977
15. The title of a book in the library on the Revolutionary War
16. Height of Mt. Everest
17. Facts about the present Secretary of State
18. History of Italian opera
19. Facts about Ralph Ellison, the American author
20. The biography of a person who has only recently become prominent in the news

Chapter 25

Vocabulary

Context, Word Analysis, Word Choice

The books you have read, the games you play, school subjects, hobbies — all your interests are reflected in your vocabulary. It is no surprise then that teachers and parents rely on vocabulary growth as one way of measuring success in school. Knowing many words, of course, does not make anyone a good student automatically. But hardly anyone does well in school without developing a good vocabulary.

Although there is no simple way to acquire a large vocabulary, there are ways in which you can learn and remember more of the words you encounter every day. This chapter will give you practice in using these methods. It will also introduce you to a number of words that are widely used in the books you will be reading this year and in the future.

To keep a record of your progress and to refresh your memory, set aside a section of your notebook in which to enter the new words you learn, together with a definition and a sentence or phrase illustrating their use. You can begin your vocabulary notebook with any unfamiliar words that you encounter in the following diagnostic test.

Diagnostic Test

Number your paper 1–25. After the proper number, write the letter of the word that is closest in meaning to the numbered word.

EXAMPLE   1. hamper   a. build   c. hinder
                          b. revise   d. search

     1. *c*

1. abashed   a. beaten   c. lowered
                b. ashamed   d. fallen

2. adept   a. skillful   c. proud
              b. bold   d. lazy

3. amity   a. boredom   c. anger
             b. hatred   d. friendship

4. belligerent   a. dull   c. swift
                   b. warlike   d. gentle

5. crony   a. old woman   c. candy
             b. tower   d. friend

6. deluge   a. opinion   c. excitement
              b. illusion   d. flood

7. dexterity   a. sugar   c. handiness
                b. duplicate   d. kindness

8. fatigue   a. war   c. fatalist
              b. weariness   d. explosion

9. guffaw   a. laugh   c. loosen
             b. retire   d. drive

10. haughty   a. moderate   c. proud
              b. smiling   d. slow

11. humdrum   a. melodious   c. aggressive
                b. loud   d. dull

12. levity   a. simple lever   c. earnestness
            b. excessive   d. lack of
               speed   seriousness

13. menace   a. army   c. song
             b. threat   d. rival

14. pallid   a. pale   c. sleepy
            b. excited   d. calm
15. pedagogue   a. teacher   c. politician
            b. learning   d. politics
16. primitive   a. undeveloped   c. violent
            b. prominent   d. religious
17. raze   a. lift   c. destroy
            b. attack   d. repel
18. remorse   a. repetition   c. justice
            b. guilt   d. reason
19. revile   a. abuse   c. rebuild
            b. correct   d. bury
20. seraphic   a. telegraphic   c. angelic
            b. intelligent   d. serious
21. sinew   a. novelty   c. disappointment
            b. excitement   d. strength
22. tepid   a. unlucky   c. alone
            b. lukewarm   d. rushing
23. unique   a. special   c. uneven
            b. together   d. heavy
24. vehement   a. energetic   c. timid
            b. serious   d. laughing
25. visage   a. cage   c. face
            b. news   d. tang

LEARNING NEW WORDS

Occasionally we see or hear a word used alone, but most of the time we encounter words used in combination with other words. When the word is unfamiliar, these surrounding words often supply valuable clues to meaning.

25a. Learn new words from context.

The *context* of a word means the words that surround it in a sentence and the whole situation in which the word is used. The context of the word supplies the main clue to the meaning of *edible* in this sentence:

> The cook was told not to use toadstools in the stew because they are not edible.

Since the cook was warned against using the toadstools in a stew, it stands to reason that something *not edible* is something "not fit to eat." If you know that much about toadstools already, you can be even surer about your guess.

Many common English words have several different meanings. The context often provides clues to their meanings. For example, *pound* means one thing in a grocery store, another in a story about a dogcatcher, and still another in a British movie. Context clues will aid you in understanding these words when you encounter them in your reading.

EXERCISE 1. Number your paper 1–10. For each italicized word in the sentences below, write the letter of the definition that is closest in meaning. You will not need all the definitions in the list. Check your answers in the dictionary.

a. calm
b. peak
c. guidance
d. magic
e. pronounced
f. honesty
g. government
h. swung to hit
i. fearful
j. confused
k. without success
l. round of applause

1. Mrs. Tompkins has been the treasurer for twenty-seven years, and no one doubts her *integrity*.
2. The angry mob gathered at the palace to express their disapproval of the *regime*.
3. At twenty-four, Lisa Chin is at the very *summit* of her tennis career.

4. The fortuneteller claimed that she had *occult* powers.
5. He is so *timorous* that he refuses to go to sleep in the dark.
6. Tired and unhappy, the baby *flailed* angrily at the bars of her playpen.
7. At the end of the play, the enthusiastic audience gave the actors a rousing *ovation*.
8. She could not solve the puzzle because it *bewildered* her.
9. The doctor spoke comforting words to *allay* the patient's fears.
10. The speaker *articulated* her words with care.

EXERCISE 2. Follow the directions in Exercise 1.

a. aloneness   g. respect
b. reduce   h. get well
c. bravery   i. disaster
d. avoid   j. insult
e. good luck   k. joy
f. ambition   l. imaginary

1. The soldiers bowed to the emperor as a sign of *deference.*
2. The earthquake, a *catastrophe* causing hundreds of deaths and thousands of injuries, came unexpectedly.
3. Harold has a *fictitious* playmate, whom no one has ever seen.
4. Luke finds it extremely difficult to make friends because he has lived the greater part of his life in *isolation.*
5. After a successful operation, a patient usually remains in the hospital to *recuperate.*
6. With a roar the crowd expressed its *jubilation* at the football victory.
7. People should not attempt to *evade* their duties as citizens.

8. If the railroad keeps on losing money, it will have to *curtail* its services.
9. José's *aspiration* is to win the lead in the school play.
10. Private Lewis showed such *valor* in battle that he was promoted to corporal.

Related Word Forms

25b. Learn the related forms of new words.

Some words can be used as different parts of speech without changing their spelling. The word *iron* can be a noun, an adjective, or a verb: a piece of *iron,* an *iron* bar, to *iron* a dress. More often, however, something is added or taken away from the word to change it from one part of speech to another. The ending *–ly* can be added to most adjectives to make them adverbs (*soft, softly*), and the ending *–ness* is often added to make them nouns (*softness*). You will study more about such changes later in this chapter. The main thing now is to be aware that a new word may have related forms that are just as useful as the one you have encountered. When you can learn two or three new words with no more effort than it takes to learn one word, why not do it?

EXERCISE 3. The first part of each numbered pair contains an italicized word used as a particular part of speech. The second part of each pair contains a blank in which a related form of the same word will fit. Number your paper 1–10 and supply the appropriate form. Use your dictionary if you need to.

EXAMPLE   1. an act of *valor*
            a —— action
          1. *valorous*

1. a *coherent* explanation
   to explain with ——
2. to *aspire* to something
   noble
   a noble ——
3. an *isolated* farmhouse
   to live in ——
4. to *evade* responsibilities
   an ____ of one's duty
5. to *coerce* a person
   to get something by ——

6. a *futile* attempt
   to try —— to do
   something
7. the *tumult* of a battle
   a —— scene
8. the *validity* of an argument
   a —— reason
9. *appropriate* behavior
   to behave ——
10. a skillful *diplomat*
    skill in ——

Using the Dictionary

25c. Learn to find the meaning you want in your dictionary.

When you cannot guess the meaning of a word from context, you should go to your dictionary. Context is still important, however. Most words have a number of different meanings, and the best way of finding the one you want is to look for the definition that fits the context in which you originally encountered the word. Consider the following sentence:

> Your jokes are in poor taste, Harold, and we can dispense with any more of them.

Dispense has the following meanings: (1) to give; (2) to distribute; (3) to get rid of; (4) to get along without. By trying each of these meanings in place of the word *dispense* in the example, you can easily eliminate all of the choices except the last one—the meaning you want.

Which of these numbered meanings for *dispense* fits the following sentence?

The Red Cross dispensed food and clothing to the flood victims.

Dictionaries often supply sample contexts to help you distinguish between the various meanings of a word (see pages 462–63). Such phrases can be very helpful in showing you how to use the new word in your own speech and writing.

EXERCISE 4. The italicized words in the following sentences have a number of different meanings. Using your dictionary, select the meaning that best fits each sentence and write it after the proper number.

EXAMPLE   1. A candidate for the presidency is likely to be an *eminent* political figure.
1. *prominent*

1. The doctor said that there was nothing to be feared from the *benign* swelling.
2. The old man gave us a *benign* smile.
3. The professor's lecture *illuminated* the subject for us.
4. With the flick of a switch, he can *illuminate* the entire garden.
5. As we drove into the valley, a beautiful *pastoral* scene unrolled before us.
6. The minister attended to his *pastoral* duties.
7. Your argument seems *valid* and has convinced us all.
8. Since this is a *valid* contract, you will have to live up to it.
9. The manager's *bland* words calmed the angry customer.
10. I don't like this cereal because it is too *bland*.

EXERCISE 5. The following two columns consist of a list of words and a list of definitions for these words. Number your paper 1–10. After the proper number, copy the letter of the definition that is closest in meaning. Refer to a dictionary when necessary. You will not use all the definitions in the second column.

1. chronic	a. calm and serious
2. appalling	b. to climb rapidly
3. sedate	c. numerous
4. forgo	d. shocking
5. prodigy	e. person having special abilities
6. myriad	f. arrival of an important event
7. debonair	g. give up
8. advent	h. slowly falling
9. decrepit	i. lively and gay
10. pewter	j. heavy silver-gray metal
	k. law or principle
	l. continuing for a long time
	m. foolishly happy
	n. feeble

REVIEW EXERCISE A. The words in this exercise have been chosen from those you have studied so far. Number your paper 1–20. After the proper number, write the letter of the word nearest in meaning.

1. evade
   a. run
   b. avoid
   c. trick
   d. lose

2. coerce
   a. cooperate
   b. lag behind
   c. refuse
   d. compel

3. pastoral
   a. finely made
   b. about rural life
   c. of the past
   d. richly perfumed

4. fictitious
   a. handsome
   b. invented
   c. musical
   d. genuine

5. regime
   a. airplane
   b. beating
   c. government
   d. regulation

6. malign   a. evil   c. kind
   - b. silly   d. worthless
7. summit   a. dessert   c. peak
   - b. rebellion   d. leap
8. illuminate   a. go as   c. argue with
   - b. light up   d. seem like
9. valor   a. courage   c. wisdom
   - b. laziness   d. vanity
10. tumult   a. disturbance   c. motive
    - b. accident   d. hatred
11. bewilder   a. prepare   c. confused
    - b. bewitch   d. lose
12. eminent   a. small   c. prominent
    - b. permanent   d. clever
13. curtail   a. correct   c. finish
    - b. build   d. reduce
14. timorous   a. unreliable   c. trusting
    - b. afraid   d. royal
15. flail   a. restore   c. beat
    - b. chase   d. impress
16. integrity   a. honesty   c. misery
    - b. loyalty   d. treachery
17. recuperate   a. lessen   c. duplicate
    - b. refill   d. recover
18. coherent   a. clear   c. mistaken
    - b. scrambled   d. recent
19. aspiration   a. relief   c. ambition
    - b. slogan   d. notion
20. benign   a. evil   c. dangerous
    - b. kind   d. pale

PREFIXES, ROOTS, AND SUFFIXES

Some words can be divided into parts, and some cannot. Those that can be divided, like *workbook* and *unhappy,* often consist of parts that mean something separately. By learning how to divide words into their parts, you can sometimes discover additional clues to meaning.

The basic part of a word is called a *root*. A part added before the root is called a *prefix;* a part added after the root is called a *suffix*. Becoming familiar with the common prefixes and suffixes discussed in the following pages will provide you with helpful leads to finding the meaning of a large number of new words.

Prefixes

25d. Learn how common prefixes change the meaning of words.

The following common prefixes occur in thousands of English words.

PREFIX	MEANING	EXAMPLE
auto–	self	automobile
bi–	two	bimonthly
circum–	around	circumference
con–	together	concord
de–	down or from	degrade
dis–	away or apart	disagree
ex–	out	expel
im–	not	impractical
mis–	wrong	misjudge
multi–	many	multiply
pre–	before	preview
semi–	half or partly	semiprecious

EXERCISE 6. Number your paper 1–10. After the proper number, give the meaning of the italicized word in each of the sentences. Be prepared to tell how the prefix of the word helps determine its meaning. Use the dictionary if necessary.

1. The assistant principal *convened* the student council to draft a new student code of conduct.
2. An artillery shell completely *demolished* the hut.
3. He gave some *preposterous* excuse for not passing the test.
4. Our newspaper is published *biweekly*.
5. Laura Chou was born in Hong Kong and was not brought to the United States until she was six years old; therefore, she is *bilingual*.
6. Some of the czars of Russia were cruel *autocrats* who were feared by the people.
7. To call Alvin a worker is a *misnomer* since he is always asleep with a broom in his hands.
8. Mrs. Boscombe cut small *semicircles* of paper with the sharp scissors.
9. The *dissident* members of the council held a protest meeting.
10. Mrs. Boone is a thorough housekeeper, and her apartment is always *immaculate*.

EXERCISE 7. Follow the directions for Exercise 6.

1. Ferdinand Magellan, the Portuguese sailor and explorer, *circumnavigated* the globe.
2. The girl held a large, *multicolored* ball in her hands.
3. The mechanic had to *dismantle* the motor to find the faulty part.
4. Holding a lantern, she slowly *descended* the cellar stairs.
5. Because Mr. and Mrs. Harrison are a *congenial* couple, they rarely quarrel.
6. The theft of the jewels showed careful planning and must have been a *premeditated* crime.
7. We finally *dissuaded* Tom from writing a letter to the author.
8. Archimedes is supposed to have *exclaimed* "Eureka!" as he made an important discovery.
9. The Pueblo Indians have observed this custom since time *immemorial*.

10. The Whitmore Construction Company is building a group of *semidetached* houses on this block.

EXERCISE 8. Follow the directions for Exercise 6.

1. Frank has become so efficient at packaging toys that he moves like an *automaton.*
2. The people, angry over years of misrule, *deposed* the unjust king.
3. Remember Shakespeare's *immortal* words: "This above all, to thine own self be true."
4. The Smiths own *extensive* lands in this valley.
5. Mrs. Slocum showed how to *bisect* an angle.
6. Is the prisoner truly sorry for his *misdeeds,* or is he only sorry he was caught?
7. Ms. Feinstein stayed in a *semiprivate* hospital room.
8. The prisoner was allowed to move freely within a *circumscribed* area.
9. Next year our city will hold its *bicentennial* celebration.
10. Melba MacHenry Gardner, who donated the money for our new Civic Center, is a *multi-millionaire.*

Suffixes

25e. Learn to recognize common suffixes when they occur in *companion forms.*

Sometimes adding a suffix will result in a word that is a different part of speech than the original word. For example, the suffix *–ly* added to the adjective *free* results in *freely,* an adverb. The suffix *–ly* occurs at the end of an adjective or an adverb but never at the end of a noun. Therefore, words ending in this suffix are never nouns. (When *–ly* occurs at the end of a noun such as *lily,* these letters are not a suffix but part of the basic word.)

There are many English words to which suffixes can be added. The new words formed by adding suffixes are *companion forms* of the basic word. Adding suffixes to the root *free* results in the companion forms *freedom* and *freely.* If you are on the alert for companion forms and learn some common suffixes, you will often be able to guess the correct meanings of new words. One fact to keep in mind is that the spelling of the root may change when a suffix is added. For example, when *–ly* is added to *gay,* the resulting word is not *gayly* but *gaily.* When *–ition* is added to *repeat,* the resulting word is spelled *repetition.*

Learn the following suffixes that occur in nouns.

SUFFIX	MEANING	EXAMPLE
–hood	condition	childhood
–ness	quality	goodness
–ance, ence	state, act, fact	independence
–ation, –ition, –tion	action or state	celebration
–ity, –ty	quality	ability
–ment	result or action	employment

EXERCISE 9. Number your paper 1–10. Form nouns from the following words by using the suffixes listed above; then give the meanings of the new words. In some cases, it will be necessary to change the spelling of the root. Check your answers with the dictionary.

EXAMPLES 1. kind
       1. *kindness* — the quality of being kind
      2. create
      2. *creation* — the act of creating

1. replace	6. man
2. likely	7. fragile
3. articulate	8. aspire
4. accept	9. improvise
5. intense	10. friendly

The following suffixes occur in adjectives.

SUFFIX	MEANING	EXAMPLE
–ish	like or suggesting	foolish
–able, –ible	able	tolerable
–ous	having the quality of	religious
–esque	like	statuesque
–some	like or tending to	tiresome

EXERCISE 10. Number your paper 1–10. Form adjectives from the following words by using the suffixes listed above, and then give the meanings of the new words. Check your answers with the dictionary, and make changes if necessary.

1. lone
2. picture
3. harmony
4. devil
5. grace
6. baby
7. luxury
8. depend
9. meddle
10. riot

Learn the following suffixes, which occur in verbs.

SUFFIX	MEANING	EXAMPLE
–ate	cause to become	animate
–en	make or become	deepen
–fy	make or cause	fortify
–ize	cause to be	motorize

EXERCISE 11. Number your paper 1–10. Form verbs from the following words by using the suffixes listed above; then give the meanings of the new words. Check your answers with the dictionary, and make changes if necessary.

1. captive
2. critic
3. strength
4. nausea
5. glory
6. active
7. civil
8. sweet
9. illumine
10. beauty

EXERCISE 12. Each of the following sentences has a word with a suffix that you have learned in this chapter. Number your paper 1–10. After the proper number, find and copy the word and underline the suffix. Then write the meaning of the word. In some cases, you may be able to guess the correct meaning. In others, the root of the word may not be familiar to you, and you will have to look up the word in a dictionary. Check *all* your answers with the dictionary.

EXAMPLE   1. Gerry's arrogance has caused him to be disliked by many people.
          1. *arro<u>gance</u>, state of being arrogant*

1. The beautiful scenery provided the artist with inspiration enough for fifty paintings.
2. The sentries in the prison camp were not allowed to fraternize with the enemy.
3. Job prayed to be relieved of his afflictions.
4. During Thanksgiving the store had a window display showing the courageous Pilgrims.
5. The two countries formed an alliance to help each other in case of war.
6. The refinement of her manners is proof of her strict upbringing.
7. This company believes that it has an obligation to please all of its clients.
8. The coat of shellac guaranteed that the table surface would be durable.
9. Factories should not be allowed to fill our waters with waste products that might contaminate them.
10. *Carmen* is regarded as one of the most melodious of all French operas.

USING EXACT WORDS

25f. Use the exact word in your speaking and writing.

In English, many thousands of words are available

to help you express exactly what you mean. If you use the same few words to describe many different people or things or actions or situations, you are not taking advantage of the variety of your language. Avoid the overworked word that is used in so many different contexts that it loses a precise meaning. *Good* is one such word. If you were to refer to someone as "a good woman," would you mean that she is capable, kind, or dependable? If you were to say, "I had a good day," would you mean an enjoyable, a productive, or a tranquil day? *Good* might be the first word that occurs to you to describe a woman or a day, but a moment's thought will usually supply a better word to express your meaning. Of course, the greater the stock of words at your command, the easier it will be for you to substitute a fresh, precise word for a trite one.

Using Adjectives to Describe

The English language is rich in adjectives. You should learn to use adjectives to express your meaning exactly. In talking about a book you enjoyed, for example, you might say it was *interesting,* but how much more expressive you would be if you called it *exciting* or *engrossing* or *stimulating!* Build your vocabulary by taking time to find the exact adjective to express your thought.

EXERCISE 13. Each of the following sentences contains a vague or overworked adjective, in italics, which should be replaced by a more precise word. Number your paper 1–10. After the proper number, write the more precise adjective from the list preceding the sentences. You will not need all the words in the list. Use the dictionary, if necessary, to check your answers and make corrections.

eccentric	customary	appalling
casual	burly	fluent
titanic	sallow	tangible
fragrant	devout	eligible
decrepit	insipid	boisterous

1. That rice pudding had a rather *flat* taste.
2. The *old* car drove slowly down the road.
3. The damage done by the hurricane was *shocking*.
4. The *muscular* sailor pushed against the door.
5. Paul is regarded as *odd* because he puts mustard on ice cream.
6. When we began to sing and shout, our counselor warned us that we were being too *lively*.
7. With a *great* effort, Samson tore down the pillars of the Philistine temple.
8. The foreman of the jury said that no *real* evidence of guilt had been produced.
9. No student who is failing one or more subjects is *qualified* for a student council position.
10. The roses were *sweet-smelling*.

EXERCISE 14. Number your paper 1–5. After the proper number, write an adjective from the list below which conveys an idea appropriate to the sentence having that number. You will not use all the words in the list. Use the dictionary, if necessary.

diverse	feasible	abundant
latent	oratorical	excessive
resolute	homogeneous	pertinent

1. Ms. Henderson's system of programing students seems to work well.
2. Once Fran has a goal in life, nothing will stop her from reaching it.
3. Your statement is very much to the point.
4. Ana has talent, but it needs to be developed.
5. All the women in this group are the same age and height, and all have the same interests.

Using Verbs to Express Action

Your ability to express yourself is directly dependent on your verb vocabulary. Verbs give action and color to your sentences. The following exercise includes a number of verbs that are important for you to know.

EXERCISE 15. Number your paper 1–10. After the proper number, copy the verb whose meaning best completes the sentence. Change the tense if necessary to fit the sentence, and use your dictionary. You will not need all the verbs in the list.

soar	liberate	restore
saturate	carouse	obliterate
diverge	pollute	browbeat
confiscate	capitulate	wheedle
restrain	stray	elapse

1. Because they could not pay their taxes, the government —— their property.
2. The fighter was badly beaten but refused to —— to his opponent.
3. Realizing that the bird would die in captivity, the girl took it to the woods and —— it.
4. As the plane —— above the clouds, the earth disappeared from view.
5. Several hours —— before the weary hikers returned home.
6. She is extremely timid and allows a great many people to —— her.
7. Skillful detective work —— the stolen painting to its rightful owners.
8. The two hunters parted company when their paths ——.
9. Two centuries of wind and weather have almost —— the words carved on the stone.
10. Although we may be tempted to overeat we should —— ourselves.

Using Adverbs to Modify Verbs

Because adverbs answer such questions as *How? When?* and *Where?* in connection with verbs, they are a very important part of your vocabulary. The exactness and vividness of your writing and speaking depend a great deal upon your using adverbs well. In the exercise which follows, there are a number of adverbs for you to learn. Many of these adverbs are formed from words in the list beginning on page 523.

EXERCISE 16. Number your paper 1–10. After the proper number, write an adverb from the list which answers the question. You will not need all the adverbs in the list. Use the dictionary, if necessary.

immensely	resonantly	superficially
covertly	scrupulously	rigidly
abruptly	urgently	cautiously
excessively	anonymously	ostentatiously

1. How did the conscientious bookkeeper keep the company's records?
2. How did the woman who found there were burglars in her house call for the police?
3. How did the opera star sing the low notes in his aria?
4. How did the audience like the actor's superb performance?
5. How did the newly engaged girl display her engagement ring?
6. How did the tired student check her homework for mistakes?
7. How did the little boy try to get a cookie from the cookie jar when his mother was in the next room?
8. How would a person stand if imitating or posing for a statue?
9. How does a doctor leave a dinner party upon receiving an emergency call?

10. How does a person cross a busy city street during rush hour?

Synonyms and Antonyms

A *synonym* is a word which means nearly the same thing as another word. Sometimes a dictionary will define a word in terms of its synonym: one definition of *benign* is "kind." While words that are synonyms are close in meaning, they rarely have *exactly* the same meaning. At times you will be able to use one of several words in a sentence, but at other times only the exact word will do.

Pleasure, delight, and *joy* all have roughly the same meaning, yet each expresses a different shade of meaning. *Pleasure* is the most general of the three words; it covers a variety of situations, none of them very specifically. *Delight* indicates a sharp feeling of pleasure that lasts only a short time. *Joy* may indicate a deep and long-lasting happiness. In the following sentence, which of the three words fits most exactly?

I receive great —— from my study of mathematics.

Pleasure fits, of course, but is not very specific. *Delight* does not fit very well because the feeling indicated in this sentence would seem to last for some time. The synonym that most exactly expresses the desired meaning is *joy*.

When you look up a word in a dictionary, you will often find several synonyms listed. Be sure you understand the exact meaning of each synonym. To help you to distinguish between synonyms, some dictionaries give *synonym articles*—brief explanations of a word's synonyms and how they differ in meaning. Your own reading will also help you. The more often you encounter a word in different contexts, the better you will be able to determine its meaning.

EXERCISE 17. Number your paper 1–10. After the proper number, write the synonym you have selected which best fits the sentence. Use your dictionary to learn the exact meaning of each synonym.

1. My jacket is made of a new (fabricated, artificial, synthetic) material.
2. Our (invincible, victorious, triumphant) army never has been and never should be defeated in battle.
3. The monks in several medieval monasteries kept (histories, annals, records) summarizing the important events of each year.
4. Medieval artists had a special (fashion, technique, system) for making stained-glass windows.
5. The young couple fondly (fed, nourished, sustained) their baby daughter.
6. You can imagine how (embarrassing, shaming, humiliating) it was to be spanked in front of all my relatives.
7. Her (guess, conjecture, estimate) that there would be a test the next day was based on the fact that Mrs. Brown had assigned no homework that night.
8. Although the lawyer stayed within the law, he relied on (guile, cunning, fraud) to win his case.
9. Under the new government, many citizens were (dispossessed, deprived, divested) of their rights.
10. After studying the problem, Dr. Paley formed a working (theory, hypothesis, supposition), which she tested by experiment.

The antonym of a word is a word with the opposite meaning. *Bad* is the antonym of *good,* and *happy* is the antonym of *sad.* Sometimes an antonym of a word is formed by adding a prefix meaning *not:* an antonym of *wise* is *unwise.* Knowing the antonym of a word will often help you to understand the word's exact meaning (or at least one exact meaning). For example, knowing that *dexterity* is the antonym of *clumsiness* will lead you to a correct meaning for this word. A dictionary sometimes lists antonyms at the end of an entry for a word.

EXERCISE 18. Antonyms for words in the first column below may be found in the second column. Number your paper 1–10. After the proper number, write the letter of the correct antonym. You will not need all the words in the second column. Use the dictionary, if necessary.

1. frustrate	a. tiny
2. contemptible	b. dawn
3. colossal	c. ornamental
4. impertinent	d. spiteful
5. upbraid	e. satisfy
6. twilight	f. wordiness
7. brevity	g. biased
8. neutral	h. probity
9. functional	i. orderly
10. random	j. eventual
	k. admirable
	l. courteous
	m. remarkable
	n. praise

SPECIAL VOCABULARIES

Each of your school subjects has special words that you must learn if you are to understand the concepts. Some of the words are new, while others, which are used in everyday speech, have special meanings in a particular subject.

A textbook often calls attention to these new words by printing them in italics or in heavy type. Printing a word in a special way shows that it is important. Often a definition immediately follows the word. If not, turn to the back of the book to see if there is a glossary — a short dictionary of special words. There you will usually find a definition for the word. Always use a glossary when a textbook provides one. It is one of the most valuable features of a book.

EXERCISE 19. The words below are used in mathematics books designed for students of your age. Write each word on your paper, and follow it by a short definition. Then write a short sentence using each word correctly. Use a dictionary or the glossary in your mathematics book.

acute	intersection	quotient
bisect	irrational	radical
diameter	numeral	radius
exponent	obtuse	rational

EXERCISE 20. The following words are likely to appear in your social studies assignments. Follow the directions for Exercise 19.

History: blockade, capitalism, carpetbagger, depression, filibuster, gerrymander, initiative, recall, referendum, sharecropper, totalitarian, vassal
Geography: fjord, meridian, monsoon, plateau, precipitation, topography, tributary

EXERCISE 21. The following words are likely to appear in your science assignments. Follow the directions for Exercise 19.

antibody	embryo	neutron
atom	friction	radiation
condensation	fulcrum	satellite
electron	nebula	spectrum

25g. Use the words from specialized vocabularies in your everyday speaking and writing.

Many words in a special field are often used outside the field. *Condensation* and *inertia* are often found in nonscientific books, while *exponent* and *radical* can be used by a political speaker as well as a mathematician. Learn the meanings of these words as used outside their fields. Use them in your own speaking and writing when they help express your ideas exactly.

EXERCISE 22. The following words used in mathematics, science, and social studies have meanings outside these fields. Use these words appropriately in the blanks below. You will not use all the words.

blockade	fulcrum	obtuse
condensation	inertia	radical
diameter	initiative	satellite
embryo	intersection	vassal

1. Harriet displayed great —— in forming a drama club and recruiting members for it.
2. When you have trouble getting started on your work you are suffering from ——.
3. The newspapers have called Mayor Tompkins " a —— of special interest groups."
4. George is so —— that he didn't get the joke even after she explained it.
5. The department store has been completely re-organized; you will discover some pretty —— changes when you go there.
6. To save space, the magazine published a —— of Madeleine L'Engle's new book.
7. The fugitive ran up the stairs to the attic and ——d the entry by pushing a heavy table against the wooden door.
8. My sister will meet us at the —— of Vernon Street and Third Avenue at two o'clock.

REVIEW EXERCISE B. The words in this exercise have been chosen from all those you have studied in this chapter. Number your paper 1–33. After the proper number, write the letter of the word which is closest in meaning to the numbered word.

1. abundant
   a. house
   b. plentiful
   c. sloppy
   d. crowded

2. affliction
   a. aviation
   b. guardian
   c. report
   d. misery

3. appalling
   a. revealing
   b. annoying
   c. shocking
   d. rewarding

4. boisterous
   a. lively
   b. supporting
   c. treacherous
   d. weak

5. captivate
   a. rebuke
   b. capture
   c. charm
   d. release

6. concord
   a. sympathy
   b. conformity
   c. agreement
   d. boredom

7. covertly
   a. swiftly
   b. gaily
   c. badly
   d. secretly

8. decrepit
   a. decoyed
   b. feeble
   c. wise
   d. proud

9. deference
   a. pressure
   b. deceit
   c. respect
   d. loyalty

10. divest
    a. clothe
    b. deprive
    c. retreat
    d. amble

11. extensive
    a. large
    b. thin
    c. visual
    d. highly respected

12. feasible
    a. expensive
    b. fearful
    c. missing
    d. workable

13. flail
    a. shrink
    b. beat
    c. reveal
    d. forget

14. homogeneous a. alike   c. thoughtful
                    b. different d. respected

15. immaculate   a. forgetful c. cowardly
                    b. spotless d. intelligent

16. jubilation   a. anniversary c. terror
                    b. ceremony d. rejoicing

17. nativity   a. birth   c. ignorance
                    b. citizenship d. innocence

18. nourish   a. hate   c. love
                    b. regret d. feed

19. obscure   a. magnificent c. unclear
                    b. rosy d. quiet

20. ovation   a. honor   c. recipe
                    b. action d. applause

21. premeditated a. deliberate c. foolish
                    b. fiendish d. great

22. random   a. close   c. aimless
                    b. emotional d. knowing

23. resolute   a. reserved c. enduring
                    b. determined d. miserable

24. restrain   a. hold back c. dress up
                    b. teach d. remember

25. rigidly   a. stiffly   c. cleverly
                    b. stubbornly d. rudely

26. saturate   a. wring out c. treat badly
                    b. imitate d. fill completely

27. sedate   a. noisy   c. calm
                    b. healthy d. honest

28. stray   a. wander   c. lonely
                    b. direct d. puzzled

29. synthetic   a. tiring   c. careless
                    b. expensive d. artificial

30. technique   a. detail   c. instruction
                b. method   d. reason

31. titanic   a. metallic   c. backward
                b. huge   d. alive

32. upbraid   a. climb   c. reverse
                b. misread   d. scold

33. wheedle   a. grow   c. coax
                b. correct   d. crawl

Word List

The following list of 240 words should form the basis of your vocabulary study for the year. You have already encountered many of them (or their related forms) in this chapter. When you encounter a new word, add it to your vocabulary notebook. Write a definition of the word, and then use the word correctly in a sentence.

abash	arrogance	browbeat
abundant	articulate	bulwark
activate	aspiration	burly
adept		canine
adjacent	attain	capitulate
advent	autocrat	captivate
affliction	automaton	carouse
allay	badger	
alliance	bayou	casement
amity	belligerent	casual
	benign	catastrophe
analyze	bewilder	ceremony
anecdote	bilingual	chronic
annals	bisect	circumnavigate
anonymous		coerce
appalling	bland	coherent
appropriate	boisterous	colossal
aristocrat	brevity	concerted

conciliate
condole
confiscate
congenial
conjecture
consecutive
considerate
contaminate
contemptible
convene

covert
crony
curtail
customary
debonair
decadence
decrepit
deference
deluge
demolish

depict
depose
descend
devout
dexterity
diplomat
dismantle
dispense
dissuade
diverge

diverse
divest
eccentric
edible
elapse
elegant

eligible
eminent
encroach
enormity

ensue
evade
excessive
exclaim
extensive
facilitate
fatality
fatigue
feasible
fictitious

firmament
flail
fluent
forgo
fragile
fragrant
fraternize
frustrate
functional
futile

glorify
gracious
guffaw
guile
hamper
haughty
hibernate
hieroglyphic
homogeneous
humdrum

humidity

humiliate
hypothesis
illuminate
immaculate
immense
immortal
impediment
imperative
impertinent

improvise
inanimate
incentive
incorrigible
indict
inquisitive
insipid
integrity
intensity
invincible

isolation
jubilation
juncture
latent
levity
liberate
malign
meddlesome
menace
misdeed

misnomer
multicolored
myriad
nativity
nauseate
neutral
nourish

nuclear
obligation
obliterate

obscure
occult
oratorical
ostentatious
ovation
pallid
paragon
pastoral
pedagogue
permeate

pertinent
pewter
philanthropist
picturesque
pollute
posterity
prearrange
precocious
premeditated
preposterous

primitive
prodigy
punctual
quadruped
random

ravage
raze
rebate
recession
recuperate

regime
relevant
remorse
resolute
resonant
responsibility
restore
restrain
revile
rigid

riotous
sallow
satire
saturate
scrupulous
secluded
sedate
seraphic
sinew
soviet

sphere
stipulate
stray

substitute
successor
summit
superficial
synthetic
tangible
technique

tepid
timorous
titanic
transcend
tumult
twilight
unique
upbraid
urgent
valid

valor
vegetate
vehement
verify
vindicate
visage
vitality
wane
wheedle
whimsical

Chapter 26

Spelling

Improving Your Spelling

English is a language that is not consistent in its representation of sounds. For this reason, learning to spell in English is a challenging task. You have already learned to spell many thousands of words, but there are probably others that give you trouble. You can increase your ability to spell provided you approach the task slowly and easily — and provided you have the will and patience to learn.

GOOD SPELLING HABITS

These are a few of the things you can do to improve your spelling:

1. Keep a list of your own errors.
2. Use the dictionary as a spelling aid.
3. Spell by syllables.
4. Avoid mispronunciations that lead to spelling errors.
5. Revise your papers to avoid careless spelling errors.

1. *Keep a list of your own errors.*

As your ability to spell improves, you will notice that some words seem to be especially difficult for you. But don't be discouraged; make your own spelling book. The best way to master your own hard words is to make a notebook list of them and review them frequently.

2. *Use the dictionary as a spelling aid.*

A dictionary is a writer's best friend. Get the habit of consulting a dictionary whenever you have a spelling problem. It's much easier, of course, to guess at spelling; but, if you want to do good work, learn to use the dictionary.

3. *Spell by syllables.*

If you have trouble spelling long words, break them up into syllables. A syllable is a part of a word that can be pronounced by itself. The word *remember* has three syllables: *re-mem-ber.* Most syllables have no more than three or four letters, and certainly you can learn that many. A long word then becomes a group of short parts, and you can learn it syllable by syllable.

4. *Avoid mispronunciations that lead to spelling errors.*

If you listen and speak carefully, you will be less likely to misspell words because you are not pronouncing them correctly. Be sure that you say *chimney* not *chimbly, library* not *liberry, modern* not *modren.*

5. *Revise your papers to avoid careless spelling errors.*

Half the trouble in spelling comes from careless haste. Whenever you do any writing, reread your paper to correct the spelling not only of difficult words but also of the ordinary, easy words that you may have misspelled through carelessness.

SPELLING RULES

The following rules are helpful, even though there are exceptions to them. If you learn them thoroughly, you will find it easier to spell correctly.

ie and *ei*

26a. Write *ie* when the sound is long *e* except after *c*.

EXAMPLES   believe, relief, field, deceive, ceiling
EXCEPTIONS   neither, leisure, seize, weird

Write *ei* when the sound is not long *e*, especially when the sound is long *a*.

EXAMPLES   reign, weight, eight, freight, height, sleight
EXCEPTIONS   friend, mischief

-cede, -ceed, -sede

26b. Only one word in English ends in *–sede—supersede;* only three words end in *–ceed—exceed, proceed,* and *succeed;* all other words of similar sound end in *–cede.*

EXAMPLES   concede, recede, precede

EXERCISE 1.   Write the following words, supplying the missing letters (*e* and *i*) in the correct order. Be able to explain how the rules apply to each word.

1. fr...nd
2. p...ce
3. rec...ve
4. c...ling
5. w...ght
6. bel...ve
7. br...f
8. h...ght
9. n...ghbor
10. fr...ght

EXERCISE 2.   Write the following words, supplying *–ceed, –cede,* or *–sede.*

1. pre...   4. inter...   7. suc...
2. pro...   5. super...   8. re...
3. con...   6. ex...

Adding Prefixes

A prefix is one or more letters added to the beginning of a word to change its meaning.

EXAMPLES   un + able = unable
             pre + arrange = prearrange

26c. When a prefix is added to a word, the spelling of the word itself remains the same.

EXAMPLES   il + logical = **il**logical
             in + elegant = **in**elegant
             im + perfect = **im**perfect
             un + selfish = **un**selfish
             dis + trust = **dis**trust
             mis + apply = **mis**apply
             over + see = **over**see

EXERCISE 3. Number your paper 1–25. Write correctly the words formed. Then choose ten of the words and use each of them in a sentence.

1. il + legal
2. in + exact
3. im + migrant
4. in + equality
5. dis + order
6. mis + inform
7. re + enter
8. over + rule
9. il + liberal
10. un + natural
11. in + active
12. mis + use
13. over + rated
14. re + establish
15. dis + similar
16. mis + interpret
17. im + probable
18. over + run
19. il + legible
20. mis + sent
21. semi + annual
22. in + numerable
23. dis + array
24. un + necessary
25. im + material

Adding Suffixes

A suffix is one or more letters added to the end of a word to change its meaning.

EXAMPLES   care + less = care**less**
                walk + ed = walk**ed**
                comfort + able = comfort**able**

26d. When the suffixes *–ness* and *–ly* are added to a word, the spelling of the word itself is not changed.

EXAMPLES   mean + ness = mean**ness**
                casual + ly = casual**ly**

EXCEPTIONS   Words ending in *y* usually change the *y* to *i* before *–ness* and *–ly:* misty – mist**iness**; happy – happ**ily**. One-syllable adjectives ending in *y* generally follow rule 26d: shy – shy**ly**.

26e. Drop the final *e* before a suffix beginning with a vowel.

EXAMPLES   line + ing = lin**ing**
                approve + al = approv**al**
                desire + able = desir**able**

EXCEPTIONS   In some words, the final *e* must be kept to keep the soft sound of a *c* or *g*: notice + able = notic**eable**; courage + ous = courag**eous**.

26f. Keep the final *e* before a suffix beginning with a consonant.

EXAMPLES   hope + less = hop**eless**
                care + ful = car**eful**

EXCEPTIONS   true + ly = tru**ly**
                argue + ment = argu**ment**
                judge + ment = judg**ment**

EXERCISE 4. Number your paper 1–20. Write correctly the words formed as follows:

1. mean + ness
2. final + ly
3. love + able
4. shine + ing
5. true + ly
6. one + ness
7. notice + able
8. outrage + ous
9. pretty + ly
10. advantage + ous
11. change + able
12. please + ing
13. hope + ful
14. place + ing
15. remove + al
16. study + ing
17. happy + ness
18. come + ing
19. sudden + ness
20. cordial + ly

26g. With words ending in *y* preceded by a consonant, change the *y* to *i* before any suffix not beginning with *i*.

EXAMPLES   cry + ed = cried
lovely + ness = loveliness
bury + al = burial
but
cry + ing = crying

Note that words ending in *y* preceded by a vowel generally do not change their spelling when a suffix is added.

EXAMPLES   pray + ing = praying
pay + ment = payment
boy+ hood = boyhood

26h. With words of one syllable ending in a single consonant preceded by a single vowel, double the consonant before adding *-ing, -ed,* or *-er.*

EXAMPLES   sit + ing = sitting
swim + ing = swimming
drop + ed = dropped

26i. With words of more than one syllable ending in a single consonant preceded by a single vowel, double the consonant before adding *-ing, -ed,* or *-er,* if the word is accented on the last syllable.

EXAMPLES   occur' + ed = occurred
            begin' + er = beginner
            permit' + ing = permitting

If the word is *not* accented on the last syllable, the final consonant is not doubled before a suffix.

EXAMPLES   tra'vel + er = traveler
            can'cel + ed = canceled
            sten'cil + ing = stenciling

EXERCISE 5. Number your paper 1–20. Write correctly the words formed as follows:

1. study + ed	11. cry + ed
2. hurry + ed	12. joke + ing
3. study + ing	13. deploy + ing
4. hurry + ing	14. prefer + ed
5. bid + ing	15. permit + ed
6. quiz + ing	16. beg + ed
7. drop + ed	17. plan + ed
8. fit + ed	18. admit + ing
9. race + ing	19. run + er
10. stop + ed	20. bat + er

THE PLURAL OF NOUNS

Plurals are formed in several ways, most of them covered by rules. To learn irregular plurals, you should enter them in your private spelling list and memorize them.

26j. Observe the rules for spelling the plural of nouns.

(1) The regular way to form the plural of a noun is to add an *s*.

EXAMPLES   desk, desks
            idea, ideas

(2) The plural of some nouns ending in *s, x, z, ch,* **or** *sh* **is formed by adding** *es.*

EXAMPLES   pass, passes
fox, foxes
buzz, buzzes
clutch, clutches
dish, dishes

EXERCISE 6. Number your paper 1–10. Write the plurals of the following words:

1. wish
2. pilot
3. machine
4. match
5. automobile

6. porch
7. dance
8. mechanic
9. reflex
10. box

(3) The plural of nouns ending in *y* **preceded by a consonant is formed by changing the** *y* **to** *i* **and adding** *es.*

EXAMPLES   army, armies   city, cities
country, countries   pony, ponies

(4) The plural of nouns ending in *y* **preceded by a vowel is formed by adding** *s.*

EXAMPLES   journey, journeys
key, keys

(5) The plural of most nouns ending in *f* **is formed by adding** *s.* **Some nouns ending in** *f* **or** *fe,* **however, form plurals by changing the** *f* **to** *v* **and adding** *s* **or** *es.*

EXAMPLES   grief, griefs
belief, beliefs
shelf, shelves
knife, knives
thief, thieves

(6) The plural of nouns ending in o preceded by a vowel is formed by adding s; the plural of nouns ending in o preceded by a consonant is formed by adding es.

EXAMPLES o following a vowel:

radio, radios
curio, curios
patio, patios

o following a consonant:

tomato, tomatoes
echo, echoes

EXCEPTIONS   Eskimos, silos, pianos, sopranos, altos

Note that many nouns ending in o and pertaining to music are exceptions to this rule.

(7) The plural of a few nouns is formed in irregular ways.

EXAMPLES   child, children   goose, geese
ox, oxen   mouse, mice
woman, women   foot, feet
tooth, teeth

EXERCISE 7. Write the plurals of the following nouns:

1. city	10. galley	19. soprano
2. chimney	11. calf	20. echo
3. company	12. knife	21. child
4. foot	13. leaf	22. tooth
5. donkey	14. belief	23. mouse
6. valley	15. roof	24. hero
7. lily	16. rodeo	25. woman
8. goose	17. volcano	
9. library	18. mosquito	

(8) The plural of compound nouns consisting of a noun plus a modifier is formed by making the noun plural.

EXAMPLES passerby, passers-by
     maid of honor, maids of honor
     brother-in-law, brothers-in-law

(9) The plural of a few compound nouns is formed in irregular ways.

EXAMPLES drive-in, drive-ins
     fourteen-year-old, fourteen-year-olds

(10) Some nouns are the same in the singular and plural.

EXAMPLES trout, salmon, sheep, Sioux, deer, moose

(11) The plural of numbers, letters, signs, and words considered as words is formed by adding an apostrophe and *s*.

EXAMPLES 1900 1900's + +'s
     ABC ABC's *and* *and*'s

EXERCISE 8. Write the plurals of the following nouns:

1. sheep
2. weekend
3. trout
4. daughter-in-law
5. *a*

6. teen-ager
7. guard of honor
8. deer
9. cupful
10. 1800

EXERCISE 9. Write the plurals of the following items. After each plural, write the number of the subrule under rule 26 j (1–11) that applies.

EXAMPLE 1. proof
         1. *proofs* (5)

1. child
2. ox
3. 100
4. *t*
5. shelf
6. belief
7. cry
8. monkey
9. sister-in-law
10. sheep
11. piano
12. spoonful
13. Eskimo
14. knife
15. clutch
16. radio
17. potato
18. lass
19. alto
20. *and*
21. baby
22. chef
23. arpeggio
24. pulley
25. wax

Words Often Confused

The words grouped together in the following lists are frequently confused with each other because their pronunciation or spelling is the same or similar. Study them carefully and learn to distinguish both their meaning and their spelling.

accept to receive with consent; to give approval to
Many of his contemporaries did not *accept* Copernicus' theory that the earth moves around the sun.

except leave out from a number; with the exclusion of; but
Copernicus' theory was accurate *except* that he thought the planets' paths were circles rather than ellipses.

advice a recommendation about a course of action
Good *advice* may be easy to give but hard to follow.

advise   to recommend a course of action; to give advice
I *advise* you to continue your music lessons if you possibly can.

---

affect   to influence; to produce an effect upon
The explosion of Krakatoa *affected* the sunsets all over the world.

effect   the result of an action; consequence
It has long been observed that the phases of the moon have an *effect* on the tides of the earth's oceans.

---

all right   everything is right *or* satisfactory; *two words. The spelling* alright *is never correct.*
Maria did *all right* in the track meet.
Was my answer *all right?*

---

all ready   all prepared *or* in readiness
The players are *all ready* for the big game.

already   previously
Our class has *already* taken two field trips this year.

EXERCISE 10. Number your paper 1–10. After the proper number, write the word given in the parentheses that makes the sentence correct.

1. Everyone likes to give (advice, advise).
2. The (affect, effect) of the victory was startling.
3. Why did you (accept, except) Carla from the class ruling?
4. The scientists were (all ready, already) to watch the launching of the rocket.

5. The coach (advices, advises) everyone to stick to the training rules.
6. Her weeks of practice certainly (affected, effected) her final game.
7. Most of the rebels were offered a pardon and (accepted, excepted) it, but the leaders were (accepted, excepted) from the offer.
8. Juan has (all ready, already) learned how to water-ski.
9. Do you think my work is (all right, alright)?
10. Whose (advice, advise) are you going to take?

altar a table for a religious ceremony
The *altar* was banked with lilies.

alter to change
The outcome of the election *altered* the mayor's plan.

all together everyone in the same place
The director called us *all together* for one final rehearsal.

altogether entirely
Your story is *altogether* too late for this issue.

brake a device to stop a machine
Can you fix the *brake* on my bicycle?

break to fracture, to shatter
The winner will be the one who *breaks* the tape.

capital a city, the seat of a government
Olympia is the *capital* of Washington.

capitol   a government building *(usually capitalized)*
The *Capitol* is one of the handsomest
buildings in Washington.

---

choose   *[present tense, rhymes with* lose] to select
Will you *choose* speech or civics as your
elective next year?

chose   *[past tense, rhymes with* grows] selected
Janet *chose* to play in the band rather
than in the orchestra.

EXERCISE 11. Number your paper 1–10. After the
proper number, write the word given in parentheses
that makes the sentence correct.

1. The building with the dome is the (capital, capitol).
2. By working (all together, altogether) we can do the
   job easily.
3. Because she loved dramatics, Alice (choose,
   chose) a difficult part in the school play.
4. Be careful not to (brake, break) those dishes.
5. That book is (all together, altogether) too complicated for you to enjoy.
6. The candles on the (altar, alter) glowed beauti-
   fully.
7. We don't know whether to (choose, chose) band
   or orchestra next year.
8. A car without a good emergency (brake, break)
   is a menace.
9. Will Joan's accident (altar, alter) her plans?
10. Tallahassee is the (capital, capitol) of Florida.

---

clothes   wearing apparel
One can learn a lot about a historical
period by studying its fashions in *clothes*.

cloths   pieces of fabric
You'll find some cleaning *cloths* in the drawer.

---

coarse   rough, crude
The beach is covered with *coarse* brown sand.

course   path of action; planned program or route; *also used in the expression* of course
The wind blew the *Gretel* slightly off its *course.*

---

consul   a representative of a government in a foreign country
Who is the American *consul* in Nigeria?

council   a group of people who meet together

councilor   a member of a council
The king called a meeting of the *council* and informed the *councilors* that the royal treasury was nearly empty.

counsel   advice, *or* to give words of advice

counselor   one who advises
When choosing a career, seek *counsel* from your teacher.
Who is your guidance *counselor?*

---

desert   a dry, sandy region
[des′ert] The Sahara is the largest *desert* in Africa.

desert   to abandon, to leave
[de·sert′] Most dogs will not *desert* a friend in trouble.

dessert   the final course of a meal
[des·sert′] Apple pie is my favorite *dessert.*

EXERCISE 12. Number your paper 1–10. After the proper number, write the word or words given in the parentheses that will make the sentence correct.

1. Each class has four representatives on the student (council, counsel).
2. The guide threatened to (desert, dessert) us as we crossed the (desert, dessert).
3. Most young people are very much interested in (clothes, cloths).
4. Your guidance (councilor, counselor) will be of great help to you.
5. The (coarse, course) for the cross-country race is a rugged one.
6. The cleaning (clothes, cloths) must be washed after each use.
7. Do we have a Canadian (consul, council) in this city?
8. (Coarse, Course) gravel lined the driveway of Margarita's house.
9. The meal didn't seem complete without (desert, dessert).
10. The members of the losing team looked to their coach for (council, counsel).

---

formally   with dignity, following strict rules or procedures
The Governor delivered the speech *formally*.

formerly   previously, in the past
Formerly, I knew the Zubalsky family very well.

---

hear   to perceive sounds by ear
Dogs can *hear* some sounds that are inaudible to people.

here   in this place
            The campsite is right *here.*

---

its   [*a personal pronoun showing possession*]
            pertaining to it
            Mount Fuji is noted for *its* beauty.

it's   [*a contraction of* it is *or* it has]
            It's an extinct volcano.
            It's been a long time.

---

lead   [*present tense*] to go first, to be a leader
[lēd]   A small town in New Hampshire often
            leads the nation in filing its election re-
            turns.

lead   heavy metal
[lĕd]   A *lead* pencil actually has no *lead* in it.

led   [*past tense*] went first
            The Governor *led* the slate with an im-
            pressive majority.

---

loose   not securely attached; not tight fitting
            If a tourniquet is too *loose,* it will not
            serve its purpose.

lose   to suffer loss
            Vegetables *lose* some of their vitamins
            when they are cooked.

EXERCISE 13. Number your paper 1–10. After the
proper number, write the word or words given in
parentheses that will make the sentence correct.

1. (Its, It's) a long way from (hear, here) to the park.
2. The plumber is removing the (lead, led) pipes and
   putting in brass ones.

3. We don't want to (loose, lose) you in the crowd.
4. Before the club takes up new business, the secretary (formally, formerly) reads the minutes of the previous meeting.
5. (Its, It's) too bad that the tree has lost (its, it's) leaves so early.
6. Do you (hear, here) me, Ann? Come (hear, here) this minute!
7. The Yankees were ten runs behind, and it seemed certain that they were going to (loose, lose).
8. The marshal (lead, led) the class into the chapel.
9. Had Ana ever done any running (formally, formerly)?
10. That (loose, lose) bolt can cause trouble.

---

passed [*past tense of* pass] went by
Our airplane *passed* over the Grand Canyon.

past that which has gone by; beyond
Some people live in the *past*.
They moved *past* the dozing sentry.

---

peace security and quiet order
We are striving for a world of *peace* and prosperity.

piece a part of something
Some people can catch fish with a pole, a *piece* of string, and a bent pin.

---

plain simple, common, unadorned; a flat area of land
A *plain* jackknife is often as useful as one with several blades.
What is the difference between a prairie and a *plain?*

plane   a tool; an airplane; a flat surface
The *plane* is a mark of the carpenter's trade.
The hangar will accommodate four single-engine *planes*.
Rhoda says she likes *plane* geometry.

principal   the head of a school; main or most important
The *principal* is the chief officer of a school.
What are the *principal* exports of Brazil?

principle   a rule of conduct; a main fact or law
She listed some of the *principles* of economics.

quiet   still and peaceful; without noise
A *quiet* room is needed for concentrated study.

quite   wholly or entirely; to a great extent
Winters in the New England states can be *quite* severe.

EXERCISE 14. Number your paper 1–10. After the proper number, write the word given in parentheses that makes the sentence correct.

1. A bright smile often makes a (plain, plane) face attractive.
2. The summer was (quiet, quite) over before the beginning of school brought a (quiet, quite) household once more.
3. This is an important (principal, principle) in mathematics.
4. On July 20, 1963, the moon (passed, past) be-

tween the earth and the sun, causing a total eclipse.
5. A (plain, plane) is a useful tool.
6. Save me a (peace, piece) of that blueberry pie.
7. Our (principal, principle) is leaving the school this year.
8. We should try to learn from (passed, past) experience.
9. The nation was working hard to attain (peace, piece).
10. Cattle were grazing over the (plain, plane).

---

shone   [*past tense of* shine]
They polished the silver until it *shone.*

shown   [*past participle of* show] revealed
A model of the new school will be *shown* to the public next week.

---

stationary   in a fixed position
Most of the furnishings of a space capsule must be *stationary.*

stationery   writing paper
I need a new box of *stationery.*

---

than   [a *conjunction used for comparisons*]
The Amazon River is longer *than* the Mississippi River.

then   at that time
If the baby is awake by four o'clock, we will leave *then.*

---

there   a place [*also used to begin a sentence*]
Go *there* in the fall when the leaves are turning.
There were no objections.

their   [a *possessive*]
             Their team seems very skillful.

they're   they are
             They're taller than most of our players.

---

threw   [*past tense of* throw] hurled
             Our pitcher *threw* four balls in succes-
             sion.

through   [a *preposition*]
             Have you ever seen a ship go *through*
             the locks of a canal?

EXERCISE 15. Number your paper 1–10. After the
proper number, write the word given in parentheses
that makes the sentence correct.

1. We go (there, their, they're) often, for the children can get (there, their, they're) instruction in
   swimming, and we can see how (their, there,
   they're) progressing.
2. She has more (stationary, stationery) than she'll
   ever use.
3. The stars (shown, shone) brilliantly.
4. The city was so much larger (then, than) I expected.
5. The new desks for our art room are not (stationary, stationery).
6. We often hear the planes break (threw, through)
   the sound barrier.
7. Sue will have the first ride; (than, then) it will be
   your turn.
8. The goalposts on the football field have been made
   (stationary, stationery).
9. We were (shone, shown) all the points of interest
   in the downtown area.
10. The pitcher (threw, through) a wild ball that al-
    most hit the batter.

to [*a preposition, also used with a verb*]
A visit *to* Chinatown is an exciting treat.
Many small nations are eager *to* become independent.

too also; more than enough
We have lived in North Dakota and in Alaska, *too.*
It is *too* cold for rain today.

two one plus one
Americans can visit *two* foreign countries without leaving the continent.

weak not strong; feeble
My mother likes to drink *weak* tea.

week seven days
Your pictures will be ready in about a *week.*

weather condition of the air or atmosphere
Weather prediction is an important branch of meteorology.

whether [*a conjunction*]
Jane Gordon is wondering *whether* the bond issue for the new school will be approved.

whose [*a possessive*]
Whose report are we hearing today?

who's who is
Who's representing the yearbook staff?

your [*a possessive*]
Your work in math is improving.

you're you are
You're right on time!

EXERCISE 16. Number your paper 1–10. After the proper number, write the word given in parentheses that makes the sentence correct.

1. Lack of exercise made the runner's legs (weak, week).
2. (Weather, Whether) we'll go or not depends on the (weather, whether).
3. (Whose, Who's) books are you carrying?
4. Find out (whose, who's) going if you can.
5. Allen thought algebra was (to, too, two) difficult for him (to, too, two) master.
6. (Your, You're) a long distance off your course, captain.
7. We took (to, too, two) (weaks, weeks) for our trip across the country.
8. The (weather, whether) was cloudy so Carmen could see very little from the plane.
9. Would you enjoy a trip (to, too, two) Mars, Flo?
10. Aren't you using (your, you're) compass?

50 SPELLING DEMONS

ache	don't	once
again	early	ready
always	easy	said
answer	every	says
blue	friend	shoes
built		since
busy	guess	straight
buy	half	sugar
can't	hour	sure
color	instead	tear
	knew	
cough	know	though
could	laid	through
country	meant	tired
doctor	minute	tonight
does	often	trouble

wear	which	women
where	whole	

250 SPELLING WORDS

In studying the following list, pay particular attention to the letters printed in heavy type. These letters are generally the ones which offer most students the greatest difficulty in correctly spelling each word.

abandon
absolutely
acceptance
accidentally
accommodate
accompany
accomplish
achieve
acquaintance
acquire

actually
advertisement
against
aisle
amount
analysis
anticipate
anxiety
apology
apparent

appearance
application
appreciation
approach
arguing
argument

article
assistance
authority
basis

beginning
believe
benefit
boundary
bouquet
bulletin
business
canceled
capacity
careless

carrier
ceiling
challenge
choice
choir
chorus
circuit
colonel
column
coming

commercial

committees
competition
completely
conceive
condemn
congratulations
conscience
conscious
control

convenience
courteous
criticism
cylinder
dealt
deceit
decision
definite
definition
describe

description
desirable
despair
develop
difficulties
disappointment
discipline

discussion
diseased
distinction

distribution
doctrine
duplicate
economic
eligible
embarrass
engineering
enthusiasm
equipped
eventually

exactly
exaggerate
excellent
existence
experience
experiment
explanation
fascinating
favorite
February

finally
flu
forty
fourth
friendliness
generally
governor
grammar
gratitude
guarantee

guardian
gymnasium

hatred
height
heroine
hesitate
humorous
hypocrite
ignorance
imagination

immediately
incidentally
individual
inferior
initial
inspiration
intelligence
interfere
interrupt
involve

judgment
knowledge
laboratory
leisure
lengthen
lieutenant
loneliness
luncheon
majority
manufacture

marriage
mechanical
medieval
military
mourn
multiplication
muscular
mystery

naturally
necessary

nickel
nonsense
nuisance
numerous
obvious
occasionally
occurrence
opinion
opportunity
orchestra

originally
paid
parallel
parliament
patience
performance
personal
personality
persuade
philosopher

picnicking
planned
pleasant
possess
precede
preferred
prejudice
privilege
probably
procedure

professor
pursuit
qualified

realize
receipt
recognize
recommend
referring
regularly
relieve

repetition
research
response
rhythm
satisfied
saucers
schedule
scissors
sense
sentiment

separate
sergeant
shepherd
similar
simply
solemn

source
sponsor
straighten
subscription

succeed
success
sufficient
suggest
suppress
surprise
surrounded
suspense
suspicion
tailor

temperament
tendency
theories
therefore
thorough
tobacco
tonsils
tradition
tragedy

transferred

tries
truly
unanimous
unnecessary
unsatisfactory
until
useful
using
utilized
vacuum

variety
various
vein
view
villain
violence
warrant
weird
wholly
writing

Speaking
and
Listening

PART SEVEN

Chapter 27

Speaking

Announcements and Reports, Delivering a Speech, Evaluating a Speech

Learning how to speak well and comfortably before groups or in unfamiliar situations is an important part of every young person's education. This chapter will help you to improve your speaking skills.

MAKING ANNOUNCEMENTS

To announce a bit of information or an event to other students, you will not need to make extensive preparation or elaborate notes. Nevertheless, you should write down the information you are to give and check it over to be sure it includes all the essential facts. Does your announcement tell *what, where, when, who, why,* and *how*?

27a. In making an announcement, be sure to include all the necessary facts.

Most announcements should include the following items: (1) the kind of event; (2) the time; (3) the place; (4) the admission fee, if any; (5) special features. The following example includes four of these items, omitting only the admission fee.

EXAMPLE   The Stamp Club meeting that was scheduled for this afternoon has been postponed
because of the storm. Instead, the Stamp
Club will meet next Tuesday, December
10, at 3:05 in Room 27. All members and
any other interested students are invited
for a program on "Stamps of New
Nations."

Go over the facts of an announcement several
times in your mind before you speak. If you are not
sure that you will remember them all while you are
speaking, carry a note card with the information
written on it, and glance at it as you speak.

Use a normal rate of speaking, and make sure that
you give your listeners time to take in what you are
saying. Speak loudly enough so that everyone will
hear.

EXERCISE 1.   Each of the following announcements
omits essential items of information. What are these
items? How would you correct the announcements?

1. Students in Ms. Bergman's and Mr. Novotny's
   classes who are going to the Science Museum tomorrow should be ready to leave at 11:15. The only
   expense will be for lunch in the museum cafeteria.
2. The Glee Club needs more members. Even if you
   are not sure of your musical talent, why not come
   to a rehearsal and join the preparation for the
   holiday program?
3. There will be a Halloween party on Saturday,
   October 27, in the school auditorium. All students
   are invited. Profits from the party will go to the
   Library Fund.

EXERCISE 2.   Prepare and deliver an announcement for one of the following events or an actual

event taking place at your school. Give all the necessary information.

1. An excursion sponsored by the Ecology Club
2. Copies of your school newspaper on sale
3. A 4-H Club meeting
4. Tryouts for the play *The Diary of Anne Frank*
5. A science fair
6. A softball game between two classes
7. An open house at school for parents

GIVING ORAL REPORTS

Learning how to plan and deliver oral reports is a skill that will be useful to you in school and in whatever career you choose.

27b. Learn to prepare an oral report.

Some instruction in preparing a written report is presented in Chapter 21. An oral report is prepared in much the same way, except that you do not write it out word for word. Instead, you may make some notes to help you remember your material as you speak.

(1) Choose a suitable topic.

If you are given a topic to report on, you have no problem of selection. If you are asked to choose your own topic, however, it is best to focus on your interests or your experiences. Select a topic that can be covered reasonably well in the time allotted for your speech. Make sure that it will interest your audience. A report on how to identify types of clouds might bore some people; a report on how to repair leaky faucets might bore others; a report on how to hang up your clothes properly might bore everybody. But a report on ways to earn money after school or on a new probe of a distant planet or on the discovery of an ancient city buried under a lava flow would be likely to interest many of your listeners.

(2) Gather material for your report.

After you have a topic, your next step is to gather information on your subject. There are at least three sources for such material: (1) your own ideas and experiences; (2) other people who know something about your topic; (3) books and periodicals. Consult all of these sources, and get as much information as you can. Write notes or brief summaries of the information you are gathering.

(3) Prepare an outline.

From your notes, prepare an outline for your talk. (Refresh your memory on how to prepare an outline by looking at pages 400–04.)

Suppose that you have decided to give a talk in your science class on shooting stars. You have often observed shooting stars and have wondered what they are and why they occur. Having discovered that shooting stars are meteors, go to the library (see Chapter 24, "The Library," page 481) and read articles on meteors in various reference works. On cards or slips of paper, copy items of information you want to use. Study these notes until the material is familiar to you. From the notes, prepare an outline. The outline might have four main headings:

   I. Time: when meteors are seen
  II. Nature: what the characteristics of meteors are
 III. Place: where and why meteors are seen
 IV. Fate: how speed, size, and course determine the final end of meteors

Under each of these headings arrange your material in logical order—the major ideas first, the details following them. Once you have settled on the content and structure of your report, you are ready to think about how to deliver it.

(4) Write note cards to use as reminders when delivering your report.

It is not necessary to write out a speech word for word and memorize it. Instead, read and reread your material and your outline until they are so familiar that you need only an occasional reminder to help you talk freely about your topic.

Write these reminders on 3 × 5-inch note cards. Arrange the cards to correspond with the order of your outline.

Write one card for each of the main ideas of your outline. Include the subheadings under the main idea on the card.

Reminder cards do not have to contain complete sentences; key words or phrases will do. Remember: These cards are not to be read aloud. They just give aid to your memory.

A reminder card for a talk on shooting stars might look like this:

I. Time
   A. More after midnight than before
   B. More in the fall than in any other season
   C. Five per hour - 500 per minute

When giving your speech, you would start with this card. The items on the card are reminders. The main point tells what this part of the speech is about; the subheadings identify details to discuss. You might start your speech by saying:

> We are all familiar with shooting stars, or meteors. Often, on summer evenings, we have seen them streak across the dark sky. Most of us, however, are unaware that we can see more shooting stars after midnight than before, and that we can see more in the fall of the year than in other seasons. Usually, about five shooting stars per hour can be sighted. However, when meteor showers occur, sometimes as many as 500 meteors fall each minute. . . .

In some cases it is wise to write full and exact details on a note card. If, for example, you want to give the ingredients of a recipe or the measurements of material needed to make a birdhouse or statistics on ships going through the Panama Canal, it is wise to write out the full details on a note card so that you can read them off when you need them.

You may want to use direct quotations from people whom you've interviewed. (Direct quotations will not only make your talk livelier but will give it the weight of authority.) Write out quotations exactly as given, to avoid misquoting the person you interviewed.

If you are explaining a process to your audience, it may be helpful to have charts and pictures. You may also want to use the chalkboard to write figures and dates or draw illustrations. A reminder card can tell you when to use these visual aids.

You may need only a few reminder cards if the material of your speech is very familiar to you — perhaps just one for each main heading, and one or two additional cards with details to support some point requiring exact information. No rule can be set for how many cards you will need; prepare as many as you think necessary.

As you speak, hold the cards in your hand. Glance at the top card, and talk on the subject it lists. Then move this top card to the bottom, uncovering the next topic of your speech. Continue this process until you have spoken on every topic listed on your cards.

As you practice your speech, practice using your note cards also. You should be able to use them smoothly so that they do not distract your audience.

(5) Plan an interest-arousing introduction and a strong conclusion.

It is helpful to write out an exciting first sentence, one that will arouse your listeners' interest. Memorize this sentence so that you can look at your audience and speak the sentence naturally.

Similarly, it is helpful to work out a strong ending statement for your talk — a sentence or paragraph that ties your main ideas together. You may write this statement out on a card. However, try not to spoil the effect of a good speech by reading the last part of it.

EXERCISE 3. Plan a short talk on one of the following subjects or on a topic of your own that your teacher approves. Go through the steps of gathering material, outlining, and making reminder cards.

1. UFO's — reality or illusion?
2. How to save the whales
3. Tree grafting: how to raise pears on an apple tree
4. What makes an airplane fly?
5. The monster called Bigfoot
6. An interesting part of the city that many people don't know about
7. The pony express

8. Why —— is the best career
9. A comparison of American football and English Rugby
10. Family customs in another country
11. Can cars run on solar energy?
12. My choice for President
13. The career of my favorite sports hero
14. Programs I'd like to see on television
15. A hobby that earns money

Nonverbal Communication

People often communicate with unspoken, or non-verbal, signals. For example, someone who cannot talk may use sign language to converse. An umpire at a baseball game raises one thumb in the air to say, "You're out!" A car driver signals a left-hand turn by extending the left arm.

Nonverbal communication is also an important part of giving a speech. An audience will read, or interpret, a speaker's gestures and body movements in the same way that they will listen to words. Such nonverbal signals, therefore, should communicate exactly what a speaker wants to say.

27c. Learn to use nonverbal signals as you speak.

You can improve your speech by using firm posture and natural gestures.

Stand straight. Keep your weight on both feet. If you are sitting, place both feet squarely on the floor and keep your back straight in the chair. Good posture communicates confidence.

Look at your audience as you speak. Glance around the room, and try to focus on the faces of your listeners. Eye contact is an effective way to hold the audience's attention. If you are using note cards, look—but do not stare—at them as you speak. You should be looking at your audience during most of the speech, not at your cards. While speaking, try to smile occasionally. Smiling usually helps to relax an audience.

Keep gestures under control. Although it is natural to feel nervous about giving a talk, avoid nervous, random gestures, such as fidgeting with your hair.

Think about what gestures may mean. Choose gestures that help rather than hinder your spoken words. Keeping your hands in your pockets, for example, is a gesture that suggests you are not well prepared to give the speech. Scratching your head suggests that you are not sure of what to say next. Avoid any gestures that detract from your message.

Pause for transition. A short pause between parts of your speech can be a nonverbal signal to your audience that you are about to introduce another topic. A pause can also give you a chance to take a deep breath and relax.

EXERCISE 4. Try to write down at least five different gestures that you notice at school, at home, on television, or anywhere else. Next to each gesture, write what you think the gesture means. Prepare to discuss your list in class.

Pronunciation and Enunciation

27d. Pronounce words correctly and enunciate carefully.

Your audience must hear your speech plainly. A talk that is not heard is wasted. An audience that must strain to hear becomes restless.

Take care to speak correctly and distinctly. In many cases the meaning of a word varies with the way it is pronounced. Remember that if your words are mispronounced or if you mumble or run words together, your audience will have difficulty in following you.

Vowel Sounds

Each vowel in our language may be pronounced in different ways. In some words vowels or combinations of vowels have sounds that you might not expect from the spelling. Make sure you use standard pronunciation for the following words:

despite	drought	opaque	thorough
despot	fertile	suite	through
draught	genuine	superfluous	victuals

Consonant Sounds

As important as pronunciation is *enunciation*, the careful sounding of every syllable. Be especially careful with words that end in *-ing* and words that contain similar consonants — *p* and *b*, *m* and *n*, *t* and *th*.

For practice, say the following groups of words aloud, taking care to make the consonant sounds clearly distinguishable so that no one in the room mistakes the word you used.

d–t		t–th	
do	to	tank	thank
dent	tent	taught	thought
din	tin	bat	bath
done	ton	tinker	thinker
dare	tear	mutter	mother
and	ant	ton	thumb
send	sent	ten	then
bed	bet	rat	wrath
wed	wet	tat	that
madder	matter	wetter	weather

b–p		v–f	
blank	plank	vendor	fender
bin	pin	veil	fail
bowl	poll	viewer	fewer
robe	rope	vault	fault
bunk	punk	veal	feel
Benny	penny	vision	fission

EXERCISE 5. Practice reading aloud the following tongue twisters. Prepare yourself to read them to the class so distinctly that they are easily understood.

1. She said severely, "Son, shun the hot sun, or your poor back will burn pitifully."
2. She sells seashells at the seashore.
3. The tinker muttered thanks in a thin, throttled tone.
4. Jane's chuckles and antics jarred her ailing aunt and uncle.
5. The tank of thin tin was dank and dented.
6. In the still, chill silence of the church, Benny's penny clattered tinnily in the cup.
7. Chunks of junk smashed the vendor's fenders.
8. The mole delved twelve feet under the thin turf.
9. His mother muttered that wetter weather would wash his wrath away.
10. Penny's robe, belted with rope, was tugged snug at the throat.

Omitting Sounds

Take care not to omit sounds that belong in words. Below are listed some words frequently subject to nonstandard pronunciation.

arctic (not ar'tic)
asked (not ask' or ast)
average (not av'rage)
exactly (not 'xactly)
finally (not fin'lly)

library (not lib'ary)
mystery (not myst'ry)
probably (not prob'ly or pro'ly)

EXERCISE 6. Use five of the words in the preceding list in sentences to be spoken aloud in class.

Adding Sounds

Take care not to add sounds to a word — either inside a word or at the end. Do you use nonstandard pronunciation with any of these words?

arithmetic (not arith*uh*metic)
athlete (not ath*uh*lete)
barbarous (not barbar*i*ous)
chimney (not chim*b*ley or chim*uh*ney)
column (not col*y*um)
corps (the *p* and *s* are silent)
elm (not el*u*m)
height (ends in *t*, not *th*)
scent (the *c* is silent)
subtle (the *b* is silent)
umbrella (not umbrell*er* or umb*e*rella)
vehicle (the *h* is silent)

EXERCISE 7. Go around the class twice with the preceding list, with each student pronouncing a word.

Changing Position of Sounds

Be careful not to change the position of a sound within a word. Sometimes such nonstandard pronunciation is based on the similarity of a word to another word that is almost like it in spelling. *Perspire* and *prescribe,* for example, having beginning syllables that are almost alike. *Perspire* is often mispronounced *prespire,* and *prescribe* is often mispronounced *perscribe.*

apron (not apern)
cavalry (not calvary)
children (not childern)
contradict (not conterdict)
modern (not modren)

EXERCISE 8. Using all of the preceding lists, let a number of students write words on the board and call on other students to pronounce them.

EXERCISE 9. Following is a list of frequently mispronounced words. Be prepared to read them aloud to the class. Use the dictionary if you are not sure of the correct pronunciation.

admirable	infamous
architect	jostle
bade	jubilant
champion	mischievous
favorite	museum
film	ogre
finale	partner
gape	remembrance
gesture	scythe
handkerchief	superfluous
hearth	theater
hurtle	toward
incomparable	tremendous
indict	yacht

Running Words Together

Another form of mispronouncing words is running them together when speaking. Telescoping words makes a wreckage of sense. Too often, for example, we run together the words of such a sentence as *I'm glad to meet you* into *'m gladdameecha.*

EXERCISE 10. Translate the following mangled words into understandable language.

didja	gonna	woncha
gotcha	whereya	harrya
thankslot	lemetry	didjaseer
gimeyahan	whadideedo	wassamadawichoo
wachasay	begyaparn	wyncha

27e. Learn to speak with expression and meaning.

We give meaning to language not only by our choice of words but by the *feelings* we put into them—the tone of voice, the grouping of words, the emphasis, the variety of tone. The tone and emphasis we use can greatly influence the meaning our words convey. Differing emphases on certain words or syllables can convey different meanings and emotions.

You can increase the effectiveness of your speech by giving attention to your tone of voice and to the amount and kind of expression you use.

EXERCISE 11. Study these sentences before reading them aloud. The class will discuss how well each person expresses the different feelings.

1. You are taking care of a six-year-old. Tell her, "Susan, put that puppy down!"
   a. Say it as if the mother dog, growling furiously, is getting out of her box to leap at Susan.
   b. Say it as if you know Susan is going to plead with you to buy the puppy and you don't have the money.
2. Someone has just walked through your room with muddy feet, leaving tracks on the rug. You ask, "Kyle, did you just walk through my room?"
   a. Say it as if you have told him before to stay out of your room.
   b. Say it as if you have just cleaned your room.

3. A new dress has just been delivered to your house. Today is your birthday. You ask, "Mom, Dad, did you buy this dress for me?"
   a. Say it as if the dress is exactly what you have been hoping for, but you can't believe that your parents would be so extravagant.
   b. Say it as if you are bitterly disappointed.
4. You have started on a long walk when you discover that your small brother is walking behind you. You tell him, "Andy, go home and go to bed."
   a. Say it as if he is feverish with a bad cold, and you are very worried about him.
   b. Say it as if you've told him before that he could not come along.

EXERCISE 12. See how many meanings you can put into the following remarks by varying your tone and the words you emphasize.

1. I'll go now, if you don't mind.
2. I'd like some steak, too.
3. Bring all your money tomorrow.
4. I told you not to play with him.
5. You earned all that money yourself?
6. Did you say yes?
7. He will do the dishes, and you, Preston, will sweep.
8. Did you promise to help him, Laura?

EVALUATING A SPEECH

27f. Learn to evaluate another person's report politely and constructively.

Often, after a student has given a report, the class is asked to criticize the talk. The purpose of such an evaluation is to help the speaker improve by hearing reactions. Another purpose, too, is for the group to give recognition to the fine qualities as well as the weak points of the talk.

Be clear and definite. Whether praising a talk for its fine qualities or pointing out its weaknesses, always give reasons for your evaluation. Be generous with praise. When you see serious faults in a talk, it is wise to begin by discussing strong points, then going on to show how the talk might have been even stronger if certain faults had been corrected.

In the examples below, study the preferred comments. Why are they good examples of evaluation?

WEAK   "I thought it was very interesting."

BETTER "His description of Mt. Rainier was very interesting because his details were so sharp that I could almost see the mountain trail." Or, "I liked her story of exploring the cave because she built up so much suspense."

WEAK   "The talk left me cold." Or, "I just couldn't follow it." Or, "He did not convince me."

BETTER "Her explanation was clear and easy to follow except in a couple of places, and I wonder if she left out some steps." Or, "He convinced me that fishing in the river should be limited for a while, but I'd like more proof that dumping factory waste into the river is the real reason why fish are scarce."

Do your part in helping the class to establish an atmosphere of kind and constructive evaluation. Your class may decide to use an evaluation sheet like the one on page 571 for criticizing speakers. After a talk has been made, each listener rates the speech, and the sheets are collected and given to the speaker.

EVALUATION CHECKLIST

1. Give praise when it is merited.
2. Avoid discussion of trifles.
3. Point out strengths as well as weaknesses.
4. Be definite and constructive.

EXERCISE 13. Deliver the talk that you prepared in Exercise 3.

EXERCISE 14. Write a paragraph evaluating a talk someone has given in class. Use the following evaluation sheet as a basis for your evaluation, but also give your opinion of the talk as a whole.

EVALUATION SHEET

Speaker _____

Topic _____

Critic _____

	Very good	Good	Fair	Weak
Introduction				
Organization				
Conclusion				
Use of notes				
Posture				
Gestures				
Voice				
Pronunciation				
Other comments				

Chapter 28

Listening

Good Learning Habits

Listening well is an important part of learning. In school, at home, and among friends, you can learn more by listening well to others.

LISTENING TO MEDIA

You may spend many hours each week watching television and listening to the radio. You may also go to the movies often. It is good to have the fun and relaxation that such entertainment provides, but you owe it to yourself to develop a critical appreciation of what you see and hear.

28a. Choose radio stations, television programs, and movies intelligently.

You can learn a great deal from radio, television, and movies if you plan ahead and decide what you want to see and hear. Newspaper reviews, suggestions from friends, and your own interests should guide your choice of these media.

EXERCISE 1. Consult the television, radio, and movie schedules for the next week. Make a list of the shows you want to see or hear. Next to each show, give the reason for your interest. In class, compare your list with your classmates'. Did you list the same shows? Do you have the same reasons?

LISTENING TO INSTRUCTIONS

A large part of what we listen to is not only enjoyable—it is informative. Our daily life depends on people telling other people things that are useful for them to know. As students, much of your listening is done for the purpose of gaining information.

28b. Listen alertly to directions and class assignments.

You can save time and avoid errors by listening carefully to directions. If the directions are lengthy, jot down each step on a piece of paper. Do not interrupt with questions while the directions are being given. Wait, and ask your questions when the speaker has finished. Be sure that you have noted *all* the instructions and have understood them. Repeat them aloud if necessary.

EXERCISE 2. Someone in the class will read the following directions aloud. See if you can follow the directions after hearing them. You may want to jot each step down on a piece of paper.

Take out a piece of paper and write your name in the upper left-hand corner. Beneath your name write the day you were born.

Draw a line down the middle of the page. Mark the left column with the letter *A* and the right column with the letter *B*. In column A write the months of the year that begin with the letter *J*. In column B write the days of the week that begin with the letter *T*. Compare the lists. If column B has more words, fold your paper in half.

LISTENING TO OTHERS

28c. Listen to talks and oral reports with an open mind.

The basis of good listening is *interest* and *purpose*. You listen very attentively to something that interests you. You also listen attentively to, and remember vividly, information that will serve a purpose that you consider important.

When listening to a talk, ask yourself: *How can this information be of real help to me?* If you can determine ways in which the content is important to you, listening and remembering will be easier.

Suppose, however, you are listening to a talk on how a particular club serves the community. You may not be very interested. The club has staged a benefit dance to buy a record player and records for a local hospital. To you, this is of no immediate concern. You could fog your mind in a daydream now if you wished. But if you pay attention, you may discover that the club also sponsors trips for students, or that it compiles job opportunities for students seeking summer vacation employment.

Sometimes you know what you are listening for—as when you listen to directions or assignments. At other times you should keep an alert, open mind—you may learn something unexpectedly useful.

EXERCISE 3. Suppose the following people spoke in assembly programs at your school. What would be your purpose in listening to each?

1. The manager of a local department store talks on "How to Tell a Bargain from a Gyp."
2. A graduate of your school gives a talk on two years spent with the Peace Corps in South America.

3. A professional guitarist speaks on "What to Listen for in Music," illustrating points on the guitar.
4. The head of a research laboratory gives a talk on new devices using solar energy.

28d. Listen actively.

If you intend to use the information you are hearing, you must be alert to grasp the ideas presented. You must select the ideas that you can use. You must retain them so clearly that you will remember them later when you need them.

(1) Listen for the speaker's purpose.

Sometimes, while listening to a talk, you want to know the speaker's intention. Is the speaker trying to persuade you to do something? Are you expected to agree or disagree with the speaker? In such situations, concentrate on grasping the speaker's point of view. Ask yourself why the speaker wants you to do something or why the speaker holds certain opinions.

(2) Listen for a few main ideas.

Listen to grasp the *main points* of the speech: the reasons the speaker gives for taking action or the ideas with which the speaker supports one side of an issue. If a speaker gives information or relates an experience, try to understand and remember each main idea presented.

When you are listening for the main ideas of a speech, it is often helpful to pay special attention to the start and finish of the talk. A speaker's introduction often presents the main points that will be developed, and the conclusion often sums them up. An able speaker makes an effort to emphasize important ideas so that you can easily recognize them.

EXERCISE 4. Select six short news stories in a newspaper. Read each story aloud. Listeners will write down, in their own words, the main idea of each story. Compare the answers.

(3) Listen for specific details.

On some occasions your purpose in listening to a talk will be to get specific details. Suppose, for example, that you are listening to a talk on how to start a model plane engine or how to decipher a secret code or how to tell edible mushrooms from poisonous ones. A general idea of the method will not be sufficient; you will want exact details.

EXERCISE 5. This activity requires listening carefully to detailed information. Close your books and listen to the teacher.

The teacher will read the following instructions to the class. When the teacher has finished, each student will write the directions from memory. When all have finished, the teacher will reread the instructions, and each student will check for mistakes.

Teacher: "If you are taking a hike in the woods, bring the following items with you:

1. A compass. Be sure you know how to use it.
2. Maps. Bring more than one map of the same area, if possible.
3. Wooden matches. Keep them in a waterproof case
4. A knife. Keep the blade in a sheath.
5. Some food. Foods such as nut mixtures and dried fruit are the best."

(4) Evaluate nonverbal signals such as gestures.

A speaker may use gestures for emphasis. Some of these gestures may be appropriate; for example, a comedian will often rely on gestures to draw laughs. Other gestures may be inappropriate; for example, nervous speakers will often wave one or both hands in the air as they speak. The best gestures add to a speech and communicate nonverbally what the speaker is trying to say.

EXERCISE 6. Watch a popular comedian or other personality speaking. Notice how gestures are used. Describe these gestures to your classmates and indicate what they mean to you.

28e. Listen critically. Distinguish fact from opinion. Judge whether statements are backed up by evidence from dependable sources.

When you listen to a speaker, you do not wish to be fooled by trickery or unreliable sources of information. Ask yourself questions as you listen: Is this statement a fact or an opinion? If the speaker is presenting it as a fact, is it backed up with proof from a dependable source or a trustworthy expert? Is the speaker talking from experience?

Know the difference between fact and opinion. A fact is a statement that can be proved true or false, such as, "Winter temperatures averaged 12° Celsius this year." An opinion is a statement that cannot be proved true or false, such as, "It feels colder this winter than last."

Study the following examples. Can you see why two are opinions and two are facts?

OPINION The library facilities in this school are inadequate.

FACT In the library, there are 10 books available for this assignment, but there are 150 students who must do the assignment at once.

OPINION The referee is being unfair to our players!

FACT The referee has given our players three penalties in the last five minutes.

EXERCISE 7. If you heard the following statements, would you accept them as fact or interpret them as opinion? After each number on your paper, write *fact* if you think the statement would be a fact, or *opinion* if you think it would be an opinion. Be prepared to explain each choice.

1. We ought to irrigate our desert lands with fresh water made from sea water.
2. A tornado in Kansas today wrecked fifty homes.
3. Sunbathing is harmful.
4. Stanford beat Oregon at football today, 28 to 14.
5. There's no place like home.
6. TV comedies are all alike.
7. Ms. Currier gives too much homework.
8. American cars give the best value among low-priced compacts.
9. The orchestra has improved greatly this year.
10. Mrs. Townsend has never been introduced to my family.

Index and
Tab Key Index

Index

Tab Key Index

Key to
English Workshop Drill

To supplement the lessons in *English Grammar and Composition, Second Course*, there is additional practice in grammar and usage, punctuation, capitalization, composition, vocabulary, and spelling in *English Workshop, Second Course*. The following chart correlates the rule in the textbook with the appropriate lesson in *English Workshop*.

Text Rule	Workshop Lesson	Text Rule	Workshop Lesson	Text Rule	Workshop Lesson
1a	13	9a	93	15e	60
1b	13	9b	93	16a	103, 104
1c	14	9c	94-98	16c-e	105
1d	13			16f	106, 108
1e	14	10a-b	74, 75		
1f	20	10c-d	76, 77	18a-e	124
1g	20				
		11a	18	19a	111
2a	1			19b	112
2b	2	12d	66, 67	19c	113
2c	3	12e	68	19d	114
		12f	68	19f	114
3a	4, 5	12g	69	19g	111
3b	6			19h	115
3c	7	13a-d	44	19i	116
3d-f	9	13f	45		
		13g	45	20a-c	120
4a	8, 58	13h	21	20d	121
4b-d	8	13i	45	20e	121
		13j	45	20h	122
5a-c	26	13k	46		
5d	27-31	13l	46	21b	120
5e	36-39	13m	47	21d-f	121
				21g	126
6a	15	14g	50		
6b	16	14h	50	22a-d	127
6d	17	14i	51	22e	128
		14j-l	50	22f	128
7a	21	14m	51		
7b	21	14n	51	23b	11, 24, 34, 72
		14q	48		
8a	83	14r	48	25a	11
8b	84	14s	49	25c	11
8c	85			25d	34
8d-f	87	15a	56	25e	54
8g-i	88	15b	57	25f	64, 101
8m	84	15c	58		

Correction Symbols

ms	error in manuscript form or neatness
cap	error in use of capital letters
p	error in punctuation
sp	error in spelling
frag	sentence fragment
ss	error in sentence structure
k	awkward sentence
nc	not clear
rs	run-on sentence
gr	error in grammar
w	error in word choice
¶	You should have begun a new paragraph here.
t	error in tense
∧	You have omitted something.